Denise Brennan

Life Interrupted

TRAFFICKING into FORCED LABOR in the UNITED STATES

Duke University Press / Durham and London / 2014

Library of Congress Cataloging-in-Publication Data
Brennan, Denise, 1964–
Life interrupted : trafficking into forced labor in the
United States / Denise Brennan.
pages cm
Includes bibliographical references and index.
ISBN 978-0-8223-5624-0 (cloth : alk. paper)
ISBN 978-0-8223-5633-2 (pbk. : alk. paper)
1. Foreign workers—Abuse of—United States. 2. Human
trafficking—United States. 3. Human rights—United States.
I. Title.
HD8081.A5B74 2014
331.11′730973—dc23
2013026436

To all those in the fight for worker justice

Contents

Acknowledgments

How can I meaningfully thank so many who have been remarkably generous throughout the years of this project—for their time, insights, wisdom, personal stories, trust, and friendship? These words seem all the more inadequate since I cannot thank by name those who have courageously shared their stories. I am deeply grateful for the trust they put in me and for their commitment to helping others in similar situations of exploitation.

There were two pivotal launch points of this project: when Ann Jordan invited me to join an antitrafficking working group around the time the TVPA was being drafted and when I met Florrie Burke, through Ann. Both women have vouched for me and reached into their Rolodexes to introduce me to the antitrafficking community. I never would have met the extraordinary individuals I have had the privilege of getting to know without their help. Thank you, Ann and Florrie.

Ileana Fohr is a gifted and dedicated case manager, from whom I learned what social service provision ideally should look like. I also have learned a great deal from many others in the labor organizing, social service, legal, and medical assistance world: Edgar Aranda-Yanoc, Christina Arnold, Susie Baldwin, Lucas Benitez, Bill Bernstein, Andrea Bertone, Cate Bowman, Kay Buck, Imelda Buncab, Stewart Chang, Namju Cho, Kenneth Chuang, Emma Cleaveland, Kate D'Adamo, Ambassador Luis C. deBaca, Alexis De Simone, Tenaz Dubash, Maria José Fletcher, Laura Germino, Gail Gottlieb, Kelly Heinrich, Darby Hickey, Minerva Hidrogo, Renee Huffman, Ashwini Jaisingh, Elizabeth Keyes, Kathleen Kim, Karina Kirana, Vanessa Lanza, Chanchanit Martorell, Fiona Mason, Allison Medina, Marley Moynahan, Heather Moore, Qimmah Najeeullah, Melanie Orhant, Nadra Qadeer,

Daniela Ramirez, Stephanie Richard, Martín Ríos, Michelle Robertson, JJ Rosenbaum, Rob Rutland-Brown, Penny Saunders, Jenny Stanger, Elissa Steglich, Aeryca Steinbauer, Bill Threlkeld, Suzanne Tomatore, Juhu Thukral, Miriam Torrado, Mily Trevino-Sauceda, Kavitha Sreeharsha, Maria Suarez, Thao Vo, Martina Vandenberg, Judy Vaughn, Gabriella Villareal, Tiffany Williams, and Joy Zarembka. Thank you for letting me into your worlds and for answering my many questions.

The Kalmanovitiz Initiative for Labor and the Working Poor has been an intellectual and activist home for me at Georgetown, where faculty, staff, and students have taught me on many levels about the struggle to ensure dignified and fair work for all workers. Katie Corrigan, Jennifer Luff, and Joe McCartin have been outstanding supporters whose deep and wide knowledge has been an apprenticeship in all things labor. The Americas Initiative at Georgetown has been another home for me over the years, where colleagues read part of the book when I first started the research, and then again as I finished writing it. Thanks in particular to Caetlin Benson-Allott, Katie Benton-Cohen, Brian Hochman, Michael Kazin, Eric Langer, Adam Lifshey, Chandra Manning, Bryan McCann, Samantha Pinto, and John Tutino for their detailed suggestions. The Washington, D.C. Labor History Group offered me a place at their learned table, where Cindy Hahamovitch and Jennifer Luff have built a lively exchange. I am lucky to continue to learn as part of a supportive community of faculty and students in the Department of Anthropology at Georgetown. Thanks to Georgetown colleagues who made specific suggestions for the book: Fida Adely, Rochelle Davis, Gerry Mara, Joanne Rappaport, Mark Sicoli, and Susan Terrio.

In the final stages of the book, experts on trafficking—practitioners and scholars—threw themselves into the manuscript and provided sharp comments on a tight deadline. Martina Vandenberg crafted some of the fiercest edits I have ever been gifted. Janie Chuang and Ann Jordan read every last word of the book and talked me through their insights page by page. Elizabeth Bernstein also shared her wisdom on every chapter pushing me in new and necessary directions. Carole Vance, Darby Hickey, and Penny Saunders likewise saw things I did not. Florrie Burke and Ileana Fohr carefully commented on my take on the social service world's practices and challenges. I am deeply indebted to all these talented colleagues who, committed to justice on these issues, generously and enthusiastically devoted a great deal of their time to this project.

My thinking on this book began to take shape at the School of Advanced

Research in Santa Fe. Thanks to James Brooks for hosting a whip-smart group of scholars whom Carole Vance so wisely assembled. The Woodrow Wilson International Center for Scholars offered a place to think and to write. Many thanks to Sara Friedman, Pardis Mahdavi, Sonya Michel, and Flip Strum for their colleagueship. Three meetings of a roundtable on trafficking that brought together legal scholars and ethnographers have provided tremendous food for thought. Working closely with Janie Chuang and Janet Halley on organizing two of these roundtables (at American University's Washington College of Law and Radcliffe Institute for Advanced Study) and on the launch of a website — http://traffickingroundtable.org/ — has been a true joy. Over the years I also have learned from the questions posed and answered by a fiercely intelligent group of antitrafficking, migrants' rights, and sex workers' rights scholars and activists: Elizabeth Bernstein, Sealing Cheng, Nicole Constable, Kerwin Kaye, Ali Miller, Penny Saunders, Svati Shah, and Carole Vance.

I have been fortunate to test ideas and benefit from thought-provoking feedback while giving lectures at the following institutions: American University's Washington College of Law, Butler University, Brown University, Cornell Law School, City College Center for Worker Education, George Washington University, Harvard University, Muhlenberg College, Pomona College, University of California (Irvine), University of California (Los Angeles), University of California (Santa Barbara), University of New England, University of Pennsylvania Law School, University of Pittsburgh, University of Virginia, and Yale University. I also am grateful to the organizers of the Freedom Network for inviting me to participate and to share my research at their annual conferences over the years.

University life is wonderfully collaborative, and I have been lucky to work closely with many talented and dedicated students. Beth Hallowell helped me jumpstart this project as we put *What's Love Got to Do with It?* to bed. Jessica Angulo-Duarte, Lindsay Du Bois, Jessica Forrest, Ashwini Jaisingh, Keely Schneider (who spent a summer doing research full time), and, most recently, Katie Farias and Whitney Pratt have been committed — and creative — research assistants at Georgetown. Kara Coughlin, Alex Fries, and Jia Zhao provided detailed research assistance at the Woodrow Wilson International Center for Scholars. Alex, a California native, also helped me navigate Los Angeles and nearby communities while doing field research. James Benton provided careful cite checking.

Writer friends have offered both comradeship and writing advice.

Maureen Corrigan and Barbara Feinman-Todd are always an inspiration. The immensely talented Marybeth McMahon read every word with her skilled editor's pen and a friend's unflagging support. A careful and patient reader, my husband, Doug Reed, has read through this book in its various forms many times. My brother Paul Brennan and dear friend Cindy Gordon offered their takes on the book as well.

I am grateful for the generous financial support from the following foundations: The American Association of University Women, The Harry Frank Guggenheim Foundation, and the Woodrow Wilson International Center for Scholars. And, my home institution, Georgetown University, has supported the research and writing with Summer Academic Grants, a senior Faculty Fellowship, and a Center for Democracy and the Third Sector Faculty Fellowship.

It has been a pleasure working with Valerie Millholland and Gisela Fosado at Duke University Press. Valerie took a chance on my dissertation many years ago, for which I am deeply grateful. Gisela has shared many terrific insights and suggestions and has been enthusiastically dedicated to this book project. Nicole Constable and an anonymous reviewer read the book with great care and skill. Their astute comments helped shape the book into its present form. Thanks.

While researching and writing this book, my amazingly loving and inquisitive kids, Emily and James, grew. Also during this time my father, Arthur Brennan, who first introduced me to the labor movement by suggesting I write on the AFL-CIO for a social studies assignment, passed away. My mother, Mary Brennan, although changed by cognitive loss, remains a loving supporter of anything I take on. It is they and my grandparents who taught me about the varied struggles that "working people" face, the unpredictable vagaries of economic security, and the constancy of a family's love.

Spending time with the extraordinary individuals I have been so lucky to meet has changed me. It brought me into the kitchens and living rooms of individuals who model a kind of grace, kindness, and patience — and toughness, focus, and determination — that continues to impress and inspire. I truly cannot understand what they have endured. Since I met them during a time of transition between acute insecurity and firmer footing, I try here to do justice to how they made it through. And how they, courageous, steadfast, and hopeful, look ahead.

Introduction Starting Over

Maria loves to sing. Her karaoke machine sits in the middle of her basement apartment in Queens. She fires it up when she has friends over, and they cook and sing. She also sings her favorite songs when she is home alone. She has sung songs into my voice mail on my cell phone. It's no surprise, then, that she describes her heartache for her son in the Philippines with the words to a song about being five hundred miles away. She left him in the care of her sister over twenty years ago, when she first traveled overseas for work. The United States is the third foreign country she has worked in. She never thought she would be gone this long. On the eve of preparing to finally see her son she turns to singing: "I don't know what I will say when I see him. What can I say? Hello, how are you, you are my son. I don't know what I will do. That's my situation. He is over five hundred miles away. So when I come home, I open my Magic Microphone and read the lyrics and sing and forget for a while."

Maria also expressed through song her love—and grief—for Felicia, her best friend in the United States. Meeting through a Filipina domestic workers' organization in New York, they became fast friends. As one another's surrogate family in this country, they looked out for each other. When Felicia had an accident and broke both her knees, Maria stopped by every day after work to check on her, to help her bathe, and to cook. It was Maria, not Felicia's husband, who nursed her back to health. Felicia loved Maria immensely, explaining over plates of barbecued meats and glasses of creamy halo-halo shakes, "Maria is my best friend. She took care of me when I could not do much. She is a real friend." Maria was also there for

Figure I.1. Karaoke machine in Maria's living room. Photograph by author.

Felicia when she learned that her beloved friend was dying of cancer and had only weeks to live. Maria nursed her as she had before, and it was she who was by Felicia's side in the hospital as she died. "I kissed her and held her hand and told her, 'I will always be with you.'" In those last days in the hospital, Maria tried to comfort her friend by singing. "I sang a lot of songs. I sang and sang and she would smile."

//////

Carmen pointed to the Long Island Rail Road tracks underneath the small bridge we were walking on. She brought me there because of the view: "It reminds me of a Chilean song about a young boy about to go on a big adventure. It makes me feel melancholic: happy, but also a bit sad." We were walking near the house she shared with her boyfriend in Queens, where she had been hiding after being physically attacked by a coworker at a housekeeping job in a midtown hotel. "Sometimes I feel like people are staring at me. Like they are going to eat me." I did not think that she would agree to go out for dessert and coffee, but without skipping a beat she said, "Sure, but let's go to Manhattan!" Back in her house, as she zipped from her bedroom to put on eyeliner, eye shadow, and red lipstick, she talked about a new start. She had been interviewing for jobs, and she pointed to her review books for the GED. As she brushed her long thick black hair, she vowed that she was going

Figure I.2. Train tracks near Carmen's house. Photograph by author.

to cut it. "I want a new look. I want to feel like I did when I wore a wig as Cleopatra last year for Halloween. I want a fresh start."

//////

Flo carried a large white envelope to the afternoon potluck at a domestic workers' organization in the Washington, D.C., area. The theme of the day was "poetry." During the workshop she helped fellow participants who were not as fluent as she with the English language. Following the dramatic tone set by a social worker leading the workshop, Flo acted out the poem she and another participant had written about the sun. The other women cheered when she was done. But she had more to share. Out of the white envelope she pulled an orange spiral notebook. She had written a poem the night before in anticipation of this day. This poem, about enjoying life and realizing how lucky she is, was an even bigger hit.

//////

Eva was carrying a book in English on dreams. She regularly goes to the library in her Bronx neighborhood to get books in English for herself and her son and explains that she looks up words she doesn't know in an online dictionary. Since she is in school to be a nursing assistant, she makes a routine for them both to study: "After school, it is rest, snack, play, homework. We don't watch television. There is no time. Last night I was up to 1:30 in the morning researching white blood cells." Since her own schooling was cut short when she was a young girl in Mexico, she wants her son to be able to focus on school while he is young. "My son picked a flower for me. He told me, 'One day I'll buy you one when I work.' I told him not to worry about work and to only think about school. I told him, 'You have years of studying ahead of you. Listen to your teachers.'"

//////

I open this book about trafficking into forced labor with these snapshots of Maria's, Carmen's, Flo's, and Eva's lives precisely because these stories have no clear connection to their time in forced labor. Rather they recount ordinary moments of composing lives in the United States. Like all newcomers, they have had to take risks, step into new relationships, and try on new experiences. The United States was uncharted territory for them; three of the women had no prior ties to the country through family or friends.[1] Building a new life in a new country is difficult in the best of circumstances. What if one's introduction to the United States is through forced labor? How individuals who were trafficked into forced labor set up their households, care for their children (whether in the United States or at a distance), find decent work, take classes, make friends, fall in love, and spend their free time is the focus of this book. While the media often has highlighted the spectacular aspects of trafficking, supplying a voyeuristic catalogue of abuse and dramatic stories of escape or rescue, this book picks up where these sensationalistic accounts leave off. Life after forced labor is a series of private daily struggles and successes, usually not the stuff of public press conferences and headline-grabbing news. This book dwells on the ordinary tasks and chores of resettlement in the United States, what I call *everyday lifework*. It recounts the ways formerly trafficked persons spend their days and nights, far from the media spotlight, quietly reclaiming their lives and making the United States their home.

The book operates on two levels: it examines the lived experience of migrating internationally for work, and it analyzes the effects of immigration policies—which may not have an ostensible connection to trafficking—on efforts to prevent trafficking into forced labor and assist trafficked persons. Both the focus on migrants' lives and the policy analysis grow out of years of anthropological fieldwork, along with migrants' and workers' rights advocacy. In this book, I introduce readers to real people, not mythologized versions of "trafficked persons," and call attention to the relationship between anti-immigrant policies and the pervasive exploitation of migrant workers. Individuals designated "trafficked" are just one part—a small part—of a much larger story of everyday exploitation of migrant laborers in the United States. Trafficking into forced labor is on the extreme end of a continuum of abuse of migrant workers.[2] A range of exploitation thrives without legal protections for all workers regardless of their immigration status. When workers fear reporting exploitation, employers can exploit with impunity. Widespread migrant labor abuse—including trafficking—is the result of robust demand for low-wage workers, the absence of federal immigration reform, ineffective labor laws, and migrants' fears of detection, detention, and deportation.

Although this is a book about individuals who suffered exploitation that was severe enough to qualify as trafficking, their experiences and insights are set within this larger political backdrop of everyday exploitation of migrant workers. My main analytical frame highlights migrant workers' vulnerability to abuse—both workers who are undocumented and those who have temporary work visas.[3] There is a huge gap between the paltry number of special visas (T visas) that the U.S. government has issued to severely exploited migrants to remain in the United States—under four thousand—and the millions of migrants who work in abusive conditions that may not be abusive *enough* to qualify as trafficking.[4] This number is particularly low in light of the U.S. government's estimate that 14,500 to 17,500 persons are in situations of severe exploitation in the United States.[5] While news headlines scream about "modern-day slavery" all around us and organizations fundraise on trafficked persons' behalf, this media attention and fundraising is fantastically disproportionate to the small number of individuals assisted as well as the vast number of migrant workers left to continue working in vulnerable and dangerous situations.[6]

Despite the media fascination and fundraising frenzy, formerly trafficked persons are largely on their own after initial government assistance. There is a striking disconnect between the splashy media coverage about trafficking, nonprofit organizations' emotional fundraising appeals, celebrity public service announcements, and the banality and poverty of formerly trafficked persons' actual day-to-day lives. Usually in the United States alone without family or any other contacts, they struggle to establish economic security and a support network. Most do not know—and often never meet—anyone else with a trafficking designation. And, they are not allowed to travel outside the United States while their applications for trafficking visas (T visas)—and then for green cards—are pending. A physician who cares for patients who had been in forced labor observes that "they are not quite free" since they start new lives in the United States with no money, family, or friends and strict limits on their mobility. Chronic financial insecurity characterizes formerly trafficked persons' lives in the United States not only in the short term but also for years into resettlement. Life after forced labor in the United States is life on the margins.

What Is Trafficking into Forced Labor?

Trafficking into forced labor is migration gone awry.[7] Individuals undertake migration strategies hoping that the crossing will be safe, they will pay off their debts to those facilitating the crossing, and that they will have better economic opportunities than they currently have. But once migrants cross borders, many lose the support of their home community and the protections their citizenship may offer them. Agreed-upon travel arrangements can fall apart. Relying on someone else to hold up his or her end of a bargain is risky.[8] Although migrants assess risk and payoff, their migration calculation often stems as well from emotion and dreams.[9] The reasons some individuals get on the road elude easy mapping. Motivations for migrants' dreams of new and better lives slip through and between researchers' neat categorizations and theories. So do some migrants' embrace of risk-filled travel plans. And, as many attorneys emphasize, not all of their trafficking clients' plans were inherently risky; some had entered the United States legally with temporary work visas.

Many capitalize on migrants' dreams: States that rely on remittances from citizenry working abroad in lieu of supplying a social safety net; recruitment agencies charging would-be migrants exorbitant fees; corrupt police officers and border guards; and unscrupulous employers. All these actors make trafficking into forced labor possible. While one person, or several persons, ultimately may be singled out as the "trafficker" or "traffickers" at the end of this chain, these other actors and forms of corruption create the conditions under which forced labor occurs.[10] This book explores what happens when individuals lose control of their border crossing. It is based on conversations I have had since 2004 with individuals whose strategies of migration to enter the United States went terribly wrong. I recount stories of individuals who ended up in forced labor in a variety of industries in cities and towns throughout the United States. Their stories of life before, during, and after forced labor provide insight into the origins and maintenance of the power relationships that undergird trafficking into forced labor. Before their experiences in forced labor begin, potential migrants may reinforce existing inequalities, particularly class hierarchies, as they sign on — and sometimes pay exorbitant fees — to travel for work. They do so with few or no assurances that recruiters, travel brokers, and employers will stick to their end of the agreement. These global workers, often from marginalized social classes, have little control over the location of work, working conditions, and pay. If they want to work in an economy outside their home country, they have to comply — even if with great reservations — to the terms of travel and work set by others.[11]

Terminology: Trafficking, Modern-Day Slavery, Forced Labor

As eager migrants set out to find work outside of their own countries' borders, the word *trafficking* obscures what is going on; the twin pillars underpinning trafficking into forced labor in the United States are abuses surrounding migration and labor. The desire, and sometimes desperation to migrate for work and the kinds of jobs available for workers in poorly regulated or unregulated labor sectors produce a perfect storm of worker exploitation — a global regime of worker exploitation.[12] Migrant workers the world over are central to local economies but enjoy few protections from abusive employers or are too intimidated to exercise them.[13] They enter new, unfamiliar labor markets in new, unfamiliar countries and may not be knowledgeable about their basic rights. Their undocumented status — or temporary work visas — ensure that they will remain quiet about these abuses. They may not have any place to turn — or fear doing so. Their employers bank on this fear and sometimes go to great lengths to cultivate it. Since there also may be an existing range of exploitative labor practices in these work sites, extreme abuse may go undetected by coworkers also experiencing exploitation.

The term *modern-day slavery* is also a flawed way to describe forced labor in the United States.[14] Slavery is not the law of the land. It is not protected by a legal framework that is based on race, and no one is born into a race-based enslaved status. No human being is legally defined as property that can be bought and sold. Nor do individuals expect to be sold. Under chattel slavery, individuals of African ancestry knew that they or a family member could be sold at any moment. In this sense, although enslaved individuals lived with chronic uncertainty, they knew what was ahead: they faced a lifetime of being bought and sold. The historian Walter Johnson writes that waiting to be sold "suffused every moment of the present with the fear of an unknown future, the heart-rending pain of losing loved ones to the traders, loss and survival in the shadow of the slave market."[15] Enslaved individuals also knew that certain destinations, such as the Deep South, meant a death sentence. Johnson quotes Lewis Clarke, who had been enslaved: "Why do slaves dread so bad to go to the South—to Mississippi or Louisiana? Because they know slaves are driven very hard there, and worked to death in a few years."[16]

In contrast, individuals in forced labor in the United States today are surprised to find themselves without control over their lives. They may not know what is ahead for them, but they know that employers may not lawfully prevent them from quitting. They know that their freedom does not have to be bought and declared through legal documents. Francisco, in his early twenties, jumped out of his abuser's van while they were parked at a gas station in California. He ran directly to police officers he had spotted. Without documentation to work and live in the United States, he expected that running to law enforcement would mean his deportation (he ended up qualifying for a T visa), but he had never expected to be held by an employer against his will. He explains his calculus: "I did not care if they arrested me and sent me back to Mexico. I had to get away."

Today's traffickers in people do not have the law on their side, nor do they have the assistance of slave patrols, fugitive slave laws, and courts.[17] They must be discreet about their coercive extraction of uncompensated labor.[18] Women who were in forced domestic labor, for example, relate that their abusers told them to stay out of sight—usually in upstairs rooms or in the basement—when their employers entertained guests. Beatrice, who had been trafficked into forced domestic labor as a teenager, suspected a young woman was in a similar situation when she met her at a party Beatrice attended. The young woman did not leave the kitchen for the duration of the party and seemed to try to make herself unnoticeable. Beatrice said, "I saw myself in her. She was afraid. She was hesitant to answer any of my questions. I told her she did not have to stay there." Beatrice reached out to her and gave her the name of her attorney and the domestic workers' rights organization that had helped her. She also followed up with phone calls. (The young woman eventually decided to go back home to Africa.)

With exploitation of low-wage migrants pervasive in the current labor system in the United States, this country's experience with sweatshops at the turn of the twentieth century is a more fitting historical reference than chattel slavery. Today many migrants labor in modern-day sweatshops where employers get away with paying poverty wages under lousy conditions because they know that their workers fear detection and deportation, or need their sponsorship for a temporary work visa.[19] Workers' debts to recruiters, smugglers, and family members back home also keep them working without complaint.[20] In some cases, such as in forestry work, which only lasts around three months and pays poverty wages, workers often leave work contracts with greater debts than before ever working.[21] Exploitative employers leverage workers' fear and debt burden by threatening to turn them over to law enforcement. Not paying agreed-upon wages, or not paying wages at all, is also commonplace in these environments where threat and fear reign. Legal scholar Jennifer Gordon writes about a kind of "super exploitation" that happens to most low-wage migrant workers who, at some point, are cheated out of their wages in what she calls "everyday sweatshops."[22] Still, meager wages — even no wages — do not guarantee an exploited worker a "trafficking" designation.[23] Routine forms of wage theft and intimidation are simply part of doing business in places where migrants labor.[24] Sweating labor — in agricultural fields, restaurant kitchens, factory floors, construction sites, brothels, and people's homes — occurs every day. Contrary to sensationalistic claims that slavery is all around us, a more mundane and politically thorny reality is that exploited migrant labor undergirds parts of the U.S. economy. Certain industries, such as agriculture, rely on paying low wages as well as employing seasonal laborers. If these workers want to be rehired, they have many incentives to stay quiet about their exploitation.

The language I have chosen to use throughout the book therefore pivots on issues related to labor. No one term accommodates a wide variety of individuals and experiences in forced labor. In fact, T visa recipients may have little in common other than their U.S. government designation as "trafficked." In order to emphasize that trafficking is about labor exploitation, I write about *trafficking into forced labor*. When I write of trafficking, I am specifically referring to the legal category created through the passage of the Trafficking Victims Protection Act (TVPA) in 2000 and a set of accompanying legal rights. While U.S. government documents often refer to trafficked persons as *victims*, social workers, trauma specialists, and medical doctors use the term *survivors*. Most formerly trafficked persons use vague, generalized phrases such as "my situation" or "back when I was with that woman" or "when I was with that man" to describe their time in forced labor.[25] The language of trafficking also has been widely criticized by social service providers. "I don't like the term *trafficking*," explains a physician based in California. "Instead, I want a term that captures that this is someone who has lost autonomy, been exploited, and abused." Concerned as well about the much larger population of exploited migrant workers who have been left out of any form of legal relief, she emphasizes that she also "would include twenty guys sleeping in a van in a field within this definition." Labor protections and immigration relief thus are at the heart of larger discussions about this wider circle of exploited individuals who do not qualify for any trafficking benefits but live and work in abusive conditions nonetheless.

Since a trafficking designation by the U.S. government confers benefits and rights—and obligations—I refer to individuals whom the government has determined qualify for T visas as "formerly trafficked persons" and "T visa recipients." With the first group of T visa recipients—like Maria and Carmen—finally having received their green cards, I realize that T *visa recipients* is a flawed term since it captures only a particular time during the legal process leading to permanent settlement in the United States. I continue to use the term, however, since it is a critical first legal step to living and working permanently in the United States. Social workers and attorneys at organizations involved in the resettlement of formerly trafficked persons consequently focus much of their energies on securing T visas for their clients. The first group of T visa recipients—pioneers like Maria and Carmen who navigated this legal regime—waited considerably longer than applicants do today. It is primarily these first trafficking clients with whom I have spent time. Their prolonged wait first for T visas and then for green cards profoundly shaped their resettlement in the United States.

A New Legal Category: Exceptions to the U.S. Immigration Regime

Those with a "trafficking" designation from the government receive T visas to stay in the United States and also qualify for a range of social services much like those that refugees receive.[26] To qualify, exploited workers must prove that they are victims of "force, fraud or coercion."[27] This is not easy to prove. Legal scholars have noted not only how difficult it is to prove coercion, particularly without physical violence, but also how this narrow definition of exploited labor that offers relief on a limited basis actually weakens the antitrafficking legal regime. Extending protections and benefits to more individuals "would have the advantage of undermining the exploitative labor practices that have been allowed to thrive at the unpoliced intersection of labor law and immigration law." Instead, by reserving relief for only a special few, the "growing chasm between the treatment of trafficked victims and all other unauthorized migrants" has "further fuel[ed] policies that limit the official scope of trafficking prosecutions."[28] And those whose exploitation is deemed not coercive enough to qualify as trafficking risk deportation.[29]

Although extreme abuse may be the exception, forms of exploitation, such as wage theft, are commonplace for migrant workers.[30] Most undocumented migrants (or those with temporary work visas) work within a kind of labor liminality. T visas are not given out for a little bit of exploitation. Providing protections for only the most extreme cases of migrant exploitation sidesteps the divisive politics of immigration reform and labor law. There is an immense gulf between these trafficking victims worthy of relief and undocumented workers regarded by many as deportable lawbreakers. When the U.S. government confers the legal designation "trafficked" upon an individual, everything changes. Unprotected migrant workers are delivered into a state of immigration grace. Not only saved from criminalization and deportation, trafficked persons also jump to the head of the line in the government's relief regime. Those designated "trafficked" are exceptions to an otherwise punitive immigration regime.

Not only is trafficking difficult to prove, but almost immediately after the TVPA's enactment, a rhetorical shift took place that sought to redefine the term *trafficking*. While many of the initial supporters of the TVPA saw trafficking through the frame of labor rights, others, particularly within the Bush administration, viewed trafficking primarily through the lens of prostitution with the goal of eradicating all forms of sexual labor through law enforcement. Thus, the TVPA's implementation has been caught between two competing principles. One view contends that the legislation is, in effect, an effort to provide labor rights protections to extremely exploited workers while the other seeks to enforce the law as a means to end all forms of sexual labor. Early in the implementation of the TVPA, the Bush administration, evangelical nonprofit antitrafficking organizations, and mainstream feminist organizations turned the campaign against trafficking into a crusade to end prostitution (the focus of chapter 1). The impossibility of such a goal notwithstanding, this war on sex work, in the name of ending trafficking, in part explains why so few T visas have been issued to date. By focusing on finding exploitation in only one labor sector—the sex sector—exploited workers in other labor sectors went unassisted.[31] In the process, sex workers have been caught in the crossfire of this assault on all commercial sexual transactions—including those between adults who were not coerced. As they have tried to work undetected to avoid arrest and deportation, sex workers—both undocumented migrants and U.S. citizens—now labor in less safe conditions. Working more in the shadow of the law than before the campaigns to "rescue" them, these workers have borne the brunt of these misguided policies. Women working in brothels fit the public imaginary of trafficked victims, men picking fruits and vegetables simply did not spur the same call-to-arms.[32] Since many workers in the sex sector are U.S. citizens, a focus on the sex trade not only provided an iconic victim deserving of assistance, but also avoided the political debates surrounding assisting undocumented workers.

Many legal practitioners and legal scholars have argued that the low numbers of T visas issued during the Bush administration resulted from the Department of Homeland Security's and the Department of Justice's focus on the prosecutorial goals of the T visa. When investigators and prosecutors identify trafficking victims, they decide both whether a victim would be a good witness and whether the individual is a victim for the purposes of the T visa. This conflict, observes the legal scholar Jayashri Srikantiah, "results in a failure to identify as trafficking victims those who do not present themselves as good prosecution witnesses."[33] Thus, even after the Obama administration backed away from the centrality of sexual labor in its approach to fighting trafficking, the predominance of the criminal justice frame still informs the U.S. government's antitrafficking efforts.[34]

Continuum of Exploitative Labor Practices

Since most undocumented workers—and some workers with temporary work visas—experience exploitation at some point, I situate trafficking into forced labor on a continuum of exploitative labor practices that low-wage migrants regularly experience in work sites throughout the United States. Low pay, no pay, unsafe work conditions, job insecurity, and no clear channels for redress are routine in work sites where migrants labor. Forced labor exists today in part because exploitative labor conditions exist and are allowed to proliferate. When some level of exploitation is the norm in work sites where migrant labor predominates, forced labor may flourish. It blends into an environment of everyday forms of normalized abuse. Trafficked persons typically are not physically restrained; thus, as they pick tomatoes or wash dishes or sew clothes alongside other migrant workers, they appear to be working under the same conditions as their coworkers. What distinguishes these coerced individuals from their coworkers is that they fear for themselves or their families if they try to leave their abuser. Intimidation works. All trafficked persons in forced labor, regardless of their particular circumstances of exploitation, have a compromised ability to walk away. For some, having no passport, money, contacts in the United States, or even seasonally appropriate clothes shapes their perception of the opportunity and safety of leaving.

There is an absurd quality to parsing out different degrees of exploitation. Although there are cases of forced labor that are so extreme that they can be mapped easily at one end of a continuum of exploitation, there also are many stories that are not so clear-cut. Rather, many of the cases of migrant worker exploitation beg the question of how to compare one exploitative practice against another. This hair splitting over different degrees of exploitation—but exploitation nonetheless—leaves many workers out in the cold. The TVPA structures new categories of labor and exploitation and sorts exploited workers into trafficked and nontrafficked categories, but this binary conceptualization obscures and effaces a broader range of migrant labor abuses. In many work sites, workers who qualify as trafficked may labor beside other employees who have a compromised ability to leave and find other work but who may not qualify for T visas. This kind of doling out of immigration relief to a few while the majority are unprotected causes tension within organizations. The staff at a domestic workers' rights organization in the Washington, D.C., area, for example, relates that there is both joy and jealousy and tension when a client receives a T visa. Those left out of any possibility for immigration relief know that if they stay in the United States, they likely will live and labor in the shadow of the law. One staff member at this organization describes their clients as living in a kind of labor "purgatory." This liminal zone of abuse and limited rights lays the groundwork for more egregious forms of exploitation to thrive unnoticed, unchecked, and unreported.

With exploitation the norm, those in severe situations of abuse that may qualify legally as trafficking into forced labor may not consider their labor experiences as significantly different from those of their similarly exploited migrant peers. Rather, there is a kind of normalization of exploitative conditions among migrant workers.[35] Importantly, T visa recipients say that they were unaware of T visas and the accompanying benefits. Instead those who eventually received a "trafficking" designation initially may have sought legal assistance for domestic abuse or for their immigration status.[36] An attorney in Florida explains that none of her trafficking clients first came to her and said, "I'm a victim of trafficking"; rather they came seeking help to avoid deportation or regarding an abusive partner. A social worker in New York similarly explains, "[Clients] talk about abuse, like 'My boyfriend beat me.' People do not talk about trafficking ever." Consequently, it is not surprising that most trafficking cases have not unfolded through self-identification. This environment of rampant abuse and employer intimidation, even when there is no forced labor, helps explain why there have been fewer than four thousand individuals designated by the U.S. government as "trafficked."

Peer-led rights-based outreach in places where migrants work and live is a first step to informing vulnerable workers of their rights. Peer-to-peer outreach as skillfully and creatively practiced by migrants' rights organizations such as the Coalition of Immokalee Workers (CIW), Lideres Campesinas, CASA de Maryland, and Damayan, protects workers against a range of workplace abuses, from wage theft to forced labor. These organizations' rights work model can be best practices for antitrafficking efforts in the United States and abroad. In the spirit of activist research, the central analytical frame of the book, which places forced labor on a continuum of exploitative labor practices, draws from these organizing strategies. It is these organizations' pathbreaking work and advocacy that inform policy recommendations in an appendix.[37] Basic rights work is the front line of antitrafficking work.

Who Are Trafficked Persons in the United States?

Often portrayed as a monolithic group, trafficked persons may share little more than their legal status. They come from many different countries, were forced into different forms of labor throughout the United States, and have settled in small towns and large cities. They speak different languages and have varying education and work histories, as well as differences in ethnic, racial, gender, sexual, generational, and religious identities. The length of time they were held in forced labor varies from weeks to years, and while most experienced psychological coercion, others also suffered physical brutality. A victim-witness coordinator for Immigration and Customs Enforcement (ICE) explains, "ICE agents ask me for profiles of traffickers and their victims. I tell them there is no one MO of a typical trafficker, there is no typical victim, and the paths that lead them here are varied. I've never seen anything like this before." A formerly trafficked person, Esperanza, who now speaks at law enforcement trainings agrees: "I've learned in trainings that every case is different. You may think you know about trafficking. But you only know your case."

Some formerly trafficked persons had never planned to live in the United States, such as young women who were persuaded by their boyfriends or husbands to travel to the United States or women who had worked as domestics overseas whose employers then moved them to the United States. Unplanned migrations such as these often capitalize on particular vulnerabilities: women manipulated by their boyfriends tend to be younger than the men. Employees following employers to the United States may be from not just a different social class but also a different nationality or ethnic group from their employers. Sometimes youth, inexperience, or traveling alone intensifies vulnerabilities. But there is no clear pattern of vulnerability that leads to forced labor. It cannot be said, for example, that trafficked persons come from the poorest classes in their countries of origin.[38] Rather in many cases these migrants had steady income-earning arrangements but could not make significant financial progress. Migration for work was a mobility strategy, a plan to attain long-term economic goals such as purchasing a home or buying a shop. In short, this is an ambitious and resourceful group, willing to avail themselves of whatever resources are within their reach.

Gendered migration patterns from their countries of origin also play a major role in determining where these resourceful and hopeful migrants look for work as well as the kind of work they seek. Out-migration for work in the caregiving industries, for example, is common among women, in particular from countries such as the Philippines.[39] Similarly migration for work in agriculture is a route for men from Mexico and Central America.[40] These individuals compose migration strategies that are not unlike those of their family members or neighbors. What could possibly go wrong when migration to the United States is a familiar path to economic mobility?

The Trafficking Assistance Regime

When all does go wrong and migrants' exploitation qualifies them for a "trafficking" designation, the trafficking assistance regime has significant shortcomings. The T visa allows recipients to stay in the United States for up to four years and to apply for permanent residence (LPR status) if they have not left the country during that time.[41] Their dependents can apply to live with them in the United States.[42] Grateful for the legal status the T visa has offered them, some of the first trafficked persons who received T visas, back in 2002 and 2003 also acknowledge the limitations of a "trafficking" designation. A major theme throughout the book is the critical lack of longer term social service assistance. Thus the actions of the state, first in identifying who qualifies as trafficked, and then in setting the terms of assistance, profoundly shape formerly trafficked persons' lives.[43]

The legal categories T visa applicant and recipient and green card applicant and recipient constitute and reinscribe notions of particular kinds of victims. These victims are deportable, while at the same time they are potential witnesses. At all stages they must be cooperative as they continue to prove their worthiness for a trafficking designation.[44] Since they cannot leave the country until they have a green card and may be called to testify against their abusers or decide to pursue civil damages, their legal status as "trafficked" subjects them to continued demands. These restrictions on mobility and ongoing encounters with law enforcement and with the justice system produce certain understandings of self, home, the United States, and place within the nation.

Maria, whose love of singing opens this introduction, was one of the first in the United States to file for a T visa, but she did not receive her green card until nearly ten years after leaving her situation of forced labor.[45] "It has been a long journey," she explained. "I've walked a long way. I have been in limbo for ten years!" She has been on the road and away from her son even longer. When she first left her home in the Philippines to work in the Middle East more than twenty years ago, Maria never imagined that she would be apart from her son for so long. Nor could she have foreseen that she would wait as long as she did for her green card. While she waited, her son grew into young adulthood in her absence.[46] With a green card in hand, she finally traveled to the Philippines to see her son. Now in his early twenties, he is the center of her life; she was truly lovesick thinking of their reunion: "I will be there for his birthday—I have never celebrated a birthday with him."

Carmen, whose story of gazing over the railroad tracks also opens this introduction, was equally frustrated that she could not travel outside of the United States to see her family while she waited for her green card. Her sisters had children she had not met, and her father's heart condition was a constant concern. "The T visa," she explained, "does not really give you much." Formerly trafficked persons are in a state of emotional and economic suspended animation while they wait to hear the result of their legal claims. Social workers who work with trafficked persons report that their clients do not find peace or calm until they receive their T visas and then their green cards. As a result, they often remain in a near-crisis state for years, unable to settle down and settle in. "My trafficking patients," commented a physician, "only begin to relax when their legal situation is more certain. When they have hope, they can sleep and eat and finally find some relief."

Everyday Lifework

While T visas allow formerly trafficked persons to live and work in the United States, removing significant fear, worry, and stress, they still face profound uncertainty and insecurity in other aspects of their lives. Consequently the overarching question animating this book is how do formerly trafficked persons rebuild their lives? How do they set their lives in motion on their own terms? Writing about how those who have suffered through brutality resume the "task of living (and not only surviving)," the anthropologist Veena Das questions how they simultaneously try to generate "a renewed capability to address the future" while they are caught up in the everyday.[47] For formerly trafficked persons, addressing immediate material needs—housing, work, health care—is more than enough to manage. As they focus on securing these basic elements of life, longer term plans for the future are stalled.

Mired in and at times overwhelmed by the demands of daily living, trafficked persons must learn, as have others who have suffered abuse, "to inhabit the world, or inhabit it *again*" through the "everyday work of repair."[48] As they once again make all the decisions in their lives, the smallest of these, such as deciding what to cook for dinner, can propel them forward. Tending to the ordinary tasks and chores of creating a home in the United States can help them move beyond the extraordinary exploitation of forced labor. This everyday lifework of home creation is a central theme of this book.

The new set of material living conditions and work options that formerly trafficked persons face after forced labor are unfamiliar at best and frightening, hostile, and potentially exploitative at worst. As these individuals plunge into a new life in the United States, factors that contributed to their forced labor in the first place may continue to shape their resettlement. Financial responsibilities to children or parents give particular direction and added stress to their decisions. Their lack of friends or family is one of the most significant factors that affects their well-being and sense of home in the United States. Nor do they have ready-made connections to communities of coethnics. In fact if their abusers are coethnics and if they or their associates are still at large formerly trafficked persons try to avoid communities of coethnics. Their level of English-language competency, marketable education or skills, knowledge of the United States, location and jail term of their abuser (in the rare cases when traffickers go to prison), and debt obligations to their recruiter, smuggler, or other travel brokers, all can aid or hinder their transition. Whether or not they are involved in court proceedings through which they have contact with their abusers, either to put them behind bars or to pursue civil awards, can prove haunting or liberating. Access to affordable health care is pivotal to their mental and physical well-being. Factors such as the economy, housing market, access to transportation, and availability of educational resources determine their longer-term strategies.

Securing an economic toehold in the United States is not easy. Most formerly trafficked persons only have access only to insecure, low-paying, and dead-end jobs. They also may face the kind of exploitative labor conditions that many workers in low-wage labor sectors face.[49] Since they do not have social networks to help them find new jobs with better wages, greater security, or opportunities for mobility, most perform the same jobs that they were doing while in forced labor. After all, if they had social networks in the United States to help secure good jobs and safe housing, they might never have been vulnerable to their abusers in the first place. And for those who want to acquire new skills or degrees, paying for school and balancing work and classes present even more challenges. They may ride out their time in a job longer than they had planned. Most formerly trafficked persons struggle to save enough money to put mobility strategies into place—for example, to go to school or to open a small business. In short, they confront the same obstacles the working poor face to getting ahead. Eva (whose story of raising her son opens this introduction) was able to go to school because, quite unusually for formerly trafficked persons, she and her son lived with Eva's brother who had been living in the United States. But since most T visa recipients have no family members with whom to pool income or other resources, social workers throughout the country have expressed concern that the deck is stacked against their trafficking clients. Even with legal permission to live and work in the United States, these individuals likely will enter the ranks of the working poor.[50] As a social worker in California explained, the benefit package can do only so much. Without more benefits and for a longer period of time, the current program often produces "a new subset of poor immigrant workers." Here are a few scenarios of life after forced labor:

> One woman occasionally sleeps in her car when she does not have enough money to pay for gas to get home from work.

> Another woman is over her head in debt following a divorce. Without her ex-husband's income, she cannot meet all her expenses as a single mother.

> A leader in the antitrafficking movement works full time where she is respected and challenged, but she can barely make ends meet and has no medical benefits.

> A number of women and men have remained in relationships that they want to end but cannot afford to move out and live on their own.

These stories of poverty and hardship, of course, are not unique to formerly trafficked persons. With both the recent recession and a tattered social safety net, stories like these are increasingly common depictions of life in poverty in the United States. What makes these challenges distinctive for formerly trafficked persons, however, are the cumulative emotional and financial impacts of being trafficked into forced labor. A Washington, D.C.–based attorney points out that this population must contend with both limited social networks and the financial repercussions of years without earnings. "These are not cases of ordinary wage theft; trafficked individuals have been deprived of their wages for years." Another attorney also in Washington, D.C., explains, "It is possible to recover from the trauma of trafficking; it is impossible to recover from years, and sometimes decades, of lost income. I have one client who was paid nothing for nearly twenty years. You cannot recover from that financial hit."

Home-Sense

Despite these many obstacles to living securely in the United States, those who pursue T visas and then green cards are continuing to choose to remain in the country.[51] They set about trying to feel at home in a country where their first experiences had been abusive. They not only have few, if any contacts, but also may have little knowledge about the United States. While social workers frequently talk about securing their clients' "stability" and medical doctors use the language of "well-being," I add to these descriptions of successful resettlement anthropological thinking on belonging and place- and home-making. Feeling at home, the subjectivity of place and belonging—what I call home-sense—takes time. But even before feeling at home, formerly trafficked persons must imagine the United States as offering possibilities worth staying for—a completely different vantage point from their first experience of the United States.

While forcibly displaced individuals assess the "degree of danger, financial viability, and reception" as they imagine returning home, formerly trafficked persons who elect to pursue a T visa imagine *staying* in the United States.[52] They take a leap, a chance that eventually they will feel at home and at peace in their newly chosen country.[53] Unlike refugees and others who were forced to leave their home as they fled insecurity and possibly violence, most formerly trafficked persons willingly left their home, in some cases undertaking complicated, dangerous, and expensive out-migration strategies.[54] The individuals who chose to stay in the United States do not look to or romanticize the past as a time of security.[55] Rather they look ahead. What they mourn is the time stolen from them by their abusers, not the loss of their past lives in their homeland.[56] In this way they do not expect or attempt to reconstitute the practices and understandings of their past homes. Nor do the formerly trafficked persons I met talk about return to their home country as a fall-back plan. Once they make the decision to stay in the United States, they focus on building a life there as if there is no other option—at least for the time being.[57] They invest in the "possible."[58]

In the course of building a sense of home, what the anthropologist Laura Hammond describes as the "affective space in which community, identity and political and cultural membership intersect," new migrants and refugees must build new personal, political, and professional ties.[59] These ties may be forged where they live, work, worship, or volunteer. Formerly trafficked persons, however, lack this entrée into a broader social network. They do not have meaningful and varied networks they can immediately tap. Thus while they face similar settlement challenges as other migrants and refugees, they do so without the assistance, knowledge, and sense of belonging that accompany membership in coethnic migrant and refugee communities that are reconstituted in the United States. They may live among other struggling newcomers, but they struggle largely on their own.

Notes on Conducting Research and Writing about Suffering
Meeting Formerly Trafficked Persons and Other Migrants

I have been extraordinarily fortunate to get to know remarkable individuals over many years. I have followed how they have been settling into their communities and jobs, as well as how they trust again as they create and maintain new social networks of friends, neighbors, and coworkers. At the same time that these individuals forge new relationships, they continue to manage old ones with family members back in their home countries. In some instances they are reunited with their relatives in the United States (since spouses and dependent children under twenty-one qualify for resettlement). While living in the United States, many have fallen in love and had children. Some also have left their partners or had their hearts broken. As they regained control over their lives, opening themselves up to new relationships has meant risking being deceived once again.

This book is based on multiple in-depth conversations with individuals trafficked into forced labor and those who have assisted them. I am indebted to the social workers and attorneys who introduced me to their trafficking clients in Los Angeles, Orange County, New York City, Long Island, Florida, Maryland, Washington, D.C., and Virginia. I first conducted formal interviews with these clients between 2004 and 2007, and since then I have continued to spend time with those who live near me (in Washington, D.C., Virginia, and Maryland) or in New York City and Los Angeles, where I visit regularly. During our first meeting, usually held in the office of a social service organization or in a client's home, a social worker or case manager was always present, and I tape-recorded our conversations. I spoke with thirty formerly trafficked persons in these formal meetings, as well as approximately twenty formerly trafficked persons in a variety of informal settings, such as potlucks held by community-based organizations, celebrations, workshops, and protests. I also met formerly trafficked persons at conferences, including participating on the same panels. I have kept in regular touch with some, and we have cooked dinner together or eaten out, seen movies, gone sight-seeing in their cities, or run errands. Many of these formerly trafficked persons, along with leaders in migrants' rights communities, social workers, attorneys, and labor organizers whom I first met as a researcher, are now trusted friends. Both formal interviews and casual dinners inform my analysis. For those of us doing research where we live, with people we know well, and on issues we also work on as activists, research blurs and blends with friendship and advocacy.

It was difficult for social workers and attorneys to identify appropriate candidates for taped conversations. Keenly aware of the possibilities of re-traumatization and of potential legal issues, social workers and attorneys were careful to introduce me to clients who had shown an interest in and whose legal cases would not be jeopardized by speaking with me. Barraged by a steady stream of requests by journalists and academics who wish to meet their clients, these gatekeepers spent time interviewing me before introducing me to their clients. I am deeply grateful for the trust they put in me. They introduced me to clients whom they believed would be strong enough to talk about their lives after forced labor. Because of this, a psychiatrist who works with trafficked patients cautioned that I may have met only particularly resilient individuals. Since I have known some of these individuals for over nine years, I have seen them confront many problems and setbacks. Their lives have taken unexpected twists and turns; domestic violence, chronic poverty, major health issues, and separation from their children are just some of the daunting challenges they have faced. Although it may be likely that initially I was introduced to individuals who are particularly energetic and determined, I have seen them struggle with a range of crises.

I also should note that social workers introduced me to more women than men since they thought we were more likely to hit it off; this is not a reflection of the gender balance of their caseload. Moreover since I have worked with half a dozen domestic workers' rights organizations throughout the United States, I have met more women than men. Consequently the book, for the most part, reflects more women's experiences than men's. I cannot emphasize enough, however, that the labor protections that I call for throughout the book are needed to protect all workers—women and men — across industries. Gender can shape forms of work and types of exploitation and abuse, to be sure, but women are by no means more vulnerable to forced labor or more deserving of assistance than men.

Assistance-givers within the trafficking care regime — social workers, case managers, attorneys, and staff at shelters — were crucial to my research. Since they are on the front lines of resettling formerly trafficked persons, I relied on regular communication with them in one-on-one meetings, telephone calls, and the annual Freedom Network conferences (a coalition of organizations that provide services to trafficked persons) and other anti-trafficking events. I cannot underscore enough how important their knowledge and experience was to this project. They generously invited me into discussions in which they exchanged concerns, successes, and best practices. Social workers and case managers who are in large agencies that oversee large caseloads know a great deal about experiences in and after forced labor. They have helped me to situate conversations with different trafficking clients in relationship with one another. I checked in with them about how they make sense of particular themes, whether recurring in many conversations or present only in one. Whereas law enforcement agents and attorneys need to produce linear accounts of what happened, social workers listen for what is not said — how events may affect individuals' self-identity and self-worth, their current relationships, health and well-being, and decision making. They ask questions that those trying to prove coercion may not, such as, "Do you hesitate when faced with a new experience or when meeting new people?" and "Is your current living situation safe?"

Living in Washington, D.C., has afforded me a front-row seat to watch antitrafficking policy unfold. Over the years I have been to a number of congressional events and hearings as well as events hosted by the Office to Monitor and Combat Trafficking in Persons at the U.S. Department of State. I have participated in small-group listening sessions convened by State Department officers who write the annual TIP Report, sessions in which these officers hear from social service agencies and researchers. I also have served as an "expert evaluator" for U.S. government grants for university researchers. And I have attended local-level antitrafficking task force meetings in Washington and in Los Angeles, as well as training sessions for law enforcement.

Because the book strongly asserts that trafficking into forced labor cannot be understood or prevented without learning from creative rights outreach in migrant communities, I also have spoken informally with migrants in low-wage jobs who have experienced a range of workplace abuses but who do not qualify for a T visa. I have met these exploited—but not trafficked—migrants through many of the same organizations that provide services to formerly trafficked individuals. They have been a part of labor-organizing meetings, potluck dinners, celebrations, health fairs, protests and other venues, some of which I attended with formerly trafficked persons throughout the country. During my travels to meet formerly trafficked persons and their assistance-givers, I also met with migrants' rights organizations and workers' rights organizations across low-wage labor sectors. When I write about the strategies, successes, and frustrations for organizers within domestic worker, farmworker, and day laborer communities, particularly in chapter 1, I draw from these conversations.

I also met workers who were exploited but not trafficked in spaces where I have been involved as a migrants' rights and workers' rights activist. In Washington, D.C., northern Virginia, and Maryland I have attended migrants' rights and workers' rights organizations' "know your rights" workshops, skill-building activities, and social events; hearings on antimigrant legislation; and coalition meetings on wage theft and other crimes against migrants. I have served as a volunteer at a day laborer center in northern Virginia and at an immigration legal clinic. I also have attended meetings of the Economic Empowerment Working Group, a coalition of organizations in New York City working to provide long-term support—including fellowships, loans, and training—for formerly trafficked persons. It is my hope that this book will bring attention to the difficulty of securing long-term economic stability. In sum, as a researcher and a migrants' rights and workers' rights activist, I am regularly in spaces where migrants and vulnerable workers assume leadership positions, advocate on their own behalf, and seek legal protections as they become part of the communities in which they live and work.

Learning through Activism

Watching membership-based migrants' rights and workers' rights organizations in action has shaped how I have framed this project both within conversations on migrants' rights as well as labor protections for low-wage workers. Scholars concerned with issues of oppression, inequality, and injustice long have explored the dialectic between theory and action.[60] Antitrafficking advocates and policymakers can learn a great deal from labor organizing strategies that improve workers' lives. For researchers, advocacy can be a form of what anthropologists' call "participant observation" that brings them into a variety of spaces where they may occupy dual roles as researchers and advocates. These political commitments also allow those who work on issues that are not site-specific to "participate" in a kind of community on an ongoing basis.[61] Getting involved locally on national-level issues can be part of an "active" and "activist" participant observation.[62] Before this research project began, I had been involved in conversations, workshops, and campaigns with a long list of migrants' rights, sex workers' rights, and low-wage workers' rights organizations. Through these various ties and commitments, I have had the opportunity to learn about resources, funds, and strategies that could be of use within the antitrafficking community. In this way, I have tried to be a conduit between the antitrafficking and migrants' rights communities. These communities generally otherwise have been siloed, in part because they have different goals and tactics, and in part because they often compete over scarce resources and media attention.

Listening to Formerly Trafficked Persons

Before meeting trafficking clients at social-service organizations, I did not read any news reports, court documents, or Department of Justice press releases about their legal cases. Nor do I use these sources here to fill in the gaps, alter, or "correct" the stories that they told me. I am not an investigative reporter, and I told them as much; I promised that I would listen to *their* stories. My primary aim is to convey their perceptions of what happened from their vantage point. Traumatic events can affect memory, and abused individuals may not be able to piece together events exactly as they happened, or place them in chronological sequence.[63] It has been up to attorneys to prove coercion throughout these events; I do not want to be in the business of proving anything with the stories told to me or of "setting the record straight." To do that, I would have to test interviewees' memories and the accuracy of their accounts. In light of controversies over getting an individual story right rather than getting out a larger representative story, I intend this project to illuminate issues after forced labor, not to retell "facts" that already may be in news accounts, court documents, or press releases. It is of critical importance that individuals who have been in forced labor keep control over their story. I would be further abusing their trust if I were intentionally to look for factual errors.[64] This is their record, an account of how they make sense of events as they lived through them. Their vantage point is significantly shaped by the vast differences in power between them and their abusers. For example, a few formally trafficked persons who had worked overseas before coming to the United States describe former employers as "like ambassadors." And a few individuals who had been trafficked into the United States also describe their traffickers in these vague terms. The view that their abusers were unassailable and did not answer to anyone or any law conveys a sense of their perceived powerlessness in the face of those more powerful.

Taped conversations and the recordings and transcripts involved can take on timeless, near fetishistic qualities. A taped conversation captures reflections at a particular moment in time. I hope to communicate how much in flux these individuals' lives are. Throughout my ongoing conversations with the same individuals over the past nine years, I have seen how they have changed their views of particular events and the choices that they have made. From these casual conversations without a tape recorder, usually over a meal, my discomfort with taped conversations has intensified. Deeply wary as well of the limits of one-time conversations, I sought to have as many ongoing conversations as possible.[65] And just as some formerly trafficked persons talk about events differently today than they did when I first met them, it is likely that they will alter them again and again in the coming years.

In the case of some of the individuals who feature prominently in the book, I shared the book in progress. Flo read page by page while we drank green tea in a Japanese restaurant. "Oh, the pictures that are coming back to my mind. I can't believe this all happened." I worried that reading about her time of escape (in Chapter 2) would be upsetting. She assured me it was in the past, "It was a terrible time. But now it seems a long time ago." While she was reading, her phone buzzed with calls and texts from some of the people that had helped her escape. She tapped her phone, reminding me, "See this is my sister's friend who helped me." And, "That's my friend from church calling." As she remembered the details of her time living with her abuser and of leaving, and we talked about the many friends she has now and "all the sacrifices" they had made to support her, we closed the restaurant. These moments when formerly trafficked persons remember, and I listen, have changed as we came to know one another over many years. As they move further away from their time in forced labor, they see past events from a different perspective. Certain gains or losses have become more important today than when we first met eight or nine years ago, while others have receded, supplanted by new concerns.

Through both formal tape-recorded conversations and these many follow-up, informal exchanges, clear themes have emerged. I listened for crosscutting themes that seem to matter to many individuals. Difficulties trusting others again, the struggles living and working on the economic margins of the United States, and the consequences of keeping silent about one's experiences in forced labor arose again and again. I attempt to convey the feelings that formerly trafficked persons — many of whom were in vastly different circumstances of forced labor — expressed about their experiences in and after forced labor. I am confident that the stories I recount in chapter 2 of life in forced labor, for example, capture the experience of being under someone's control as well as the mechanisms used to control, even if the specific details vary from case to case. My ongoing conversations with those who assist trafficked persons — social workers, case managers, attorneys, and shelter staff — helped me to draw connections and understand distinctions between individual cases.

Other circumstances of conversations with formerly trafficked persons also shaped my understanding of their resettlement. I spoke with individuals from all over the world, and consequently had to rely on their limited English, on translators for those who spoke only Vietnamese, or on my own Spanish. Having social workers present who vouched for me certainly helped me gain trust with clients I was meeting for the first time. Their presence also may have unintentionally spurred their clients to talk about certain themes, as well as to downplay or avoid others. Getting to know formerly trafficked persons outside of their social workers' offices has allowed for wide-ranging conversations — and a great deal of fun. Our interactions have not always been about telling and listening, but are also about sharing our lives, cooking and eating, meeting friends and partners, and family, and going to parades, protests, street fairs, museums, movies, and concerts.

For cases that have been covered in the press and are easily identifiable, I leave out identifying characteristics. Some individuals are among only a handful of trafficked persons from their home country who have resettled in a particular town or city (and in some cases there may be just one person). As a result, I am vague about their country of origin to keep my promise of confidentiality to them. In these instances, I refer to the continent of their home country or the state in which they live now, not the specific country or city or town. I use pseudonyms throughout the book. Out of extra caution with particularly identifiable cases, in some parts of the book I do not use any name (not even an assigned pseudonym) but instead write generally that "a woman's trafficker is still at large" or "a woman fell out of love" with a live-in boyfriend. In the sections where I reproduce what formerly trafficked persons said to me, I have at times altered verb forms to make clear the sequence of time. For example, I have added the word *had* in front of verbs to indicate an event that happened earlier. Otherwise I have not copyedited their accounts.

In sections on programs and policies that could help prevent forced labor and find individuals in an abusive situation, I identify migrants' rights and workers' rights organizations by name that are models of innovative peer-led outreach. I do not identify specific organizations by name, however, when I quote particular member-activists, peer leaders, labor organizers, or attorneys, but write generally about a "farmworker activist in California" or a "day labor organizer in the Washington, D.C., area." Nor do I identify by name specific social workers, attorneys, or shelter staff or the organizations for which they work. Instead, to protect their clients and their organizations' funding—and in some cases, their own jobs—I quote a "social worker in New York City" or a "shelter staff worker in Los Angeles." In sum, the practice I have followed is to call attention to creative and effective migrant- and worker-led and centered rights work while protecting the specific names of these organizations' worker-members and staff. I also hope that the expertise and dedication that so many social workers, attorneys, and shelter staff bring to crafting new best practices with trafficking clients shines through.

The Currency of Victimhood

Unlike attorneys who must produce a full narrative of events for legal cases, I made clear to the formerly trafficked persons I met that they need not tell me anything they did not want to. I encouraged them to talk about things that matter to them. I explained that I was writing about life *after* forced labor. In every conversation, however, formerly trafficked persons wove their present-day experiences together with their past ones in forced labor. Thus the book also includes portraits of life before and during forced labor. Some details remained murky. While I did ask questions about their lives today—such as what they do to relax or what they think of their current working conditions—I did not ask questions intended to prompt them to elaborate on information about their time in forced labor.

It is hard to know why so many formerly trafficked persons returned to the period of forced labor in our conversations; they may have done so because this was one venue in which they could control the terms of the telling. Asked by many law enforcement, attorneys, and social service providers to talk about their time in forced labor, they ironically are silenced. They know that in these spaces of proof they must tell stories of victimhood. In contrast, talking in venues that they choose to be in, such as community events, is a way to present themselves as they want to be seen. I also think that they spoke about their time in forced labor because it has shaped who they are now. They are reminded of this when they return to their social service providers' offices, which may be the only spaces in which they talk about their experiences in forced labor.[66]

Since the formerly trafficked persons I met explain that they are shaped, but not stopped, by these past events, how much of these past events should I retell? In an essay on suffering, the anthropologists Arthur Kleinman and Joan Kleinman ask a powerful question relevant here: "To what uses are experiences of suffering put?"[67] Images and stories of human suffering help organizations raise money, fuel social movements, and persuade governments to act. Eyewitness accounts of the horrors of the Middle Passage (from ship doctors or members of the ship's crew), for example, were powerful tools for nineteenth-century abolitionists to gain public support.[68] The forum or audience also informs the storytelling; whether bearing witness in a truth commission, testifying against one's abuser in a court of law, or proving one's legal status, the venue influences what is said and unsaid.[69] Fiona Ross found that women's testimony before the South African Truth and Reconciliation Commission, for example, "permitted the expression of certain kinds of experience while eliding others." "Any telling," consequently, "is produced of silences and erasures."[70] Similarly, while participating on Peru's Truth and Reconciliation Commission, the anthropologist Kimberly Theidon found that only "certain victim categories became 'narrative capital.'"[71]

In the United States only certain conditions of "victimhood" qualify the tellers for trafficking status. The language in the telling of suffering is measured and assessed. In the chapters that follow, I write about the dilemmas inherent in measuring labor exploitation, which result in leaving abused workers — but not abused *enough* — out of assistance and immigration relief. Language is central to proving these different degrees of victimhood and thus worthiness for legal protections and of assistance. Evidence of suffering on the body is another. During my research with Dominican women (in the Dominican Republic) who had been trafficked into forced labor in

Argentina, a young woman took off her shirt during our conversation in her social worker's office. She wanted to show — not just tell about — the abuse she endured in Argentina.[72] Not everyone, of course, finds the process of recounting suffering as empowering or healing as others want it to be for them. The anthropologist Maria Olujic achingly demonstrates this point when she describes Croatian women who killed themselves after speaking to journalists about being raped during the war.[73]

Recounting abuse in great detail has been a cornerstone of human rights reporting. Careful accounting of gruesome human rights violations makes it more difficult for governments and international organizations to do nothing.[74] With the TVPA guaranteeing assistance to trafficked persons and with state and federal laws in place to prosecute traffickers, the fight against trafficking in the United States does not lack political will or legal tools. Nonetheless news accounts and organizations' fundraising materials generally recount stories in which trafficked persons emerge either as heroes who courageously escape or as beaten-down victims who need to be "rescued" by "modern-day abolitionists." Either way, accounts of their suffering are essential to the creation of an iconic image of a trafficked person.

Instead of fitting real lives within these two extreme representations of trafficking, I try to make clear the context of coercion in which trafficked persons make decisions. I do not want to trade in stories that reduce individuals to particular details of their suffering. Nor do I want to overstate their active strategizing when there may have been few opportunities to do so. Forced labor is not always a physical state of coercion, with locks on doors preventing individuals from leaving. It can be a mental state with chains built out of fear (the focus of chapter 2). Forced labor takes place within a zone of power differentials — class, race, ethnicity, gender, and religion. When writing about forced labor, therefore, there must be an interplay between recounting the specific forms of coercion and suffering that individuals endured and the larger systems in which such profound injustice, inequity, and abuse could exist and thrive. In the details of life in and after forced labor, real lives come into view, not a monolithic portrayal of victims of trafficking. There simply is no unified narrative about living through forced labor, exiting it, and recomposing a life afterward. The narratives of survival through and after forced labor that are celebrated and circulated simultaneously produce a particular body of knowledge about trafficking and trafficked persons' needs as well as constitute a popular understanding of trafficking and trafficked individuals. A frustrated social worker in New

York observed, "We like stories of a young woman who was trafficked into a brothel—and does amazing things and then ends up on *Oprah*. We never hear about women who stay in sex work. This is not recorded anywhere. But many stay—because the money is so good."

The Chapters Ahead

With fewer than four thousand individuals in the United States with trafficking visas, trafficked persons' stories, often sensationalized, frequently unfold in the media. I hope this book allows readers to learn about the daily concerns and successes of real people. These individuals are not just one-dimensional statistics in a chart or a three-sentence harrowing vignette in a news article. Maria, Carmen, Flo, and Eva are far more than their experience in forced labor, their story of exit, or their current visa status. Those with T visas explain that nearly everyone they know in their low-income neighborhoods and at their low-wage work sites struggles as they do. This shared struggle at marginalized communities throughout the United States is rarely depicted in the dominant narratives about trafficked persons. Instead the main story line is about sex trafficking. The conflation of trafficking with prostitution has led, as chapter 1 explores, to "rescuing" individuals in the sex sector who are not trafficked and do not want assistance, but want to continue working. At the same time, migrant workers who experience actual instances of abuse—but not severe enough to rise to the level of trafficking—risk deportation if they come forward.

These claims about who trafficking "victims" are and what they need—expressed in U.S. government documents, the media, NGO mission statements, and fundraising campaigns—extend and rely upon mythic notions of trafficking victims. A ferocious and evidence-bereft battle over sexual labor has set the terms of debate on how best to undertake antitrafficking activities in the United States. While extending labor protections to workers (regardless of immigration status) in unregulated industries (such as agriculture) is critical to preventing forced labor, this war on sex work—along with an assault on undocumented migrants—instead has dominated U.S. antitrafficking policy. I devote chapter 1 to the sexual and immigration politics of trafficking. Chapter 2 examines the conditions of and exit from forced labor. Formerly trafficked persons settle into new lives, solving crises immediately upon exiting forced labor (the focus of chapter 3), and facing more crises over the long term (the discussion in chapter 4). Chapter 5 examines their new relationship to labor *after* forced labor. I close the book by offering some ideas for action.

Conclusion

Formerly trafficked persons quietly settle into towns and cities throughout the United States. They soon time-out of government benefits and find themselves dogged by bills, obligations to send money home to family, and the everyday assaults of living in poor neighborhoods. Tires blow, gas tanks empty, kids' shoes tighten, teeth need dental work, and rents rise. They face ordinary financial stressors, usually on their own, without family. They create a sense of home. They imagine what is possible. As bills mount, a recession wracks the U.S. economy, and they and their migrant friends, coworkers, and neighbors struggle in low-wage jobs. Making ends meet is a monumental challenge.

Nothing is resolved overnight. A string of small and large setbacks, surprises, and accomplishments punctuates formerly trafficked persons' resettlement process. These individuals tell their own stories. Julia, now a marathon runner, anchors her description of building a new life in California in the races she has run. Flo maps her time in the United States by ticking off the goals she has methodically accomplished: obtain a GED, driver's license, and nursing assistance degree. Yet while Flo was able to save enough money to invest in her education by living rent-free with a family she had met at her church, most formerly trafficked persons tread water financially. Bills and other immediate responsibilities regularly sideline longer-term plans. A $500 speeding ticket cut into Beatrice's goal, for example, to take a full course load at a local college. Trafficked into forced domestic labor as a young teen, Beatrice is determined to make up for the time taken from her. Now in her early twenties, money is tight. Securing an affordable apartment and a job that accommodates her school schedule has meant that she practically lives on the highway. With work, school, and home at least a forty-five-minute drive from each other, Beatrice operates on the brink of logistical and financial disaster. Like the majority of formerly trafficked persons who have no family or established social networks in the United States, she confronts one crisis after the next on her own. Having to raise herself, she has learned to drum up resources from all corners. She texted me, for example, to see if I knew of any programs to help defray the costs of filing for her green card. (Her pro-bono attorney eventually was able to secure a fee waiver.) Years into their resettlement, long after their government benefits have ended, formerly trafficked persons like Beatrice and Flo must rely on the knowledge and generosity of their new friends and colleagues, as well as their own savvy—and luck.

Over time their legal status as a trafficked person determines their choices less and less. Their life experiences and education and skill sets that they brought with them to the United States become all the more important. So do local factors—job opportunities in the local economy, housing costs, and the presence or absence of coethnics. This status as a new migrant and not a trafficked person is what the outside world knows about them. Short of becoming a locally or nationally known antitrafficking activist and publicly referencing their past exploitation, formerly trafficked persons look, sound, and struggle like their migrant friends, coworkers, and neighbors. Since most formerly trafficked persons do not talk about their trafficking status and only invoke it in private bureaucratic encounters, they move further away from this juridical label and the benefits it carries. The cards in their wallet announce this legal status—and reference past abuse—but once put away in purses and pants' pockets, there are no other visible ways that they are marked as trafficked. They do not live in a separate community of formerly trafficked persons or enjoy long-term social benefits stemming from their legal status. As they time out of case management and the benefits accompanying their trafficking designation, and later receive their green cards (and possibly receive criminal restitution or civil damages), they no longer have the formal guidance of social workers or attorneys.

They struggle. Their struggles resemble those depicted in a rich array of migrants' testimonials, memoirs, novels, and art that tell of the compromises and losses—along with the surprises and joys—involved in making a new home in the United States. Racial profiling by law enforcement, unwelcoming communities, and inflammatory media pundits have demonized individuals simply trying to make a living in low-wage jobs that are essential to the U.S. economy. At the same time that antimigrant vitriol floods prime-time TV and drive-time radio, trafficked persons are mythologized and trafficking is popularly understood as a major human rights issue of our time. Central to this mythologizing has been the removal of trafficking from the domains of migrants' rights or workers' rights. Trafficking instead has come to signal sexual victimhood even though the sex sector is just one labor sector among many into which individuals are trafficked.

This book squarely situates trafficked persons' experiences in and after forced labor alongside those of other exploited migrant workers. It tells the early story of resettlement of the first trafficked persons, who are the object of public fascination but who remain unknown as *trafficked* in the communities where they live and work and whose stories may not resemble those told in the media. It has a viewpoint—that of formerly trafficked persons themselves. Through their stories we will learn what they identify as hallmarks of forced labor, how they exited it, and what they need and strive for afterward. This is a book about them, their concerns, their struggles, and their successes—their everyday lifework.

Part I. *The Assault on Workers*

Chapter One

Dangerous Labor

MIGRANT WORKERS and SEX WORKERS

In her office in a run-down neighborhood in Los Angeles, an organizer with a migrants' rights organization was worried. They were getting more calls every day. With the recession and recent anti-immigrant legislation in Arizona, migrant communities were rattled. Fear was palpable. Those living on a razor's edge were losing their minimum-wage jobs or having their hours scaled back, falling behind on rent, and getting evicted. Those working, the organizer explained, "tolerate all kinds of abuses to keep their jobs; they don't complain. They don't complain about terrible housing conditions either." Fearful of getting deported, they keep quiet and hold on.

//////

At a press conference at a community center in Washington, D.C., a collaborative team of researchers reported that the D.C. police were targeting anyone who "looked" like a sex worker. Racial minorities, transgender individuals, anyone wearing certain kinds of clothes or walking in certain areas of town were being harassed (with verbal slurs, physical battering, and sexual assault) and arrested. They recounted what they heard throughout Washington: "We can't work—or even just walk—safely in our neighborhoods."

Figure 1.1. The Alliance for a Safe and Diverse D.C. holds a press conference to announce the report "Move Along" on policing of prostitution in Washington, D.C. Spring 2008. Photograph by PJ Starr.

////////

The story the organizer in Los Angeles tells—of worry, vulnerability, exploitation, and poverty—is one told by migrants' rights organizers around the United States. An organizer in the Washington, D.C., area tells of domestic workers who fear that their employers would fire them if they know the women attend domestic workers' rights meetings. A day laborer organizer in Virginia explains that he has never met a worker who has not been cheated by an employer. Farmworker activists in California tell of foremen sexually assaulting women workers, widespread wage theft, and regular exposure to pesticides.[1]

The story the community researchers in Washington tell of danger at every turn is similar to what sex worker rights activists and researchers have heard throughout the United States.[2] Seeking to "end demand" for prostitution as a strategy to end trafficking, antiprostitution forces have engaged in an all-out attack on anyone presumed to be in sex work.[3] In the name of "rescuing" trafficking victims, those who choose to work in the sex sector—both U.S. citizens and foreign nationals—have been incarcerated (and deported in the case of undocumented migrants).[4] Justified as saving women from coercion in the sex sector, the "rescues" themselves can be coercive and push already vulnerable workers further underground.

Two Communities under Attack: Migrants and Sex Workers

At first glance, these two communities—low-wage migrants (undocumented and documented) and workers in the sex sector (undocumented and documented)—may seem to have little in common. Yet both communities labor at the margins of legality, and thus both constantly face the possibility of arrest and incarceration. Those who lack legal status in the United States also face the possibility of deportation. Both communities have experienced targeted raids and arrests. Both have been trying to labor undetected. And both face great risks if they report abuses that either they or their coworkers experience.

This chapter focuses on the immigration and sexual politics shaping antitrafficking policy in the United States. I examine the fallout of anti-immigrant and antiprostitution policies on vulnerable workers and, ultimately, on the effectiveness of antitrafficking work. With local policies (such as 287(g) agreements and "secure communities" programs) and state-wide legislation (such as in Arizona and Alabama) targeting undocumented migrants and coercive rescues occurring in all kinds of sex sector venues (massage parlors, dance clubs, brothels) and in public spaces, workers are unlikely to report any level of exploitation.[5] The hyperscrutiny of the sex sector, meanwhile, often has eclipsed efforts to expose exploitation in other labor sectors. In common parlance trafficking has become synonymous with prostitution. Forced labor is simply invisible, overshadowed by the dominant discourse of sex trafficking. The reality of migrant exploitation, however, is all around us. With migrants often performing some of the most low-paying, insecure, and dangerous jobs throughout both rural and urban United States, their precarious labor is an essential element in today's economy. Low-wage migrants do work that is ubiquitous: picking crops, washing restaurant dishes, building houses, and taking care of children. But since undocumented migration is a political hot button, the link to forced labor is ignored. Instead, those who control the terms of debate, images, policies, and resource allocation focus exclusively on trafficking-as-sex trafficking. The failure to enforce labor laws and to protect the rights of all workers— including undocumented migrants and those working in the sex sector— creates the conditions that allow forced labor to flourish.

This chapter is divided into two sections: the assault on migrants in section I and the assault on sex workers in section II. While the rest of the book focuses on life in and after forced labor, section I examines the less abusive—but more widespread—exploitative practices that characterize many work sites where migrants labor. I highlight a number of factors that prevent exploited migrants from seeking help from community-based organizations or law enforcement to underscore how unlikely it is for *extremely* exploited workers to do so. Section II continues to explore this connection between vulnerable communities' fear of law enforcement, silence about abuse, and the paltry number of T visas issued. I argue that the conflation of trafficking with sex trafficking, particularly during the George W. Bush administration, resulted in a myopic focus on exploitation in only one labor sector: the sex sector. In the process, exploited workers in other labor sectors have gone unassisted and sex workers have become more vulnerable, with their livelihood under attack in the fight against trafficking.

I. THE ASSAULT ON MIGRANTS
Almost Trafficking

The story of living and laboring precariously in Los Angeles that opens this chapter—and the abuses that stem from this precariousness—is a recurring tale in the political economy of migrant labor. To understand cases of extreme abuse—trafficking into forced labor—we first need to understand the forms of abuse that happen every day in places where migrants work and live. Migrants stay quiet about this everyday exploitation. Employers and landlords try to get away with all they can. They are able to do so, in large part, because of workers' and tenants' undocumented status (or visa status that ties them to one employer).[6] These vulnerable workers know that at any time they may be cheated out of their wages and asked to do dangerous work. For some, threats of violence as well as instances of actual violence have been regular features of their experiences working in the United States.[7] Conceptualizing the effects of policing legality, the anthropologist Susan Coutin describes undocumented migrants as living in "holes" within the national territory, where laws and courts protect everyone except them.[8] Exclusion produces silences. Silent about everything from domestic abuse in their home to robberies in their community and assaults and exploitation in their workplace, undocumented migrants strive to remain unnoticed. As they parent, live, and work alongside citizen family members, neighbors, and friends, they navigate the United States with only minimal protections that are woefully underenforced.[9]

The domestic worker organizer mentioned earlier who reaches out to fearful domestic workers describes an extensive web of employer control: "Their employers know they don't have family here. And since they control their hours so much they [the employers] know that they [their employees] have not made friends. They know the women are alone here, so if they say they have to leave for a few hours, they may even follow them." This threatening work environment, in which employers monitor their employees' down time may not be trafficking, but it is close. Worker-activists and labor organizers describe cases that teeter on the brink of forced labor. Although these cases may not qualify as trafficking, they involve daily abuse and powerful forms of intimidation nonetheless. Within this gray area of exploitation, there can be bad working conditions and really bad working conditions, none of which may amount to a trafficking case. The roughly 3,500 individuals who have received the DHS stamp of approval as "trafficked" (in the form of a T visa) are on the extreme end of the more widespread phenomenon of everyday exploitation of migrant workers, both documented and undocumented.[10]

The Migration Politics of Trafficking

Two major anti-immigrant actions during President Obama's first term profoundly affected migrants and their communities: U.S. Immigration and Customs Enforcement (ICE) ramped up workplace raids at work sites where undocumented workers were presumed to labor, and states and localities passed anti-immigrant legislation. All told, roughly 1.6 million individuals were deported during the Obama administration's first term.[11] Highly publicized ICE raids on workplaces have sent clear messages to exploited migrants to not report abuse. They also have torn apart families and communities. During an ICE raid in 2008 at a meat-processing plant in Postville, Iowa, agents apprehended 389 undocumented workers and charged, convicted, and sentenced nearly three hundred of them within ten days. Group trials were held at temporary fairgrounds. The American Civil Liberties Union commented that the close coordination before the raid between the prosecutor and the chief judge to hasten the process and structure plea agreements was highly irregular and raised due process concerns.[12] A translator at the plant later reported, "In some cases both parents were picked up and small children were left behind for up to 72 hours."[13] Abuses abounded at another high-profile ICE raid, just months after the raid in Postville. At least 595 workers were detained at an electrical transformer plant owned by Howard Industries in Laurel, Mississippi. An organizer for the Mississippi Immigrants Rights Alliance described the event: "It's just horrific. We've got two families where the mom and the dad were released with ankle bracelets. They've got bills to pay and kids to feed. We've got a woman who is 24, 26 weeks pregnant, and she's got a husband, brother, father and brother-in-law who were detained."[14]

Secure Communities programs and 287(g) programs—which empower local police officers to check the immigration status of individuals stopped for other possible violations—have critically damaged trust between migrant communities and law enforcement.[15] Taken together, these offensives have created a state of siege in communities where migrants, documented and undocumented, work and live. This erosion of trust compromises community members' safety. Among the unreported abuses that the community organizer in Los Angeles references (in this chapter's opening) is the rape of a teenage girl by a neighbor who had taunted her that he would report her family to immigration if she told anyone.[16] "This is what is happening. People are not reporting crimes in our communities."

With local law enforcement now functioning as border patrol agents, there are, in effect, patrols hunting for undocumented migrants deep within U.S. borders.[17] At the same time, some community members lobby for the deportation of "illegal aliens" along with creating an unwelcoming atmosphere as a way to reduce immigration.[18] "Attrition through enforcement" has become a mantra among these antimigrant activists.[19] As a result, migrants without documentation live in chronic fear of detection, detention, and deportation. And the assault on migrants takes new forms every day. For example, a front-page story in the New York Times reported on a new technique to hunt down migrants: U.S. residents along the U.S.-Mexico border text Border Patrol agents if they see anyone trying to cross.[20] The effects of this policing by law enforcement agents as well as ordinary citizens terrifies and unmoors. These efforts also are at odds with campaigns to prevent trafficking, which rely on timely reporting of abusive employers from migrants themselves.

These ICE raids and the Obama administration's expansion of 287(g) agreements have deepened the atmosphere of fear and silence around labor abuses. As states pass Arizona- and Alabama-style anti-immigrant legislation, and localities continue to enact and enforce policies that target migrants, more and more foreign nationals are likely to mistrust law enforcement, both local and federal. The very real risk of detention and deportation (with a ten-year re-entry ban) allows unscrupulous or abusive employers to threaten, exploit, and even physically harm their employees. An H-2B forestry worker from Guatemala recounted how employers deployed the threat of deportation as a silencing mechanism: "When the supervisor would see that a person was ready to leave the job because the pay was so bad, he would take our papers from us. He would rip up our visas and say, 'You don't want to work? Get of here then. You don't want to work? Right now I'll call immigration to take your papers and deport you."[21] Since in many instances employers take workers' passports and visas, those who decide to take their chances and leave may have to do so without any of their documents. One H-2 worker who was recruited to work in the southeastern United States explained: "Since I couldn't prove that I was in the country legally, I was nervous to even go out to the store for fear that I would be stopped by the police."[22]

While immigration raids and programs that target migrants strain notions of justice and morality, the legal relief and social service benefits that trafficked persons receive expose the contradictory logic that undergirds U.S. immigration policy. Although there is widespread consensus among law enforcement, migrant labor organizers and attorneys, and social workers that large numbers of migrants are working in situations of forced labor, finding them has been a challenge in this anti-immigrant atmosphere. With the TVPA allowing up to five thousand T visas to be issued every year, in theory, by the end of 2012 as many as sixty thousand persons could have received T visas. Even the scale of trafficking to the United States is uncertain. After years of fluctuating statistics, as I write this, the latest numbers the U.S government circulated was an estimate of 14,500 to 17,500 persons trafficked to the United States every year.[23] But there is little doubt that egregious forms of exploitation occur every day at work sites where migrants labor—for example, in restaurant kitchens, fields, and factories.[24]

Today's Jim Crow

This widespread abuse of migrants—both documented and undocumented—often in communities with a long history of racial discrimination, has prompted labor organizers and civil rights leaders to refer to life in certain counties and states as life under "Juan Crow."[25] Migrants, particularly those whose racial identities are not "white," fear being stopped by law enforcement at any moment.[26] The Southern Poverty Law Center (SPLC) reports, "Like African Americans during the height of Jim Crow, many Latinos in the South live in constant fear of being unfairly targeted by the police as they go about their daily lives. Just the simple acts of driving to work or taking a child to a soccer match can result in intimidation or abuse—regardless of a Latino's immigration status." In fact a number of those interviewed for the SPLC report described the South as a "war zone" for immigrants, "a place where harassment and routine inconvenience is a way of life and where life-altering consequences are always just one false step away."[27] One grower in North Carolina put it plainly: "The North won the War on paper but we confederates actually won because we kept our slaves. First we had sharecroppers, then tenant farmers and now we have Mexicans."[28] An attorney representing low-wage workers in the South explains: "With or without documentation, no matter how you arrange it, it's not a level playing field. The workers don't have a life. One grower said to me, 'Why would I want a U.S. worker—he may have to take off work to take his kids to the doctor.'"

A labor system of extraction, exploitation, and intimidation unfurls in spaces where there is a history of racism, disenfranchisement, and unchecked employer control. An attorney in California describes an underregulated environment in the Central Valley, where growers operate knowing that labor inspectors will not be paying a visit. In these more remote areas, this attorney estimates "it would take about forty years to reach all the farms with the current number of government inspectors." Consequently, the lawyer reports, "workers are mistreated everywhere. Historically, these growers have been Neanderthals in their approach to labor. These are people whose families fought against the elements. They survived by exploiting others. This is the way they have done their business. They'll be damned if the law is going to get in their way!" Referencing the historical loopholes in the Fair Labor Standards Act, the attorney asks, "How do you change a system that has survived where abuse can happen legally? The abuse is rooted in the system, in our separate laws for agriculture where workers have to work ten-hour days and get paid no overtime. Big AG businesses do not suffer penalties if they get caught. There is no real penalty to change their ways. "Critiquing "the idyllic notion of a small family farm," he explains that only a few families own nearly all the farmland in entire counties: "Farms just don't look as they once did." The lack of government surveillance ironically may provide an incentive for undocumented workers to keep working in these remote areas. "Workers may be abused in places like the Central Valley," explains a worker-organizer, "but it may be better than having an ICE presence. Workers know they won't get harassed after work. A bad situation is a hell of a lot better than going to jail and getting deported."[29]

Working for decades with U.S. citizens who also have been exploited in farm labor, an attorney in the South describes that some kind of vulnerability, such as homelessness or substance abuse, keeps these "lifers" in farm labor.[30] Just as they do for undocumented workers (and those with temporary work visas), employers often create an extensive system of control and indebtedness placing African American crews in a "spiral of debt" by paying for employer-supplied housing and food. Workers stay because they have nowhere else to go and no means to travel. Without a vehicle it is difficult to pursue other housing and work options, or even to go to the supermarket. So their indebtedness mounts. An African American farmworker explained his situation to the anthropologist Daniel Rothenberg, "What can you do, man? You're out there. You're alone. You're somewhere way out in the fields. You can't buck the man. You ain't gonna fight him." The same worker told Rothenberg about the theft of his wages when he was picking onions in Georgia: "I never made minimum wage. Never. One week, I earned ten dollars. Other weeks, I was paid two dollars, three dollars, four dollars. Some weeks, I got nothing." He heard "guys sit and argue with [the contractor]," but "what could they do about it? Ain't nothing they could do."[31]

This cycle of vulnerability, hopelessness, wage theft, and debt can tip into forced labor even for marginalized U.S. citizen workers. "In terms of trafficking," the attorney representing vulnerable U.S.-citizen workers explains, "you kind of know it when you see it." Those who work at the camp to pay for alcohol or drugs but "can't work off the debt—that's servitude." These workers have few labor choices, and thus they "accept work conditions that would be unacceptable to others." A U.S.-citizen farmworker's description of escaping one evening resembles foreign nationals' stories of waiting for the right moment to slip away from their abusers undetected: "I walked away and didn't stop." He walked for twelve hours. "It's nothing that you'd put your worst enemy through. I mean, they work you to death. . . . That ain't even living. You're just existing."[32]

Staying Put and Enduring Abuse

If U.S. citizens feel stranded, cheated, and without forms of redress, what chance do undocumented workers (or workers with visas tied to one employer) have of landing jobs with fair treatment? Workers whose immigration status stops them from making demands, reporting abuses, and pursuing back pay have a slim chance of finding jobs that will pay well and offer opportunities for mobility.[33] Walking away also guarantees they will receive no wages while looking for new work.[34] To what new possibilities are vulnerable workers heading? They may end up trading one set of exploitative practices for another. A farmworker-activist in Oxnard, California, describes meeting many farmworkers over the years who had left agriculture to work in construction, only to find that their employers were "just as abusive and just as likely to not pay wages." With the housing crash in California, many have returned to farmwork. And, in cases where visas are tied to employers, the act of leaving catapults a documented, legal worker into undocumented status.

Geographic and linguistic isolation also can play a role in workers' decision to stay put. Many of the agricultural workers in and around Oxnard are part of a close-knit community of workers from La Mixteca region in Mexico, for example, and their crews are made up of family members and friends from home. One worker-organizer observed, "it's more important for them to keep everyone together on the same crew than to find higher wages elsewhere." Without Spanish- or English-language skills, they also are insulated from outside information. Familiar with discrimination, these indigenous workers, reported the organizer, "can't imagine anyone listening to them. So they fall into a pattern of remaining silent." Since they "equate the idea of being undocumented with no rights, they do not come to us seeking help. So when we do have the opportunity to tell them that there are companies that pay better, or that without documentation they still are entitled to back wages, the workers often think it is a setup." Their contractors have waged a "propaganda campaign," telling them that lawyers and organizers will charge them fees for finding new jobs. Contractors threaten that they will fire an entire crew if one worker complains, seeks outside counsel, or attends any worker-related meetings or events. "It's power abuse, plain and simple," pronounces the organizer. "And companies turn a blind eye. They know what the contractors and foremen are doing, but they pretend that these men are out there on their own. They are cold-hearted. Why can't they pay the workers for the work they do? They are thieves."

A worker at another farmworker rights organization in California explains the logic of staying, hoping for pay: "They will work for weeks waiting to get paid. They sleep under their cars in the field. They may get paid for just a part of the onions they pick. They hope for the rest." An attorney representing farmworkers in California comments on the larger backdrop of individuals' stories of wage theft and abuse: "It's difficult to wage a large campaign. Each company pays differently. Some pay piece rate, some hourly, some combined. Workers talk about having a good employer, but then the employer does not pay them, sometimes for two months. They stay, hoping that they will get paid soon. If they file a wage complaint, they may find that the person who hired them is using a fake name. It's a shell game. The companies of course are still liable. But the workers don't know who the employer is. For day hires, they may think it is the person who took them in a van to the field, but it turns out this person is just a neighbor." In the case of new arrivals, they "may be desperate to work and may be willing to put up with abusive conditions. They may not even know about minimum wage."[35]

Migrant workers also accept inadequate wages, particularly in farmwork, to guarantee future seasonal work. And there is a kind of demonstration effect: when they see others, often coethnics, doing the same work, presumably for the same low pay, a process of normalization of lousy pay under lousy conditions begins. Risks of border crossing also convince workers to stay with exploitative employers. As an organizer in Oregon explained: "People stay because of the highly publicized militarization of the border. Rather than go back home and return for the harvests, they stay during the winter and do canning and work on tree farms. They take what work they can find."[36] After working throughout the United States over many years, Arturo, a poultry-processing worker, told the anthropologist Steve Striffler that he still could not access good-quality jobs, so he returned to North Carolina from California: "We [Mexicans] are all trying to get the same jobs."[37]

Contractors and foremen exact a host of trumped-up fees to siphon money from workers' paychecks. In farmwork, for example, employers charge workers for tubs to hold produce and sometimes even charge for ladders. If something breaks, the workers must pay. Contractors often charge a fee for transportation to and from a work site every day. One homeless day laborer in the Washington, D.C., area, for example, reported that the round-trip fee is typically $6. But paying for one's return trip ahead of time does not guarantee a ride, since employers use "abandonment" at work sites to threaten workers who challenge wage theft.[38] In this unrelenting con game, workers feel they cannot effectively challenge—much less beat—the system.[39]

Even workers with visas face abuse. Guest-worker arrangements rest on and intensify inequities. Living in what the historian Cindy Hahamovitch describes as a "no man's land," guest workers find themselves tied to specific employers with no long-term possibilities of staying legally in the United States.[40] Thus many legal guest workers "quickly learn," an attorney in the south explains, "that they have to please the boss." They not only "have to suck up," but foremen squeeze them for bribes, demanding, for example, $100 to get hired again. The attorney marveled, "It's amazing how much people will pay." Guest-worker arrangements render workers vulnerable to being "exploited and abused without having recourse to other jobs in the external labor market" and offer no "prospect of future permanent residence or citizenship."[41]

Structuring Exploitation: Sweatshops Past and Present

Sweatshop conditions are pervasive across low-wage labor sectors dominated by migrant labor—documented and undocumented.[42] Worker-activists and organizers within garment manufacturing, agriculture, poultry processing, the restaurant industry, day labor, and domestic work all describe their industries as rife with worker exploitation. Commenting on rampant exploitation in agriculture, an attorney representing low-wage workers told me, "In factories it's abusive—the wages are bad. But it's practically all trafficking in agriculture." These industries often rely on subcontractors to provide a highly flexible, expendable, and replaceable workforce, rendering real employers invisible. The low-wage worker operates within a labor system that forces the worker to expect underpaid and insecure employment. In garment manufacturing, for example, Bonacich and Appelbaum describe workers "toil[ing] at breakneck speed for long hours and low wages," who "do not require coercive oversight to achieve the desired effect."[43] The workers tolerate "abuse and harassment that pervade the industry," such as "favoritism, the demanding of sexual favors, arbitrary punishment, and arbitrary firings," and complain of "being yelled at by factory owners and supervisors and sometimes even of being hit."[44]

A restaurant worker similarly describes employers who demand that workers pull double shifts: "After being around food all day, I would go home hungry after 14 hour days with no break." Sick employees also know, he explains, that they "either have to come to work sick or get fired." This worker reports that employers might pay for injured workers' cab fare to the hospital, "but they do not tell undocumented workers about workers' compensation." Workers, he emphasizes, "are too intimidated to complain" since their employers "threaten to call ICE." And, a farmworker tells of employers not supplying enough water, or breaks to use the bathroom or to eat. He too describes workers going hungry while surrounded by produce.

Abuses like these go almost universally unreported. As such, they become part of the everyday practices in these low-wage work sites. Wage theft is particularly common. At a community meeting on wage theft in the Washington, D.C., area, worker-activists described the problem as widespread. One worker compared wage theft to swine flu: "It's everywhere, but no one sees it." A farmworker-organizer in Oregon recounts, "Growers always testify that they pay workers well. But there is not one person we have spoken with recently who has been paid more than $4 or $5 an hour [below the $7.25 per hour minimum wage]." Likewise an organizer in the Filipino community in Los Angeles constantly battles wage theft: "I know the workers will stay quiet. We can be particularly ashamed if we are being abused because so many come here with a high degree of education. This adds a layer of complexity." One farmworker-organizer in Oxnard explained that workers know that they will not be paid minimum wage when contractors are involved: "They are supposed to make $2 a box [of strawberries], but if it's a contractor who has hired them, they will actually make 75 cents a box."

As it did in the nineteenth century, the term *sweatshop* still describes work sites where labor protections do not exist or are rarely enforced.[45] I use the term in the same way as the legal scholar Jennifer Gordon, who writes of "new sweatshops" to refer to many kinds of work sites, not just those in a factory setting.[46] Where migrant labor predominates, workplace conditions eerily resemble conditions before legislation to protect workers' and children's rights. At the turn of the century photographers such as Jacob Riis and Lewis Hine captured appalling living and working conditions in urban,

Figure 1.2. Lodgers in a crowded Bayard Street tenement, "five cents a spot." Photograph by Jacob Riis, *How the Other Half Lives* (New York: Dover Publications, 1971), 58. Originally published in 1890.

industrial settings. Later photographers hired by the Farm Administration during the Great Depression documented rural poverty.[47] Whether they required dump picking, coal shoveling, construction and ironwork on beams in the sky, or farmwork without protective gear from sun and pesticides, job sites were dirty and dangerous. Workers were expendable. These photographers' iconic images depicting women, men, and children laboring under horrendous conditions helped enact legislation and ignite social movements. Commissioned by the National Child Labor Committee to document child-labor abuses, Hine's more than five thousand photographs between 1908 and 1921 helped persuade lawmakers to pass child-labor laws.[48] Dorothea Lange's photos of migrants in California were influential in securing federal funds for housing. Later in the century, in 1960, the television broadcast by Edward R. Murrow on the plight of farmworkers in Florida, *Harvest of Shame*, also offered images of worker exploitation and poverty wages in the United States. In the documentary, Murrow refers to fieldwork

Figure 1.3. A ten-year-old spinner in a South Carolina cotton mill. When this photograph was originally published the caption was: "The overseer said apologetically, She just happened in. She was working steadily when the investigator found her. The mills seem full of youngsters who just happened in or are helping sister. Newberry, S.C., December 1908." Photograph by Lewis Hine, 1908. Still Picture Records Section, Special Media Archives Services Division (NWCS-S), National Archives at College Park, 8601 Adelphi Road, College Park, MD, 20740-6001.

as a "sweatshop of the soil."[49] The Coalition of Immokalee Workers (CIW) and numerous journalists have described today's farmworking conditions as virtually unchanged from Murrow's time.[50]

Abysmal working conditions in both industrial and rural settings exist today. One practice that links contemporary labor conditions to those of the past is subcontracting, and hence the concealment—and easy denial—of employer responsibility.[51] Riis describes the role of the "sweater" in the nineteenth-century labor market: "The sweater is simply the middleman, the sub-contractor, a workman like his fellows, perhaps the single distinction from the rest is that he knows a little English; perhaps not even that, but with the accidental possession of two or three sewing-machines, or of credit enough to hire them, as his capital, who drums up work among the clothing-houses. Of work-men he can always get enough. Every ship-load from German ports brings them to his door in droves, clamoring for

Figure 1.4. Morning "shape-up" in Florida, 1960. From the CBS documentary *Harvest of Shame*, Fred Friendly, producer.

Figure 1.5. Morning "shape-up" in Florida today. Photograph courtesy of Coalition of Immokalee Workers.

work."[52] Today's sweaters are part of an invisible chain of command that obscures employer responsibility and thus muddies any transparent channels for redress.[53] Garment manufacturing and the fast-food industry in particular depend on a chain of underground subcontractors. As clothing and produce are passed up a chain of intermediaries, it can be difficult to link any one supplier with any one major corporation. Two legal practitioners have noted that "any strategy to ameliorate the harms of subcontracting must focus on the entities that have the economic power to change the system: the companies that retain the subcontractors"; otherwise subcontractors are too numerous and new subcontractors will "always replace ones that are put out of business."[54]

This strategy of holding accountable those at the head of and along the supply chain is essential to improving labor conditions for all vulnerable low-wage workers. It is also a key to preventing forced labor. The CIW has done so to great effect. Their Boycott the Bell campaign with the slogan "No Quiero Taco Bell" resulted in winning one more penny per pound for tomato pickers in Florida. The boycott brought to light the otherwise invisible web connecting the Yum! Corporation (which owns Taco Bell) with its system of tomato suppliers. Since then, the CIW has been engaged in an ongoing Campaign for Fair Food aimed at compelling other large tomato purchasers to pay one penny more per pound of tomatoes.[55]

Threats and Retaliation

Workers do not know whom to trust. Farmworker organizers in California explain that "workers are so fearful that they don't trust who we say we are. Sometimes we have to impress on them that we are not with a government agency." Contractors make it clear that they will fire any workers who go to an organization's office. A farmworker-organizer in California noted with frustration, "The few who do come here to the office are literally scared to be here. It's easier to meet folks out and about in town and to tell them what I do, than to get them to come here." Organizers at another farmworker organization in California also report workers' fear of coming forward: "Two workers recently were fired for calling us. So we'll tell workers to not tell other workers that they called us." A worker-activist in Oxnard regularly encounters widespread fear and intimidation: "Even when I tell them that whatever they tell me is confidential, they say there is no guarantee." An organizer for farmworkers in Oregon also paints a picture of unbridled abuse:

"Exploitation happens in small companies and large companies. There are multiple avenues to rip off workers, especially because of a lack of English. This is so common, these things happen all the time, to all the workers." A farmworker-activist in California sums it up: "There is bad pay or no pay all the time. If you complain about the safety conditions or if your check is short, you get fired. This sends a message. So no one else complains." Women endure sexual harassment. When a few women on one farm spoke out about sexual assault, they were fired. "After that," the California activist reports, "none of the other workers wanted to file any complaints. This is what they have been shown, that there is no other outcome."

Workers not only worry about getting fired but also endure a barrage of insults and forms of bodily control. Foremen hound and harass the workers. One worker-organizer in California relates: "The foremen will say you have to keep moving, you can't stand still or talk. They time workers when they are in the bathroom or getting water." The foremen constantly pressure workers to work harder: "We can not go like a machine and pick more than usual. But the foreman asks us to. Most can pick three or four boxes of strawberries but are pushed to do six. If not, they get fired." They also mock the workers: "The foremen make fun [in Spanish] of workers who speak Indigenous languages. They treat them as inferior." A manager of a mushroom-packing plant in Oregon posted threatening flyers of a picture of ants being crushed under a large boot—after workers had asked for better pay and complained that the bathrooms were dirty. He also attached photocopied pictures of pigs to their paychecks, explaining, "This is your own fault. You made them dirty." He made clear that if they complained again they would be fired. Pointing to the exit he told them, "The door is very large."[56]

Confident that undocumented workers (or workers with visas that tie them to their employers) will not report them, employers can become violent. A Mexican couple in Oregon endured a farm contractor's escalating abuse. They had been returning from their home base in California to work for this same grower for more than ten years. The contractor who had hired them squeezed every dime he could from them and the other workers living there. Since he arranged their contracts, and in some cases provided Social Security numbers, he extorted 10 percent of their paychecks. Over time, the living conditions worsened. The last straw was his decision that the workers could no longer cook on site; instead they would have to buy over-priced meals from the contractor and his wife, who prepared the food. The Mexican couple contacted a migrants' rights organization and quit working for this particular contractor. In retaliation, the contractor torched their car—their lifeline to travel to other work sites and back home to California, where their children were living with relatives. They surmised that he was angry that he was losing out on his 10 percent fee. He told them, "There are no witnesses. What are you going to do? I'll report you."

Dirty and Dangerous Work

In addition to experiencing chronic wage theft, and the constant threat of getting fired or reported to ICE, undocumented migrants—and those with temporary work visas—also often work in dangerous conditions.[57] Many of the low-wage jobs that are available to low-wage workers are not inherently dangerous, but the lack of protective gear and proper training makes them so.[58] A day-laborer organizer in Virginia described the contractors who look to pick up workers at day labor centers: "Many contractors do not know how to properly supervise a job site. They are not trained themselves. They are day laborers with vehicles."[59] While working as an attorney at the workers' center she founded on Long Island, the Workplace Project, Jennifer Gordon kept the telephone log from the center's opening days. "Pain flies from the pages," she writes, documenting calls like the following from a man who worked as a rug cleaner: "Blood fr. Nose. Eyes burn and tear. Chemicals. No gloves. Headache. Stomach. Hurt back on job. Emplyr won't pay bills." Another entry reads, "Machines; doors slide up and in. So hard to open and close that you have to hit them with hammers. Closing door is how he lost fingertip and so did another man." "The question is not whether any workers will be hurt," explains Gordon, "but how often, how many, and how badly."[60]

As risky as it may be, workers find ways to make demands. A worker-organizer who worked in a mushroom-packing plant in Oregon described unsafe conditions that eventually sparked a work stoppage: "The workers couldn't take it anymore. There were eight beds of mushrooms stacked on top of one another. They would shake—because you have to climb them. And the wood was rotting. Sometimes they would collapse with workers on them." When possible, workers also set limits according to their own standards.[61] A day laborer from Peru, for example, explained why he turned down a job offer with an employer who had a granite business: "I have worked with them before. They don't give tools or masks. They say, 'Work fast, fast,' because they pay by the hour. But you can't. If you do, you might break something, and then you don't get paid. I would rather not have any work at all." Others pursue justice following unjust treatment. A staff attorney at a migrants' rights organization in the Washington, D.C., area says one of her favorite cases was representing a client who was owed $60. The outraged client pursued the money, explaining, "This is money that I worked hard to earn."

Building Workers' Protections

In this environment of racism, criminalization, orchestrated exploitation, and unregulated and underregulated labor sectors, members of vulnerable, migrant communities take great risks when they fight these injustices. Rights-based outreach in collaboration with community members in places where migrants work and live is essential to finding and possibly preventing cases of forced labor. Creative organizing, particularly peer to peer, can begin to build trust, rights knowledge, and a sense of belonging. Organizations use a number of strategies to assist workers. Lideres Campesinas, a farmworker women's membership-based organization in California, empowers women to make demands. Members hold house meetings around the parenting and work schedules of their fellow worker-members, many of whom regularly confront sexual harassment in the fields. Still others face domestic violence in their homes. A leadership-training institute develops new leaders to fan out throughout agricultural communities in California. Domestic workers in the Washington, D.C., area who are members of CASA de Maryland and those in New York City who are members of Damayan, also conduct peer-to-peer outreach. They approach women waiting at bus and subway stops and playing with the children in their care at parks and playgrounds. Places where day laborers gather become sites for know-your-rights workshops, English-language classes, and the circulation of lists of dead-beat employers.

Even if migrants have a clear understanding of their legal rights, protecting oneself is still a challenge. An organizer in Los Angeles explains, "The workers may be vigilant and take down an employer's information. But the guys hiring at a hiring site may use a nickname. Once cheated, the workers think they will see a contractor again, but not always. And if they are taken to a town far from home, like Malibu—to do construction, landscaping, or housekeeping—they are not sure where they are." Farmworker organizers have a hard time just getting their message out. Particularly with new

Figure 1.6. "Know your rights" house meeting, organized by Lideres Campesinas. Photograph courtesy of Lideres Campesinas. Fall 2011. Photograph by Ramona Felix.

Figure 1.7. A community fights together. Lideres Campesinas. Photograph courtesy of Lideres Campesinas. April 2012. Photograph by Ramona Felix.

Figure 1.8. Domestic worker organizers from CASA de Maryland protest outside the Embassy of Argentina in Washington, D.C., December 11, 2012. Photograph courtesy of CASA de Maryland.

arrivals they have had to refine their outreach methods. As organizers in Oxnard explain: "Flyers don't work because not everyone can read. Radio doesn't work, since not everyone has a radio, especially new arrivals. So now we go house to house and work in Mixtec, Triqui, and Zapotec [languages]." They also conduct outreach and rights workshops in the fields late at night, between midnight and dawn. These organizers worry, however, that with so much abuse they cannot possibly "fight every battle." "We don't want to do outreach, raise expectations, and then destroy our credibility. We don't have enough attorneys to take on all the cases out there." Overwhelmed by the number of cases of abuse, this farmworker-organizing team empowers workers to secure their own rights: "We try to impress [on them] that they have the right to earn the minimum wage and receive lunch and a break time. They have a right to water, individual cups, and clean bathrooms. We also teach where to go if you have trouble." But making demands does not always yield results. A day-laborer organizer in Virginia recounts what happened when a young man from Mexico pursued the $100 he was owed: "He called the guy a couple of times, who did nothing to pay him. He eventually stopped calling explaining, 'It's only $100.'" A farmworker-activist in California found similar frustration among workers who were "resigned to the fact that nothing will happen."

Figure 1.9. Tomato pickers receiving a "know your rights" education session facilitated by CIW farmworker staff, April 2011. Photograph courtesy of Laura Emiko Soltis and the CIW.

Figure 1.10. Tomato pickers "punching in" at the beginning of work on a participating farm to ensure their receipt of minimum wage, April 2011. Photograph courtesy of Laura Emiko Soltis and the CIW.

Despite these challenges, worker-designed and -conducted outreach and advocacy can transform individuals' lives as well as create systemic change. Fighting to raise farmworkers' pay, improve their working conditions, and end forced labor, the Coalition of Immokalee Workers (CIW) has been a national leader. CIW conducts both worker-to-worker local organizing and membership-led national-level fair wage campaigns.[62] Through their drop-in center, regular meetings, radio show, block parties, and ongoing outreach in places where farmworkers work and live, CIW's worker-activists are ideally placed to learn of abuses. While monitoring potential abuse, they inform workers of their rights. These kinds of ground-up information streams are critical. They both expose daily exploitative practices and bring to light more cases of forced labor.[63] Remarkably, CIW members also have gone undercover as workers on farms to gather information on forced labor and debt bondage cases. Several of these cases have been federally prosecuted. CIW's investigative work revealed that over a thousand tomato and orange pickers had been working in debt bondage, leading to prosecutions by the U.S. Department of Justice in 2002.[64] Workers' leading role in fighting everyday practices of exploitation is the centerpiece of CIW's organizing strategy. Lucas Benitez, one of CIW's veteran organizers (and winner of the Robert F. Kennedy Memorial Human Rights Award in 2003), recounts that when crew leaders used to "'forget' a check or insist that it was not due," "40 or 50 of us would walk to the boss's house, knock at the door, and say, 'Here we are!' Like a magic trick, the pay would appear."[65] But migrants who are cut off from peers face down their exploiters on their own, without any co-workers at their side.

II. THE ASSAULT ON SEX WORKERS
The Sexual Politics of Trafficking
Modern-Day Abolitionists

Not only have anti-immigrant policies had a profound impact on finding individuals trafficked into forced labor, but obsessions over sex work also have played a colossal role shaping antitrafficking policy. Prostitution has been at the center of antitrafficking policy debates ever since the crafting stages of the TVPA, before its passage in 2000 during the Clinton administration.[66] The George W. Bush administration decoupled trafficking from forced labor in all labor sectors and reframed it instead as about sexual exploitation.[67] Fighting trafficking in the United States became a way for

Figure 1.11. Sex workers' rights slogan on a T-shirt at the International AIDS Conference in Washington, D.C., 2012. Photograph by PJ Starr.

antiprostitution activists and policymakers to crack down on the sex sector and its workers—both foreign nationals and U.S. citizens. Left out of discussions were sex workers themselves, as activist for sex worker and transgender rights Darby Hickey emphasized in her speech to the UN Human Rights Council in Geneva in 2011: "It is critical that the government work to systematically involve sex workers in policy decisions that affect them. Specifically . . . eliminate federal policies that conflate sex work with human trafficking, investigate and prevent human rights abuses perpetuated by state agents against sex workers, and examine the impact of criminalisation on our communities."[68]

The split over how to conceptualize the selling of sexual services has occupied two camps. The antiprostitution "abolitionist" position maintains that all forms of commercial sexual exchanges are not only exploitative but also coercive.[69] Therefore, this camp argues, all commercial sex activities should be eradicated.[70] In contrast, advocates and scholars who embrace a sex workers' rights perspective acknowledge that although work within the sex sector can be exploitative, it also is work that adult women and men may choose free from coercion.[71] This workers' rights approach argues that granting greater labor protections to workers in the sex sector would prevent them from working underground, making them far less vulnerable to violence from clients and the police, as well as exploitation by potential traffickers.[72]

Instead, in implementing the TVPA, the Bush administration launched an antitrafficking campaign that primarily was an antiprostitution platform. The administration made explicit its goal of eliminating all forms of sex work—not just forced labor in the sex sector—as part of its fight against trafficking in the United States and worldwide. A fact sheet issued by the U.S. Department of State's Bureau of Public Affairs, "The Link between Prostitution and Sex Trafficking," reiterated a presidential directive that voluntary prostitution involving adults leads to sex trafficking of women and children: "The U.S. Government adopted a strong position against legalized prostitution in a December 2002 National Security Presidential Directive based on evidence that prostitution is inherently harmful and dehumanizing, and fuels trafficking in persons, a form of modern-day slavery."[73] "Ending demand" for prostitution became a cornerstone of the Bush administration's antitrafficking policies. Since then, "end demand" policies—which include sending clients to "Johns' schools," confiscating condoms as presumed evidence of participation in a commercial sexual exchange, and enacting laws that target cab drivers as traffickers in women—have proliferated on the local and state levels in the United States as well as overseas. Taken together, these policies have not reduced sexual transactions, but rather have driven them underground. These policies harm already vulnerable workers. A New York City Department of Health and Mental Hygiene survey revealed that 42.8 percent of sex workers interviewed had condoms confiscated from them by a police officer. Of those who had condoms taken away or destroyed by police, 50 percent reported engaging in unprotected sex work afterward.[74] A worker-activist for sex workers' rights assesses the far-reaching consequences the fight against trafficking has had for sex workers. "We are collateral damage. If one operates within a framework that all sex work is inherently violent, then it is easy to justify everything else as collateral damage. For those who can not imagine that a sex worker would choose her work, they see sleeping in a jail cell as better than being in sex work."

The politicians and antiprostitution activists pushing this "end demand" agenda used the language of *abolition*. For a period of time a number of antitrafficking activists—including John R. Miller, the director of the U.S. Department of State's Office to Monitor and Combat Trafficking in Persons—signed their emails, "Abolition Now!" The term has a double meaning, referring both to ending prostitution while calling on the moral claim-making of slavery abolitionists—both the African slave trade and the so-called white slave trade of previous centuries. The foot soldiers of this movement included the strange bedfellows of feminist abolitionists and conservative Republican politicians and pundits.[75] A lobby composed of politicians, conservative pundits, antiprostitution scholars, abolition-ist nongovernmental organizations, and abolitionist evangelical organiza-tions, as well as mainstream feminist organizations, pushed an antipros-titution agenda as an antitrafficking one. Antiprostitution organizations rose to prominence as national leaders on trafficking and are still widely featured in media stories on trafficking. Funded by the Bush administra-tion's "charitable choice" initiative, "evangelical Christian groups secured a growing proportion of federal monies for both international and domestic antitrafficking work."[76] According to this vocal group of allies, trafficking is about prostitution and all prostitution leads to trafficking.

The similarities between the moral claim-making inherent in the lan-guage of abolition and sexual panics of the past are hard to ignore. Carole Vance traces a straight-line narrative from "white slavery" scares to today's fight against "modern-day slavery" that justify "rescuing" women—any woman—in the sex sector: "Virtually unchanged from its nineteenth-century versions, the modern melodrama of trafficking performs various reductions that erode the innovations of international law: trafficking again means prostitution (forced or voluntary); the trafficked person is a woman or female minor; the danger and injury are sexual; and the nature of the crime is an offense against society and morality (for evangelical activists) or against women's equality (for antiprostitution feminists)."[77] Conflating traf-ficking with sex trafficking and modern-day slavery with sex slavery, these abolitionists have mobilized the right and the left alike. Who today would stand with slavery? But "galvaniz[ing] action through moral outrage," the anthropologist David Feingold points out, can "cloud reason."[78] Politics—and ensuing panics—have trumped common sense and facts about traf-ficking at every turn. As a Pulitzer prize–winning journalist observed, anti-trafficking efforts under the Bush administration became so "pervert[ed]" that it was "largely a campaign to abolish prostitution. . . . Put simply, the administration concocted the view that every prostitute, worldwide, is actu-ally a slave; the very nature of the work amounts to slavery."[79]

The assault on commercial sex work did not end at the borders of the United States. In two efforts to regulate sex work internationally—one a 2002 National Security presidential directive, the other a federal statute—the U.S. government declared its opposition to recognizing the legitimacy of sex work. The presidential directive, NSPD-22, declared prostitution "inherently harmful and dehumanizing," and adopted an "abolitionist" approach to ending trafficking.[80] The federal statute, United States Leadership Against HIV/AIDS, Tuberculosis, and Malaria Act of 2003, required that any entity accepting federal funding to fight these diseases must explicitly reject prostitution.[81] Because a number of health NGOs work with sex worker advocacy groups to distribute condoms or educate sex workers, they were frozen out of federal funds. As a result of these and other federal policies, "private, nongovernmental organizations (NGOS) must have a position in opposition to prostitution in order to participate in the U.S. antitrafficking effort."[82]

The Bush administration's obsession with prostitution thus affected a range of policies—and quickly.[83] This antiprostitution agenda defined who trafficking victims were, who was worth finding, and which organizations would assist with rescues and aftercare. With ending prostitution a clear priority, attorneys for foreign nationals who were severely exploited in labor sectors other than the sex sector were frustrated that investigations and prosecutions were more aggressively sought in cases classified as sex trafficking. For example, of the fifty-nine prosecutions initiated against traffickers in fiscal year 2004, "all but one of those cases involved sexual exploitation."[84] The focus on sex reached a frenzied peak during the reauthorization process of the TVPA in 2007, when the version proposed in the Senate effectively redefined all prostitution in the United States as trafficking and made it a federal crime. Although this version did not pass, if it had the U.S. Department of Justice would have been charged with prosecuting all cases in all states related to prostitution. The Department outlined its "significant concerns" in a letter addressed to the Committee on the Judiciary in November 2007, saying that "the Federal government lacks the necessary resources and capacity to prosecute these offenses." It warned, "To the extent that this expansion of the Mann Act would federalize the criminal prosecution of pandering, pimping, and prostitution-related offenses, it is unnecessary and a diversion from Federal law enforcement's core anti-trafficking mission."[85]

Low-Hanging Fruit

While abuses within the sex sector are horrific and need attention, one kind of abuse and one kind of victimhood should not be privileged over others.[86] With rhetoric focused on and resources directed to finding trafficked individuals in the sex sector, limited efforts were made to reach those in other forms of work.[87] I contend that the low numbers of persons found during the Bush administration in forced nonsexual labor nationwide was, in part, a consequence of not looking.[88] De facto U.S. antitrafficking policy largely was to search for—and, as a result, find—only one kind of trafficking victim. Prior to the reauthorizations of the TVPA in 2005 and 2008, members of Congress questioned where money allocated to fight trafficking had gone and why more individuals had not been found. The pressure resulted in increased resources to find trafficked persons. With funds from the Department of Justice, antitrafficking task forces were created in cities and towns throughout the United States.[89] Intended to be "victim-centered," these task forces are composed of staff from social service and other organizations that provide assistance to victims of trafficking, along with law enforcement. Since many law enforcement officers were or are part of vice crime units, these task forces focused on the sex sector.[90]

Another effect of the pressure to produce trafficked persons dovetailed with the Bush administration's framing of trafficking as sex trafficking. Increased attention and resources focused on one part of the TVPA that grants protections to U.S. citizen youth in the sex sector. In my conversations with some attorneys at the U.S. Department of Justice and staff at abolitionist organizations, they described domestic youth involved in the sex sector as the "low-hanging fruit" in the fight against trafficking in the United States because it is assumed they are easier to find than non–U.S. citizens in situations of forced labor.[91] In the scramble to produce trafficked persons, these "low-hanging fruit" provided evidence that antitrafficking policies were working.

The 2005 TVPA Reauthorization also earmarked a $50 million grant for local law enforcement and social service agencies to "reduce demand" and investigate and prosecute buyers of commercial sex. Sex workers came under attack.[92] "Feminist fights over prostitution and pornography are old news," writes sex worker rights activist Melissa Gira Grant. But by repackaging old messages about women's exploitation into new antitrafficking battles, anti–sex work activists pushed an agenda that advocated stepping up vice enforcement.[93] Embracing what Bernstein calls "carceral feminism," these activists "view calling the cops to 'rescue' people from the sex trade as the model of a successful human rights intervention. They don't count their victories by the number of people they help; they count them by arrests."[94] With two hundred "johns" arrested in a sting in New York between January 12–14, 2012, and another 156 "johns" charged in a sting in June 2013, NYPD commissioner Raymond Kelly has made clear that the NYPD "is focusing on the demand side of the equation."[95] Moreover, since ten sex workers were arrested in the 2012 sting in which undercover officers posed as sex workers, and since 97 percent of the charges in prostitution-related felonies in Chicago between 2008 and 2011 were made against sex workers, "protect[ing] women by 'going after the johns' doesn't exempt sex workers from arrest."[96]

Urban Legends and Wild Claims

While the Bush administration crafted antitrafficking policy, popular understanding of trafficking as sex trafficking began to take root. With the U.S. government circulating such large estimates as fifty thousand persons trafficked into the United States, sensationalism followed in the media.[97] Both government figures and news stories defied logic. For example, stories about the summer 2006 World Cup events in Germany illogically suggested that up to one million women and children would be trafficked into Germany, where prostitution is legal, to fatten up the brothels for the influx of soccer fans.[98] And a much-criticized front-page story, "Sex Slaves on Main Street," in the *New York Times Magazine* featured a cover photo of a young girl (from the lips down) on a bed clad in a Catholic-schoolgirl's uniform (plaid skirt and knee socks). The story cites wildly unproven statistics that "perhaps tens of thousands are held captive and pimped out for forced sex."[99] This kind of hysterical story line incited panic. A manager of an online antitrafficking project explained, for example, that she received a flurry of emails the day after a *Lifetime* TV miniseries, with a similar name to the antitrafficking website, first aired in October 2005. Parents feared that their daughters would be kidnapped and trafficked into the sex trade in the United States.

Despite the Obama administration's increase in prosecutions of forced labor cases that do not involve sexual labor, the legacy of the Bush administration is clear. An antiprostitution frame continues to dominate discussions on trafficking in the media. Years ago, when I was just beginning this research project, I wrote about Landesman's *New York Times* article as a low point in myths replacing evidence about trafficking.[100] Yet the same kinds of stories, with shoddy and shady reporting based on unsubstantiated figures and sensationalized photographs and text, still appear regularly today. On the eve of the 2011 Super Bowl, for example, Sergeant Louis Felini of the Dallas Police Department told the *Dallas Morning News* that "between 50,000 and 100,000 prostitutes could descend on the metroplex." "His estimate was astonishing," wrote Peter Kotz in the *Dallas Observer*. "At the higher figure, it meant that every man, woman and child holding a ticket would have their own personal hooker."[101] The press coverage of the past two World Cups also embraced and fueled similar urban legends. Mainstream media outlets reported, for example, that several hundred thousand women and girls would be trafficked during the World Cup in Germany in 2006, and then again in South Africa in 2010. In this process, myths replace evidence, ideology poses as fact, and moral claims infantilize workers by proclaiming what is best for them. This emotional claim-making that later gets fact-checked and then retracted is like a "Trafficking Ground Hog Day." As this feedback loop of invented data and the media's parroting of them indicates, the antiprostitution lobby has been wildly successful in producing the dominant narrative on trafficking.

While the ideologically fueled assertion that the way to prevent trafficking is to end demand for prostitution circulates in the media and shapes policy, it does not hold sway in peer-reviewed scholarship.[102] Scholars across disciplines have written critically about the lack of evidence for claims that forms of commercial sexual labor contribute to trafficking into forced sexual labor.[103] Evidence-based research, however, cannot recapture the ground lost to fiction—especially when the source has a large audience, such as celebrity tweets and public-service announcements.[104] Expressing his opinions on trafficking through Twitter—where he had over seven million followers—and during an appearance on the Piers Morgan show, the actor Ashton Kutcher has had an instant audience. Unfortunately his claim that there are "between 100,000 to 300,000 child sex slaves" in the United States today is not grounded in empirical research.[105] In an investigative series, "The Truth behind Sex Trafficking," the *Village Voice* traced the original source of this inflated figure to two University of Pennsylvania professors, Richard J. Estes and Neil Alan Weiner, who wrote that the numbers do not represent the *actual* numbers of cases in the United States but rather the number of children "at risk" of commercial sexual exploitation.[106] The authors used geographic proximity to borders—living near the Mexican or Canadian border—as a factor that places children at risk. Estes clarified to the *Village Voice*, "Kids who are kidnapped and sold into slavery—that number would be very small."

Trafficking Care Regime
Antiprostitution Organizations' Ascendency

The politics of sexual labor also spilled over into the trafficking assistance regime. There were few "experts" in the United States on trafficking into forced labor prior to the passage of the TVPA. In the first few years after the TVPA's passage, social workers throughout the country charted new territory, drawing on their past experience with refugee resettlement, domestic violence, and torture in the migrant community. One veteran social worker in a large social service agency in New York explained, "Of course we had seen clients over the years who would be considered trafficked under today's legislation. But back then they were part of our domestic violence program, immigration clinic, or torture treatment program." For seasoned social workers and attorneys, the past experiences and urgent needs of their new trafficking clients were not unfamiliar—the new legal designation was.

Staff at community-based organizations that long have been dedicated to migrants' needs also had an expert understanding of the conditions of forced labor. Yet these advocates within the migrants' rights community, along with other frontline service providers with extensive experience (sometimes developed over decades) working with refugees or domestic violence survivors, were not necessarily the organizations that government agencies consulted during the Bush administration. Instead new players, freshly minted antitrafficking organizations with little or no experience on migration, labor, or violence, assumed major roles in advising on antitrafficking policies and programs. They gained funding and eventual prominence during the Bush years, particularly if they agreed with the administration's strategy of ending prostitution worldwide as a way to combat trafficking. Trafficking became, as the anthropologist David Feingold has observed, "the flavor of the month," launching a cottage industry of organizations seeking to end trafficking, prostitution, and modern-day slavery.[107] Many of these start-up antitrafficking organizations that grew during the Bush administration only focused on domestic youth and adult women in the sex sector. And some antitrafficking organizations shifted their focus from assisting foreign nationals to focusing on U.S. citizens in the sex sector. These organizations use the language of rehabilitation and recovery as they bestow victimhood on workers in the sex sector who often have been demonized as unredeemable lawbreakers and deviants.[108]

Experience Assisting Individuals Trafficked into Forced Labor

Under the Obama administration, more established social service agencies with actual experience assisting trafficked persons since the passage of the TVPA have emerged as national leaders in the trafficking care regime. Government agencies have sought the advice of social workers and attorneys who, after a decade of working with trafficking clients, are particularly knowledgeable and skilled. Such expertise also has been on display at the annual Freedom Network conferences over the past few years, where panelists and audience participants — primarily social service providers and attorneys — display a remarkable amount of knowledge.[109] In audience questions and small-group discussions, it is clear that dozens of attendees know as much as the "experts" giving presentations. This is quite different from the first Freedom Network conferences (in spring 2002 and winter 2003), which consisted primarily of panels that introduced the then-new and flawed trafficking legal and social service provision framework. Everyone — panelists and attendees — was learning on the job in those early years. With so many experienced legal practitioners throughout the country, much has changed. And, the Vermont Processing Center, which reviews applications for T visas as part of the Department of Homeland Security, takes considerably less time to respond to T visa applicants' attorneys' requests than in the years immediately following the passage of the TVPA.

Much also has changed in terms of personnel at social service organizations that work with trafficking clients. More than ten years after the first TVPA, a core group of these critical early knowledge-shapers have retired or left the issue. As staff leave, new staff members can seek guidance from other Freedom Network members through regular conference calls. What may prove indispensible, however, is experience working with a number of different kinds of clients. I have been with social workers and case managers in clients' living rooms who spend hours playing with their children or helping out in the kitchen. This kind of roll-up-your-sleeves investment of time to build trust and slowly assess how their clients are faring is not something learned out of a manual. It is a patient approach that requires a light touch and a genuine interest in the small details of lives unfolding.

Collaboration versus Competition

This approach also requires sufficient funding to have staff who can spend this kind of time with clients. Because most social service agencies' budgets are stretched thin, they often rely on ongoing collaborations with other organizations. They hand off clients to other agencies in town that may have housing available or have expertise with a particular language or ethnic group. "I'm so relieved and can not wait for the new social worker to come on board," explained a social worker assisting Spanish-speaking clients in the metropolitan D.C. area about another organization in town that assists domestic workers. Organizations such as these that provide a range of legal and social services to different kinds of clients—not just trafficking clients and not just individuals in the sex sector—must cobble together resources, funds, and partnerships to meet their clients' multiple needs. They rely on one another and willingly pool information and resources. Tellingly both of these organizations belong to the Freedom Network, through which they regularly exchange information.

In contrast, organizations that focus on getting women out of the sex sector not only do not belong to the Freedom Network and thus do not exchange best practices and learn from others but generally take a go-it-alone approach in terms of clients' services as well. In fact some organizations across the country have become known as secretive and proprietary, which is out of step with the transparent work practices and collaborative ethos that have evolved among social workers within the antitrafficking community. For example, for years social workers in the Washington, D.C., area never knew how many clients—if any—were assisted by one particular trafficking start-up. Operating without a trained social worker, its staff called other organizations' social workers seeking information about what to do with clients but would remain elusive about where the clients were, what kinds of services they were receiving, and who was providing those services. In addition to the questionable ethics inherent in the proprietary treatment of clients, organizations' involvement with raids and rescues has stirred criticism. One social worker in Washington, D.C., for example, was particularly troubled that this organization was involved in raids. "It's a problem if you've participated in a rescue as a social worker and then, later on, you ask the client if they want to join something or to consider doing something. They may feel obligated or pressured. I don't want to put clients in that position."[110]

Organizations that are reluctant to transfer a client's case to another organization that may be better positioned to assist the client may be overly interested in keeping up their client rolls. The number of clients an organization has—a body count of sorts—can be critical to future fundraising and securing government grants. This competitive approach also may be the product of these organizations' origin stories. While the proprietary D.C. organization sprang up after the TVPA was passed and its only mission has been to fight trafficking, organizations that work with a particular migrant community or with workers in a particular labor sector often came to the issue of trafficking only through their other programs. These multiprogram organizations, such as CASA de Maryland, Damayan, Break the Chain Campaign, Ayuda, and the Coalition of Immokalee Workers, have members or clients who were trafficked, but their antitrafficking program is just one program among many. While new antitrafficking organizations have come and gone during the funding frenzy of the Bush years and have continually shifted their mission and programs to suit funding trends, organizations that existed before the TVPA added services for trafficking clients to their existing programs. Trafficking clients are just one additional kind of client they assist. Unlike organizations that likely would close their doors without their antitrafficking funds from the U.S. government as well as from their antitrafficking fundraising campaigns, these organizations with broader workers' and migrants' rights missions are not dependent on trafficking funding. Their potential longevity is evident in their collaborative—not competitive—work with other organizations. Without trafficking as the primary mission, multiprogram organizations include their trafficking clients in their larger activities, and their other clients may not know their trafficking clients' legal status. Rather all the clients share the experience of being a new migrant and/or low-wage worker.

Sector-based organizations, such as domestic workers' and agricultural workers' organizations, and social service agencies that do not depend on government funding can set their own programmatic agendas. Some migrants' rights organizations and social service agencies with long-standing programs assisting refugees, migrants, and survivors of domestic violence have not pursued U.S. government antitrafficking funds, in part to avoid the politics of sexual labor. Thus most of these organizations work outside of the trafficking assistance regime, and most of their members or clients would not qualify for trafficking relief.

Conclusion

The absence of federal immigration reform has had a monumental effect on efforts to find and prevent forced labor in the United States. Without protections for migrant workers (both those with temporary work visas and those who are undocumented), everyday forms of exploitation can thrive, which in turn facilitate or mask conditions of forced labor. Industries that rely on low-wage migrant labor, such as agriculture and domestic work in private homes, have a history of routine labor violations. In these environments of chronic and unfettered exploitation, workers come to expect and to normalize poor working conditions and lack of clear channels for redress. Threatened, intimidated, and frequently isolated, abused workers are difficult to reach even for seasoned rights-based outreach workers. With some immigration reform proposals requiring migrants to show proof of work and tax payments in order to advance toward citizenship, the most vulnerable workers will remain unprotected, even if reform legislation is enacted. Without a paper trail of employment and tax history, day laborers in construction, agriculture, and domestic work, for example, likely will continue to labor in conditions where employers can threaten, steal, and abuse. The most economically vulnerable migrant workers currently in the United States—and those who arrive in the United States in years to come—will continue to keep quiet and keep working.

The protection of migrants from exploitation across labor sectors has also been caught in the firestorm over sex work. In the wake of the Bush administration's framing of trafficking, two conflations continue to characterize discussions in the media, among policy makers and politicians, and among celebrity activists. First, sex trafficking has come to stand in for trafficking into all forms of labor. Second, voluntary sexual exchanges between adults for money have been described as "sex trafficking," thereby linking forms of chosen sex work to forced sexual labor. Both of these conflations divert attention away from the relationship between migrants' legal status and exploitative labor conditions. The conflation of trafficking and sex trafficking has profoundly hindered progress on preventing forced labor at work sites other than in the sex sector. At the same time, workers in the sex sector have become less safe. Both immigration enforcement raids and sex sector raids have driven vulnerable workers further underground. And those who come forward with claims of abuse or are rescued—sometimes coercively—risk detention and deportation if the U.S. government determines that they have not been trafficked.[111] Providing protections for a range of forms of exploitation, not just for cases that meet the standards of trafficking, may encourage witnesses to forced labor to report it. Coerced workers' coworkers—including in the sex sector—are a critical link to reporting instances of severe abuse. But without protections for these whistleblowers, they too fear coming forward.[112] And they have had good reason to remain quiet about abuses. There have been cases of undocumented workers—such as those known as the "Southern 32"—who ended up in deportation proceedings after reporting abuse or organizing on behalf of immigrant rights.[113]

As arrests, detentions, and deportations have soared, and employers' threats and abuse continue, members of vulnerable communities—much like the Southern 32—are nonetheless taking great risks to organize and demand justice. "I felt so free," said a domestic worker from the Philippines, as she described marching and chanting in a protest in New York City. An organizer within the domestic workers' rights movement explains that by marching, "Workers see justice in action. Their employers threatened them all the time that they would call the police. By marching, they see others demanding justice and now they do too. They get courage and inspiration. They feel a weight lifted."

Chapter Two

"I was full of dreams about coming to America. So many dreams. I was so happy that maybe I was going to change my life," explained Tatiana about what she expected to find in the United States. She paid smugglers to bring her from Russia through Mexico and into the United States. "I thought I would be independent and that I would build my own life. I thought I would get an education and do certain things in my life that I've wanted to do. I wanted to prove that I'm open—that I can take a challenge. And then, when you face challenges, you say to yourself, 'It's here, take it!'" Tatiana's plans for an education and economic mobility were shattered once she realized her employers would be taking most of the money she earned as a dancer.

//////

Iconic images of newcomers arriving in the United States often depict them kissing the ground as they set foot in their new country or running to reunite with relatives. They approach their new land with a sense of boundless optimism. Many leave behind places of limited opportunities and believe that they are heading toward limitless possibilities. In forced labor, migrants' hope for a bright future give way to the realization that something has gone terribly wrong. As hope evaporates, fear sets in. The individuals I

Figure 2.1. Welcome to land. "New York—Welcome to the Land of Freedom—An ocean steamer passing the Statue of Liberty: Scene on the Steerage deck." Sketch by staff artist in *Frank Leslie's Illustrated Newspaper*, July 2, 1887, 324–325. LC-USZC2-1225, from Library of Congress, Prints and Photographs Division, Washington, D.C.

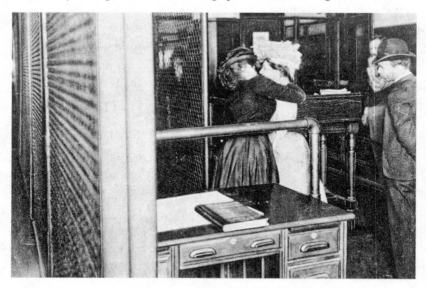

Figure 2.2. Kissing Gates of America. "Kissing Gates of America—Friend greeting emigrant just discharged." Black-and-white photograph by unknown artist in Quarantine Sketches (New York: Maltine Co., 1902), 24. LC-USZ62-122834, from Library of Congress, Prints and Photographs Division, Washington, D.C.

met tell of such turning points—of realizing, as Tatiana did, that what was ahead for them was far from anything that they had ever imagined.

But proving that trafficking cases are not run-of-the-mill cases of exploitation but something more has not been easy. What makes them different? How much more exploitation is *enough* to prove trafficking and thus justify a legal remedy? And what about those whose exploitation is not great enough to seek protections under the new trafficking law—what happens to them? Kathleen Kim, a legal scholar who has represented trafficking clients, sums up the difficulties of proving trafficking: "Identifying psychological coercion is not a simple task."[1] This chapter lays bare the invisible and elusive characteristics of trafficking cases. It examines the circumstances in which individuals in forced labor find themselves, the resources from which they draw, and the methods of coercive control that traffickers typically use. The first part of the chapter explores how individuals in forced labor make sense of their abuse while it is unfolding and how they assess whether, when, and how to leave. A discussion on forms of resistance and of power frames my understanding of how individuals live through conditions of forced labor. The second and third parts of the chapter consider how abusers capitalize on individuals' vulnerabilities and deploy multiple forms of control to keep their victims fearful and compliant. Part four explores the risks trafficked persons take to escape. These experiences inform formerly trafficked persons' decisions and expectations in their lives after forced labor, the focus of the remaining chapters.

I. GLOBAL WORKERS AS VULNERABLE WORKERS

Taking out loans to finance travel for work and paying smugglers, as Tatiana did, or signing up with travel brokers requires a mix of moxie and discounting of risk. One woman from Indonesia, Liza, did not know of anyone from her rural rice-farming community who had migrated overseas. She had never considered traveling before. But when a travel broker came to her town, his propositions of work in Saudi Arabia dangled economic possibilities that she and her husband could not have achieved if she had stayed in Indonesia. Although her husband earned money as a truck driver, she decided that the only way the family would ever make any more money would be through a bold move.[2] She knew it was a risk. As she was preparing to leave, she met women in a nearby city who were clear about how hard the work was in Saudi Arabia for migrant women. "They said it was a twenty-four-hour job and that sometimes women end up beaten." With this knowledge about the lack of protections for migrant workers, Liza nevertheless got on the plane. (She later accepted a job in suburban Washington, D.C., where she ended up in forced domestic labor.)

Liza's decision to put her faith in a travel broker raises questions about how migrants assess the relationship between risk and payoff. Migrants like Liza who dare to leave the familiarity and wage ceilings of their everyday lives are entrepreneurial. What makes these ambitious individuals vulnerable to forced labor? Are some more vulnerable than others? Are their vulnerabilities linked to earlier abuses? These issues are critical to policies and strategies to prevent trafficking into forced labor as well as to providing assistance afterward. These questions also illuminate how such extreme experiences shape one's sense of self and place in the world. This subjectivity of coerced labor—both while it is unfolding and afterward—is the overarching theme that connects this chapter and the chapters to follow.

Two broad viewpoints on trafficked persons' vulnerabilities have emerged along disciplinary and ideological lines. While social workers, case managers, and attorneys are likely to describe their clients as highly resourced, some trauma experts (psychologists and psychiatrists) as well as self-described "abolitionists" emphasize past experiences, such as childhood abuse or domestic violence, and their influence on individuals' vulnerability. By claiming that past sexual abuses set the stage for trafficking, antiprostitution advocates strengthen their case for rescuing all sex workers.[3] Implicit is a denial that adult women and men would ever *choose* to work in the sex sector. In striking contrast, social workers and case managers generally explain their trafficking clients' vulnerabilities to forced labor as no different from that of their other migrant clients who undertook either the risks of undocumented border crossing or of signing a contract to work in the United States with a temporary visa. Their trafficking clients were simply unlucky that the worst-case scenario happened to them.

With Inflexible Citizenship Migrants Need Luck

The potential for losing control over one's border crossing and working conditions increases when individuals have what Aiwha Ong terms *inflexible citizenship* and consequently entrust their safety to a smuggler, travel broker, or recruiter.[4] Since nation-states simultaneously "refine immigration laws to attract capital-bearing subjects" while also "limiting the entry of unskilled laborers," those who are trafficked into forced labor in the United States are vulnerable to exploitation because of this politics of border crossing.[5] While the "managerial class" that Ong describes can rely on employers—corporations and international organizations—to arrange their visas, the migrants I write about here rely instead on luck. Migrant workers take a leap of faith when they pay someone to help them cross borders, sign a contract with a legal recruiter, or an employer who sponsors their visa.[6] They only can hope that their travel broker will deliver them safely as agreed upon and that the working conditions spelled out in labor contracts with recruitment agencies or individual employers will be followed.

Elsa, one of the women I met, knew that if she wanted to work outside of her home country in Africa, she would have to comply with the decisions and actions of her recruiter and her employers. Her acceptance of the travel and work plans they made for her demonstrates, on one hand, her resourcefulness and gutsy willingness to pursue a potentially good-paying job. But, it also underscores the lack of control that global workers like Elsa ultimately have over where they work and their working conditions.[7] The anthropologist Nicole Constable goes so far as to refer to some Filipinas in Hong Kong as "*like* exiles" since they "feel forced by economic and personal circumstances to go abroad."[8] Frustration over one's working conditions, including the necessity of migrating for work, has its limits. What can low-wage workers like Elsa do with their anger? If these individuals want to work outside of their home economies, they have to agree—even if with great reluctance and many reservations—to the terms of travel and work set by intermediaries and employers.

Migration and Debt Calculus

The poor and working poor (and, in some cases, members of the middle class) in formerly trafficked persons' countries of origin may dream of more economically secure lives and actively craft out-migration strategies to expand their economic opportunities, yet they may not expect their economic plans to catapult them into a more secure social class. While significant economic mobility may seem like a long shot, making enough money that could help build a house or start a business may seem possible. And some see overseas work as the only solution to immediate needs that they otherwise cannot meet in jobs in their home communities and countries. I heard this belief that migration strategies only rarely deliver big pay-offs among a group of Dominican women in a "safe migration" workshop that I attended in a rural town a couple of hours' drive from the capital, Santo Domingo. The workshop was designed to prevent trafficking into forced labor overseas. The participants pointed to the houses around us that were owned by women who had migrated off the island for work and were still living overseas.[9] These participants alternated between buying into the stories of the money to be made overseas and acknowledging that it is not easy to come home with a lot of money without getting into illegal activities. They asserted that "no one makes money cleaning houses" and that women who return with a lot of money "sell drugs or sex; they find easier ways to make a lot of money." The women also expressed contradictory attitudes toward debt: they were willing to take on debt to travel, but they also acknowledged that they probably would lose their homes if they used them as collateral for loans from banks or the town's loan sharks.

One explanation of their willingness to take such risks is the absence of economic opportunities in their small town. As an outreach worker and I drove through this and other nearby towns, we saw only a couple of small grocery stores and no other open businesses. The towns were like ghost towns, their streets lined with boarded-up storefronts. Although some residents engaged sporadically in seasonal agricultural work, there was no way to earn cash steadily in rural communities like these without migrating internally to other Dominican towns or internationally for work. One woman who was willing to incur the debt—and the risk—of migrating overseas had just had her electricity turned off. She only earned money occasionally at her cousin's hair salon washing clients' hair. It was not nearly enough to take care of her two kids. She had been thinking about migrating overseas for work, while also acknowledging that "many of the women who have gone overseas have lost their houses." The debts are so large—reaching anywhere from US$2,000 to US$7,000—that they seem unfathomable, like board-game currency.[10] She explained her thinking: "How can I make money here? There are no jobs in this town." With no opportunities for the poor to significantly change their economic lives in local economies like this small town, why not take a chance and migrate for work?

When Exploitation Tips into Abuse: Passage into Forced Labor

Once potential migrants determine how they will pay for travel and get on the road, anything can happen. No matter their country of origin, age, gender, class, or physical strength, they are at risk of being abused in transit and then once they reach their destination and start working. Forced labor is not an easily recognizable or obvious condition, signaled by a guard with a gun. Living and working conditions may worsen over time, and those caught in these deteriorating conditions may not realize the gravity of the situation until the conditions reach an extreme. Individuals react quite differently when they realize they are in trouble. Some tell of their desperation to find a safe moment to get away and immediately begin to plan their escape. But others may stay even if they have the opportunity and means to leave. Flo had been in danger before. Beaten up by thugs for her political activism in opposition to her corrupt government in Africa, she had experience standing up for herself. Once in the United States, she tried to negotiate with her employer, but to no effect. Her treatment worsened over time. This gradualism—both of employers' abuse and of employees' resistance—helps explain why individuals stay. They also stay because, at least at first, mistreatment may be familiar. Since forced labor unfolds within a matrix of class, racial, ethnic, and gender hierarchies that may also undergird exploitation in workers' home country, they may be accustomed to feeling less powerful than their employers.

This tipping point between familiar mistreatment and unfamiliar, extreme abuse may evolve over time. When formerly trafficked persons speak of their life before forced labor, they describe acting in ways expected from workers in their social class. Women who had previous experience working as domestics or child care providers in employers' homes, for example, tell of employers who treated them in ways that reinforced their status as subordinates. Maria, for example, had experience traveling overseas from her home in the Philippines with wealthy families as a domestic worker. She had come to expect a certain amount of demeaning treatment when working for families that were far more economically and socially powerful than she. She had never shared a meal at the table with employers before; she did not expect this arrangement to change when she moved to the United States. But like so many other migrants, she discovered that she was treated more harshly in the United States than she had been overseas. Being fed scraps and forced to eat on the floor was a level of abuse that she never before had encountered. For global workers like Maria, eating separately from their employers was familiar and acceptable. She may never have expected—or wanted—to eat with her employers, but being treated like an animal came as a shock that Maria still cannot explain. Some of the workers I have met in farm work, restaurant work, and domestic work—those who were in forced labor and those who were exploited but not trafficked— described always being hungry. The control of food is a common form of control and abuse.[11] Global workers like Maria may resign themselves to certain forms of mistreatment, but not to its extreme and violent forms— such as chronic hunger.

Subjectivity of Coercion

Although they resoundingly reject and are often terrified by extreme forms of mistreatment, those in forced labor may appear complicit. In her now-classic essay on resistance and the importance of ethnography, the anthropologist Sherry Ortner observes, "In any situation of power, there is a mixture of cultural dynamics. To some extent, and for a variety of good and bad reasons, people often do accept the representations which underwrite their own domination."[12] The complexities and contradictions of accepting lousy work are central to the labor subjectivities of low-wage migrant workers in the global economy, documented and undocumented. Making sense of why some workers do not try to leave their abuser underscores not only that individuals subjectively experience coercion, but also that they have vastly different capacities for waiting out abuse. Some walk out the door; others fear doing so.

Many formerly trafficked persons' explanations of why they stayed with their abuser as long as they did (assuming that there were opportunities to leave) echo what Nicole Constable found among Filipina domestic workers who "passive[ly] acquiesce" to their "employer's every desire and view their work situation as their 'fate.'"[13] Maria fits this description. "You know me, I work," she says. "This is what I've always done. I'll work my whole life." While in forced domestic labor, Maria put up with her employer's abuse as she waited for the right time to make the next move. She knew what her employer was doing was wrong. Her hesitancy to leave is in keeping with Constable's observation that there are a "complex set of ambiguities and contradictions" such that workers "resist oppression in certain ways but also simultaneously participate in their own subordination."[14] For some, escape seems impossible. Those with work visas tied to their employers may fear the instant undocumented status that results from walking away. Gender ideologies and practices also play a critical role in shaping women workers' expectations and decisions. In Russia, as her mother was dying, Tatiana's older female relatives told her, "It is the fate of women to take care of themselves. It's our destiny." Having lost both of her parents (her father had been murdered and her mother eventually died of cancer), Tatiana felt the weight of this responsibility. "I knew I did not have parents to ask about me or to come and get me. So, I thought, well, I've been working my whole life. I'll continue to work." She decided to stay in her situation of forced labor as a dancer in a strip club and work off her debt.

Although there were bouncers at the club, Tatiana was not watched twenty-four hours a day. What stopped her from walking away? Why some individuals walk through an open door and others do not is not easily explained. Social workers and attorneys who have conducted workshops on how to identify trafficked persons for the Freedom Network Training Institute report that workshop audiences have particular difficulty grasping what keeps trafficked persons from leaving their abuser or from seeking help. One service provider told the audience of a workshop I attended that it has been easier to "prove" that her clients were trafficked if they had been physically restrained or abused, even though the law says otherwise. In order to secure T visas for clients who have not been physically harmed, attorneys must demonstrate why their clients feared walking out an open door or telephoning the police. The necessity of proving the perception of danger has had the unintended effect of emphasizing trafficked persons' victim status. But many do not fit the image of a victim. Underscoring that not all trafficked persons appear fragile, a social worker from New York posed the question, "What do we assume about how trafficked persons present? I have clients who are very quiet and reluctant to talk. But last week a woman came into the office who was very aggressive, not at all fragile. I had to check my assumptions about what a trafficking victim should look like." Similarly in a profile of a social worker in Moldova, the journalist William Finnegan writes about a seventeen-year old trafficked girl who did not cooperate with law enforcement but instead was determined to find her trafficker herself, explaining, "I know how to find her. I will beat her."[15]

I have been asked if a kind of "Stockholm syndrome" sets in and prevents those in forced labor from leaving their abuser. Fear, not identification with one's trafficker, is the hallmark of the power dynamic (although women who had a romantic relationship with their abuser and with whom they may have children may also have a difficult time severing ties).[16] The sources generating this fear may not be evident to outside observers. A guard with a weapon is an obvious deterrent; locks on doors and a system of informers may make it impossible to leave. When no guards or locked doors prevent exit, threats to families back home can be just as potent. To keep their workers from calling the police, abusers weave frightening stories about law enforcement in the United States being corrupt and violent. They also remind workers that the police will deport any migrant without documentation. Esperanza explains why she did not seek help: "They [traffickers] know that people who are here are of course not going to go to law enforcement. Most of the time these people take any identification. My trafficker told me, 'Who is going to believe you! You are nobody in this country and you don't even have an ID. You don't speak English, you don't have an education and you don't have money. So the police might think you are crazy and they will put you in jail and you will never see your children.' And in some way it is true." Flo, too, believed her abuser's lies that people in the United States did not like people from her home country in Africa, "I believed her because she was a diplomat."

Class, citizenship, race, ethnicity, religion, and gender can inform individuals' perceptions of their power in relation to their trafficker. They may never have placed demands on someone from a more powerful social stratum before. These power dynamics may be nearly undetectable. "Proving" forced labor means explaining migrants' perception of threat, danger, and compulsion to work.[17] Researchers have tried to pinpoint factors that contribute to forced labor, as well as those that may increase the likelihood of exit. One research team combed through news accounts to document the circumstances of trafficked persons' exit; they charted different contexts of "exposure/discovery" such as through the help of a "Good Samaritan" or through police intervention.[18] But where do power dynamics that may lead to, delay, or prevent an individual from leaving fit in a chart? How can one's readiness for resistance and action be quantified and charted?

The anthropologist Lila Abu-Lughod's discussion of resistance and power helps us understand why a threat against one individual may not have the same coercive effect on another. Shifting the focus away from forms of resistance toward a focus on "forms of power," argues Abu-Lughod, helps explain the often elusive and deeply contextual reasons that compel individuals to stay with their abuser.[19] Her rejection of "some sort of hierarchy of significant and insignificant forms of power" reminds us that one form of power between an abuser and the abused may not have the same coercive effects on others.[20] Simply put, what scares some individuals does not scare others. Every individual in an exploitative situation has his or her own subjective understanding of the dangers of leaving and of what constitutes extreme abuse.

This subjectivity of coercion explains why many trafficking cases "appear to fall somewhere between consent and coercion." Even though the TVPA criminalizes the use of psychological means to induce labor, it "lacks specificity," especially regarding nonphysical harm.[21] These cases pivot on identifying the "subtle methods of control" that constrain "the workers' freedom to quit."[22] Proving an individual's perception of threat and danger and the fear that it generates is not easy. Kim notes that in some cases without proof of physical harm, attorneys have decided to not move them forward as trafficking cases.[23] Moreover these non-overt methods of coercion that induce workers to continue working may go unnoticed by law enforcement officers and other first responders, such as medical personnel or housing inspectors.[24] In these confusing moments of legal assessment, those in forced labor can be hastily—and wrongfully—categorized as undocumented lawbreakers, put in detention, and be slated for deportation. Legal scholar (and legal practitioner) Dina Haynes warns that "unless the victim is 'rescued' or found chained to a bed in a brothel, she will be forever unable to establish that her traffickers ultimately had something more 'severe' and 'exploitative' in mind" since "the victim bears the burden of proving her traffickers' intent to exploit her."[25] Haynes worries that since the vast majority of trafficked persons are not rescued by U.S. government officials but leave their situation of forced labor on their own, they are less likely to be perceived as "victims."[26]

Scholars' efforts to understand why the world's marginalized may appear resigned to subordination helps make sense of the contradictions, discontinuities, and fissures in formerly trafficked persons' narratives about how they viewed their traffickers and their opportunities for leaving. Many trafficked persons like Maria (from the Philippines) and Liza (from Indonesia) come from rural, agricultural settings and have work and family histories as part of the rural peasantry who do not own their land; they are intimately familiar with being treated badly. Yet, as enslaved individuals' writings from the eighteenth and nineteenth century show, there is a chasm of difference between navigating safely within and out of systems of oppression and subscribing to ideologies of domination. Individuals in forced labor today may appear beaten down while they wait for an opening to act, but they do not believe "actively in values that explain and justify their own subordination."[27] Abu-Lughod, for example, struggles to account for Bedouin women's resistance to and support of "the existing system of power" without "resorting" to explanations of false consciousness.[28] The political scientist James Scott also tackles these questions in his masterful exploration of Malay peasants' forms of resistance, *Weapons of the Weak*. He rejects assertions of "false consciousness" or other forms of mystification to explain "apparently acquiescent" behavior and a seeming acceptance of the social order.[29] Carefully attending to the thorny relationship between thought and action, he emphasizes that action is tied to the material world. He elaborates: "It is possible and common for human actors to conceive of a line of action that is, at the moment, either impractical or impossible. Thus, a person may dream of a revenge or a millennial kingdom of justice that may never occur. On the other hand, as circumstances change, it may become possible to act on those dreams. The realm of consciousness gives us a kind of privileged access to lines of action that may—just may—become plausible at some future date."[30]

Remaining with one's trafficker thus can be understood in terms of tactics and strategy, not consent or resignation.[31] Consciousness of one's subordinate treatment is not at issue; the timing of when or how to challenge it is. There are many, often not readily apparent, reasons for waiting, holding steady, and not blowing the whistle. Formerly trafficked persons tell "stor[ies] of rational calculation," not passive acceptance of oppression.[32] What may appear as passivity may be better understood as stalling. This waiting game reflects the level of confusion and uncertainty that accompanies brutality and fear. While waiting for the right time to make their move, formerly trafficked persons make clear that they looked for ways to outsmart their traffickers. Many recount being told that they were filthy, worthless, and stupid and how they manipulated their abusers' perception of their incompetence to their advantage. Nanci tells of secretly collecting spare change that she brought with her when her abuser sent her to the corner store. She describes how she capitalized on his view of her as passive: "He thought I was submissive and would not try to leave him. But I had those quarters with me when I was out on an errand and I called 911. The police came." Saving loose change over time, picking up a flyer from a community-based organization that could be of assistance to them in the future, or eavesdropping on conversations in the household, all became small acts that played a critical role in their future escape plans.

When abusive employers make demand after demand, have expectations that can never be met, and give little or nothing in return, workers learn to gauge just how much to ask for. Individuals in forced labor know that they have scant leverage to make demands. Ultimately every individual evaluates exploitation—what can be endured and what goes too far—by different criteria. Steven Lukes's description of "willing" and "unwilling" "compliance to domination" as not "mutually exclusive" helps explain why individuals in forced labor do not escape through unlocked doors at the first possible opportunity.[33]

Elsa: Global Worker

Elsa, a woman in her early twenties from Africa, stayed in an unlocked apartment where she cooked and cleaned for no money, in part because she was waiting for the paycheck that her abuser kept promising her. She also stayed because actually walking out of the apartment was daunting: she had no passport, money, friends to call, or seasonally appropriate clothes. For those who are holding out for payment—any payment—the decision to leave guarantees that they will receive no money at all. And once they leave, then what? To what new uncertainty would they be running?[34] For some, working for no pay is less risky than leaving and sleeping in the streets—or worse, ending up in a jail cell and raped by a corrupt police officer, a common scenario that their abusers use to intimidate. As Elsa kept asking for her pay, her abuser eventually sent a couple of money wires to her family. And since he was not physically abusing her, she made the decision to wait a while longer.

Elsa's forced labor in the United States began when a Saudi family hired her from an employment agency in Bahrain. She explains her initial decision to go to an employment agency in her home country in Africa to arrange a job as a child care provider overseas: "I did not have enough money to support my family [she lived with her parents] or to help myself." Like many hopeful migrants, she took a gamble that her migration for work would be worthwhile in the long run. She worked in Bahrain for three years: "It was not good. It's hard, you know, every day, every day I struggled to work there. But I had to finish my contract." She almost never left the house and had no clearly defined hours but "worked all the time, day and night." She was paid, although it was "a small amount," and not the salary that had been agreed upon by the agency. "I would ask for it, and every day my employer would say, 'Tomorrow, tomorrow.'" Fed up with the low salary and long hours, Elsa told her employer that she wanted to go back to the agency, and he took her there.

At the agency her employer talked with the owner, but Elsa still did not receive any back pay. "The owner of the agency told me he owned me and that I would work in his house. I stayed at the office a couple of weeks [where there were beds], until a woman came and wanted to take me to Saudi Arabia." Elsa found herself going straight from the office to Saudi Arabia, with just a small bag of her things. She had no idea—let alone assurances—of what she was getting into next. "I didn't have any money. It was hard. I didn't have anything. In the office you watch other employees get taken by employers. Some employers asked me questions. This lady pointed to me and said, 'Okay, I will take her.'" Elsa was not involved in the negotiations; travel arrangements and the terms of her labor contract were discussed between this new employer and the owner of the agency. "They did everything, they took care of everything by themselves." The agency had been keeping her passport while she was in Bahrain: "When I entered Bahrain, the agency took my passport from me. After that, the agency gave my new employer my passport." Elsa traveled to this second job in Saudi Arabia in a car driven by a hired driver. (Her new employer was not with them for this thirty-minute drive.)

Elsa believed her new employer was "an ambassador of some kind" since her house was quite large, with a swimming pool. Her new employer employed not only a driver but two other women to work in the house. One woman was from Elsa's home country in Africa, and the other was from the Philippines. The three women shared a room in the house. Once again, Elsa worked all the time. "While I was there I did everything! I cooked, I cleaned, and sometimes I took care of my employer's son's baby. I did all the work. When I finished with something, they gave me something else. I did everything." The employer abided by the agreement worked out at the employment agency in Bahrain and paid Elsa every month. Elsa worked there for a year and three months. She was less lonely than she had been in her first job since she could speak her language with her coworker. However, Elsa did not know that everything was about to change.

Elsa's Unintended Migration to the United States

The family for whom she had been working unexpectedly announced that Elsa would accompany them the next day on a three-day trip: "I did not even get a chance to get my stuff, nothing. My employer told me to pack three uniforms." When they arrived at the airport she still did not know where she was going. She was told there was a problem with her passport, that it had expired, and a driver she had never seen before took her to her country's embassy, where he handed over her passport to the officials. Not once since her first trip to the employment agency in her home country had she touched her own passport.

In the embassy Elsa managed to speak for a few minutes with one of the office staff. She told him that she did not know where she was going. He helped her, as she explains: "He told me that he would make a copy of my passport for me. He said, 'Don't show them, it won't be good for you. Don't lose this passport. Every day put it in a secret place. And if you go to new places, bring this, it is your ID, do not throw it away.'" He then surreptitiously passed the photocopy to her. She showed me how he placed it under her armpit, undetected from behind. During the ride back to the airport, she was able to hold her passport for a fleeting moment. Once at the airport, the driver handed it back to her employer's son, who, though Elsa didn't know it at the time, would be her new employer in the United States.

She became scared when she realized the family had been lying to her. By withholding information, they exerted a new dynamic of control over her: "They told me, 'We're not going far. We'll be there in two or three hours.' But you know, I read the board. I read New York. I wept." She felt she had no way out. "I did not know what do to. I was scared. I did not know where I was going. Or what I would be doing. Nothing. I knew nothing. So I had to follow what they did." She could understand them some of the time (they spoke in Arabic), "but mostly I could not understand what they were saying to one another."

Once they arrived in New York, her employers and their son continued to treat her differently than when she had worked for them in Saudi Arabia. They signaled their control over her by amplifying her state of confusion. At various stages of the journey, including during the drive from New York to the Washington, D.C., area, they kept on asking her where she thought she was. When she asked where they were going, they would reply, "Someplace." Her employer teasingly asked her, "Do you have any fears of America?"

She began working for the entire family right away in the hotel where they all stayed for a couple of weeks. She unpacked their clothes. The rooms had kitchens, so she cooked meals for them. "While they were out, I stayed back at the hotel. They told me that if anybody comes to the door, don't open it. And if anybody calls on the phone, don't answer it. They explained that maybe the workers of the hotel have the key to the room. That I have to be careful." When she asked why, they told her, "People here are not good. Everyone here is bad." Not knowing much about the United States since she had never planned on traveling there, Elsa thought, "Maybe they are right." Even though she had her own room, was not locked in, and as far as she knew was not being watched, she did not leave.

She continued to work around the clock—and still had not been paid anything—when, after a few weeks in the hotel, the woman brought her to the son's high-rise apartment in the suburbs of Washington. "When I got there, she told me, 'You clean the fridge, the bathroom, everything. Wash his clothes and put them away.' Then they all went out to dinner and I started to clean. Around ten they came back and asked if I was finished. I explained no. The house was so dirty, so dirty. 'What kind of job have you done?' they asked. I said I washed half the clothes, cleaned the dining room, but that the kitchen is not done and it is too much work for me to finish all by myself. They said we would go to the apartment again tomorrow and I would continue working." It was at this point that the woman informed Elsa that she would be living with the son in the apartment. "I cried when she told me this, but I turned my back so she wouldn't see. She told me, 'You are good. There is too much work here for my son. You stay with him. You and him. There is nobody else here. You cook for him. You clean for him. You wash his clothes. You take care of him. You do everything and there will be more salary.' I was so tired and did not know how I could continue working like this. But I did not say anything to anyone. I did not know how I could do what was expected."

Elsa's Demands

With more than one member of this family demanding work and refusing payment, Elsa had no opportunity to build a relationship or an understanding with any member of the family—the only people with whom she had any contact. She did, however, protest. "How could they just bring me here and leave me like this! I told him [the son] that I did not get to say goodbye to my friends! He told me, 'You will get good money.'" But he did not pay her. As the weeks and months passed she continued to ask for payment. The son made light of her demands: "You don't need money, for what? Why would you need money?" She told him that she wanted to send money back home to her parents, and he promised that he would do so. She describes his response: "He would say, 'Tomorrow, tomorrow, tomorrow.' But he never did." The situation continued—Elsa stayed and the son verbally berated her and refused to pay her salary—but she is uncertain of the exact length of time. She did not leave the apartment except to go with him to the supermarket. She was not allowed to go to church, even though she asked him every day. When she was sick, he refused to bring her to the doctor and instead would buy her over-the-counter medicine.

The son finally wired $1,500 to her family. Hoping to speak with her family, she pleaded that she needed to call them to notify them to pick up the money. But he would not let her make a phone call. She angrily explained: "He told me the phone was not working. But it was!" Finally he let her use his father's mobile phone. "When I reached my family, my sister answered and she cried and cried. 'Where are you!' they screamed. It had been a year and a couple of months since they had heard from me. My sister told me she thought I was dead! I said, 'I am sorry.' I told her what happened and said 'Please, please if you can get somebody to help me. I don't know anybody.'" Elsa gave her address to her sister, which she had learned by chance: "One time when I was cleaning his clothes, I found a letter in his suit pocket. I read the address on the envelope with the apartment address and found the telephone number written in the letter. I copied it and put it in my pocket. I told my sister all this information and to give this to somebody to help." One night her brother called. "I was sleeping and the phone rang. It was my brother. Oh the son was pissed. His face was red. He gets red when he is angry. I thought he would kill me—he shouted 'Who gave him this number!' I had to lie. He called his family right away! I thought the mother would send me back to Saudi!" Her abuser punished her by ignoring her. "After that everything changed. Everything. He would not even say hello to me when he came into the apartment from outside. He would come home, go to his bedroom, change his clothes, and then go back outside. He changed the telephone number. He told me never to answer the phone." She did not; she feared him without his ever raising a hand. Elsa knew very little about her abuser, such as where he worked during the day or where he went when he left the apartment in the evenings.

Months later the employer claimed that he had sent money again. Unconvinced, Elsa asked to see the receipt. "He told me he threw it away! After that I was very hungry to see my family. I asked if I could give them the address to write me letters. But he told me it would take too long for letters to get here from home. He wouldn't allow this. He told me to give them the address in Saudi Arabia, and they would send the letters here. I did this. I wrote letters and he said he mailed them for me. But when I did not get any in return, I asked him for receipts to show that he had sent my letters. He would say to me: 'Why do you need the receipt? Everything you say, I need a receipt, I need a receipt! Why do you need this? If I sent the letter, I sent the letter.' He stopped talking to me for a week."

Elsa's Loneliness

Elsa's isolation was stifling. She describes her time in the house as like being in jail. "All the time I was crying. Even sometimes at night I could not sleep. I would cry so hard I would have a headache. I would dream and see my family. It was a very hard time. I was the only one in the house. I never saw anyone or anything. I never even saw an animal. I only moved between this room and that room and did not see anybody." Her employer prevented her from having contact with anyone by telling her, "People here are not good, they will hurt you." He also told her, "If you go outside without your passport or any other ID, you will get in trouble." "I had to stay and do my work. I was scared by all of this." Looking out the window she explains, "I could see people outside, but since I was up in the apartment I never got to talk to them." Several times a year Elsa found companionship with the man's thirteen-year-old son when he came to visit. She describes these visits: "He is a nice boy. Before he came I felt lonely. I did not talk with anybody. But then when he came I had him to talk to. I was happy around him. Even though I had to do everything for him—cook for him and clean his clothes—he was like my friend when he was at home."

Elsa eventually left her abuser with the help of her sister back home in Africa, who gave her the phone number of a friend living in Colorado. Elsa phoned this friend when her abuser was out, and he put her in touch with a coethnic radio personality in the Washington area. At one point all three were on the phone at the same time and hatched an escape plan for Elsa. The local contact would pick up Elsa down the street from her apartment in a week and a half. Elsa knew her abuser monitored the phone records and would see these outgoing calls. She began to monitor him as well. He pretended to leave to go to work every morning. "I could see his car sitting in his parking space. He was not going anywhere. He would get up, change his clothes, eat his breakfast, and then head downstairs. But he never left the building." She watched him as carefully as he watched her. "One day it was raining very hard. But he came back home supposedly from work and he was completely dry. Even his shoes." While he monitored her, Elsa mapped out the details of her escape. She packed a small bag of her things, which she would stash in a garbage bag that she would take out of the apartment. She would wear her white uniform, as she always did, but over some street clothes that her abuser's mother had given her to wear on the rare occasion she went to the supermarket with her abuser.

All went as she had planned. On the Wednesday evening that she was going to meet her accomplice, she took the garbage out. But instead of garbage, she threw out her white uniform and walked out of the building in her regular clothes, carrying her small bag. She soon spotted the car of her sister's friend's friend. He took her to his mother's home. "It was so warm. She fed me and made me feel at home. It began to sink in that I was free." She stayed with this elderly woman from her home country, and together they contacted a social service agency that helped Elsa secure temporary housing and, eventually, a T visa.

Elsa tells of humiliating treatment from the first moment the Saudi family hired her from the employment agency in Bahrain. But being treated in a demeaning manner as a subordinate did not foretell her future treatment in forced labor. She could not possibly have known at the initial bureaucratic and transit sites that she would end up working without pay in an apartment in the United States, where her only contact with the outside world was through a window. Her decision to move forward with plans to travel with this family even after they had taken her passport underscores the few choices migrants with "inflexible citizenship" have.

II. CHAINS OF INTIMACY: RELATIONSHIPS
BETWEEN ABUSER AND ABUSED

Work to control others involves planning and strategy.[35] In her landmark book on the effects of violence, the psychiatrist Judith Herman writes that the methods of control in abusive situations are "remarkably consistent."[36] In trafficking cases in the United States, abusers' mechanisms of control typically have included taking workers' passports, restricting their contact with the outside world, and withholding money. Without identification, contacts, money, or even the right clothes for the season, many are over-whelmed by the uncertainty—and perceived danger—of leaving. They may not know English, anyone in the United States, or the country's laws. Like Elsa, they may not even know where they are. If they are young, they may have fewer experiences from which to draw. And if a woman is in love with her abuser or has children with him, these ties of intimacy will complicate leaving—and later prosecuting—her abuser. Those who have been beaten or raped or have witnessed others being beaten (including members of their abuser's family) worry about the consequences for them or others if they are caught leaving. In short, their world turns upside down.

Young Women and Older Men

In many trafficking cases, men (usually in their twenties and early thirties) seduce young girls (in their mid- to late teens) and woo them with romance to eventually channel them into forced labor. A social worker in California has observed that the "nature of the relationship between young women and older men looks like that of domestic violence. This is a personal relation-ship, and it is very different from trafficking cases that involve strangers."[37] Young women's frustration with their own family's restrictions on them often prepares them to accept the promises of these men. They cite prob-lems with their father—in particular, their father's patriarchal control and rules—as driving them out of the house. As one woman from Mexico ex-plained, "My father was coming from another time. I couldn't wait to get out of his house." "They want to do something on their own," asserts a social worker with a number of Mexican clients in New York. "But they are young. In many cases they are not actually that interested in these men but are eager to get out of their parents' home."

These relationships can quickly take an abusive turn. The New York–based social worker has clients who were raped the first night they were away from their parents. The young women, she explains, "blame them-selves for not listening to their parents." Years after not heeding her parents' warnings about her "boyfriend" who trafficked her into forced labor, one young woman from Mexico carries her regret with her. She feels an over-whelming debt to her parents since she ignored their counsel and casts her current struggles to resettle in the United States as a kind of test or punish-ment for being so rash. Formerly trafficked persons of all ages express anger over the time their abusers stole from them, but younger individuals can be particularly eager to recapture this lost time — and their youth. Gladys, who was trafficked in her late teens from Mexico into forced domestic labor in the Midwest, angrily declared that her abuser "destroyed a big part of my life." Although he is now in jail, Gladys is clear that his sentence "is nothing compared to what he did in my life."

Imagining one's boyfriend or husband as a potential trafficker is difficult for anyone; who could foresee that one's partner is weaving an elaborate trap to eventually make money from one's labor? The journalist Benjamin Skinner tells a story of a young woman getting into her boyfriend's car in eastern Europe just moments after her mother handed her a safe-migration pamphlet from the antitrafficking NGO La Strada warning of the "loverboy phenomenon." Suspicious of the boyfriend and well aware of patterns of trafficking into forced sexual labor in their country, the mother had prepared for foul play. Her daughter, perhaps in love, and in need of a job in Holland that the boyfriend had promised would finance the remainder of her university studies, waved the pamphlet away. Once on the road, away from the protection of her family, the young woman was forced by this man into sexual labor.[38]

Nanci too tells a story of falling in love and believing false promises. Growing up in a small rural community in Mexico, she had not planned on traveling to the United States. Her family, which included eight brothers and sisters, lived hand-to-mouth making bricks. In her late teens Nanci met an older man (he was thirty-two). Her parents were impressed by his family, who ran a successful store in a nearby town. He showered her with presents and took her out to restaurants and dance clubs. She fell in love and was excited by his plans for them. He paid a coyote for them to travel to Los Angeles. But soon after they arrived in the United States, he started treating her harshly. Almost overnight he changed from loving boyfriend to cruel captor. They crossed the country to New York City, where he moved her between different brothels. Knowing no one in the United States, Nanci realized that she had to help herself. I recounted earlier how she took advantage of her unsuspecting boyfriend's confidence in his control over her as well as his presumption of her passivity by phoning the police when he sent her unaccompanied on an errand. Because of her age and lack of familiarity with the United States, he had counted on Nanci remaining in fear and always returning to him.

Coercion through Domestic Violence

When men manipulate ties of intimacy to force women into work, domestic violence usually permeates their relationships. Sofia, a mother of two small children in Mexico, was regularly beaten by her husband who demanded that she work in the sex trade in Tijuana. "We never had a lot of money. It was very difficult. My kids outgrew their clothes. When there was a hole in the front of my son's shoe, I cut the front of the shoe off so that he could still wear it. My husband had been asking me to work in prostitution. He said we could make a lot of money. I said, 'Why don't you work?' He never worked. But we needed basic things: clothes, rent, food. I came to realize I had to work in prostitution. And the beatings got stronger. Especially when he was drunk. Over time the beatings were anytime for any reason." Sofia relented and worked in Tijuana's sex trade for five years, while family members raised her children. "They were hard years. I would work six months and return home for a month. My husband would hit me. Always. He drank and took drugs. Eventually he wanted me to go to the United States. He wanted more money, not me. He said, 'I promise it will only be one year. Then you'll come home.' He arranged for me to go with a coyote."

Sofia diligently sent money home regularly from the United States. She earned a substantial sum over the course of a few years; she had sent home over $130,000 and kept all the wire transfer receipts to prove it. She shook her head, explaining that her husband "had a great time with my money." He spent it all: he built a couple of stores and a gym and paid off debts to shady business associates. When women migrate internationally for work and remit money to family members at home, they can only hope that their family members will keep their promises to save the money or spend it on their children.[39] Sofia's husband did more than live large off her earnings: "[He] turned my children against me. They refused to speak to me when I called." Their relationship remains strained today. Convinced her husband will kill her if given the chance, she fears returning to Mexico to see her children. She ignored his urgings for her to come home one Christmas. "I made excuses," she laughed. "I said, 'I'll be there in January.' And it went by. I said at that point that I had to stay in the United States because of passport issues. He was very angry." She laughed with pride, recounting how she evaded her husband and his beatings. It is an uncomfortable reality that, in Sofia's calculation, she had to leave her children behind in order to stay alive. Afraid of her husband's long reach to New York City, she also avoids certain neighborhoods where he has friends. She takes precautions in her new home to keep safe from the violence of her old home. Even after forced labor has ended for her, she still lives with the fear of being brutalized.

Family Business and Towns' Economies

Trafficking into forced labor can become a way of life in places where corruption thrives and builds on the normalization of abuse of women, children, and the poor. Social workers throughout the United States describe clients from towns in Mexico, for example, where many families are involved in trafficking. In these towns, falling in love can be dangerous, and romantic relationships that become abusive can involve more than one abuser; the abusive partner's family members may be complicit as well. In these cases, individuals in forced labor cannot trust anyone with whom they come into contact since their partner's mother, father, sisters and brothers, extended family, and other girlfriends maintain the conditions of threat and coercion. Trafficking into forced labor is a family business with roles for everyone. Within these ties of familial intimacy, there can be grotesque cruelty. I spoke with a few women whose husbands took them back to the men's home communities in Mexico when the women were about to give birth. Their husbands' mothers took these women's babies immediately following their delivery. The abuser and his family would then use these babies as a form of collateral—a twisted means to induce these bereft mothers to continue working under their control and to stay silent.

It is difficult to make sense of this involvement of multiple members of a family; it can be easier to grasp one individual's greed or particular penchant for cruelty. Women from these towns who remain separated from their children point to rampant and entrenched corruption and violence unprosecuted by the authorities. Sofia, for example, comes from a town in Mexico that has become known as a "sending" community into trafficking, where corrupt local officials and law enforcement turn a blind eye to and profit from spectacular forms of lawbreaking. Sofia says that nearly every family has a member who is touched by trafficking, either as an abuser or as a victim of abuse: "In my town everyone is somehow involved. Husbands, sons, uncles, grandfathers." In these towns, individuals learn to justify control of others. Young boys talk about growing up and pimping girls. Sofia was shaken to hear that her young son was parroting what his father and his father's associates talk about. Her son had boasted to Sofia's sister that when he grows up, he was "not going to work" but rather would "have a few girls do the work." Horrified, his aunt prodded, "And what if they do not want to work for you?" Without hesitation he replied, "Then I will beat them."

III. THE WORK OF CONTROLLING OTHERS' WORK: MECHANISMS OF CONTROL

To understand everyday life in coerced labor demands attention to the interplay between abusers and those they try to control. Defiant acts may appear insignificant and ineffectual in comparison to the techniques abusers use to control, which may include surveillance, violence, and informers. Particularly in the press and in movies, traffickers' control has been depicted as so totalizing as to crush any resistance. Traffickers are portrayed as unstoppable. The movie *Taken*, starring Liam Neeson, for example, features a gang of ruthless Albanian traffickers who are portrayed as elusive and unstoppable until they meet Neeson's character.[40] In many instances in the United States, however, it is not an absolute level of control that prevents individuals from exiting situations of forced labor but their perception of control. The biggest hold Nanci's boyfriend had over her, for example, was her assumed devotion to him; he wrongly believed that she would never leave him. When she left, she used simple means: a few quarters to make a telephone call. Individuals in forced labor plan and take action while facing techniques that abusers use to intensify fear, disorientation, confusion, and silence. At the top of the list is isolation.

Isolation

Abusers seek to isolate their workers by preventing them from contacting their families in their home country as well as from having any contacts where they live in the United States. Herman explains that "perpetrators universally seek to isolate their victims from any other source of information, material aid, or emotional support."[41] The isolation imposed upon Elsa, the woman transported from Saudi Arabia to an apartment in suburban Washington, D.C., no doubt intensified her fear and insecurity. But while certain jobs, such as domestic work in private homes, may be carried out alone, jobs with coworkers may not lead to any relationships either. Those who work in settings where there are clients or coworkers may confront a system of informers that creates a sense of isolation—even while they are surrounded by others. Linda from South America, for example, worked in the kitchen of a national restaurant chain. She received a weekly paycheck, traveled unaccompanied to and from work, and worked alongside many coworkers. She lived in a house owned by her abuser, which she shared with a dozen compatriots. Her housemates also headed out to workplaces every day, where they too worked alongside others, and returned home each night. They all handed over their cashed paychecks to their abuser. What kept them there was debt, fear of detection and deportation, and, at least in Linda's case, the abuser's promise to bring her son to the United States.

Surveillance and Informers

Formerly trafficked persons tell of feeling watched and monitored. This perception of constant surveillance helps explain why some did not walk away or why some, like Elsa, did not use the phone while their abusers were out. Tatiana describes always feeling watched by the owners of the strip club where she was a dancer: "They knew information that nobody knew. How could they know these things? And then they would say with a kind of smile, 'Oh, you think we don't know anything about you. We know everything. Every single move.'" She asserts that the effects of this real or implied surveillance made her feel like a "freak." "It got to be that I would look at something, like a smoke detector, and would think maybe there is a camera taking pictures of us? Maybe when I'm in the shower there is somebody watching me?" She and her only friend, another dancer at the club, developed ways to communicate to evade what they believed was their abusers' monitoring. "We would go outside or put on our TV very loud because we didn't know if there were bugs. Sometimes we would go into the bathroom and run the water, just like in the movies." They also bought a tape recorder to surveil the surveillants. "I was thinking one day we could record them and we could take it to the police, so we would be prepared. I gave the tape recorder to my friend. But, she ran away [from the club]. After she ran away, they broke into her locker and they found it. They said to me, 'She is really dangerous. Do you know what we found that she had?' I made myself look stupid when they told me this." Tatiana likens this immensely stressful atmosphere to that of combat: "I felt like soldiers who try to survive even while maybe somebody is watching them. We were like spies. They lied to us, so we were going to lie to them."

After her friend had run away from the club and their abusers, Tatiana

felt completely alone. Since she had no family left in Russia, she did not imagine ever returning. During this time the cat-and-mouse games with her abusers took a new turn. "My friend called me, and I got scared because somebody had called her and asked about me. The caller had claimed they were Homeland Security. At first I was worried that it was, but then I realized this was a trick. They did not want her to have any contact with me." Without her friend by her side, Tatiana says, her sense of isolation increased exponentially, as did her distrust of everyone around her. "When you are far away from friends, it is hard. You start to be weaker. It's better to stay together."

Feeling constantly watched induced Tatiana to keep secret what she could about her life. She learned that being lied to demands lying in return. She dated an owner of another club and found herself having to lie to him. "He did not understand why I did not have a car and why I was living in such a small place while making so much money." Once she started lying, she found it difficult to remember which lies she had told to whom. Between lying to her boyfriend and lying to her abusers, she was in a state of constant confusion. "It was like a spider web. Who can you trust if you are a big liar? You don't want to lie to people, but you have to. People are not going to understand me. So it goes on. It gets even deeper. It's depressing. How can you build a nice healthy relationship if you are lying to people?" Tatiana believes that all the lying changed her: "When I used to not lie, I was so open to the world. I was dreaming all the time. I was kind of a fighter, and they made me quiet. I'm afraid to take certain steps in my life now. And I often get confused and wonder if I'm making the right decision or not. I'm always thinking about this." Like many formerly trafficked persons, she is flummoxed by how to explain to potential employers what she was doing during the years she was in forced labor. The lies that she continues to tell to conceal that time wear her down and make it difficult to settle into and open herself to a new phase of her life.

The use of informers is a bedrock strategy in controlling others and generating a state of fear. All relationships become suspect. Tatiana describes being on guard at all times, including with her boyfriend, with whom she did not use her real name. His loyalties remain as unclear to her as anyone's she met through the club. She maintains that he seemed unaware that his associates were taking all the money that she earned, but was this a front he put on? As an owner of a club, he was powerful in this social world. It is not clear if Tatiana believed that she could not turn him down or thought that he could offer her some degree of protection. At the very least, any time she spent with him took her out of her abuser's orbit. (Her abuser let her spend time with him only after she had earned her daily quota.)

Debt

Debt — money borrowed from loan sharks, travel brokers, or other middle-men or -women, or family and friends — can keep individuals from walking away from their situation of forced labor. Considering the investment that migrants have put into their travel, some develop a "nothing more to lose" approach and decide to stick it out for possible improvements. Ba, for example, owed money to family members in Vietnam. He was one of 270 workers locked in a Korean-owned factory in American Samoa. "If I left, I would have to pay a fee for breaking my contract. And my family would have to pay the damages since my older brother had signed my contract. My father-in-law also signed it since my parents are dead." In his calculus, he had determined that migration for work to American Samoa was a sure way to change his family's economic position in Vietnam in the long run. He and his wife had struggled to save money to grow their business, a tailor shop in a "small country town," while also taking care of four children. "If I stayed at the tailor shop, even after five or ten years, it would be no bigger, no smaller. But if we traveled, we could get a lump sum." Before he and his wife signed on with a labor recruiter in Vietnam, they watched a video and had opportunities to ask questions. They were led to believe that American Samoa was "part of the United States" and thus banked on receiving the "protections and benefits that Americans have." In short, they had done their homework, traveled together, and had a plan for their earnings.

Once they arrived in American Samoa, however, the factory owner took their passports and threatened them and their coworkers with deportation if they did not follow orders. Although the owner did not threaten to hurt his family in Vietnam, deportation would have meant that he and his family would never be able to pay off his contractual debts. Ba also was worried about his wife; workers were not allowed to have traveled with a spouse, so he and his wife had hidden their marital status. But the owner figured out that they were married and separated them. Ba describes a pattern of verbal and physical threats by thugs hired by the factory owner, who did not pay them for six months but then gave each worker $300.[42] This kind of sporadic payment keeps workers like Ba, with large travel debts, holding on.

Ba weighed whether to stay and hope for more pay or to cut his losses and try to get out. Not only does debt prevent individuals from leaving exploitative situations, but many also believe that it is shameful to return home empty-handed. Ba could not bear to return home without accomplishing his plan to help his extended family.

Abusers also siphon their workers' paychecks—and further indenture them—by positioning themselves as the sole source of food and housing. Linda's and her compatriots' abuser supplied not only their housing but all of their meals as well. Linda says that there was never enough food and that they ate the same meals every day. The abuser then added these costs to their travel fees, and their debt deepened day by day. Reminiscent of the permanent indebtedness of peasants working on haciendas in colonial Latin America or sharecroppers in the American South under Jim Crow, these contemporary workers could not extricate themselves from their ever-mounting debts to their abuser. Between the abuser's promises to bring over Linda's son and her threats about the money Linda allegedly owed her, Linda felt she could not walk away.

Physical Abuse

Violence, of course, powerfully intimidates and terrorizes. It also can inspire bravery and action. Tatiana and her best friend decided to tape-record their abusers after they had brutally beaten this friend in front of the other women at the club. "She was bruised. And a little piece of her tooth was gone," Tatiana reported. She believes her abusers beat her friend because she had spoken up about the treatment of the women: "She got beaten because she said the truth." This one beating had long-term reverberations at the club. The possibility of another beating kept Tatiana from leaving her friend unprotected: "I was out of town for the weekend with my boyfriend when she was beaten. When my friend called me, I told him I had to go back. I couldn't sleep." Once she returned, she vowed to stay. "I mean, I couldn't leave because if I left, they would beat her. How could I leave her? Yes, she has a temper, but she's also full of trust. She's truthful. And she stood up for me all the time." Despite the surveillance and threats, Tatiana and her friend managed to form strong ties of friendship, mutual assistance, and respect. The atmosphere of deception, mistrust, violence, and personal gain brought these friends closer together and deepened their devotion to and reliance on one another.

Subhuman Treatment

Formerly trafficked persons tell of their abusers treating them as subhuman. By "instill[ing] terror and helplessness" and by "supervis[ing] what the victim eats, when she sleeps, when she goes to the toilet, what she wears," the abuser seeks "to destroy the victim's sense of self in relation to others."[43] Lack of control over one's body also compromises health in the short and long term. Across a spectrum of abusive experiences, formerly trafficked persons tell of being denied medical care. A report on forced labor in the United States describes workers in an Oklahoma factory who suffered work-related injuries and illnesses and were not allowed to seek medical attention. In one instance, one worker who was a U.S. citizen attempted to take a coworker to the doctor, but the employer stopped them. Workers at the same factory were also malnourished.[44] Women and men I spoke with throughout the United States talked about being given over-the-counter medication when they asked to see a doctor. Elsa lived with constant headaches: "They got worse and worse. I asked to go to the doctor. But all he [her abuser] did was hand me Advil." Flo suffered through chronic back pain and kept on asking to see a doctor. Her abusers also told her to take over-the-counter medication. Women who lived in their abuser's home as child care providers were often required to sleep in the children's room; on call to tend to the children's needs twenty-four hours a day, they were chronically deprived of sleep. A Thai worker locked in a factory in El Monte, California, had no choice but to extract eight of his own teeth that had "rotted from long neglect."[45] Lack of dental care during their time in forced labor hounds many formerly trafficked persons today.

Nearly all workers, no matter the industry, have been denied food. Maria judges her current employer's generosity with food as a barometer of her treatment. She places a higher value on money left on the kitchen counter for her to order take-out for lunch or dinner, for example, than on the same amount of money she may receive as a bonus for working on the weekend or particularly late. When I first met Maria, not long after she had exited her situation of forced domestic labor, she boasted, as have many other formerly trafficked persons, about how much weight she had put on since her time in forced labor. In a workers' rights meeting in New York City, all those who had been in forced labor—in domestic work and farm work—described being "always hungry."

A constant barrage of verbal assaults is also standard fare in the debasement of workers in forced labor. Every formerly trafficked person with whom I spoke recounts having been insulted. Most often they were told they were "stupid." They still recall the sting of these words. Gladys says of her abuser, "[He] worked on my mind" by repeatedly "tell[ing] me I am nothing." She is particularly proud of her strong English skills since her abuser had taunted her that she would never master the language: "He said that there are people who have been here twenty years and never learn English. But I did it."

Fear of Deportation

The threat of deportation shapes migrants' lives in the United States and keeps them from reporting a wide variety of crimes and abuses. In the well-publicized case of the Kosher meatpacking plant in Postville, Iowa, in 2008, one of the workers, Elmer L., explains why the workers did not report long hours and abusive conditions: "They [the supervisors] told us they were going to call immigration if we complained."[46] Angela, from Brazil, answered an advertisement in a Portuguese-language newspaper in the metro New York area for a live-in child care provider in Texas. She had been living and working in New York and New Jersey for over a decade and had built an impressive résumé and a network of close girlfriends. With the recession, good-paying full-time child care jobs were not as plentiful as they once were, so she decided to take a risk and accept the job in Texas. She regretted her decision immediately. She was not allowed to use the phone or to leave the house. She worked seven days a week and was paid $250 a week, a salary that was significantly lower than what had been agreed upon before she arrived. One day, while out shopping with the family, she surreptitiously managed to buy a phone card and call her friends in New Jersey, a tight-knit group of Brazilian women who also worked in child care. They urged her to leave and pooled their money to buy her an airplane ticket. One of the women, who is bilingual, offered to come down and get her. She left Texas — on her own — and returned to New Jersey and her supportive friends.

What is striking about Angela's experience in Texas is that even with knowledge about the United States, a long work history in the country, a strong network of generous friends, and a community to which to return, she did not immediately leave out of fear that her employers would make good on their threat to contact the authorities and have Angela's green card revoked.

IV. ESCAPE AND LEAVING

Once faced with forced labor, individuals have different choices available to them. Liza, from Indonesia, began to make plans right away: "I had to get out, I did not know how, I had to get out from these people." She surveyed her options from the living-room window in the high-rise apartment in which she had been living and working as a domestic in the suburbs of Washington, D.C: "I was trying to look for somebody to help me — down on the street. I did not know where I would go, but I did not care. I just wanted to get out from them." She waited for an evening when the family was away and snuck out of the apartment. She remained hidden in the building out of fear that the family would see her in the parking lot. "I waited until it got dark to get out from the building. Then I walked to another apartment building that was pretty far away." Along the way she "looked for people who might speak my language." She approached two different sets of people and spoke to them in Arabic. "I said, 'I need help and can work for you.'" One couple told her to go to the police, but Liza was too scared to do so. "Maybe the police would be like the police in my country, because in my country they are bad, and you have to give money to them."

She continued walking until she came to another apartment building. "I was tired, so I slept on the couch by the mailboxes." An elderly Pakistani couple who managed the building found her early the next morning. They brought her up to their apartment, where Liza lived rent-free for a year and a half. She worked in the building cleaning apartments, at $70 an apartment. Because of this couple's generosity, Liza was able to save all her earnings to get a financial footing in the United States before she moved out on her own.

Rights Knowledge and Demanding Rights

Experience making demands, as Elsa had while working in Bahrain and Flo had while working in Africa, does not easily translate into better treatment. Flo came to the United States experienced in identifying and redressing injustice. As a former activist who worked against the corrupt government in her home country, she is a self-confident leader and experienced worker who tried to negotiate with her employer in the United States, but to no avail.

Before coming to the United States, Flo had worked for "rich" families in her home country, where she always had been paid the wages for which she had agreed to work. "I always got paid, and was paid extra if I worked extra hours. At one point, I think I earned more than any housekeeper I knew." Despite her history of securing good wages, she is "astounded" by how poorly she understood the work environment in the United States. "I can't believe I did not have a bank account." She was receiving only $250 a month. "They came up with the $250 as my salary in the United States by converting it from money at home. By those standards, it was a good salary. I was earning the same that teachers do at home." But once Flo saw how much everything cost in the United States, she realized that she was being cheated. "They told me it was so much money! But I knew better. I could see the prices in the stores." She also befriended her neighbor and a family she met at her church, who informed her that she was abysmally underpaid.

Flo tried regularly to set limits on her employers' endless list of tasks for her. She pointed out inequities and refused particular demands. She protested, for example, about the wife's demand that Flo wash the wife's underwear by hand. "The first time I kept quiet and I didn't say anything. But then I said, 'No, it's too much. I can't wash anybody's underwear.' And then she [the wife] became quiet." On another occasion she suggested a less messy and labor-saving approach to cooking oatmeal for breakfast: "I had to make everyone oatmeal in the morning, but all at different times when they woke up. So instead of having four pots on the stove, I said, 'Let me cook just one pot so that when everyone wakes up I can put oatmeal in the microwave to heat it up.'" The wife insisted that Flo make everyone fresh oatmeal. Flo saw this as unreasonable, particularly since she was busy doing "everything" for the morning routine: "I got the kids dressed for school, made their lunches, and walked the youngest to school. After the kids were at school, I would clean the house top to bottom. I did all the wash, ironed, cleaned the carpets, and even wiped down the walls."

After Flo's refusal to wash the wife's underwear by hand, the wife stopped speaking with her. During this time the husband had been visiting (he lived in Africa), and Flo knew he would be returning to Africa in a couple of days. She made sure to speak with him before he left. "I wanted to understand what these people were thinking and why they were treating me this way. I knew the way that they treated me was not right. They had to know what they were doing was not good. I said to him, 'I am not satisfied with the way I am staying here. Your wife and I are not getting along in this house.'" During his periodic visits, Flo always called attention to his wife's treatment of her and also strategically revealed that the wife sometimes disappeared while the husband was out of the country. "I asked her in front of the husband, 'You always leave the house. Why is it you always go and come back later?'" Sometimes the wife would take the kids with her and come back home around midnight and wake Flo up "to bathe the children, feed them, and put them to bed." "This was too much. So I asked her in front of the husband. I said, 'You don't need to take the children. I can bathe them and put them to sleep after I feed them. If you want to go, you can go on your own and leave the children with me.' I wanted to be able to rest. There was no time. Even if they were out, I knew that she would call. If I didn't pick up the phone, she would keep calling. She would call to tell me, 'We are on our way home and then you will have to bathe the babies.'"

Flo's meager wages for on-call work twenty-four hours a day, seven days a week, put her in a situation of severe exploitation. "From the time I came here everything was upside down. I wanted to work in a fair way. Not for only $250, when I have to do everything in the house, sometimes working sixteen hours a day, and sleeping with the baby." The wife tried to justify her chronic exploitation of Flo by emphasizing that "everything here is cheap and that you can find things for a dollar." Flo believes that the wife kept her from doing the food shopping because it would give her too much freedom. "I really was not free. She would not let me do the shopping because then I would meet people and then they would tell me that I was not being paid well." The wife continued to justify the wages by valuing them according to their home country's currency.

Flo lost count of the many occasions when she spoke out about her treatment. She tried to pin down her abuser to clearly define her hours. She raised the issue regularly with both the husband and the wife: "I asked them, 'I want to know the way I am working here. I want to know my working hours, because my working conditions are not good.' They said, 'What do you know? You don't know anything about working. You don't know anything about hours.' And then I said, 'Am I a slave?' And the wife said, 'Yes, you are a slave. I am paying you $250. If I tell you to work twenty-four hours, you have to work twenty-four hours because of that money.' I said, 'No. Do you know that I also have rights?' She responded, 'What kind of rights do you know? You don't even know any rights.' I said, 'I know my rights and I know your rights. I have to work for you, but I am not supposed to be like a slave.'"

Flo began to build a case against her abuser. She learned about the U.S. justice system from TV shows, particularly the role of evidence. "I watched *People's Court*. I learned that in America you need proof when you make claims. I knew I needed to have proof of how this lady was treating me if I was going to report it." She wanted to show that the work she was being asked to do was unreasonable, so she asked her abuser's daughter to take a picture of her scrubbing the carpet on her knees with the baby on her back. After showing me the photos, Flo explained that her abuser does not know to this day that Flo had these photos. "She didn't know that I was so smart."

Flo asked for her passport, which so angered her abuser that she ordered Flo out of the house, screaming, "I brought you here, now get out of my house! Get out of my house!" Flo stood her ground and told her, "I am not getting out of your house right now. I want my money first because you have been underpaying me." Flo decided she was not leaving without her passport, back wages, and an airplane ticket home. "I told her that she can't kick me out of the house without buying me a ticket home. And when I demanded my passport, she said it was at the State Department." After Flo repeatedly demanded her passport, her abuser told her, "I am not going to give you your passport. Flo, your pride is not going to help you with these things." At an impasse, Flo was distraught: "At this point I thought that if she wasn't going to give me my passport I might try to commit suicide. I thought if I could get some tablets, then I could go to the hospital, and once there they would ask me why I did this and I could try to explain to them what was going on." Flo did not know where to turn. Her neighbor told her to call her embassy. "But I explained that I couldn't. These people are the same people, they were not going to help me!" Flo also was in contact with her best friend's sister who lived in Maryland. Flo reached out to anyone with whom she had some connection, no matter how marginal. Because of her chronic back pain, she took note of television commercials for a mattress company and even contacted them. A sales representative came to the house. When he wanted to show her a video of their product, she would not let him inside the house, explaining: "If my employer finds out you were in the house, she will kill me." Perplexed, he asked her questions about the terms of her employment. He gave her the name of a social service organization in the area, telling her that there were "other people who are just like you." This organization eventually assisted Flo with her resettlement. At the time, she told herself, "God is sending me people now."

During a fight Flo had with her abuser over leaving the country, Flo called the police, who dismissed the call as a run-of-the-mill wage dispute. Flo recounts the call: "They said, 'You believe this woman owes you some money? She doesn't owe you anything because you agreed to work for that $250.'" While Flo was speaking with the police, the abuser picked up the phone. Flo countered her abuser's lies to the police: "I continued telling them that this woman owes me loads and loads of money and that she needs to pay me back that money. She [the wife] started crying and saying, 'I don't owe her anything. I don't have anything.' Finally, the police asked me, 'Ma'am, do you want to go to jail or do you want to go to your own country?' I told them I wanted to go to jail. I thought I would get my money if I am in jail here. When I explained that I could not leave anyway since my employer had my passport, the policewoman asked to speak to her. She told the police officer, 'No, I'm not refusing her the passport. It's in my office. I bought her a ticket and she is leaving today at five o'clock exactly.' Then I spoke with the police officer again. She told me that if I wanted to report this lady that I should go to the DA in my country. I said that I would be leaving today at five."[47]

The employer bought Flo a plane ticket, but Flo had no intention of leaving the country. She describes conversations with her neighbor: "I learned that no one can force anyone to get on a plane. Only Immigration can. This was a relief when I learned that no one could force me to leave." Armed with this knowledge, Flo had been putting a plan in place with the help of her neighbor, the family whom she had met at church, and her sister's friend in Maryland. She phoned them and told them today was the day she would be leaving. The friend had told Flo, "'Once you get to the airport, leave the area where you get on the plane. Leave your bags if you have to. Sleep in the airport. Then come out, get the shuttle to the bus station, and come to my address.' I did not even know what a shuttle was. But she told me to bring $100. So I had been saving the money little by little, sending some home and putting some away." Flo went to the mall that afternoon with her friend from church to buy a big suitcase. "I packed my real bags and moved all my things to my neighbor's house. My employer did not even stop to think why I didn't have a lot of bags. She didn't even ask. She just was trying to get rid of me."

During this time of planning, deception, and waiting, the uncertainty made Flo sick. "I could not eat, and my stomach hurt because I was so weak. I was crying all the time. I think I looked very sick the day I left. It's hard to explain. I had on this little sundress, but I forgot to put on a bra." It is little wonder that Flo was not herself that day; four couples arrived at the house to help her abuser take Flo to the airport. Their intent to intimidate Flo was clear. She describes the caravan: "When she took me in her car to the airport, there were four cars following us. All to take me to the airport!" And the abuser had not paid Flo for the previous month, "not a cent." Once in the airport, the abuser "cried and cried," but Flo had the last word. "I said to her in front of her friends, 'You don't have to cry, because this is what you wanted. You told me to get out of the house.' I told all the ladies and men who were there that this lady had treated me badly. She had me working seven days a week, twenty-four hours a day." In this final moment with her abuser Flo did not hold anything back. "They told me, 'Well, she told us something different. People don't say the truth.' Then I said, 'This is the truth! That is why she wouldn't let you all talk to me before.'" She left them, pretending to head to her flight. Her suitcase was empty, except for a teddy bear. She was afraid that she would not be able to get out of the airport. "I saw a worker, a man from Africa, and asked him if I would be able to walk back through the airport. He said, 'Sister, I will take you,' and he walked with me and helped me leave the airport. I then talked to the driver of the shuttle and told him my story. There was no point in keeping my story a secret."

Once she was on the shuttle, with her abuser nowhere in sight, Flo was still scared. "I was scared that maybe my employer was looking for me. It wasn't until I woke up the next morning at my friend's house that I realized I was free." She thought about what the pastor of her church had told her: "'Flo, everything is going to be all right. You need to move by faith, not by sight.' He was right. God was with me that day." The teddy bear still sits on her bed, a reminder, she explains, of her strength.

The Confusion of Leaving

Exiting forced labor is often a time of confusion and fog. Flo had made use of all the contacts she had in the United States: she had called the police, a friend of her sister in another city, a neighbor, a family from church, and even a mattress company. Learning about the U.S. justice system from *People's Court*, she took photographs to gather evidence of her abuse, and she asked her neighbor questions about workers' and migrants' rights. Yet despite Flo's multiple attempts to generate assistance, they did not yield a clear path ahead. Her story of feeling sick before taking a leap into uncertainty brings into focus why individuals put off leaving.

As in other cases, the generosity of acquaintances and strangers played a crucial role in Flo's ability to learn her rights and make a plan to leave. Her neighbor had pieced together that something was amiss since she often heard Flo's abuser yelling. She reached out to Flo and asked her what was going on in the house. They arranged a weekend outing, with the abuser's consent. They spent a day going to museums and walking past the White House. Up to that point, Flo had not yet seen much of Washington. During their time out, the neighbor and Flo talked about Flo's wages. Flo explained that she was responsible for the children day and night. "She told me how much people get paid for child care here in the United States. She told me to get out of the house—that no one works seven days a week, twenty-four hours a day."

While Flo knew her abuser's treatment of her was wrong, she did not know about the new trafficking law and its specific legal remedies and forms of social assistance. Like most formerly trafficked persons, Flo was not aware that there was a trafficking law or social organizations to assist her. Rather they cast their experiences in forced labor under a net of domestic abuse or employer abuse. Social workers and attorneys around the country tell of trafficking clients who first came to their offices for assistance with abusive partners or for help with their immigration status. A social worker in New York explains, "Many of our trafficking clients first come to us to get help with domestic violence or with legal issues. They often lack knowledge of basic human rights. It is only after we hear their stories that we point out to them that they may qualify as 'trafficked.' They do not come to us talking about trafficking. We have a client, for example, a woman from West Africa, who, when asked why she stayed with an employer who did not pay her, said, 'But he brought me to this country.'"

Another client, a woman from Mexico, endured years of forced sexual labor under the control of her boyfriend (and father of her child), who regularly beat her. She was desperate to leave but feared the police and did not know how to leave without assistance. It was not until she saw a Spanish-language news broadcast about the arrest of a trafficker in a case similar to hers that she realized there was a system set up to punish abusers like her boyfriend and assist women like her. She worked up the courage to leave with her child. She went to a shelter, but had no idea what was ahead of her: "I was young and did not know that there were organizations that could help me."

Conclusion

Abusers may seem unassailable, especially to those unfamiliar with the United States and its justice system. Targets of their abuse may continue to fear them even after these abusers are in jail or living outside of the United States. This fear reflects the image these abusers work hard to project, of having endless power and reach.[48] Formerly trafficked persons have good reason to continue to fear their traffickers since some of these criminals have friends who will inflict violence at their request. Eva from Mexico, for example, reluctantly testified against her trafficker in court. "I did not want to speak. I had to cooperate with the lawyers and so I did. But they [the lawyers] do not understand that they [the traffickers] have people on the outside." Her trafficker attempted to intimidate her in court: "He kept on turning around and staring at me." Even though her trafficker was sentenced to many years in prison, Eva still felt unsafe. "I worried about parole and that the sentence would be cut in half because in Mexico they count days and nights."[49]

Abusers' control of all aspects of trafficked persons' lives can induce paranoia, distrust, and chronic anxiety. Many tell of thinking that they see their trafficker when they are out in crowds. They also spin revenge fantasies in which they imagine showing their traffickers how well they are doing. Gladys's version is typical: "I imagine running into him in the street and showing him how great I am doing—telling him about my job and having him hear how good my English is now." While some avoid going out until they get their bearings, those who venture out often describe feeling watched. Flo, for example, could not shake the feeling that she was being watched when she was shopping. Carmen too tells of freezing with fear when she thought she saw her abuser on the street. The fear their abusers instilled in them—along with the sense of loss of control—is not easily overcome. The effects linger long after formerly trafficked persons exit their situation of forced labor.

Part II. *Life after Forced Labor*

Chapter Three

Imagining the Possible

CREATING HOME

I want to eat New York!—GLADYS, a twenty-one-year-old woman
from Mexico who had been trafficked into domestic work

I was done thinking about this and was healing. But it's like you have a kind of
tape in your head, like you are making a movie. It's like you are running back and
forth. And you are still lost because you are in a kind of veil. You have a veil over
your face and you are seeing through this veil. You see only through this veil. You
don't really see things. You think that you see everything, but no.—TATIANA,
a Russian woman in her mid-twenties who had been trafficked into dance clubs

Moving into the Possible

As they look forward, formerly trafficked persons are enmeshed in and at
times overwhelmed by setting up a new life in a new country. Tatiana's and
Gladys's expressions of what lies ahead capture both the excitement of moving forward after forced labor and the challenges of putting the past en-
tirely behind. Most days are unremarkable, filled with mundane tasks. With
enduring effects of emotional abuse and physical injuries as well as travel
debts, life after trafficking in the United States is not necessarily the fresh
start that Carmen wants (see introduction). With no clear path ahead and
no family or friends in the United States, formerly trafficked persons begin
building a sense of place and home on their own. Those who had migrated to

the United States intending to work only for a short while must now assess what life would look like if they stayed. Staying involves seeing whether there are new and better possibilities than those available in their home country. As they set about "the delicate work of self-creation," what I call lifework, they must believe that these possibilities are worth resettling on their own, with no money, and far from family.[1]

After spending years of living under the control of her abuser, Gladys is now living on her terms. Particularly outgoing, she actively puts herself in unfamiliar social spaces, and seeks out new experiences. Enrolling in English classes and then courses to prepare for a GED, Gladys works to create opportunities for herself. She eventually wants to open her own store and has been fortunate to have found a mentor in her boss, the owner of a small retail store that sells perfume and other cosmetics. This mentor has been teaching Gladys how to run her own business and is willing to share her wholesale contacts. She also enables Gladys to schedule her work hours around her school schedule.

Gladys exudes confidence—in herself and in the possibilities ahead of her. Not everyone moves forward with as much enthusiasm and forethought, but social workers emphasize that their trafficking clients move forward nonetheless. These clients have little time to waste since U.S. government assistance that accompanies their status as "trafficked persons" runs out quickly—in about a year.[2] They begin with their resettlement checklist—housing, job, English-language classes—right away. While a variety of programs around the world that assist trafficked individuals use the language of recovery, not everyone feels the need to "recover" or to "heal." This language of recovery and healing pathologizes individuals at a time of acute economic uncertainty and legal limbo.[3] There is extreme dissonance between what formerly trafficked persons say they want and need and what some antitrafficking organizations claim they need.[4] Social workers and case managers at direct-service providers, however, take cues from their clients who often defer mental health counseling until their material needs are settled. "Clients say to me," explains a social worker in New York, "'I'm not crazy! I'm in touch with you and talking with you all the time. I don't need therapy.'" Formerly trafficked persons are clear about what they want: steady jobs that pay well, legal assistance, and their abusers put in jail. They want to regain control over all aspects of their lives and to resolve their legal status. Like Gladys, they want to make up for lost time.

A problem arises when clients decide to seek counseling at a later date but they have already timed out of their eligibility for benefits.[5] In such cases the trafficking care regime falls short of what clients need, particularly in the long term. There is constant tension between social workers trying to create an environment in which clients make decisions on their own and the reality of the benefits clock pushing both assistance-givers and clients to get the clients settled quickly. Even the best-trained and most seasoned social workers regularly encounter new issues and needs. They are kept on their toes by the diversity of this client base and restricted, time-sensitive funds. Thus both trafficking clients and those committed to assisting them have to improvise as they navigate bureaucratic agencies that are often unfamiliar with these clients' legal rights and ill-equipped to serve their needs.

After Violence: Living with Loss and Suffering

The formerly trafficked persons I have met, like Gladys, emphasize that they look forward and try not to dwell on past abuses. As a consequence, the remaining chapters of this book address how individuals who suffered through abuse and possibly violence begin to move through the world again. I take as a starting point that formerly trafficked persons have had widely divergent experiences in forced labor and thus face different challenges settling in the United States.[6] Since each trafficking case has its own characteristics, it is not possible to assert that forced labor presents a particular or fixed set of traumas.[7] The analytical limitations of the "trauma concept" remind us that suffering through abuse does not necessarily render individuals "traumatized." Rather some people end up profoundly sad, scared, or lonely. I heed Derek Summerfield and other mental health professionals' warnings about the overapplication of a PTSD diagnosis to all who have experienced traumatic events.[8] For many, it is possible that what medical doctors refer to as somatic signs of stress and anxiety—such as stomach, head, or back aches—would dissipate with greater economic and legal security.[9]

Tatiana's struggles, however, are evidence that moving beyond traumatic events is not something one simply wills. Immediately after exiting her situation of forced labor, she found herself drinking before going to sleep to help her "forget about things." She describes having nightmares that transported her back to her time in forced labor: "I was depressed. I had certain things in my dreams. People telling me scary stuff. One time I saw my trafficker and he was talking to me as a friend and was saying 'I need your help.' It was kind of weird because it was in the dark and the police came and I disappeared from the scene." She wanted to rid her life of these nightmares.[10] "I'm trying to put an end to them. Like any stage in your life, you have to fight with the monsters. When you fight them, you go to another level, like in a game; then I start to be stronger." Tatiana's difficulty moving forward illustrates Das's critique of "sanitized" terms like *posttraumatic stress disorder* and her embrace instead of Langer's description of pain and loss after the Holocaust as "the ruins of memory."[11] Writing is one way to relax. "Sometimes when I feel bad I write poetry or I write something," explains Tatiana. "When something hits me like a flash, I write it down."[12]

Esperanza sees a therapist. She thinks that she would put her experiences in forced labor behind her, however, if she were reunited with her children. I am not suggesting that individuals like Esperanza would not benefit from seeing a therapist even after they are reunited with their families or have secured well-paying jobs. Indeed Tatiana's description of seeing through a "veil" is troubling.[13] But formerly trafficked persons — and their social workers — often reject the mantle of "traumatized victim" and bracket their time in forced labor as a break from their past that does not irrevocably determine their future. For them, this time of "emergency" was not "the rule" but "the exception."[14] As formerly trafficked persons express their feelings of extreme loneliness, concerns about their future, and sadness and anger over the time their abusers stole from them, they do not put their suffering at the center of their lives. They describe hesitancies, anxieties, and fears about their future — as do many new migrants finding their way in a new country — but are not necessarily chased by their past. Rather they throw themselves into anchoring their future in the United States.

Others' Suffering

Some formerly trafficked persons do not dwell on their suffering because they see other migrants in their communities with the same struggles, scratching out a living in low-wage work while separated from their family. There is a common longing for good jobs, decent pay, citizenship, and family reunification. At an event hosted by a Filipina domestic workers' rights organization, the key topic of discussion was the fate of family reunification policies under different immigration reforms proposals bandied about in

Washington, D.C. Living without family members or chronically worrying about possible separation by arrest and deportation permeates everyday life in migrant communities. In light of these common worries, trafficked persons' particular forms of grief and loss may not stand out. Thus we cannot compare formerly trafficked persons' past abusive experiences with one another nor with the experiences of their migrant roommates, coworkers, and friends. They are not the only group of migrants to wrestle with past experiences of suffering; many others have experienced civil war, other violent conflicts, or state-sponsored persecution.

The consequences of experiencing or witnessing violence are multiple, not just for individuals but also for communities. Linda Green's ethnography with widows in post–civil war Guatemala, for example, shows that violence was not "simply the historical background" but that "violence and fear suffused people's everyday lives."[15] The violence during the civil war in Peru was so inconceivable that one woman told Kimberly Theidon that it "was another life."[16] Traumatic events and chronic emotional and physical abuse can have both short-term and long-term effects. Individuals may not be stopped by abuse, but they are changed; violence can be "formative" such that it "shapes people's perceptions of who they are."[17] Yet, although individuals and communities must cope with the violence that they endured, there is no monolithic response to violence.[18]

Challenges Particular to Formerly Trafficked Persons' Resettlement

Up to this point I have argued that it is not possible to assert that trafficking into forced labor causes a particular set of traumas. But there are characteristics of formerly trafficked persons' resettlement that diverge from other populations that have experienced violence, such as refugees displaced after war or genocide. Unless they were prisoners of war or pressed into fighting, other migrants' experience with violence may not have included the experience of being held against their will.[19] And while violence that splits apart communities usually involves multiple members of a community who may be targeted because of their alleged political affiliations, ethnicity, or religion, trafficked persons are not singled out for abuse because of their group identity.[20] Nor do they undergo resettlement collectively, as members of a group that experienced violence in a particular locale.[21] As a result, their experiences are individuated and typically are not understood as part of a common and known experience among a group of migrants. In contrast, migrants and refugees may discover that their new neighbors and coworkers are familiar with their home country's struggles, for example, with war or natural disaster.

To add to their isolation, formerly trafficked persons describe not telling their new friends in the United States about their experience in forced labor. Most do not tell their families back home either. Their legal designation of "trafficked" largely remains on paper; they do not reference it in their daily social interactions but usually only in private bureaucratic encounters. With fewer than four thousand individuals in the United States with this legal status, it is likely that no one in their social circle has the same legal designation. They remain silent about their past abusive experiences and present immigration status in part because, under current immigration laws, their new friends and coworkers may have little chance of obtaining documentation to live and work legally in the United States. T visa holders report that their exceptional legal status has sparked gossip and jealousy among coethnics. They also may conceal their status for fear that it may signal some kind of weakness or foolishness on their part that they were not able to outwit their abusers. And of course, confiding in others requires trusting them, which can be a fraught proposition for those whose trust has been so profoundly broken.

Step by Step: Building a Sense of Home and Belonging

A group of best friends living in Los Angeles who met at the only shelter in the United States dedicated to trafficking clients explain how they approached piecing together their lives after forced labor: "You take it step by step. You need to survive first. And send money to family back home. And learn English." The making of home—and feeling at home, what I refer to as "home-sense"—involves concerns related to housing, work, legal documentation, and health care as well as trusting others and making new friends. All these issues affect formerly trafficked persons' safety, peace of mind, and well-being.[22] Although the trafficking legal regime opens a legal place in the United States for these exceptions to the immigration regime, legal residence does not necessarily convey a sense of belonging, or what anthropologist Renato Rosaldo refers to as "cultural citizenship."[23] Alone in the United States, formerly trafficked persons become immersed in legal issues as an individualized pursuit, not a shared project with family or larger community. Rather the pursuit of the legal right to stay in the United States evolves among them, their lawyer, and possibly a social worker. Building a sense of home and belonging is intimately tied to resolving their legal status. While they wait for word on their legal fate, the uncertainty can intensify what already is a disorienting time.

Research on refugee resettlement provides some insights into understanding formerly trafficked persons' resettlement into new communities or into the same communities where they had been living while they were in forced labor.[24] Writing about Ethiopian refugees returning to their old communities, Laura Hammond found that a degree of uncertainty creates "confusion" that can be "uncomfortable, dangerous, and at times even life threatening."[25] In an "unstructured transitional state," these Ethiopian refugees were "like actors rehearsing a play, holding a script in their hands, but not sure whether they would be required to read from the script in its entirety or would be compelled to improvise here and there in order to enact a new story."[26] Unlike refugees, however, formerly trafficked persons have no such script. Where their resettlement significantly diverges from refugees' and other migrants' home-making is the extent and form of ties to a larger community.

Home, by definition, implies a shared life with others.[27] The "refrain of home" that Ilana Feldman heard among Palestinian refugees was not singularly expressed but was constructed and reproduced by many members of this displaced community. Engaging together in the "repetitive details of daily interaction" was essential not only to reconstitute a sense of home for Palestinian refugees but also to "hold chaos at bay."[28] Many of the women and men I have met do not have a ready-made community with whom to share, inherit, reconstitute, or invent the practices of home-making. As the first in their immediate family and kin networks to migrate to the United States, they navigate the United States on their own as "pioneers."[29] Those who are fearful to tap into coethnic social networks in their new community relinquish ties to assistance, knowledge, or friendship that well-established migrant networks potentially could provide. And since most do not know a single other formerly trafficked person, they cannot look around at members of a community of formerly trafficked persons and see how they are doing after years of living in the United States. Instead they have to build new networks by opening themselves up again—a trying process for individuals who have been lied to, taken advantage of, and cheated.

Trust in a Time of Confusion

Every formerly trafficked person I met talks about how difficult it is to trust again. I use the term *trust* in ways similar to the anthropologists Valentine Daniel and John Knudsen, who write about how refugees "mistrust" and are "mistrusted," to capture both how difficult it is for someone who was duped and abused to trust others as well as the role that community support can play.[30] Almost immediately after they exit their situation of forced labor, formerly trafficked persons are asked to put their trust in a cast of strangers: local police, immigration officials, state and federal prosecutors, their own attorneys, and social workers. Many talk about how hard it was to trust others — anyone — again. When speaking with FBI agents, one woman from the Philippines, Eliza, feigned not being able to speak English, explaining, "I could not trust anyone!" She describes being alone and "scared and nervous" and also not having any of her possessions with her: "I had nothing. Not even a change of underwear." Nor did Suzanne, from Indonesia, know whom to trust: "Especially after I got out of that place and there were all these people asking me questions. I was not sure if I had to talk to them and tell them what happened or not." Julie, also from Indonesia, echoes this confusion: "You do not know anyone. It's hard to trust other people. After I got out, everyone was asking me questions. I thought what if *they* do the same thing to me again?" Formerly trafficked persons who today self-identify as antitrafficking activists and speak at law enforcement trainings about how to identify trafficking into forced labor have urged police officers to call them when they encounter formerly trafficked persons who are scared. Kathy, from the Philippines, explains, "I told the police and FBI how scary it feels. It is a really scary time. I told them to give women my telephone number if they ever want to talk. Especially women from the Philippines who may not speak English."

Tatiana was overwhelmed by the many questions posed by lawyers and law enforcement officers soon after she left the dance club. "I had to start to trust people, the people trying to help me out. They were asking me questions. They needed information to help me." Adept at lying to her abusers to protect herself, she described feeling "lost" during this time that she was expected to trust those helping her. "It's hard when everybody is asking questions and trying to get to know you. They ask about things you cannot really answer." After lying to her captors for so long, she continued "to make up stories" and say that everything was all right. "It was hard to trust anyone at first because I was thinking maybe I said too much because I am a very talkative person. I thought, you have to keep information a secret because you never know where it goes. You can't control it!"

Just how much information individuals should reveal in order to make a legal case can be particularly difficult to gauge since doing so challenges their instincts for self-preservation. Trusting others—whether a police officer, social worker, bunkmate in a temporary shelter, or coworker—runs contrary to the techniques of concealment that may have helped them endure abusive conditions. In Tatiana's case, her abusers had deepened her anxieties by lying to her about the police: "They told us not to trust the police—that they [the police] would take us to jail and then send us home with stamps in our passports that would make it impossible to come back here again. And they told us we would be sent home as prostitutes—that the stamp would say this!" The notion of building a legal case with law enforcement's cooperation also can be perplexing for individuals from countries where law enforcement officers do not actually conduct the investigations that they claim to be pursuing—and may in fact be working alongside traffickers.[31] Tatiana explains, "In my country you cannot trust anybody. So you think, 'Oh my god, maybe these government people don't want to do anything for me.'"[32]

Tatiana ultimately decided to talk with law enforcement: "I made the decision to go and talk about this, and to be protected. It was the right decision, but it was hard for me to realize it. If your life is controlled by other people, you can't do anything. You know people are using you, and you never know when it is going to stop. But you have to realize that it won't change." When prosecutions are possible, T visas can be quite hard-won, entailing a demanding and frightening process of interviews with investigators and lawyers, and testifying against one's abuser.[33] Tatiana took many risks by providing evidence. She also put her faith in law enforcement's relocation plans for her. "They told me if I was not comfortable here I could move somewhere else. They were really nice." She began to cry, recalling that she would not leave without her cat: "They even helped me to live with my cat. I said I will not move without my cat. They had to run around and catch him. He was scared and running, but we caught him." She brightened when recalling the comical scene: "They told me it was the first time they had to run after a cat. It was like a movie, watching them run all over. Like *Kindergarten Cop*!"

Much like refugees and migrants after forced displacement, formerly trafficked persons face a "remaking of self" while enduring multiple losses.[34] First leaving Russia after losing both her parents, and then the midwestern city where she had been in forced labor, Tatiana has been through several rounds of losses. She took a huge leap of faith by trusting her assistance-givers' relocation plans for her. Skilled assistance-givers recognize that their role may not be apparent to trafficking clients nor their trustworthiness evident. A staff member of a domestic violence shelter in Los Angeles describes how a trafficking client became agitated when someone on the staff asked her for a receipt for reimbursement. The client believed that the staff member had doubted her. The staff member explains, "These clients have been emotionally battered. Some, like one of our clients who had to sleep on the floor, were treated like dogs." It takes time for formerly trafficked persons, she emphasizes, to "breathe" and to trust again. "It doesn't matter if people tell them they can be trusted. It only happens over time."

Trust: Over Time

Although social workers, attorneys, and other frontline assistance-givers may see themselves as trustworthy, new trafficking clients may not see them as such.[35] While some, like Maria, talk of their social worker or case manager as a valued friend, others keep their private lives private. Peers—coethnics or fellow workers in the same labor sector—can also represent support. Of particular relief for Flo, for example, was the opportunity to meet other domestic workers who also had been exploited by their employers. She began attending Sunday potlucks at a domestic workers' rights organization in Washington, D.C.: "I realized that I am not the only one, that there were many others who have gone through the same thing." Those who experienced abuse may find calm and connection with those who have had similar experiences, while they also may feel "different and misunderstood by others who had not shared their experiences," including "friends, doctors, or lawyers who were trying to help."[36]

But communities of coethnics are not unproblematic and all-embracing; they can be sources of judgment, stigma, and gossip. Migration scholars long have heralded social networks within coethnic communities as a way to facilitate finding jobs and housing.[37] When formerly trafficked persons turn their backs on these communities, they have to start making new friendships from scratch. Running from gossip in their own coethnic communities, the group of friends who met at the shelter for trafficking clients in Los Angeles found that they could trust one another with anything. Although they are from different backgrounds in Latin America, Indonesia, and the Philippines, they describe having more in common than they do with their compatriots who had not been in forced labor: "Your own community can judge you. They blame you." "They say you knew you were here illegally, and look what happened! They make it your fault." These friends explain how their coethnics harshly criticized them for receiving benefits that eluded others in their communities. "With one another and other survivors, we feel free. We can laugh. We can cry. We can help one another. We understand. We can share with one another like a family." One woman, who had experienced particularly vicious scorn from her community of coethnics, explains, "With [formerly trafficked persons] I am not ashamed. I never feel judged. But I do with others in my community." As if on cue, her friends jumped in: "There is nothing to feel ashamed about. We have nothing to be ashamed about." They emphasized that they were there for her, reminding her, "We are a sisterhood."

With intense distrust of coethnics comes increased isolation. Knudsen found that when Vietnamese refugees mistrusted their communities of coethnics, they saw their problems shift from being "shared ones" to private ones, and they became "alone in a new and heightened sense."[38] Those betrayed by close friends or relatives in particular "may never again have quite the same confidence in anyone" and "may also find [their] personal world philosophy is irreparably dented by the experience."[39] When coethnics have perpetrated violence and killings, it becomes even more difficult to trust compatriots.[40] In such cases of pervasive and profound distrust and disconnection, meeting others with similar experiences can provide a lifeline.

Opening up about one's past may be off-limits. Suzanne explains, "It takes longer to trust others than before. You just don't tell people about your life." Nor did she share details with her new friends about the benefits her legal status carries: "I don't talk to them about how the [social service] agency has helped me." Guarded, Suzanne has decided with whom and in what settings she will open up. Moving in and out of multiple social spaces, she meets many people through her job, her children's schools, and her advocacy work in the trafficking community. She is outgoing and charismatic, and people gravitate to her. While Suzanne can choose whom to let in to her life, most formerly trafficked individuals meet fewer people. One trafficking client takes risks and opens herself to new relationships, but with extreme caution. She is dating a man but will not let him know where she lives. On their first date, she had a friend with her to greet him and to write down his car's license plate. After months of dating, they still meet in locations where there are security cameras and a lot of other people. This relationship unfolds on her terms. "Who else is going to take care of me?" she asks. "No one—just me."

Nuts and Bolts Resettlement Issues

A social worker in New York expressed discomfort with the advocacy necessary to get more resources for her trafficking clients: "Do my trafficking clients need more assistance so that they can stabilize? Yes. Should we ask for more for these clients? Yes. But all my clients need more resources. This is the idea behind the social safety net." An attorney in Washington, D.C., who has been on the front lines of advocacy for greater social and legal benefits for individuals trafficked into forced labor acknowledges that many U.S. residents are struggling in poverty. As a result, the social service community needs "to spell out why trafficked persons are a population that needs substantial assistance for a long period of time." She, like every other attorney and social worker working with trafficked persons, emphasized that these clients have few or no social ties in the United States, no place to go, and often do not have a single possession with them other than the clothes they are wearing. "Trafficked persons are victims of crime who have nothing. They are a fragile population who, since they are not U.S. citizens, would not qualify for social assistance without a trafficking designation." While U.S. citizens living in the same shelters as trafficked persons are in a desperate situation, "they may have some family somewhere." "They can apply for food assistance. They may speak English. But trafficked persons have no one to turn to. They do not trust a soul. Some are highly traumatized. At the same time they have no resources to take care of themselves." Distinguishing trafficked persons from other migrants, she points out: "Trafficked persons are not going to the church, market, or community center so they don't run into anyone associated with their abuser. Think about it, they may not even be able to eat their own food if they feel they can't go to the markets. And, on top of facing poverty, trafficked persons also may be waking up with nightmares every night."

The First Night

Immediately following their exit from their abusive situation, trafficked individuals have no place to stay for the night. They have little choice but to follow the advice and arrangements of law enforcement agents and the attorneys and social service providers whom law enforcement officers contact.[41] At this point they may not know what trafficking is, that their abusers have committed a crime, or that they may qualify for social services as well as for immigration relief. Even if a plan had been in place ahead of time, decisions happen quickly. When law enforcement or a social service organization is not involved, and individuals leave on their own, they have to figure out where they are going to stay and how they are going to get there. In the previous chapter, I recounted how Flo had duped her abuser at the airport and took an airport shuttle to her sister's friend's house, as well as how Liza had spent the night on the couch in the lobby of an apartment building within walking distance of the apartment in which she had been abused. These on-the-fly plans can intensify an already frightening and profoundly uncertain moment. If a social service organization is involved, its staff may make housing arrangements, but their choices are often few and ill-fitting for this particular population with its particular needs. With only one shelter in the United States, in California, that provides housing exclusively for trafficked persons (women only), there is a chronic shortage of housing for individuals exiting forced labor.[42] This housing shortage for this population unfolds within a larger landscape of poverty, deprivation, and struggle that the New York–based social worker points to: "It's not just about trafficked persons and housing. This is about a housing crisis and shelter crisis for many!"

Since trafficked individuals leave forced labor in large cities and small towns all over the United States, the local organization assisting them may not have emergency housing plans in place, let alone plans for clients who may need housing assistance for months or longer. With waiting lists throughout the country for a handful of temporary apartments owned or rented by social service organizations, assistance-givers often have to improvise and collaborate with other organizations. Social workers' and other first responders' breadth of experience, contacts, and goodwill all come into play as they try to locate housing.

In some instances, social service organizations use hotels, but for the most part they turn to shelters, both domestic violence and homeless shelters. A case manager in New York also reports that there have been instances when convents, seminaries, and private housing have been available for short-term stays. With no other housing options, shelters have become more than a stopgap in emergency situations; rather trafficking clients end up staying in shelters much longer than they or their assistance-givers had intended. Suzanne, from Indonesia, lived in a domestic violence shelter for about fourteen months. Trafficking clients like her stay in shelters longer than expected in part because they have no family or close ties to anyone or any place in the United States. Yet, staying on the couch or floor of relatives or friends from one's hometown is a common housing solution for new migrants. Refugees too benefit from previously established social networks. The logistics of their resettlement usually are worked out through voluntary agencies long before they even travel to the United States.[43] Once in the United States, refugees can tap into a network of coethnics where they are settling, or if they are among the first from their country to move to a particular town or city, their resettlement agencies can put them in contact with compatriots in other locales. These are highly bureaucratized processes that have been hammered out over time, not pieced together with little time to prepare, as they often are with trafficking clients.

Housing: Homeless Shelters and Domestic Violence Shelters

Social workers around the country insist that homeless shelters can be a particularly bad fit for trafficking clients. Staff at a domestic violence shelter in Orange County, California, who have assisted trafficking clients (both men and women) expressed concerned about the safety of trafficking clients in homeless shelters: "We knew one woman who had to be at the Salvation Army shelter by seven every night, and out by eight. How can this be a safe and secure arrangement? She had no place to go during the day."[44] Their residents also have complained about the lack of privacy in homeless shelters: "Homeless shelters generally do not have private rooms, so clients say, 'I didn't feel safe that everyone was always looking at me.'" "If they don't feel safe," the staff worried, "how are they going to work with you to move forward?"

Nor can homeless shelters provide the one-on-one case management that trafficking clients often need. "Our trafficking clients have at least one question every day," explains the domestic violence shelter staff. One of their trafficking clients had been living in a homeless shelter when he needed assistance with his legal case. But since the staff at the homeless shelter was not trained on issues related to trafficking cases, he missed a series of deadlines and opportunities. Without trained staff available around the clock, "some clients actually feel that their trafficker was more available for them than the staff at homeless shelters." Alone in the United States and living on the streets, one client told the domestic violence shelter staff in Orange County that he would have killed himself if he had not found out about their shelter.

Nor do the rules that are appropriate for domestic violence clients work well for trafficking clients. Staff at domestic violence shelters throughout the country have learned through trial and error that the guidelines for their domestic violence clients can backfire with trafficking clients. A staff member of the Orange County shelter explains, "If we applied the same rules, our trafficking clients would have to leave the shelter before they are ready." Instead staff improvise with their trafficking clients: "There are rules and protocols, but we also need to look at the client and possibly look beyond the rules. We want these clients to get on their feet. We want them to have saved money, and to have housing lined up. We don't want them in the streets." Thus the shelter operates according to clients' needs, not according to a one-size-fits all timetable that is largely dictated by state and federal funding guidelines for domestic violence shelters. "We had one trafficking client here for two years, long after our other clients." Of course this timetable-blind approach is costly and requires unrestricted funding sources. "[The U.S. Conference of Catholic Bishops] gives us very little money. We make it stretch."[45] They get around these government restrictions by holding fundraisers. They also rely on volunteers from the community who donate money as well as clothes and household items specifically designated for their trafficking clients. Outraged that some of their clients "had earned tens of thousands of dollars for their traffickers," the Orange County shelter staff fumed, "There should be a way to take money from busts and put it into clients' care."

One-on-one case management is not only costly but is also time-intensive. Like their counterparts at social service organizations, shelter staff working with trafficking clients around the country report a tremendous learning curve. The director of the Orange County shelter needed two hands to hold up a weighty three-ring binder bursting with papers outlining guidelines for assisting trafficked persons. She explained, "Everyone said it wouldn't work, that this population is too different from our domestic violence clients. But we have been assisting them for years now—we never turn down a client. But it's not easy. The regulations for our trafficking clients are always changing." For the shelter staff, whether or not their clients have an experienced attorney matters. The shelter works closely with an organization that specializes in trafficking, and their attorney "files everything for us—from soup to nuts." But with other clients who have attorneys with little or no experience with trafficking, the staff "had to take the lead and learn what needs to be done and when." This kind of dedication to shelter residents, from fundraising to getting up to speed on their legal cases, underscores the pivotal role particular experts may play in the trafficking care regime. This model is not easily replicable around the country, especially for shelters with smaller staffs.

Without access to organizations that have enough staff and sources of unrestricted funding to do whatever it takes to get clients stable, trafficking clients' legal, health, and other needs may go unidentified and unaddressed. This story of slipping through the cracks of the trafficking care regime, however, is not reported by the media. But saving money for a rental deposit or to purchase a mattress, kitchen pots and pans, or bus fare is the main story line in these first weeks and months of formerly trafficked persons' exit from forced labor. It is the difference between living indefinitely in shelters and living on one's own. While they work through these mundane challenges, formerly trafficked persons begin to make the United States their home.

Relationships with Social Workers

Social workers and case managers are among the first individuals in whom formerly trafficked persons put their trust. These social service providers not only facilitate access to a range of services, but they also become confidants and cheerleaders. Vigilant against their clients becoming overly dependent, staff at social service organizations and shelters walk a tightrope as they set professional boundaries. Ultimately their role is to help their clients make decisions on their own, pointing them to the resources necessary to do so. They try, as a social worker in Washington, D.C., explains, to provide services "but not meddle." A California-based social worker echoes this goal: "Clients need to make their own decisions. There are limits on what we can do. Some refuse, for example, to address mental health issues, which can lead them to hop from job to job. If they don't address the cause of destabilization, we'll sit down and try to work out another plan. This is a big moral, philosophical, and professional issue. They have to make things happen for themselves. We can't do that." "Ultimately we are working up to not being that first call when they have a stomach ache," explains a social worker in New York. "Eventually they should be calling a neighbor or friends."

Getting to this point in a trusting relationship with trafficking clients takes time. "We are strangers, and they do not know who to trust," explains a staff member at the shelter in Orange County. "We have to gain their trust. It's about proving ourselves." One trafficking client who had a bad experience at another shelter was particularly wary, as the director explained: "She wanted to know how we were different. We don't expect people to trust us immediately. We know it will take time. We emphasize letting them take part in this process — making a phone call, speaking a bit of English. In this way they do things for themselves." Their assistance begins by handing over the reins of their clients' cases to the clients themselves. At the same time they try to always be there, just as the clients' abusers were. Caught in the confusing logic of various bureaucracies, trafficking clients — like any vulnerable client — can get lost in and pushed around by institutional exigencies. While the shelter staff has their clients make their own phone calls, for example, they suggest using a speakerphone together so that they can chime in on their clients' calls if necessary. They also accompany their clients to face-to-face appointments. The director explains, "Our domestic violence clients know the system and they will speak up." U.S. citizen domestic violence clients also may have jobs, family and friends, a faith community, and other sources of information and support. But with trafficking clients they start in an information vacuum. It does not help that "the process is confusing, and takes longer (than with domestic violence clients) because often the agencies don't know how to fill out the forms. And different agencies will ask them, 'Are you legal? Do you have children? No, okay, you don't qualify for anything.' They then shrink and stay quiet." The staff's own credibility is on the line: "If we don't go with them, it can compromise their trust in us. They will come back to us and say, 'Why did you send me there? They didn't help me.'"

As much as they try to stay in the background of their trafficking clients' lives, social workers and case managers find that their clients may place them in prominent roles. Some clients insist that their only "real" friend is their social worker and that they cannot talk about their experiences in forced labor with anyone else. It is easy to understand how some organizations and individuals on staff become a lifeline for their clients. Suzanne describes crying at a graduation ceremony that marked the formal closing of her case management: "I was crying both because I was sad and also out of happiness and thankfulness. It was a bittersweet day. They have helped with a lot of things. Not just about trafficking, but with everything." Similarly Maria, from the Philippines, has told me on many occasions how much her case manager and attorney have done for her. She is in awe of their kindness, skill, and loyalty. After she received her green card, she said, "I can't thank them enough. They have done so, so much for me. For nothing."

Trafficking clients' gratitude can sometimes get in the way of their fully disclosing their needs or concerns. As one trafficking client in California explains, "I did not want to tell my social worker that I was having a hard time in the shelter. She was already doing so much for me. I did not want to complain." A social worker in Chicago worries: "These clients are not complainers." Once they start working, her trafficking clients often "are so grateful for opportunities that they won't tell us about any bad conditions at work. So we have to be very aware of their needs, because they won't present them to us. For example, if they have an accident at work, they will not tell us." Not only do most formerly trafficked persons regularly talk about how thankful they are for their assistance-givers, but they also often describe feeling lucky. "I'm just so lucky," explains Esperanza in Los Angeles. "I've been helped so much." In the midst of setback after setback, Maria finds strength in being grateful and emphasizing how lucky she is. "I'm luckier than others. I have my son and my friends at Philippine Connections."[46]

But thankfulness not only empowers but also can indebt. Assistance-givers may make arrangements on which their clients have no intention of acting. Enrolling clients in English-language, computer, or other skill-building courses may place the clients in an uncomfortable position. Not wanting to disappoint their assistance-givers, clients may not know how to turn down these opportunities. A social worker in New York City learned, for example, that one of her clients had not been attending a course only when the program director phoned her. Perhaps knowing that her social worker had lobbied the director to take her name off the waiting list and that the social service organization had paid the course fees, the client did not know how to tell the social worker herself. Clients' gratefulness and worries about losing their assistance-givers' respect, consequently, can constrain them from speaking up. Anticipating what clients need takes skill and experience. Seasoned social workers and case managers have a kind of sixth sense with their trafficking clients and have learned to ask questions about issues their clients may not have brought to their attention. When clients still do not make clear their worries, needs, or plans to their social workers or attorneys, being around other trafficking clients and shelter residents can open channels of advice and support.

Opening Up while Maintaining Privacy

"In shelters, the clients, no matter their past, naturally bond," explains a social worker in New York. Shelter life for trafficked persons "can help create a sense of community where clients learn that 'I am not the only one.' You find community and sisterhood and become a resource for one another." But there can be a fine line between not feeling alone and feeling overly scrutinized. Social workers and shelter staff worry about their trafficked clients revealing too much, too fast—which clients later regret. As the social worker in New York City explains, "It can feel funny if someone knows too much. The same is true with domestic violence survivors. If you form friendships too fast, and someone knows a lot of horrific things about you, [you] may regret it later. Privacy is power." And for trafficking clients who had experienced sexual abuse "there can be such shame that it is very hard for them to tell anyone."

Consequently bringing clients together in a support group setting is a potential minefield. The social worker in New York cautions, "Clients must be ready for it; they must be able to tolerate other viewpoints and disagree with others and have a sense of boundaries. Otherwise group sessions could make things worse, and the participants could retraumatize one another." Suzanne, the woman from Indonesia who had lived in a domestic violence shelter for over a year, participated in a support group at the shelter: "We talked about our experiences." She found, "It helps a lot to talk, especially since some people want to keep it inside. But it's good to let it out. This way people are not wondering, 'Why is she acting like this?'" Suzanne saw commonalities between herself and the domestic violence clients: "Most of the women there had experiences like me. You know, they had been abused by their husbands. It is kind of similar."

Staff at a shelter in Los Angeles that has a range of clients echo Suzanne's positive experience with a support group: "Whether living homeless with kids, or living through trafficking, everyone here has horrors behind them." A staff member at the domestic violence shelter in Orange County notes particular benefits of these larger support groups: "Our trafficking clients prefer the larger empowerment groups, so that they are not singled out as trafficking clients." They also doubt the value of a trafficking-only group: "Even if we had a trafficking support group, these are cases that are all so different that it would be hard. And some clients are here with a family member—and they don't want them to know. There also is the problem of sharing with other clients who could become witnesses and subpoenaed. It's a problem because we have their trust, and they want to tell us everything. But we are here as advocates, not to determine if they were trafficked. You have to know the boundaries."

Home Is Where the Space Is

Having a place to meet for social gatherings can make a significant impact in formerly trafficked persons' lives. Community organizations are more likely than social service agencies to have space where its members can meet for formal meetings, workshops, or social events that they themselves organize. Social service agencies generally do not have spaces or ongoing formal or informal events to bring clients together. Since they are not membership-based, these organizations tend to be hierarchical and funding-driven. In other words, social service organizations' staff, not their clients, design programs and organize events. If staff do not seek funds for and implement programs that bring together clients—for example, skill-building workshops, empowerment support groups, or a speaker's bureau— they will not happen. Clients otherwise have no way of meeting one another and possibly organizing an event together. One social service organization in New York City set aside some unrestricted funding to hold yoga and relaxation sessions and empowerment groups for their Spanish-speaking trafficking clients. But the timing was difficult—both for the clients, many of whom worked evenings and weekends, as well as the staff, who were donating their free time to hold these extra activities.

The design of the one shelter in the country that is dedicated to trafficked persons is perfect for hosting small intimate activities as well as larger events. Its kitchen, living room, and patio are well used as the staff, current and past residents, and current and former clients—some of whom never resided there—organize all kinds of events. Its presence in these clients' lives cannot be overstated. One of Suzanne's friends moved quite a distance away, but Suzanne could count on seeing her at the big parties held by the shelter: "If they have a Mother's Day party or a Christmas party, I know I'll get to see her." Holiday parties and other special celebrations not only are opportunities to catch up with old friends, but are events at which clients can feel understood and at home. They can let their guard down. Esperanza met her closest friends at the shelter in Los Angeles: "I've made friends in different ways. I have friends at school, and I have friends in my neighborhood. Different kinds of friends." But it is with friends that she made through the trafficking shelter that she feels particularly understood: "We feel very close even when we just talk by phone. We are confidants. We know each others' secrets and worries, everything." In contrast, she is careful with friends she meets outside of the trafficking community. "I really care about confidentiality, so I tell them some things but not a lot about my past situation." At the shelter, where she makes a point to not miss out on any potlucks and other events, she feels at home, trusted and trusting. "I feel like I can trust the women there because in some way we all identify ourselves in the same way, so I feel comfortable with them."

Elsewhere in the country, I have heard over and over again from trafficking clients that they met their closest friend in a shelter. Many of the former clients at the domestic violence shelter in Orange County, for example, have moved into apartments near the shelter, fostering a tight-knit community. There also are a number of cases of formerly trafficked persons now living together as roommates, such as two women who met in a shelter in Los Angeles who are from the same country. Older, and with limited English skills, they look out for one another and even traveled to their home country together soon after they received their green cards.

Language

Shelter clients come from different countries and speak different languages, so they often have no choice but to speak English with one another. Esperanza, a native Spanish speaker who now lives in a Spanish-speaking neighborhood, looks backs on her time in a domestic violence shelter as prompting her to learn English: "Most of the people in the shelter spoke English. I was the only person who spoke Spanish, so it was difficult for me at the time." In fact some of the other residents took advantage of her limited English and bullied her to clean up the kitchen. Esperanza explains that this dynamic pushed her to study English: "I learned English because I wanted to speak up for myself. This was my main motivation." As part of her activism on antitrafficking issues, Esperanza now encourages other formerly trafficked persons to make learning English a priority: "The huge, huge barrier to everything is English. Without it, I don't know where I would be. English was the number one thing that I had to learn because everywhere you go, you need it. If you go for an appointment, you have to speak English. If you ask someone a question, they answer in English. You have to know it." She dedicated herself to continue studying English, even though Spanish was spoken all around her in her neighborhood. "When I left the shelter it was hard to be in a new country and learn the language. It was a challenge because I could say, 'Oh, I don't need to learn language because I am living in a neighborhood where everybody speaks Spanish.'"

Getting together at events sponsored by social service or community-based organizations also often entails speaking in English. And some formerly trafficked persons use English on Facebook with one another and with one another's teenage and young adult children. While hanging out at a McDonald's in downtown Los Angeles where their children could run around in an indoor playground, a group of friends who met at the trafficking shelter laughed as they told me—in English—that their older children have "friended" one another on Facebook. "We can tell anything to one another. We understand one another," they said. They rely on one another, communicating daily through texts, email, Facebook, telephone calls, and outings like this one—all in their shared language, English.

Living on One's Own

A constant challenge for service providers and shelter staff is how to arrange their trafficking clients' long-term housing while meeting their immediate need for shelter. A social worker in New York is upfront about how long it takes to "stabilize" sufficiently to earn enough money to cover one's rent without assistance: "Realistically no organization can continue to pay rent for years until someone has stabilized." She is frustrated that her organization does not offer enough assistance to their clients. As a result, she believes, her trafficking clients leave her office's programs only steps away from the economically vulnerable position that they were in when they first sought assistance after forced labor.

Establishing economic stability takes time—for any low-income client, not just trafficked persons. Thus the domestic violence shelter in Orange County prepares all its clients for life after the shelter. They require all residents to save 30 percent of their benefits and/or paychecks so that they have money available for security deposits for their housing after they leave the shelter. The residents are able to put money into this rent fund because the shelter provides a variety of on-site services, including a preschool offered free of charge so that parents can go to work or attend school, support groups, and appointments related to their legal cases. The staff also encourages them to enroll in free English-language classes, held within walking distance from the shelter, while they are waiting for a work permit or looking for a job. They explain, "Learning English is critical. It also helps them feel busy. We don't want them just staying in their rooms watching television. Going to classes gets them out every day." Before they live on their own, the shelter transitions these clients to a second-step program in which they move out of the shelter and into a rent-subsidized apartment complex. The complex has a courtyard in the center, with picnic benches and a barbecue. There is also a small, enclosed playground for children. In this space that facilitates community but also provides privacy, clients can choose how much time to spend on their own or with others. Impromptu barbecues and play-dates at the playground offer opportunities for the women to socialize as much or as little as they want.

Romantic Partners, Friends, and Housing

Subsidized long-term housing options such as this second-step program are rare. Once trafficking clients leave shelters or other temporary housing arrangements, finding safe, affordable housing is a monumental challenge. Some women elect to work as live-in child care providers or housekeepers. Living-in allows them to save money toward their own apartment. Others move in with friends they meet at a shelter or at work. Carmen has had many different types of shared living arrangements since I met her in 2004. When she exited forced domestic labor, she lived in a domestic violence shelter outside of New York City. Then she moved in with a friend she made there. When her friend remarried, Carmen moved to an apartment with another friend, whom she had met through her housekeeping job in a hotel. In both situations she only had to furnish her own bedroom, since her roommates had furniture for the living room as well as items for the kitchen. She then moved in with her boyfriend (whom she also had met at work). Like many in New York City, where housing is expensive and leases difficult to break, she remained living with her boyfriend even after their relationship ended. She eventually moved out and lived on her own, which she found lonely and expensive. She now lives with a few friends she met through work.

In many U.S. cities, the rents are so high that it is not financially feasible to live on one's own. Consequently romantic partners have figured prominently in many formerly trafficked persons' housing arrangements. Francisco relied on his older girlfriend to pay the bulk of the rent in the New York area. While he worked intermittently in construction, she had a steady job. Living on one's own requires a security deposit plus first and last month's rent, as well as cash to set up even the barest of households. Suzanne could not afford to move straight from the shelter to her own apartment; instead she moved in with her boyfriend (who eventually became her husband). They paid $650 for a one-bedroom rent-controlled apartment in Los Angeles. (Most apartments in her neighborhood cost $900 to $1,000 a month.) Yet she worried about how safe their neighborhood was for children. With no outdoor space for kids to play nearby, her toddler's only play space was in the building's large lobby.

Sharing household expenses also allows formerly trafficked persons to take time out of the labor market to go to school. It is not only romantic partners with whom they may share expenses. Although most do not have family members in the United States—a factor that may have shaped their vulnerability to their abusers in the first place—those with family in the U.S. experience less social isolation and fewer financial pressures. Eva and her son moved in with her brother in New York City. Her brother not only paid their rent but also took care of his nephew while Eva worked the night shift bartending. With this significant savings, Eva was able to pay tuition for English-language classes, preparation courses for her GED, and eventually a nursing assistance program. Flo saved money for tuition for GED classes, driving classes, and a nursing assistance program by living rent-free with the family she met through her church (they also helped pay for her various classes). During the time that she lived with her friends she also was able to save enough money to eventually live in her own apartment, without a roommate. This head start paid off considerably in the long run, when, years later, Flo's husband moved to the United States and Flo had to support them both until he could find work in construction.

Not only do soaring rents and gentrification make living on one's own impossible for many working low-wage jobs, but anti-immigrant politics also prevent formerly trafficked persons from moving to more affordable towns. For example, Prince William County, Virginia, has a 287(g) agreement, making it difficult for social workers to suggest living there, even though rents are cheaper there than in nearby Washington, D.C. "When we say, 'Why don't you go to Virginia?,'" explains a D.C.-based social worker, "our clients are afraid. They have heard about the new policies. They know that the police ask for ID. Even though they have green cards, it is a scary situation they want to avoid." Having a severely limited housing budget also pushes formerly trafficked persons into arrangements they otherwise would not have chosen. Gladys, whose eagerness to "eat New York" opens this chapter, faced rental prices she could not afford when she first relocated to New York City after exiting a situation of forced labor in the Midwest. She knew no one in New York except for an old boyfriend. She moved in with him but soon found herself the object of his wife's wrath when she unwittingly answered the phone when the wife called from Mexico. To avoid further drama, Gladys scrambled to find other living arrangements.

Tatiana had a different set of concerns: she was sheepish about telling people where she lived after restaurant coworkers questioned how she could live on her own in an enviable neighborhood on their meager paychecks. "They talked about how I could afford to live there because they know I don't make much money." A former client from the club in the Midwest where she had danced helps pay her rent. He visits her from time to time in Washington, D.C., and drops by the restaurant. She did not tell her colleagues that he helps pay the bills and is rattled by their eager interest in her personal life. "One time it was really hurtful. They asked, 'Are you a prostitute?'" She cried as she continued, "Maybe they were joking, but you know, I took it seriously. It took a little bite out of me." She decided to protect herself by staying silent: "It's better to be quiet and not say anything so that they don't hurt me." Her decision to not socialize with her work colleagues (who are not coethnics) illustrates how formerly trafficked persons often choose to keep themselves and their business private and apart. Relationships thrive on openness and honesty, and yet dissimulation and evasion often help individuals survive persecution, violence, and genocide.[47] Hurtful encounters like Tatiana's can result in even greater isolation and loneliness. She feels watched: "Other people are watching this, and I don't know what they think." She started to cry. "It's just like bombs. [They] go off. You are trying to do something positive and [they] go off."

Being around Others

Feeling watched is a common paranoia among formerly trafficked persons. They describe feeling that "Everyone is looking at me." Some express a desire to retreat from the world.[48] Being around others, particularly in crowds, can be difficult. At the other extreme, some search for public spaces so that they are not alone. Before they have permission to work, trafficking clients usually have a lot of free time on their hands. Those living in the suburbs tell of going to the mall, while those in cities describe riding public transportation with no destination in mind. When Tatiana first arrived in Washington, D.C., for example, an FBI agent had told her that admission to the museums was free, and she went to the Smithsonian every day. "The agent thought I would like all the history there. They have everything! I was not working and I just moved here and I did not know what to do. I would walk around and meet people when they would help me out, you know, getting directions." Heading out to the museums those first days when she had nowhere else to go gave a rhythm to her otherwise unplanned days. She spent all day there. "It helped me relax. I never had enough time; you just start to think and then it's five o'clock, everything closes, and you have to come back the next day."

Flo too was not used to having free time. "The first days after I had left I was feeling scared. Even once I could go out, I did not want to." It was hard for her to forget her abuser's lies. "She had told me over and over how people in the United States do not like people from my country and how they could do all kinds of terrible things to you. I was scared at first, even to say hello to people." When her friend from church with whom she was living wanted to take her shopping, Flo balked. "She said, 'Let's go to Walmart.' I did not want to go. I was too shaky. And when I went, I saw somebody that looked just like my employer and I thought she was looking at me. She [the friend] laughed. She tried to calm me down. She said, 'Flo, you know that wasn't a normal time.' It wasn't. I wasn't normal."

Since her abuser was a diplomat and did not go to jail, Flo also avoided going to places her abuser had frequented.[49] She was unprepared, however, when she actually ran into a friend of her abuser in a store. "She [the abuser's friend] must have told my employer that I was still in the United States. She [the abuser] sent me an email and told me that I might think I'm clever for not leaving, but that I really was stupid." The abuser also called the pastor of Flo's church and complained, "That lady is illegal. She needs to leave because if anything happens to her, I am the one that is going to be in trouble." Once the abuser figured out Flo had been living with a family from the church, she also telephoned them. "She called my friend. She [the abuser] tried to be nice on the phone. She tried to get information. She said to my friend, 'Oh, Flo is a good lady; she looked after my children nicely.'

But my friend never revealed that she knew where I was. She told her, 'I don't know where she is.' But I was standing right there!" As her abuser called all over town for her, Flo was on edge. "She tried and tried to find me. By then I had been working with a lawyer and my case was moving fast." After Flo began conversations with social workers and an attorney, she found some peace of mind. Up to then, in legal limbo, she had been losing a lot of weight. After her legal case was under way, she was able to eat again. Flo says of this legal and emotional turning point, "I was relieved, finally."

Time and Freedom to Explore

Formerly trafficked persons may not know much about the towns or cities in which they had been living when they were in forced labor. Only after their exit do they have the opportunity to move about in their new country. Suzanne, who was from a rural village in Indonesia, spoke about how overwhelming it was to get accustomed to living in Los Angeles. "The first time I was traveling by myself it was difficult. I was trying to go to Hollywood and I got lost. I took the train back and forth three times. I did not know which train to take. Finally, the conductor asked me where I was going. He saw me ride the train for so long and never get off!" There were many firsts for Suzanne. "Everything is hard the first time you have to do it. I had not really had any experience being on my own. And I did not have experience working other than housekeeping or babysitting. And if you don't speak English, it's hard to get around." Tatiana tells a similar story of getting lost when she was on her own for the first time in a new city: "Somebody told me which train to take. And I got a map in one of those stores that sells souvenirs. But I still got lost."

Driving affords a considerable amount of independence and cuts down on commuting time. Tired of waiting for the bus at late hours after work, Tatiana was taking driving lessons when I met her. Flo's plans to become a nursing assistant hinged on her getting her driver's license. With little time to spare between school during the day, studying in the afternoon, and working the night shift at a nursing home, having control over her transportation relieved a great deal of stress. She could even squeeze in a quick nap. Moreover it was safer. Once she got her license, she no longer had to ride the bus late at night to her shift at a nursing home. Although she had liked taking trains and buses around town and felt that it had helped her learn her way around Washington, D.C., she could not have juggled work, school, and studying without a car. Taking driving classes and passing the test to obtain a license also provides a kind of gateway school experience. The driving test is often the first formal test formerly trafficked persons take in the United States. But enrolling in driving school and buying a car and insurance require savings—money that Jamie, from Malaysia, lamented she did not have. She had no choice but to spend a couple of hours every day taking several buses to get from her home in Virginia to her job as a child care provider in Maryland.

While most formerly trafficked persons had not traveled within the United States until they exited their situation of forced labor, Sofia had learned how to traverse the country by bus, visiting over a dozen states to work short stints in brothels both before and after forced sexual labor. Self-reliant and daring, she explains, "I had the courage. Not everyone is willing to travel far." She quickly learned to protect herself: "When I first came to this country, I was in Nebraska for Christmas. A client tried to take advantage of me. He was drunk and insulting. I said I have to handle this situation well. I knew I would have to find a way other than yelling and hitting. Girls end up dead or beaten up. So you have to learn many ways to survive." She also outsmarted law enforcement in Cleveland when they boarded the bus and inspected luggage. "I had a lot of condoms, so I went to the bathroom and put them in a cereal box." "I learned how to take care of myself," she proudly asserted, "so I'm not scared of anything."

Conclusion

Sofia now lives with a boyfriend. She had to move in with him when she left behind the steady money she was earning in sex work. It was not an easy decision for her to leave the sex sector, as she explains: "It takes a lot of strength to not return to it. You get used to the money. And life is very expensive here." Since making this move, she has been exploring New York City for the first time, with her boyfriend, a welcome break from always working: "I never took the time before to see New York. I only thought of work." They have walked over the Brooklyn Bridge, visited Central Park and the Empire State Building, and gone to movies. She lights up when she speaks of her boyfriend. "[He] is so different than my husband!" (We learned in the previous chapter that Sofia's "husband" had beaten her regularly and forced her into the sex trade, first in Mexico and then in the United States). Her new boyfriend is a former client: "He was unlike other clients. He was always polite. He is a good person, a good man. He doesn't yell. If he gets angry he goes into the street and then cools off. And when I yell, he says, 'Are you done yet?' I was afraid to get into a relationship again. But he has a very calm way about him. And he accepts me for me." She also has opened herself up to friendships with women she has met from around the world in her English class. "They are from India, Bangladesh, Ecuador, Colombia, Sri Lanka. We all went to a Mets game together. I told them I didn't have the money, and they said, 'You've got to go with us.'" They chipped in and bought her a ticket.

Enjoying a new city and marveling at its sights comes with time; so does entering new romantic relationships and friendships. Over time, formerly trafficked persons become less scared and jumpy and more trusting. They begin to feel at home. But as much as Sofia describes feeling supported by her new boyfriend and new friends, she desperately misses her children: "I wanted to live differently than in the past. And I am. But I want to be a mother to my children; they've never been with me."[50] Without her children with her in the United States, Sofia has a hard time putting her experiences in forced labor completely in the past. Living with grief and such devastating loss is a constant: "I try [to move forward]. But because I am not with my children, of course the past is in some ways in my present."

Chapter Four

Living the Possible

SETTLING into HOME

As one of the emcees at a green card party, Suzanne was at ease moving the evening's events along. Unfazed by the microphone, the size of the crowd, or speaking in English, she seemed an old hand at hosting large events. While she spoke, her daughter whirled around the room with other kids. She spun over to us and beamed: "I just won a spelling bee at school!"

Dee commanded respect. Sitting behind the front desk of a domestic violence center, she firmly explained to a young man that he had missed his appointment. Apologetic and deferential, he thanked her profusely for giving him a second chance. Watching these dynamics, I thought she ran this organization. I was surprised to learn that she was a counselor and, as a part-time worker, had no medical benefits.

Maria marched in the Philippine Independence Day Parade holding the Philippine Connections banner. She was out in front of many colleagues and friends. Her boyfriend marched with her, as did I. She is not alone in the United States, but with her only child living in the Philippines, she constantly talks about how much her heart hurts.

Even after years living in the United States with a T visa and eventually a green card, formerly trafficked persons' lives are still in flux. Many who have been out of forced labor for a long time, like Suzanne, Dee, and Maria, have made the United States their home, but they still have a great deal of insecurity in their lives. Their economic hold in the country is fragile, and other sources of insecurity shape their ability to settle in. Divorced, Suzanne has tremendous financial responsibility as a single mother. A charismatic speaker at antitrafficking events, Dee is in great demand, but her activism does not pay her bills. And as I write this, Maria just started working a new job; child care as a career means a constant rotation of employers. Nor will she feel at home or at peace until her now-adult son is by her side in the United States. After more than a decade of U.S. government assistance for a relatively small number of individuals, the resettlement of formerly trafficked persons is still a work in progress. As they build a sense of home in their new cities and towns, they skate on the edges of poverty. Most formerly trafficked persons face a resettlement double burden: the burden of the memory and possibly physical effects of pervasive insecurity and violence and the burden of the economic, social, and health hardships that they experience working in low-wage jobs and living in low-income communities.

Legal Limbo: Waiting and Waiting

Maria phoned with the good news: "I just got my green card! Now I can go to the Philippines. And finally hold my son. I want to be there before his birthday. My phone keeps ringing, everybody is calling from Philippine Connections. I waited for this. I never complained. I've suffered so much. But I never did anything to the people who hurt me. Everyone told me to get a lawyer, so I did. And I did what she told me to do. I did not feel sorry for myself. I never surrendered. I never thought about losing; I put 'winner' in my head. I waited and told myself to stand strong. I still can't believe it. My boyfriend wanted to go out and celebrate. I said, 'Let me be for a while.' I needed to think about it all. I could not believe it."

Maria had been in legal limbo, unable to leave the United States. The waiting period for green cards for Maria and the other first T visa recipients dragged out over years — considerably longer than the average waiting period today. This waiting—for T visas and green cards, for family members to arrive, for full-time employment with medical benefits, for enough savings to move to safe neighborhoods or to enroll in school—creates an enduring state of anxiousness and disconnection.

During their long period of legal limbo trafficking claimants must put their legal fate in their attorneys' hands while their applications work their way through the U.S. immigration system. (Their applications are reviewed at USCIS's Vermont Service Center.) This period of waiting—and of scrutiny—profoundly shapes how these claimants experience life in the United States. Philippe Bourgois's description of subjectivity as "the process of becoming subjected to power" captures well how individuals are affected by their particular engagements in the world.[1] Formerly trafficked persons continue to be subjected to various forms of power and authority years after exiting forced labor. Not only can they not leave the country while they are waiting for their green card, but they also may be continually cooperating with ongoing investigations or trials.[2] Even after they have a T visa, formerly trafficked persons continue to be suspect subjects in their ongoing bureaucratic encounters, in part because of the rarity of T visas.[3] Formerly trafficked persons often end up informing those in positions of power about their legal rights. As potentially empowering this may be, for many it is intimidating and can delay benefits that they may need immediately.

Unless trafficking clients meet other trafficking clients at a shelter or through group activities at their social service provider or a community-based organization, they have no way to learn from those who already received the legal status and benefits they seek.[4] Consequently their dependency on the legal knowledge and advice of their attorneys cannot be overstated. But even the most seasoned attorneys in trafficking cases can never be sure of how things will turn out. The pace at which the Vermont Service Center has reviewed T visa applications has been uneven, particularly in the early years of processing claims following passage of the TVPA. The T visa holders I have met and the experts who helped prepare their claims (as well as those who judged their claims) were among the first to test the new trafficking legal regime. Now that they have completed this legal process, these early claimants face other sources of insecurity and uncertainty that accompany life on the economic margins of the United States.

Collisions with the Past: Court Appearances,
Civil Litigation, and Run-ins with Coethnics

Despite formerly trafficked persons' best efforts to start anew, their past sometimes catches up with them. Events that recall their former circumstances can be particularly painful: court appearances to prosecute their abusers, conflicts with current coworkers, or random encounters with individuals associated with their time in forced labor or with individuals who resemble them. One woman who had been in forced sexual labor in New York City was having more nightmares than usual during her trafficker's trial: "Sometimes I have nightmares about that life. I dream that I am with women, I'm not sure where, but with people where I'm working. I don't dream I'm having sex with anybody, but that I'm there in that place. I'll always have to live with that. It's difficult to live with that. But then I wake up and it's just a dream." She observed that the dreams began to intensify during the time that she had been having "a lot of conversations" with law enforcement agents and lawyers. Although she had terrible nightmares during the time of the trial, during sentencing she witnessed her abuser's own terror. "For the first time I saw him scared. He looked like a little boy in that jump suit. He was terrified when he heard the amount of time he would be in jail. I had never seen that face of his before."

With one of her abusers still at large, she lives with a knot of paralyzing emotions: fear, anger, and resentment. But she does not allow her feelings toward him to overtake her: "I wish the police could find him. I wish that I could send him to jail because he really destroyed me. He took a lot of time from me. But I don't feel like I live with this; I don't bring my past with me now. I think these things make you stronger. But if I have the opportunity to send him to jail, this would be great." For her, the U.S. justice system helps ease her suffering: "There is justice here. It's fair here. I feel strong because I now know when I can say no and when I can say yes. I have choices."

Pursuing civil litigation can affirm formerly trafficked persons' sense of control and choice. It also can be immensely stressful.[5] Ideally, attorneys Kathleen Kim and Charles Song advise, trafficking clients would have received their T visas, be living in a "stable and supportive environment," and any criminal proceedings would have concluded.[6] Civil litigation can be "the best thing and the worst thing a victim can do. In a good sense, the civil process is incredibly empowering. It is the most empowering thing I have seen a trafficking victim do because they have total control of the lawsuit." "The flip side," however, "is that the civil process is the hardest thing I have seen a trafficking victim go through, more difficult than the immigration process, even more difficult than the criminal process. Civil discovery is so intensive and so permissive in the U.S. that victims have a difficult time dealing with it."[7] But, as an attorney in Washington, D.C., emphasizes, "these awards—some of which can be considerable—change lives." Having seen the life-altering economic security that civil awards can deliver, social workers and attorneys throughout the country have made more efforts of late to help their clients secure civil awards. Frustrated that their first clients to receive awards sent nearly all the money home, social workers and attorneys who help clients pursue awards today do so within the context of financial literacy training.

Even without pursuing civil litigation, taking control of one's immigration case can restore confidence and spur a sense of calm. For trafficking clients who had been trafficked when young, their dealings with their lawyers and law enforcement may be the first time that they have negotiated anything on their own behalf. The woman having nightmares had been trafficked when a teenager. Living in her parents' house, where she resented her father's patriarchal control, she had jumped at the chance to move out and live with her older boyfriend, who coerced her into sexual labor. Now living on her own for the first time, she relishes her decision-making authority, no matter how tough the decisions. "I'm mature now. I know what I have to do." After relying on attorneys early on in her case, Flo explains that she has filed—on her own—for citizenship. "It's not hard, I just followed instructions on the Internet." Flo also has managed to send regular remittances to her parents and just finished building a house for them.

Not having a welcoming family to help out, or return to in one's home country (to visit or to live permanently), can intensify feelings of being alone. Going back to Russia holds little emotional or economic promise for Tatiana. With both of her parents dead and her brother addicted to heroin— and, she worries, possibly dead from his addiction—she has no emotional safety net there. Another formerly trafficked person feels she cannot return home since her family had arranged for her to live with and work for her eventual abuser. In telephone conversations, her family expressed disbelief in her story of abuse. Their lack of faith in her fuels self-doubt. As it has for Tatiana, the world has shrunk for her; although she has a green card, she has not traveled to visit her family. She also regularly confronts gossip in a tight-knit community of co-ethnics that blame her for blowing the whistle on her employer and bringing unflattering media attention to their community. Her abuser "has a lot of money." "This is what I don't like about Africa. The corruption. People care more about money and rich people than the way they treat children! So, I try not to give people my last name when we meet so they don't know who I am."

Staying away from judgmental or dangerous coethnics involves strategy; so does avoiding places and people linked to their time in forced labor. While waitressing in a restaurant serving an African clientele, this young woman from Africa came face to face with her abuser's brother. "He slammed his beer down and screamed, 'this is not what I ordered.' He made a scene." She quit. "I knew I couldn't work there with everyone from the community coming in. He told the owner, 'Do you know who this is and what she did?'" A Mexican woman who was forced to have sex in Mexican-run and -frequented brothels in New York City ran into a former customer at her waitressing job in a restaurant. He recognized her and told one of her friends that she used to work at a brothel. Since then she vowed never to work in a restaurant in the Mexican community.

Esperanza also tells of a run-in with her past when her abuser phoned a migrants' rights organization whose meetings she knew Esperanza had been attending. And, in the previous chapter I recount how a friend of Flo's abuser spotted Flo in a store in the Washington, D.C., area. By deciding to stay in the area where she had been in forced labor, Flo had to second-guess her plans and at times alter her movements. Settling near the same community where they had been in forced labor can complicate formerly trafficked persons' best-laid plans to make a break with the past and to start a new life in the United States.

"Trafficking Plus": Joining the Working Poor

Years into living in the United States, formerly trafficked persons face a range of events and circumstances that contribute to their stability or instability, well-being or anxiousness. A crisis like a death in the family or the loss of a job can bring on episodes of depression. Not telling friends and family about past experiences, or not having family alive—or having accusatory family members—can create an ongoing sense of isolation. Keeping sources of income secret, such as income earned in the sex trade, may also induce stress even while it provides financial stability.

An attorney in New York City refers to the new problems that crop up in her trafficking clients' lives—sometimes years into their resettlement—as "trafficking plus." They may face medical problems after years of non-existent or inadequate medical care. Many, this attorney reports, increase their financial vulnerability by not safeguarding their earnings from their family's requests for remittances. The social workers with whom she works help their clients keep track of their earnings and remittances. Financial literacy is critical since their clients often face back-to-back financial crises. As a staff member at a domestic violence shelter in Los Angeles points out, "Everyone needs a rest after coming out of a trauma. The buzz word right now in housing circles is *rapid rehousing*. But it won't work on its own for these clients. They don't just need a home and then resources. They desperately want to re-create their lives. They have dreams and goals and need time to establish them. They struggle to clean up their debt and get a job they can live off of in an expensive city like Los Angeles, where so many people are struggling." Some solutions are uncomplicated. Recognizing the widespread problems associated with the cost of transportation in the Los Angeles area, this shelter program began issuing gas cards.

"Over the long-term, in terms of well-being, we are dealing with poverty," pronounces a social worker in New York. Poverty—and the injustices it is rooted in—delays formerly trafficked persons' dreams, compromises their economic futures, and has long-lasting health effects. The conditions of living in unsafe neighborhoods, working in low-wage and often physically demanding jobs, and not having access to decent health care thwart many formerly trafficked persons' long-term plans. The current recession adds to their economic insecurity and vulnerability. In today's economy, even those with professional degrees and marketable skills who were on a steady course have seen their jobs evaporate or their hours rolled back. A nurse, for example, lost her job when her employer, a hospital facing budget cuts, laid off a number of its newer staff. For years, during the low tourist seasons, Carmen has been furloughed in her housekeeping job at a hotel in New York City. She also has suffered through a number of repetitive-motion injuries. Since the recession, families employing Maria as a child care provider have cut her hours considerably. And as construction projects dried up close to home in Queens, Francisco has traveled to work sites out of state, sometimes two hours each way.

"Controlled Poverty"

Unless formerly trafficked persons live with a family member, friend, or romantic partner, they are their own safety net when trouble hits. Since government support runs out in a year, long before many formerly trafficked persons are financially stable, they and their social workers have been frustrated by the limits of what their status as a "trafficked person" actually provides them. The refugee expert Roger Zetter's critique of well-meaning assistance for refugees that nonetheless disempowers and sets them up to live in "controlled poverty" parallels the finite nature of assistance for trafficked persons in the United States.[8] A seasoned social worker in New York sums up how her trafficking clients are doing years into their resettlement: "They are hanging on by their fingernails."

Florrie Burke, the former senior director of antitrafficking programs at the largest service provider in New York City, underscored the gap between needs and assistance in her remarks at the conference Rethinking Trafficking: "Financial support is awarded and then stopped, seemingly without thought to what happens to the victims and to the case. The timelines for service provision put forth by government-funded programs do not match the reality of a survivor's life."[9] "Long-term care is a huge issue," echoes a social worker in Washington, D.C. Since the social service system is not designed to help clients over time, agencies maximize what they can offer by partnering with other organizations that can provide specific services, such as legal assistance or job preparation. However, these niche organizations may not understand clients who had been in forced labor, as the D.C.-based social worker explains: "In graduate school, we learned the refugee resettlement model was to ask clients, 'Do you want to be a nurse's aide or a domestic worker?' This is not really listening to the clients. And now we send folks to refugee resettlement agencies, and they do the same thing. Yet they [refugee agencies] should focus on the particular needs of a particular client. Sure, some clients want to become a live-in nanny; this works great for them. But not for all clients."

In contrast to this one-size-fits-all approach, the long-term needs and interests of formerly trafficked persons veer off in multiple directions. "Perhaps the most important factor in the long term," asserts a social worker in California, "is the education and skill set that they bring with them to the United States." Their economic stability and mobility largely depend not only on the skills they already have when they first arrive in the United

States, but also on their opportunities to expand these skills. A staff member at a domestic violence shelter assesses: "The gap between being an RN and being a nursing assistant in elder care is enormous." To enter nursing programs, however, prospective students need proof of graduation from high school and proficiency in the English language. They also need time away from work to go to school and a way to finance their schooling. The staff member at the domestic violence shelter explains, "Everyone wants to learn English. Everyone wants to achieve. But not everyone has the time, money, and skill set to become an RN." Meanwhile formerly trafficked persons face an onslaught of challenges, large and small. Here are examples of the economic precariousness of formerly trafficked persons years after they exit forced labor:

Jamie, from Malaysia, is the sole financial provider for herself and two children in the metropolitan D.C. area. She worries constantly about how to stretch her paycheck. There is no room for any extras. Her salary as a child care provider barely covers the family's monthly expenses: rent, food, and her hour commute by bus and Metro to her job. On the weekends, when buses do not run between her neighborhood and the Metro train station, she does not mind the hour walk to the station, but she refused to follow a case manager's suggestion to have her children wear their jeans more than once to save money at the laundromat. Distraught, she explained, "The laundromat is expensive. But I'm not sending my kids to school in dirty clothes."

Nanci, who had been trafficked into a Mexican-run brothel in New York City, lived with her husband and baby in a Spanish-speaking neighborhood in New York City. They occupied one room in a railroad apartment where several other families lived. Their every belonging was there, displaying their current lives. Baby clothes — onesies and pajamas — were drying next to a brown restaurant uniform on a makeshift clothing line. A bulky kit of English-language tapes and accompanying guides revealed future dreams.

Visiting Nanci a couple of years later in a new apartment, she and her husband — and now two kids — had the privacy they had craved. Although they all shared one bedroom, it was *their* apartment. The living room allowed them to stretch out beyond the bedroom, but they still had to take in a boarder, who occupied the second bedroom. He bothered Nanci since he often came home drunk late at night and never cleaned up after himself in the bathroom. As in the case of their first apartment building, this new building was filled with tenants like Nanci and her boarder sharing the rent. As music videos played on their large television in the center of the room, Nanci shared worries about the quality of the kindergarten and the all too frequent presence of drug dealers and users in the park where she takes her children. Her worries had shifted over the years from those particular to trafficked persons to those indistinguishable from her Spanish-speaking neighbors living with the noise, garbage, and drug dealing in the streets of her neighborhood.

Jamie's and Nanci's fragile economic state is not remarkably different from that of other newly arrived migrants working low-wage and insecure jobs. The radiating effects of poverty no doubt also shape the lives of the other residents living in Jamie's immigrant suburban neighborhood and Nanci's apartment building in Spanish Harlem. But there are aspects of formerly trafficked persons' settlement that are distinctive and may not be apparent in their neighborhoods or workplaces. Perhaps the most striking difference between formerly trafficked persons and other new migrants is that they live on an economic precipice without a network of family or kin with whom to pool resources. They have no family with whom to share income, invest in small businesses, learn of job opportunities, or trade baby-sitting.[10] Without family or romantic partners to share household expenses and responsibilities, which the sociologist Nazli Kibria aptly describes as "patchworking," formerly trafficked persons like Jamie scramble to stay in place economically.[11] Jamie, for example, could not scrape together enough money to take driving lessons or to buy a used car. She continued to spend hours each day on buses rather than with her children, as she wanted. Her teenage son's part-time work busing dishes at a pizza parlor after school helped them to stay afloat but could not defray the costs of a car. Incomes can stretch only so far, and plans that would increase quality of life are suspended.

Even as formerly trafficked persons expand their social networks, they still may be locked out of upwardly mobile opportunities. "Trafficking survivors only know other poor people," observes a New York–based social worker. "Poverty is not about money, it's about access. It's about certain social networks. These survivors have been isolated. Lack of access defines their existence."[12] Their networks begin to take shape when they first leave their situation of forced labor: "In New York, shelters are not in high-income neighborhoods, and they may be in violent ones. We struggle just to keep them safe." This social worker worries about how her trafficking clients will ever move beyond poverty: "It is an American notion to do it yourself. Yet there are very few opportunities for trafficking survivors to pull themselves out of poverty. We lack the safety nets to do something long term for our clients. Instead we say, 'Okay, we gave you a visa, now go ahead and better yourself.' We help them in the shelter, but then we ask [them] to move it along." She reluctantly forecasts, "They will be poor in the United States. How are they going to get out of it?"

Structural Violence: Health and Well-being on the Edge of Poverty

When war, genocide, or other forms of extreme violence end, the debilitating effects of structural violence, what Green calls the "violence of everyday life," can linger.[13] Even though their period of abuse is over, formerly trafficked persons contend with a new set of constraints that grow out of their social location on the margins of life in the United States.[14] Their choices are shaped by the structural violence that they and their neighbors and work colleagues confront daily. "They may face the same problems our other clients have in the projects, where violence is a symptom of the poverty they experience," explains a social worker in New York. "So once they leave the interpersonal violence, they may be surrounded by community violence. They are basically entering the underclass." Since a sense of home and belonging can be intimately tied to personal safety, formerly trafficked persons' stressors can undermine their home-sense.[15]

Visualizing concentric circles that depict overlapping health issues that result from poverty and violence, a physician places the issues facing her trafficked patients alongside those of her other disenfranchised patients: "I see homeless people who are raped on the streets share in the same difficulties with those who suffered political violence or violence in trafficking." This physician points to her own limitations as an expert within the care system as contributing to her patients' suffering. "We find ourselves in roles where we are reinforcing inequitable policies. It's not the level of trauma that my trafficking patients have that makes them complicated patients; it's the care that I can give them. If we have a complicated patient, we cannot spend enough time." "I'm kind of part of the problem," laments a frustrated social worker in New York, "when we have to ask people to leave shelters after 135 days. We try to get people on their feet. But many are not ready yet. We are not really addressing the larger issues surrounding poverty."

Moreover, trafficking clients typically face a number of urgent issues simultaneously. "Everything has to happen at once," explains the social worker in New York. "It is even more complicated since there is an interaction between mental health and everything else." Simply having access to healthy foods can be a challenge. One of the physician's trafficking patients is homeless—there are fewer shelter options for men than for women—which compounds his health issues. "He is totally motivated to be healthy and would rather eat fruits and vegetables. But he can't afford anything beyond ninety-nine-cent burgers. He has severe gastrointestinal problems as a result." Another one of her patients feels that she was healthier when she was making steady earnings in sex work; now she struggles to pay her bills.

With interrelated needs, patients need integrated care, yet the "trauma-informed care" that these trafficking patients need is not available at the low-income clinics on which they rely. For a while, until the agency lost its funding, there was a collaboration in California between doctors and a social service agency in which they held regular case management meetings that were interdisciplinary and team-based. A patient needing mental health counseling, nutritional advice, and medical testing would find his or her case overseen by a team of health care professionals. In this integrated approach, clients hear the same messages from different caretakers. "I shouldn't be the only one talking with them about how to get healthy food," explains the doctor. She lauded the model, practiced by Planned Parenthood, among others, in which patients meet with various staff before seeing a physician. By the time the patients see a doctor, they have been given a number of opportunities to ask questions. "I would love a trafficking model that has an intake about diet and physical ability." Instead her patients receive care that is incomplete, inconsistent, and dispersed. "The integration of mental and physical health shouldn't be so hard. Any trauma survivor needs them integrated. This is true, for example, for veterans. We need one-stop shopping, a human rights clinic, where, from the front desk to all the other staff, everyone would be trained." Instead trafficking patients—like their low-income friends, neighbors, and work colleagues—often experience neglect in clinic settings.[16] One of the doctor's trafficking patients had been having chest pains and trouble breathing. She went to a free clinic, where, after her X-ray was read, a staff member yelled into the waiting room that this patient had tuberculosis and should leave the waiting room immediately. She was humiliated by this public disclosure of her private medical status. But the mistreatment did not end there; it turned out that she had been misdiagnosed. She did not have tuberculosis; she had end-stage lung cancer.

Clients' personalities also play a role in how they confront past abuses and present stressors. "People have different dispositions—some are positive, others negative. Some navigate the United States with greater ease than others," observes the New York–based social worker. "For example, not everyone can learn English at the same pace. We know what needs to be in place in order to survive and stabilize. . . . But everyone has a different timetable." A social worker in Texas finds that many clients insist they do not want counseling: "But issues related to trauma come up later. Six months later they will want help or they will show problems. One client was acting strange, fidgety, smiling a lot, acting uncomfortable in familiar settings. I asked her what was going on. She was having flashbacks." Those who decide to work with a therapist often explain that they cannot confide in family or friends. One of the first trafficking clients in the country to receive a ⲧ visa relates that she started to see a counselor because she could not talk to anyone about her time in forced labor, including her husband. She believes the therapy helped: "I just told my counselor last week that I don't need to go back anymore. I'm fine right now. Most of my problems are out."

Thickening Social Networks through Large Organizations

Once they time-out of social service provision, trafficking clients miss out on regular opportunities to build ties to other clients or to staff. Large direct-service organizations, ethnically based community organizations, and workers' rights organizations offer opportunities to expand social networks. Through involvement in these organizations, clients and former clients not only meet other individuals who were trafficked into forced labor but also meet other migrants and volunteers who can serve as mentors and cultural brokers. Large organizations in particular have resources that smaller agencies do not have the funds or staff to offer. A large social service organization in New York City, for example, has a connection with a hospital and a particular doctor who sees trafficking patients on a sliding scale. One of this organization's social workers worries, "Here in New York we have lots of resources to draw on. This just isn't possible in places like Oklahoma."

The large organization in Los Angeles with its own dedicated shelter for trafficking clients has a packed roster of trained volunteers and close relationships with domestic violence shelters, other social service organizations, pro-bono attorneys, and doctors in town. The shelter has been central to the growth of community that simply does not exist in other cities and towns in the United States. Current and former trafficking clients and staff, as well as a corps of dedicated volunteers, regard the shelter as a meeting space that brings together this extended trafficking community. As a result, trafficking clients in Los Angeles do not enter this vast city alone but as part of this organization's orbit.

The stress that accompanies concealing or rewriting one's past may be mitigated while one is with members of this community.[17] The past need not be hidden off-stage, but is an acknowledged part of one's identity. In stunning contrast to the isolated experiences of formerly trafficked persons in other cities and towns, these clients benefit in multiple ways, even long after they have timed out of assistance. Attending an event, and usually preparing food to share there, they become part of a larger community. This network spurs the active exchange of support, advice, and knowledge. It also is a fun group; no opportunity for a celebration passes by.

This spirit of celebration was on joyful display at a "green card party" for twelve former clients who had received their green cards over the previous year.[18] It was a big night that allowed for splurging on new outfits or a trip to the hair salon. Not only did guests arrive showing off their new dresses, or traditional outfits from their home countries, but they also proudly displayed home-cooked dishes. No one arrived empty handed. An African client who had taken the evening off from work, like many of the partygoers, exclaimed, "I was not going to miss this!" The green card holders, along with other former clients, had prepared thoughtful speeches and moving thank-you's to former and current staff. A slide show was deeply affecting as a visual archive of past events. Shout-outs, applause, and roars of laughter underscored that this was a close-knit community, one that had not been built overnight.

The sense of devotion to one another was perhaps the most overwhelming feeling of the night; these women and men had known and supported one another for years. Spoken and unspoken, explicit and implicit acts of generosity, compassion, and inclusiveness were evident in the way they greeted one another at the party. They had overcome generational, linguistic, ethnic, and class differences through years of friendship. Everyone had different tasks at the party: some were at the microphone, while others stayed in the background, helping with the food or with the children racing around. Those who did not speak English found themselves accompanied by those who could translate for them and introduce them to fellow guests. These intermediaries acted as a kind of social glue. Those with limited English found ways to communicate, particularly to express thanks. One older woman who did not speak any English, for example, brought cake to volunteers throughout the room.

Overwhelmed by the warmth and sense of community at this gathering, a pro-bono attorney with a client in Orange County mused, "I've thought about recommending that she come to Los Angeles. She is all alone there without family." Staff at one of the shelters in town had a similar reaction to the evening: "Oh, it's hard to not know anyone in the L.A. antitrafficking community and to not have any friends. This is an instant community." But not all trafficking clients open themselves to this supportive network. One former client explained that she generally avoided the celebrations that involve looking to the past: "I like to forget and move on; I don't like these memory things." Pro-bono attorneys who had worked with Korean clients surveyed the room and saw that none of their clients were there. After they received assistance, they did not stay in touch with the attorneys or any of the staff at shelters or social service organizations. "They want to put all this behind them." Another observer, a medical doctor, also worried about "who is not here."

Volunteers and Mentors

Just as it was remarkable to gather so many former and current clients in one room, it was also astonishing to see how many volunteers have pitched in over years of service with the Los Angeles antitrafficking community. A few years earlier while visiting the shelter, two volunteers were there giving an English-language workshop. I also have met volunteers at various conferences over the years which they attended to support trafficking clients who were speaking. On this occasion, the party's filled room revealed the ties of connection between the diverse members of this community. Directors and staff of the various shelters that have housed trafficking clients stood next to pro-bono attorneys who have taken on clients' legal cases. Clients introduced their language tutors and doctors to friends. By developing a robust roster of volunteers and collaborating with other organizations and shelters in town, this large antitrafficking organization brings together a range of people who otherwise might not meet. The volunteers have offered not only their professional expertise but also advice on applying to school and for financial aid, buying a house or a car, and navigating children's schools. They also have served as references for jobs. Through them, trafficking clients find friendship and mentorship with more established members of the community who live in different neighborhoods and have secure employment.[19] These volunteers open up new ways of living in Los Angeles to which most trafficking clients likely would not have access otherwise.

Connections to established members of the community, whether volunteer mentors or peers, offer incalculable social and economic benefits. Ager and Strang describe such volunteer mentors as "facilitators" in refugee communities and underscore the importance of the "bridging capital" that can develop from "intensive involvement with the local people."[20] More established refugees also mentor, assist, and guide newcomers in their community. These more established refugees and volunteers both can serve as cultural brokers or even as surrogate parents or grandparents.[21] The more people newcomers know and the more activities they are involved in, the more they may feel at home.[22]

Outside of this trafficking community in Los Angeles, most formerly trafficked persons throughout the country have to generate new connections on their own to feel part of a community.[23] Flo did just that. Her relationship with the family she initially met at church is a story of friendship, mutual trust, generosity, and the multiple benefits of close ties with long-established members of the community. Flo had first met this family when her abuser dropped her off at church every week with her children in Flo's care. "This family thought, 'Oh, this must be a single mother with all these children by herself.' They introduced themselves one day after church. They invited me to lunch. That's when I told them that these children were not my own and that I was working for this family. They were surprised. They said, 'You are so nice to these children, we did not know they were not your own. Everybody thinks they are yours!'"

Ever since Flo first met this family, they have been at the center of her building a life in the United States. They offered her a place to live, a job (providing child care for their children that fit into Flo's class schedule), helped with the tuition for her nursing assistant courses, and often drove her to class. Their friendship, support, and guidance obviously cannot be quantified. While tuition, inconvenient class schedules that compete with work, and transportation needs can pose insurmountable obstacles for many new migrants, Flo's friends made it possible for her to move beyond poverty. Flo constantly acknowledges their help: "I would not have managed work and school without them. They were always there helping me. They really pushed school and made it possible for me to go. They introduced me to people I didn't know. They also sent money to my parents. They made a lot of sacrifices for me!" Another woman, who had been in forced domestic labor in California, has likewise benefited from the regular counsel of a married couple who recommended her for jobs, helped her apply for school and financial aid, and hired her to work for them. These friends and mentors helped both these women imagine and make real new opportunities in the United States that would not have been possible in their home countries.

"Good Samaritans" can help formerly trafficked persons "get a foothold in the world," observes an attorney in New York City. One of her clients made money while she was in forced domestic labor by cleaning the apartments of neighbors. (Her abuser never knew of this arrangement.) By the time she exited her situation of forced labor, she had money saved. But this attorney cautions that these first friendships after forced labor can become overly significant in formerly trafficked persons' lives. Having few friends can be problematic if they make uncomfortable suggestions. The New York attorney explains, "These relationships can turn negative. It can get weird. Sometimes they ask my clients things like 'Join my church.'" A social worker in New York also cautions that "Some young women enter in relationships with their rescuers. They then feel obligated to these good Samaritans for having helped them and because they need a place to stay." Formerly trafficked persons may be reluctant to end these relationships even when they sour. Particularly in the early days of making the United States their home, they may perceive that they cannot afford to lose any emotional or financial support.

Conclusion

Surrogate kin networks that bring friendship and support can be vital lifelines for any new migrant to the United States.[24] Over time, Flo and her husband have built a large circle of friends who are from their home country in Africa. Flo regularly babysits for friends while her husband has helped friends move furniture or given them rides when their cars need repair. They also are part of a pool of thirty participants in a money exchange.

By putting money into the pool every month, they know they can withdraw money in a time of crisis. Crises can be particularly hard-hitting when endured far from family. Upon arriving at a Sunday afternoon potluck for domestic workers in the Washington, D.C., area, a woman from Sri Lanka started crying as soon as fellow Sri Lankans greeted her. Her brother had been killed earlier in the week in a bomb attack. Her grief was palpable. Her compatriots immediately shared in her despondency about being so far away from her family during this tragic time.

For formerly trafficked persons, being unable to visit one's home country and to see one's family complicates settling into the United States as a new home. The waiting period for green cards can exacerbate their sense of dislocation. When I first met Suzanne, she had been waiting for her green card to visit her parents in Indonesia, whom she had not seen in over seven years: "I want to go back. I can't wait to see my parents, especially now that I have children, and I really want them to meet the baby! I have been telling my mother to come here, but it is too expensive for her to travel here." Years later when she finally received her green card she was ecstatic to travel to Indonesia with her children. After returning to the United States, she was uncertain whether she would stay. While deciding where she would set up her household, she sent her children to live with her parents where they would "learn our culture and language." She enrolled them in school there for a semester. But more visits and her children's academically disappointing school experience helped her decide: "I have opportunities in the U.S. — and the kids do too — that are not in my hometown."

This chapter opened with Suzanne's daughter spinning around the room at the green card party, gleefully announcing her spelling bee win, a clear testimony to her intelligence and English fluency. Such literal wins, along with the more intangible gains of feeling at home in the United States, helped Suzanne decide to stay. After years of limbo and uncertainty, she finally has some clarity and calm as she looks ahead.

Chapter Five

Laboring after Forced Labor

Eliza works two jobs as a caregiver, one during the day, and the other at night. Two days a week she wakes up at 3 A.M. to take a shower and walk forty minutes to the bus stop to work the early shift. Sending money back to the Philippines, she explains, "I work for my kids." Living in sprawling Los Angeles, Eliza spends her time between jobs riding buses. "I'm never home. It takes me three hours to get to my job that begins at ten P.M. So I leave the first job at six P.M., and then get on a bus, then a train, then another bus. At least I can sleep while I travel."

//////

Formerly trafficked persons reenter the workplace changed. They have altered expectations of what constitutes good working conditions, relationships with employers, and colleagues. At work they can voice demands and set limits on others' demands on them. The income they earn offers relief from temporary housing arrangements, independence from the financial support of others, and is essential to staying in the United States. They often draw strength from their work and feel valued, despite low wages or few chances for mobility. Over the years Maria's various employers have remarked, for example, on her loving dedication to the children in her charge. She knows she is good at her job. She also knows she does not have the skill set to find work that offers more money, security, or status. With her modest wages, and the money she received from a civil award from her abusers, Maria has transformed her son's future in the Philippines by paying for college and building him a house. She has changed the lives of her extended family by purchasing a banana farm along with a truck to bring their produce to market. She has paid the college tuition for several nieces and nephews. She even has helped pay for part of the tuition costs for a total stranger — a young man whose number she dialed by accident while she was trying to reach her son. After talking a long time, and learning how much he longed to finish his studies, she offered to help. Maria mentions his success with the same pride she expresses about her son's.

Maria also has transformed her own life. Instead of working into her old age in fields, as her mother did, Maria has a job that does not demand constant physical labor. And, she has had the opportunity to travel with the families for whom she works, seeing places in the United States she would not visit otherwise. But the vagaries inherent in child care as a profession have meant that Maria has worked with at least six or seven different families since I first met her in 2004. She often works with employers for too short a period to earn raises, she does not receive any health care benefits, and she has no retirement fund. There is no doubt that her career in the United States allows her to earn significantly more than she could in the Philippines, and, as a result, she is able to remit funds that make her extended family's life more secure. Yet while her remittances make a considerable impact on her family in rural Philippines, Maria has lived with tremendous financial insecurity in the United States, often relying on her boyfriend to pay the household bills when she was between jobs. Without the civil award, and her boyfriend's steady salary, Maria could not have afforded to make large capital investments in the house and the farm or to send remittances. (She has since broken up with the boyfriend after she found out he had been cheating on her. She is now married to a man she knew for seven years before they started dating; he is a doorman in one of the apartment buildings in which she used to work.)

A recent typhoon devastated the banana farm that Maria has worked so hard to underwrite. While they wait for their trees to grow back and bear fruit again, her extended family does not earn the same kind of money working on nearby farms that Maria earns. The timing of the typhoon could not have been worse for Maria. Around the same time, a fire in her apartment destroyed her and her new husband's belongings. And, just two days before the typhoon she had been dismissed, once again, from her child care job. Yet despite her precarious economic state, she knew that she would land another job and soon would be able to send money to help her family get through the lean times ahead (she ended up being out of work for about two months). While they try to get on sure economic footing in the United States, formerly trafficked persons continue to be tied to families' needs and calamitous events in their home countries.

The anthropologists João Biehl and Peter Locke describe the strategies that resilient individuals like Maria use to maneuver around foreclosed "life chances."[1] Over time formerly trafficked persons pursue new work and school opportunities that were not open to them in their home countries. Out of coerced labor a new labor subjectivity emerges, which shapes their sense of self and future possibilities in the United States. Security and success are subjectively experienced and measured against a backdrop of what is and is not possible in their home countries. Flo moved from working as a child care provider in her home country in Africa to obtaining a nursing assistant degree and is now saving to go to college to become a nurse. Also a nursing assistant with plans to continue her studies, Eva affirms that such opportunities would not be open to her in Mexico — or to anyone in her social class.

Work as Zone of Empowerment

In Paul Willis's classic ethnography on British working-class "lads'" relationship to work, work impedes connections and cuts the young men off from the world, not the reverse: "Labour power is a kind of barrier to, not an inner connection with, the demands of the world. Satisfaction is not expected in work."[2] But for formerly trafficked persons, the workplace becomes a crucial site to feel valued and a part of something of their choosing. They also often first make friends and learn about the United States through the workplace. Since most work before they are reunited with their children (or have children in the United States), they do not have the opportunity to build such networks through their children's schools or activities. And, they are anxious to get to work. Aside from women who followed boyfriends, most formerly trafficked persons came to the United States to work. Work and its transformative possibilities had featured prominently in their imagining of opportunity in the United States even before they entered the country. After forced labor they finally have the chance to actualize what they had come to the United States to do.

While other low-wage workers may be surrounded by family, kin, and friends who over time have learned that the workplace usually does not offer economic mobility, formerly trafficked persons often have expansive expectations for what work can bring into their lives. They can be less concerned about the particular form of labor than the respect that work conveys — as well as the ability to finally keep all of their own earnings. The anthropologist Daniel Dohan found that new migrants from Mexico and Vietnam in a northern California barrio similarly are "eager to hold a job — any job" since they view working low-wage jobs as "part of a difficult but sensible path toward higher status."[3] Embarking on a strategy of "overwork," they work long hours at multiple jobs.[4]

Working also can be therapeutic. Social service providers throughout the United States report that while their trafficking clients often put off mental health therapy, they want to work right away. It gives structure to the day. Without work, many complain of having too much time on their hands and of replaying their past abuse in their minds. Soon after Maria had exited forced domestic labor, she spoke of wanting to work all the time: "Ever since my situation I wake up every morning at four-thirty or five. I think about my past situation. I wish I could go to work early in the morning." Julia designs her day so that she is almost always working, going to school, or studying: "It's hard juggling it all, but if I don't do something, I have to think about what happened to me. So if I am in school and busy, I don't think about it too much." Work is often central to a sense of control in one's life. Work helps trafficking clients, according to one California-based social worker, "move ahead." "They usually are fast planners. It keeps them from getting emotionally depressed. Even when there is a setback they say, 'Okay, this was a setback, so now what do we do, what's next?'"

Work thus can be a reprieve from racing thoughts and worries and also help stave off loneliness and homesickness. When I first met Flo, she was running from school to work, with little time for sleep. Before they were reunited, she missed her husband terribly (at the time his paperwork to enter the United States was stuck in a bureaucratic black hole). She was constantly worried about the economic hardships her family faced while her home country experienced political upheaval, violence, and economic decline. Working was a refuge from these worries. "I don't mind working so much. If I sit and read a book I start thinking about my husband's paperwork and about my family. It makes me so sad. I would rather keep busy." Her social worker recommended that she speak with a therapist, but Flo declined. "You don't go just once. You go over time. But I really don't have time to do this."

The workplace is also one of the first sites formerly trafficked persons negotiate on their own, without the guidance of social workers or attorneys. Reclaiming the experience of work can deliver a profound sense of accomplishment. After moving to New York City from the Midwest, where she had been trafficked into forced domestic labor, Gladys threw herself into school and work: "I wanted to forget everything. I wanted to do something in my life. I suffered a lot." Her abuser had regularly demeaned her. "He told me I would never learn English. He told me, 'You think you are going to learn in just a couple of years?' And I did and proved him wrong." Learning English, passing the GED exam, and working in a retail job where she feels respected by her employer—and has considerable responsibilities such as opening and closing the shop—are the steps that Gladys has taken to put new possibilities in place. She summons strength to take risks by recalling how she had crossed the border: "I did it myself. It took three days with no water. I tell myself now that I am not doing that for nothing."

When I met Gladys, her parents and younger siblings were about to join her in the United States (a benefit associated with her T visa), and she was buzzing with ideas about their future together. Not cowed by the responsibility of being the only member of her family with English skills and an income, she instead was determined to get her family "strong." As Gladys prepared for the arrival of her parents and younger siblings, she imagined what she could help make possible for all of them. Feeling obligated to her parents while also eager to have their approval (they had forbidden her to go out with an older man, which led her to run off and to her eventual trafficking into forced labor), she shouldered a great responsibility. "I want to change my parents' minds about me." She also wants her sisters and brothers "to think for themselves." "I want to change things for them and make sure that they have choices here that they don't have at home." She has a tentative business plan for the family. Since they sold fruit in Mexico, she hoped that they could sell it on the street in New York and one day open a restaurant. From mourning over the childhood taken from her, to moving to a city in which she knew only a former boyfriend, she now readied herself for the role of family breadwinner, translator, and cultural guide. "They will have me here to help them. I want to teach them. I want to show them everything."

Work as Zone of Disempowerment

As much as formerly trafficked persons try to open new opportunities for themselves and their families, they face many obstacles in the low-wage marketplace.[5] Work and school can be sites in which formerly trafficked persons are reminded of their limitations. While some, like Flo and Maria, deliberately overbook themselves, others cannot find full-time work. Some describe not being able to focus or follow through. One woman in the Washington, D.C., area had enrolled in a course to prepare for the GED but did not finish the program because she "couldn't stand sitting still and studying." She was overwhelmed by balancing school, work, and running to many appointments related to her case. A formerly trafficked person in New York has started and quit a GED review course a number of times. Pointing to the review books lying around her apartment, she was exasperated: "I don't know where to begin. I just can't do the math no matter how many practice tests I take." After years of feeling that their lives were out of control, some formerly trafficked persons quickly abandon challenges that unmoor rather than empower. Social workers consequently walk a fine line between building up their clients' confidence to pursue challenges and assessing what they realistically can manage and possibly master. Potentially constructive experiences can become dispiriting and destructive. The trafficking client in the Washington, D.C., area, for example, says, "[People] are always mad at me because I do things last minute and I'm unorganized."

Not earning enough money causes constant worry. Pushed and pulled by outstanding travel debts and family expectations to send money, formerly trafficked persons see their low-wage salaries quickly disappear. "They feel stuck because of debts," comments a social worker in Texas. "I just met a client who told me she cannot survive on her minimum-wage job. But she doesn't speak English well and cannot find a better-paying job."[6] With so many obstacles to landing jobs that pay well, the social worker in Texas reluctantly concedes, "it may be their kids who succeed, not them. These are truly resilient people who are working and studying. But most are just staying afloat. It's their kids who are doing well. They are in school, learning English. And with them here, the parents no longer worry about who is taking care of them back home."

Some formerly trafficked persons do not have the time, skill set, or personality to strategize about using work (and the school it may require) to get ahead. Those without a high school degree or strong English-language skills are not likely to move into better-paying jobs with greater status. A staff member at a domestic violence shelter in Los Angeles emphasizes that many of the formerly trafficked persons she meets know full well that their jobs in housekeeping or child care will not catapult them into a new social class. The shelter meanwhile gets calls from people who want to donate "interview clothes." Clear-eyed about the limitations of low-wage work, the staff member explains, "Our residents are going into housekeeping. They don't need these clothes. They need steady work."

Subjective Valuations of Good Jobs

Formerly trafficked persons' relationship to work not only is remade by their time in forced labor but is also shaped by their work experiences before forced labor. Whatever they achieve in the U.S. labor market may surpass what is possible and expected back home where work choices may depend on class, racial and ethnic categories, gender, and generation. They also may cut a new path away from their family's labor histories that often are tied to one geographic space and one labor sector. If they come from a place where everyone works in fields or factories, they may believe they have no other work choices open to them. They also may not have experience creating opportunities. Unfamiliar with choosing among or cultivating different options, some formerly trafficked persons seize the first opportunity that presents itself, assuming that no better option will become available.

Trafficking clients' assessments of what are good jobs and what are unacceptable vary widely. These subjective valuations keep social service providers on their toes. Jobs that have an easy commute, use existing skills or teach new ones, and involve working with one's coethnics — or not — may be highly valued. Jobs that offer the opportunity to speak one's native language may be chosen over those that offer higher pay. This was a priority during the resettlement process of Thai workers who were held in forced labor in a garment sweatshop in El Monte, California. Since this case was reported in 1995, five years before the TVPA was passed, their resettlement was uncharted territory. Every step was a learning experience for all involved. A community advocate described how at first it was "bewildering" to the social service community that some of those who went to work in garment manufacturing jobs with solid benefits were unhappy. They wanted to work with Thai contractors in their own language, even if that meant giving up higher wages and benefits. For many of these workers, explains the community advocate, "not working on a farm was an achievement."

Social workers' and community organizers' notions of a "good job" have been frequently challenged as they help formerly trafficked persons find work. One social worker in New York learned from years of working with domestic violence clients to not make any assumptions about what clients may value. One of these domestic violence clients, a woman from Bangladesh whose children were grown, wanted to find a new husband. "This was her main goal," recounts the social worker. "For her, it meant being independent. Otherwise her adult daughter would have taken care of her. In the United States women who seek to be taken care of often are seen as passive and looked down on. But she felt empowered and active since she had a plan." What one client may value and pursue, another may dismiss. A social worker in Texas explained that she had helped a few trafficking clients find jobs as seamstresses, but when she suggested this as a possible route to other clients, "they thought this kind of work was terrible." Esperanza identified respect as her main priority. After working in retail, where she had felt invisible, she sought out a position as a security guard. The pay was only marginally better than what she had been earning in her retail job. But the job commanded respect: "People respect what the guard says. This is the most important part of my job to me. To have respect."

Since her English-language skills were not strong, Jamie, from Malaysia, knew she had limited job choices and earning power. Her first job as a bagger in a supermarket paid minimum wage and offered only part-time hours. At the time, her two children were soon due to arrive from Malaysia. She assessed her options. She had years of experience working in child care both at home and in Saudi Arabia, so she decided to look for a job in child care. She made the calculation that she would not land a better-paying job. "I don't know how to use a computer, so this is a good job for me." She sees her child care jobs in the United States as a major improvement over her work in Saudi Arabia, where she had been "cooking and cleaning all the time. And not sleeping. All for very little money."

Social workers and other assistance providers try to guide clients to work options they may not have considered, while also respecting the clients' own understandings of success and priorities. An attorney with trafficking clients in New York City pointedly asks, "How do you measure success?"

She runs through various scenarios: "Some have small children, so they don't work, and thus their English is only marginally better. It takes a certain type of person to think ahead. Many clients have a third-grade education. They married at thirteen. But a better way to frame this is to ask, 'Are they on track with their peers in their community?'" Hoping to spark ideas, she asks clients what they would like to do if there were no "barriers," such as language. She also connects clients with job counselors at social service organizations, suggests a financial literacy workshop, and follows up to make sure they are getting paid their agreed-upon wage.

Similarly a social worker in New York tries to lead clients to "see themselves differently." She makes suggestions that her clients may not have contemplated: "When someone says 'I want to be a home health aide,' we can suggest being a nurse." She also pushes her colleagues and herself to ask themselves if they unintentionally expect different plans from different clients. "Do we treat white clients and black clients equally? Do we have higher expectations of some clients—from certain countries—over others?" Ultimately, however, it is up to the client to make decisions: "If you are working harder than the client, then there is something wrong." Overwhelmed, some clients "shoot themselves in the foot by 'oversleeping' and missing an interview. They undermine themselves before they even get a chance to fail. Self-sabotage like this can be an outgrowth of how some formerly trafficked persons see themselves and what they deserve. People at the margins of our society can't participate fully and manipulate their environment to their advantage. There can be a learned helplessness, a disempowerment. They don't expect things to work out. They may believe 'Whether I do this or not, everything sucks anyway.'"

Labor Histories and Making Demands

To explain workers' politicization, labor scholars examine past injustices suffered as well as workers' involvement in fighting them. In his book on Mayan workers in a furniture factory in Morganton, North Carolina, the historian Leon Fink connects these workers' past experience with "boss control" on coffee plantations to their present workplace protest.[7] During conversations with formerly trafficked persons, I asked about their past work experiences, mistreatment, and activism. Many told of intermittent income-earning opportunities in their home communities (often in back-breaking agricultural work), a culture of migration for work, and normalization of debt. Suzanne explains that if she had stayed on her family's farm in Indonesia, where they grow vegetables and rice, she too would be working in the fields like her parents. Many in her hometown opt instead for work overseas, arranged by recruiters. "They go to Singapore, Malaysia, Hong Kong, Saudi Arabia, Taiwan and work in child care and housekeeping." Even after Suzanne told her younger sister about her abusive experiences in forced domestic labor, her sister still made arrangements to migrate internationally for work: "I told her what happened to me. And she still wanted to go. I said 'Just stay home and help out our parents.' But she doesn't want to because there is more money if you work in Saudi Arabia. She can make about $800 a month, which is a lot of money in Indonesia."

Many formerly trafficked persons' previous work experiences unfolded within a logic of employer invincibility. Maria says there were few chances to make demands in her past jobs, but today she is assertive about what must be in place before she accepts a job, such as overtime pay and vacation days. Over the years she has increased her demands, learning from employers' unfair treatment. When she was working for a family as a child care provider soon after her exit from forced labor, her employers did not pay her while they visited their home country in Scandinavia for three weeks during the Christmas and New Year holidays. Maria was furious, asked for back pay, and quit when they refused. Referring to her time in forced labor, she is emphatic that she will never be taken advantage of again: "I make the decisions in my life now. No one else tells me what to do."

Maria was in a position to walk away from this paying job in part because at the time she was living with her boyfriend. She also knew she would not be out of work for long. She easily could tap into extensive social networks at the community-based organization where she was an active member. Since the majority of the organization's members work as child care providers, they operate as a kind of informal job bank for each other, passing on names of friends to prospective employers. Impressed by her loving care of the children in her charge, other families living in the same luxury apartment building where one of her past employers lived also offered Maria jobs. Once fair, respectful arrangements are made, Maria does not allow herself to take a break. When asked to work late or on the weekends, she always says yes. Her self-identity, formed as part of a rural peasantry, is modeled on that of her parents: "I will always work, just like my parents. They worked [as farmers] until they were old and sick."

Some need time to develop the courage and skills to make demands.

Often this evolves after they make decisions they regret. Carmen wishes that she could revisit a series of decisions that she made in the months immediately following her exit from forced labor. "I was young, only twenty when I left. I wanted to move on. I've changed. I was so naive." Like Maria, she is clear about her standards: "No one will ever tell me what to do again." Emphatic about calling out mistreatment, Carmen and Maria nonetheless have weathered instances of firings and reduced hours.[8] Carmen, for example, experienced a traumatic firing from hotel housekeeping following a fight with a coworker who had cornered her in a shower, enraged by Carmen's suggestions that she clean the toilet more thoroughly. Carmen's brief time as a supervisor had yielded several run-ins with coworkers, all of which were noted in her employee file. Management treated this incident as the last straw. Even though Carmen sought help from an attorney, she remained out of work for close to a year (she was living with a boyfriend at the time). Her short-lived experience taking on more responsibility at work convinced her to turn down other offers, at least for now. For example, when offered the opportunity to work at the hotel switchboard, she decided to stick to cleaning, explaining, "I'm good at what I do and I have more of a chance of getting raises since I have been there a while."

Politically active in her home country and beaten up by its corrupt government's henchmen, Flo has had extensive experience identifying injustice and speaking out. She had always negotiated the terms of her work contract with past employers back home. Once in the United States, she pointed out her abuser's exploitative practices on many occasions, even though her demands went unmet. And, after ICE informed her that they had lost her husband's file, Flo wrote to Eleanor Holmes Norton (a Delegate to the U.S. Congress representing the District of Columbia). Flo took action without her lawyers explaining: "I wrote her because she is my Representative. She helped get the file opened the next month." In short, Flo has a history of political consciousness and of action. Thus it was not surprising when her fellow classmates picked her to speak with the director of their nursing assistant training program. They had felt dismissed and demeaned by the faculty, one of whom would not answer their questions during class, directing them instead to look up the material in their textbook. Fed up, the students selected Flo as their spokeswoman to relay their frustration. "We were not learning what we wanted to learn," Flo explained to me while lifting her massive textbook. "We all want to be the best nursing assistants we can be. But many are not passing the tests because they are not prepared properly."

Esperanza too had experience making demands in her home country, Mexico, where she had tried to launch a woman's textile cooperative. "There was a group of women, and we went to talk to our governor about the factory where I was working. It was really hard to get in to see him. There were guards protecting him and they stopped me and said, 'No, you are not going to talk to him.'" She persuaded them to let her in to see him. He told her to write him a letter, which she did. "I wrote a letter asking him for the government to invest in the business." Unable to secure any local investment, however, Esperanza took it upon herself to earn the money. "All I had was the dream, just the project in my mind. I had never been out of the country before. I thought I would go to the United States and earn enough money to start the collective." Today Esperanza is an experienced, confident, and charismatic public speaker who presses for workers' rights: "I think there is a lot of work to do. When I go to conferences [on trafficking] I learn a lot and I see that there is so much ahead of us. I learn from other activists, especially the ones at the Coalition of Immokalee Workers. They really listen to workers. We have a lot in common. We all have a lot of work to do."

Speaking out has not always been easy. Esperanza recounts a story of attending her first conference, at which a Mexican official tried to chastise and belittle her. "There was this woman from the Mexican government who didn't know anything about trafficking and she wasn't willing to listen. There were two of us survivors at the conference. She just judged us, everything we said. She asked questions that blamed us. She asked us things like 'Why didn't you go to the Mexican Consulate? Why did you go to the U.S. government?' I told her 'Because I don't believe in Mexican law enforcement.' And I said that she did not understand trafficking and did not seem willing to learn about it. So how can they combat trafficking if they don't know anything and they are not willing to listen to learn?" Esperanza continues to speak in a variety of venues, including legislative events and trainings for law enforcement. "Survivors have to tell law enforcement how to look for trafficked people. I speak for those who can't."

Sources of Inspiration

Esperanza's experiences as an activist are rare, however. Few formerly trafficked persons attend antitrafficking conferences, legislative sessions, or other events such as those where Esperanza speaks. When it does happen, though, it can have a substantial effect on formerly trafficked individuals.

Even if the advice is the same as that of their social workers, friends, or colleagues, it can seem more within reach coming from somebody who has been through the same struggles. In these instances, the messenger can matter more than the message. In addition, having access to other formerly trafficked persons at confusing junctures can make a big impact, and can help them learn how to make demands in their current workplace and take steps toward more secure jobs. At a workers' rights training, the woman I sat next to sucked in her breath when she realized that one of the other participants, a farmworker, had been in forced labor like she had. "Oh he was held," she whispered.

Eva prepared to lead a workshop for Spanish-speaking trafficking clients at a social service organization in New York City. She wanted to inspire her fellow participants to draw on their own strength to hold on and to slowly take steps forward. "In the beginning you often think you are wasting your time. But if you take it step by step you can do it. It looks really hard and really big. But they will get help from the program—they don't have to do it alone. I hope to let them know that if they were strong enough to get out, they can work to move further. I don't want to talk about myself and say, 'I did this, I did that.' But we've been in the same situation. I was one of them before; I know how they think and what they say. If you work a little, you can pass through the situation. They may be younger or older than me. But it's just time that everyone needs to get through. It's effort and time. And dedication—to try to believe that they can do this." Moving forward also involves risk-taking. "They have a fear of making mistakes. It's hard to say yes again. Some want to do things almost perfectly. But of course, they may make the wrong decision!" Eva explains that she also will emphasize that she took advantage of any assistance offered, including training on how to be successful in interviews and write a résumé. "I'll tell them that since I knew I wanted to keep on studying, I told my social worker. The organization paid for my course and computer classes. I'll encourage them to ask for help and take risks."

Esperanza dispensed advice to a fellow trafficking client at their social service provider's office in California. "One day I was in the hallway and this client was talking with her case manager. She said she wanted to leave the shelter where she was staying, and that things were really, really hard, and that she couldn't see anything positive. When she went to the waiting area I asked her how she was. She told me, 'Not good.' I asked her, 'Why are you so mad?' I told her how lucky she was because she had support from the organization and was living in their shelter and did not have to worry about the house or food. Everything was free. I told her that I am living in my own apartment, but I have to worry about rent, about everything. She was angry with me and told me I was attacking her. But a week later I went to the shelter where she was living to see her. She jumped up and was crying. 'Thank you, thank you, I just received my work permit.' She explained that when I had seen her in the waiting room she was ready to leave the U.S. and go back to her country. She told me, 'I thought I was the only one who had this kind of situation.' I told her that all the clients that come here have similar problems."

Julia did not know any other formerly trafficked persons, but she maximized the networks that she made through her work as a housekeeper in a senior living community. "While I was working there I asked the nursing assistants how they got their licenses. They told me what classes to take and what to do to get a license." Julia set a course of study that involved a series of classes — English-language classes, classes to prepare for the GED, and courses to obtain a nursing assistant degree. She also took driving lessons. She explains how she developed her map for the future. "I do not know many people from my country. This is why I had to learn English. I had to rely on myself." She also knew that she had to begin to trust others again: "I only had this organization and the other lawyers who helped me. I didn't know too many other people. It is hard to make friends. It is hard to trust them. It's hard, but I try."

In spaces of exchange and energetic support, new and old migrants — some with a "trafficking" designation and some not — take inspiration and guidance where they can. Potlucks and other social events sponsored by community organizations can unintentionally turn into job fairs. At a regularly held Sunday potluck at a domestic workers' rights group in the Washington, D.C., area, much of the chatter over lunch — before the official workshop theme of the day was under way — was an information swap about how to apply for jobs, the best kind of employer, and how to negotiate for better wages and working conditions. Other places where new migrants gather also can become informal job resource centers. Calling them "lateral partners," anthropologist Katherine Newman notes the benefits of "maintaining a constellation of friends" who can "facilitate movement from one position to the next and shorten spells of unemployment."[9] In the Washington, D.C., area, for example, Indonesian women meet one another at prayer services at the embassy and find out about child care jobs that become available. Those renting out weekend shares in apartments and those seeking a share (women who are live-in domestic workers during the week) also make arrangements at the services. In New York City, Filipina domestic workers' rights organizations offer a wealth of information on jobs, workers' rights, and how to make demands to secure those rights. Composed of new migrants and long-established residents, these organizations offer a large, experienced, well-connected, and passionate membership.

With limited social networks, and little time or money to learn new skills or to pursue new degrees, a focus on the future and formerly trafficked persons' belief in themselves become sources of capital from which they can draw. But Gladys's plans to open her own perfume shop and for her parents to open a restaurant also require significant financial capital. Julia's and Eva's courses cost money and time away from earning it. Julia almost never slept while working and going to school. Both Eva and Flo are clear that they never could have gone back to school if they had not been living rent-free (Eva with her brother, and Flo with her friends). Without family or friends to help out, Carmen has indefinitely shelved her dreams of attending school to work in a salon. She has not come close to saving enough money on her hotel housekeeping paycheck to cover the nearly $10,000 tuition.

Since not everyone can lead a workshop like Eva or testify in legislative settings like Esperanza, social workers and shelter staff help create other kinds of opportunities for formerly trafficked persons to pitch in and feel a part of a community. "We all have different roles. We all need our niche," exhorts a staff member at a domestic violence shelter in Los Angeles. She offers the example of a quiet but powerfully steady and unflappable trafficking client: "Look at Carolyn. She may not speak publicly, but she gives so much support to other women." A leader who does not take the lead, Carolyn's offstage mentoring—and remarkable compassion and kindness—make a huge impact in the lives of her fellow formerly trafficked persons.

Decent Wages

There are a host of vulnerabilities built into the kinds of jobs that formerly trafficked persons find in the low-wage market, such as child care, elder care, housekeeping, construction, factory work, waitressing, nail salons, and retail. Finding jobs that pay a livable wage is a constant challenge both for the most recent T visa recipients, as well as for formerly trafficked persons who have been in the United States for years. These kinds of insecure jobs rarely offer medical or other benefits. Nor do they offer opportunities to move into better-paying positions with greater security or the possibility to learn new skills.[10] And it becomes all the more difficult to earn raises if one is frequently starting over with a new employer.

Social workers have counseled trafficking clients to not take jobs that do not pay well. But their clients often have few other options.[11] "We give them T visas and then say, 'Go ahead and make a life,'" an exasperated social worker in California explains. "Their desperation to work is so high, but their skill sets may not always be strong. So if a client looks for work in a restaurant, she very well may be offered a job below minimum wage. There are ten other people waiting to take that job. It's hard to tell a client to not take this job and to hold out for a higher wage, which may be difficult for her to find." She emphasizes what social workers report throughout the country: "My trafficking clients' number one goal is to work." But, "without the English language, education, and skills, they can only find low-wage exploitative work. Many will choose to go back to a situation of exploitation. What can we do? We tell them this is not legal and that these are sweatshops with exploitative conditions. They go to places like restaurants and get paid under the table. It's a dilemma. But they see their larger community of co-ethnics is in the same situation." For clients starting from scratch with no family or friends to help out, some pay is better than no pay. "If they do hold out for minimum wage and full benefits, they may be waiting a long time."

Quitting is a huge risk. Dora was out of work for a year after leaving a job in child care. Relieved to be working again, she now is "afraid to ask for more pay." "I can't afford to lose my job." Working for a family as a child care provider, she points out that asking for more pay requires "going up against your employer." "You are alone in the workplace. It's just you and your employer. And usually it's you up against a couple!" A worker-organizer in the domestic workers' rights community in New York City explains: "Even after the Domestic Workers' Bill of Rights passed, the culture did not change. Workers are still afraid to report their employers. It's a big challenge for workers. Not many cases have been brought forward." Experts also let down workers. Social workers tell of battling with other social service organizations that have referred their trafficking clients to jobs, such as elder care, with no minimum wage and no system for documenting how many hours employees work. If they quit, as did a trafficking client in California who was not being paid minimum wage in a garment factory, they may decide not pursue any legal actions. This particular client did not seek back wages because a member of her coethnic community owned the factory, and she did not want to be ostracized.

An attorney does not mince words about the kinds of jobs her trafficking clients in New York City are able to find: "They take jobs that are on a road to nowhere. Like as a nursing assistant. You break your back for minimum wage. Some even pay around $350 to shady middle companies. They could be making more money and getting benefits at Starbucks!" In some job markets where there is a high concentration of migrant labor, the competition for jobs increases the likelihood of low wages. The options available for one trafficking client's husband in California bears out the limits of the low-wage marketplace — even for migrants who have legal documentation. A U.S. citizen originally from Mexico, he has had little formal schooling. He worked in two different restaurants, essentially around the clock, cooking in one and washing dishes in the other. His wife explains, "He took any kind of job, like his dishwashing job. He is a hardworking guy. He does not care as long as it pays the rent." While she attended a GED class after work, he went to his second job. "He thinks the same way as me about education. He would like to study since he does not want to always live like he is right now. He does not want to work and work and work and never enjoy life. If we ever have enough money to pay the rent and buy food, he would like to go to school and get a better education. He likes to study. He does not only want to live this life."

Those working in the sex sector are among the highest earners. Since money often passes directly from the clients' hands into the workers' hands, women who had been in forced sexual labor knew how much money their abuser was making off of their labor. Some tell of being able to keep a portion of their earnings — just never enough to pay off the debt that their abusers kept on increasing. Since sex work requires a particular mix of moxie, resourcefulness, and independence, women's experiences working in the sex sector may serve them well as they take new risks and set about building secure lives in the United States. Outside of work in the sex sector, few labor options pay well and are accessible to most formerly trafficked persons with limited language and other skills.

Getting Ahead

One solution is to generate income from as many sources as possible. In New York City, an attorney has several trafficking clients who have rented apartments with a number of bedrooms that they, in turn, rent out. They offer cooked meals for a fee, and some also babysit for their tenants' children. Nanci and her husband became landlords out of necessity: by living with their two children in one bedroom and renting out the second bedroom, they were able to afford their relatively spacious New York City apartment. Liza, from Indonesia, also seized a similar entrepreneurial opportunity within her community of live-in domestic workers in the Washington, D.C., area. She rented out the beds in two bedrooms in a bright apartment to women during their time off on the weekends. She had been fed up with her poorly paid job as a live-in child care provider that paid $300 a week for workdays that started at 7 or 8 A.M. and did not end until 8 P.M. She had learned of the apartment through the network of women at the Indonesian Embassy. Explaining that few ever leave her rice-farming town, Liza sees herself as a risk-taker. She also describes her pursuit of more than one income stream as setting her apart from other women in her community: "They don't mind living-in because it is easier; they don't know this country or English very well." She made gradual moves to greater economic security, first by saving all the money she could while still living-in and not paying rent. With her strong English-language skills, she eventually transitioned out of child care and now works as a hostess at a restaurant.

Generating more income by earning additional degrees means having the time and money to do so. Elsa, the African woman living in the metropolitan D.C. area who had exited forced domestic labor with the help of the coethnic radio personality, made course work a priority while she worked the night shift at a 7-11. After living in the United States for a few years, she had decided that without a GED and other course work, the only jobs available to her would be those like her current minimum-wage job. "I knew I had to get a degree. Otherwise I would always be working in a job like this." Unlike Flo and Julia, who already were working in health care settings and asked work colleagues how to become a Certified Nursing Assistant, Elsa did not know anyone working in health care. Instead she researched the degree on a school computer where she attended classes for her GED. She had earned a high school diploma in her home country in Africa and found the GED prep course relatively easy. But without documentation proving her degree, she worked the night shift so that she could go to school during the day.

Suzanne did not come to the United States with the same high level of schooling as Flo and Elsa. In Indonesia, she explains, "people don't ever think about education. They don't want to get an education and get a nicer job. They just think about money. They just want to work and work, and don't care what kind of job they are working." She was determined to make up the gaps in her schooling. "When you live in this country you know that if you want to have a better life you have to have a better education." Her strong English-language skills made it possible for her to work in high-end retail, take courses in accounting, and learn how to use several computer programs. As an office manager, she learns new skills every day. Once her children are a bit older and more independent, she plans to get a college degree in night classes—while working full-time during the day.

Trying to move into better-paying jobs by learning new skills—either on the job or by enrolling in courses—can be particularly challenging for older formerly trafficked persons. Social workers have observed that trafficking clients who juggle work and school and homework generally are younger (in their twenties and thirties), like Flo, Eva, Elsa, Julia, and Suzanne. A social worker in New York describes, "Those in their early twenties are ready to go and try new things. Older clients are more cautious and lack confidence." Maria, in her early fifties, has never seen school as part of her future. With scant educational opportunities for girls of her generation in the Philippine countryside, education was not part of her past either. As vulnerable as she is in an unprotected occupation, however, she describes feeling strong and self-reliant. By changing her extended family's lives, she has tremendous social and economic status in the Philippines. The house she has built there, the investment in her son's education, and the expansion of the family's produce business guarantee Maria a secure place to live in the future. This is the retirement plan that she does not have in the United States. Thus the same jobs that allow formerly trafficked persons to just "get by" in the United States can put them in a position of considerable economic security and status in their home country.

At the same time that remittances build a secure future in formerly trafficked persons' home countries, they also are an immediate obstacle to anchoring their lives in their new country. They often feel compelled to show their family they are doing well and send hefty remittances as well as most of the money they may receive from civil awards. A staff member at a domestic violence shelter in Los Angeles explains, "Trafficking clients feel a lot of guilt for not being able to keep in touch [while they were in forced labor]. They know that their family's needs back home are so great. They want to help out as much as they can." A Chicago-based social worker similarly observes that "They are intent on remitting money. Even if they only make a small amount, it is incredible how committed they are to sending money back home." With these kinds of obligations hanging over them, formerly trafficked persons frequently dedicate themselves to making as much money as they can from as many sources possible — even if it means working under conditions only marginally better than when they were in situations of forced labor. One young woman, stretched thin paying for school and all her own household expenses, sends regular remittances home to her family, against the advice of her attorney and social worker. They want her first to secure her own financial stability in the United States. Explaining that her family blames her for ending up in a situation of forced labor, she is eager for their approval. Other families, in the dark about their loved ones' experiences in forced labor, remind them that they are lucky to be in the United States and have a financial obligation to them, who have been left behind. As far as these family members know, there is no before and after forced labor. They also may have little understanding of how hard it is to make significant earnings in the low-paying jobs available.

Remittances also can create unbalanced relationships, including cruel and perverse dynamics involving children. I have met several women from Mexico whose "husbands" (in consensual unions) demand remittances in return for letting the women speak to their children on the phone. In these cases, the men and their families have held the children for ransom. Using children as pawns is a tragic twist on the benefits available through the T visa. One woman explains, "My boyfriend is not cooperating with me and won't let me communicate with my children, but the money I send is welcome. So when I can't send it I feel badly. But another [trafficking] client told me that when she stopped sending money to her family they told her she could finally bring her daughter to the U.S. She told me if I do that he will say, 'Oh, take your children with you,' so this is why I am going to stop sending any money." This other trafficking client who had given this advice had been trying to reunite with her daughter who was in Mexico. Her husband's family had refused to gather the documents necessary for the child to move to the United States with her mother. But once this client stopped sending money, her husband's family said that she could take her daughter. "The child became a burden," surmised the client's social worker, when she "no longer was a source of money."

Conclusion

Living in low-wage United States, most formerly trafficked persons are, at best, in a financial holding pattern. A domestic violence shelter staff member in Los Angeles relays a typical story of staying one step ahead of poverty: "What happens to them is classic: they only can afford cars that will break down. Or old tires. So they are always having car troubles. But they cannot afford any emergencies." One of the residents' father had just died, and she needed $200 to contribute to the funeral service. "If you are just holding on the edge, this $200 pushes you over. If you are just making it, you go into debt."[12] A formerly trafficked person in Los Angeles tells of having to pay $1,300 to get her boyfriend's car out of impoundment. Yet another lives under a mountain of debt, over $8,000 for failure to make car payments after she and her husband divorced. She had no choice but to let the payments stack up: "It was either pay the rent or the car."

As formerly trafficked persons throughout the United States recount similar stories from poverty's edge, they explain that if they could endure their abuser they can handle a few bills. Their time in forced labor changed them; so too do their experiences afterward. The woman who paid for her boyfriend's car is fed up with working more than he. This is not the first time she has bailed him out of debt, and she is on the brink of kicking him out. "I don't want to take care of anyone anymore," she says. Although battered by bills, debt, and obligations to send remittances, they nonetheless focus on the future. "I have opportunities here others from my hometown will never have," Esperanza explains. "And I have my son with me now. Just the other day was his birthday, and he was crying. He told me he hated his birthday since it reminded him of all the birthdays we were apart."

Esperanza and other formerly trafficked persons are realistic about what they can accomplish. Emboldened, inspired, and spurred on by fellow activists, Esperanza joins in workers' rights campaigns, locally and nationally. At the same time she faces her own challenges paying bills and sending remittances to her family in Mexico. "Sometimes it is very difficult, but we have to continue living." Suzanne doubts she ever will own a house, but she has started a small college fund for her children. Maria waves away any concern about all that she lost in the fire. Instead she sets her sights on helping her family in the Philippines recoup after the typhoon. Finally reunited with her husband, and with her nursing assistance degree in hand, Flo still works the night shift at a nursing home. She kept their household afloat during the many months her husband was looking for steady work in construction after he first arrived. She sends most of her earnings to her family and puts some aside for college to study nursing. She knows her economic mobility will take time, and she is patient. Her income sustains so many in her family. This is success.

Closing Comments

The idea of a conclusion is strangely out of step with the ever-changing lives of the women and men I have introduced here. I have settled instead on offering some of the latest turns of events. I also include recent observations by assistance-givers in the antitrafficking community who are frustrated by the continued funding shortfall, limited opportunities for past and current clients, the politics of immigration reform, and the violence of deportation.

//////

A woman had a beautiful baby with an active member of the U.S. armed forces; he was deployed out of the country throughout her pregnancy. They now live in separate cities. He has yet to pay any child support. Hopeful that he will decide to live with her and their child as a family, she is reluctant to take him to court.

A woman's live-in boyfriend started berating her and threatening to hurt her. In the whirlwind of their fighting he revealed he was gay. She left him when he made good on his threats and began hitting her.

A formerly trafficked person tries to raise funds to start her own organization, but she faces stiff competition for antitrafficking funds, including with some of the organizations that have assisted her.

Another trafficking client regularly receives invitations to speak at various events hosted by women's rights and human rights organizations. They pay for her travel and lodging, but she usually does not receive any other compensation for her time and expertise. When she is on the road she not only does not earn her hourly wage, but also has to pay a babysitter to take care of her children.

Every few months I learn of formerly trafficked persons who, like other low-wage workers across the United States, have lost their jobs. But, unlike many laid-off, low-wage workers, formerly trafficked persons often financially support households outside of the United States. Their precarious position in the U.S. labor market reverberates throughout the globe.

Frustrated by years of working without a break or benefits, a woman who had lost many years to her abuser's control, asks when she will "find her place." "I would like to have more than part-time jobs the rest of my life. I don't have dental or medical. I want what you and others have. Everyone else goes on vacation, and returns from vacation. I've never had a vacation."

After years of touting nursing assistant programs as an accessible pathway to security for their trafficking clients, a number of social workers and lawyers have concluded that these programs are a "racket" that ultimately lets down their students. Charging fees to place them in the same kind of jobs that they had before, these programs have not transformed clients' lives as they had hoped.

A lawyer is concerned about trafficking clients who get involved in protests. Distrustful of the long reach of Immigration and Customs Enforcement (ice) and the black hole of the t visa process, she worries that speaking out at a rally or other events can jeopardize clients' legal cases.

The longer a veteran social worker has worked with trafficking clients, the more he is on guard with ice. Over the years he has seen ice send potential trafficking victims to detention instead of a shelter. "ice just doesn't get it. They want it right away. If they can secure some witnesses, they don't care what happens to the rest. Until ice gets a change in their cultural paradigm, we won't find more victims."

Those who are not trafficking victims continue to be framed as such. Bearing the brunt of "rescues," workers in the sex sector have become entangled in antitrafficking activities. "We were at a moment to secure more rights, and then trafficking sucked all the air out of the room," explains a leader in the sex workers' rights movement. Increased police surveillance, moralizing fundraising campaigns, and a feedback loop of ideologically tinged data cited by antiprostitution researchers and eager celebrities keep activists "dispersed and fearful." More than ten years into the fight against trafficking in the United States, people profiled as sex workers have been hounded to enter "rehabilitation" programs, jailed, and deported.

There have been some bright spots. After a decade of hysteria and beefed-up police surveillance at large sporting events, reason and research finally outpaced panics about sex trafficking at the London Olympics. Gross exaggerations and trumped-up claims about tens of thousands of visitors buying sex were quickly dispelled when British politicians and the media criticized police in London for their overly zealous crackdown on commercial sex establishments in the run-up to the games.[1] At the Freedom Network Conference in 2012 and 2013, panels composed only of survivors of trafficking into forced labor presented their experiences, insights, and proposals for combating trafficking and assisting clients. The ballrooms were packed. Previous annual conferences featured panels mainly of attorneys and social workers, but in these most recent forums the torch was passed from service providers to clients. The audience crammed themselves into any space available to hear these new experts. And President Obama's commitment in June 2012 to waive deportation of some undocumented minors was a first step toward long-awaited migrants' rights–centered immigration reform. As I write this, the nation and our elected officials are debating major federal immigration reform proposals.

Editors often caution writers not to include policy material that quickly will be out of date. After this book goes to print, much in the fight against trafficking into forced labor will still be in flux: there likely will be more policies incited by sex panics, more racial profiling, and more policies that target undocumented and other vulnerable individuals of our communities. There likely also will be more calls for evidence-based policy, and for survivor-led forums and agenda-setting. As these policies come and go, the particular contours of formerly trafficked persons' lives likely will not change considerably. Reading through this book I am most struck by the similarities between the daily challenges of formerly trafficked persons and those of other low-wage workers. Other than the chapter on living through the conditions of forced labor, the book largely tells a story of acute economic insecurity, no new or better opportunities on the horizon, and communities and networks of poor people. Anthropologists are not in the business of prognosticating, but it does not take a crystal ball to predict the role that these structural factors will continue to play in the lives of formerly trafficked persons. This is not to say that they and their neighbors, coworkers, and friends are not making it, proud of their accomplishments and still putting future plans into place. It is to say that those plans are all the more difficult to implement for individuals who generally do not have extensive networks — familial and otherwise — to help them through financial rough spots or to lend a hand with basic household demands such as child care. As new members of their communities who may go out of their way to avoid coethnics, they are disadvantaged. Their accomplishments are all the more impressive in the context of intentional distancing from these ready-made communities.

These accomplishments have been hard-won, sometimes even within the care regime intended to assist formerly trafficked persons. A service provider told me how mortified she was a few years ago when, during her trafficking client's meeting with lawyers to prepare a civil case against her abusers, the client was sent out to get lunch. With some formerly trafficked persons homeless, still separated from their children, or living with a romantic partner they want to leave, the uncomfortable realities of life after trafficking into forced labor do not produce easy or eye-catching storylines that raise funds or sell newspapers. Basic, pragmatic concerns are neglected while other dimensions of their "victimhood" are emphasized in the media or in programs offered by moralistic charities. Car ownership, for example, is of major concern to formerly trafficked persons. Throughout the United States (other than in New York City) they frequently mention the need for financial aid to attend driving school, as well as resources to purchase a car and insurance. But I know of no fundraising campaigns, media accounts, or government programs designed to help formerly trafficked persons drive. At the same time new antitrafficking organizations pop up, staffed with untrained personnel with no prior experience with issues related to trafficking into forced labor.

This proliferation of new NGOs working on trafficking (usually sex trafficking), the growing media attention on trafficking (usually sex trafficking), and frequent conferences about trafficking (usually sex trafficking) leave most formerly trafficked persons' everyday struggles unrecognized, misunderstood, and unaddressed. At once both visible and invisible, trafficked persons are known and unknown. Trafficking is a topic in some high school curriculums and around workplace water coolers, yet trafficked persons are not known as individuals but as a category of extreme suffering. Unlike refugees who have been resettled in the United States in large numbers, formerly trafficked persons are few in number.[2] Under four thousand individuals have been granted this legal status; as a result, most of us know formerly trafficked persons only through news stories and fundraising slogans that largely portray them as helpless victims. This storyline of unimaginable suffering—most often in the sex sector—inspires many concerned individuals to act, volunteer, and donate money. Organizations that work on trafficking receive inquiries almost daily from job seekers, students, and community members who want jobs or to volunteer. (I too regularly get emails from students around the country who are looking to work on the issue of trafficking—usually sex trafficking—or who want advice on graduate programs that focus on trafficking.) Often, however, organizations that "raise awareness" about trafficking do not offer direct services. Far removed from the everyday needs of formerly trafficked persons, they frequently leave the fundamental issue that confronts formerly trafficked persons—poverty—unaddressed.

As formerly trafficked persons figure out how to pay their bills, finance their schooling, take care of their kids, and wire money to their families back home, organizations send out fundraising mailers and email alerts about "what you can do to end modern-day slavery" and how to be "everyday heroes." I need not point out that the language of heroism to describe those fighting "modern-day slavery" on behalf of those *in* forced labor is an offensive misstep. The image of the hero loses credibility when broadly applied to those who write a check, run a race, or hold a benefit concert. The trainings of students and members of the public at an "abolitionist academy" to learn how to "set captives free" is particularly concerning.[3] This mass-market, all-hands-on-deck approach begs the question: In what other circumstances are ordinary citizens asked to assist those held by potentially violent individuals? Is this not territory for trained law enforcement? In the name of fighting trafficking, such inflamed rhetoric and dubious claim-making has sustained the dangerous idea that anyone can and should "rescue" those who have been trafficked into forced labor.

Formerly trafficked persons often are called upon to recount publicly their suffering. In one instance, a formerly trafficked woman was little more than a prop at a prayer meeting and fundraising event for a large Christian antitrafficking organization. Summoned by the organization's director to the stage, she told her story of horrific abuse in forced sexual labor. A group of men who self-identified as overconsumers of pornography were then called to lay their hands on this woman by forming a "healing circle" around her. Barely five feet tall, she became enveloped by these men; all that remained in view was their reaching hands placed on her body. The organization's director claimed from the podium what other antiprostitution activists also have contended: that consuming pornography can lead to buying sex, which can in turn lead to trafficking girls and women into forced sex. The same logic underpinned a fellow panelist's presentation at a conference I participated in at the University of Pennsylvania Law School.[4] Similarly, at a conference at Yale University, a fellow panelist showed police mug shots of women whose faces were badly bruised. Although she provided no evidence, this panelist claimed that the women were engaged in sexual labor and that the violence inflicted on their bodies was the inevitable consequence of selling sex. I saw students in both university audiences shake their heads and laugh a little. During the question-and-answer period some disputed these claims and asked for evidence.

Forums on trafficking that focus exclusively on sex ignore the risks of migrating for work and the abuses committed by recruiters and employers. The lack of respect toward low-wage workers, sex workers, and formerly trafficked persons — by denying their choices and abilities — undergirds these kinds of sideshows that take place in the name of helping them. The bizarre juxtaposition of real people's every day needs (such as steady wages, safe places to live, and decent cars to drive), with the lurid depiction of their lives by organizations and media outlets driven to sexualize their identities is a troubling facet of the "fight against modern day slavery."

Outlandish claims and circus-like performances now must compete with the powerful and persuasive voices of formerly trafficked persons as they take the podium themselves at conferences, inform the policy-making process, and participate in media stories that they help shape.[5] They not only talk about their time in forced labor, but also address what is needed in social service provision and local and national policy. New stories are being told by new speakers like Esperanza: "If somebody is willing to listen to you and you have something important to tell, you have to do so. For me, it was time. Life gave me a chance to prove myself. It was time." There also is a new national network of survivors that has held conference calls over the past year, has a private Facebook group, and recently met for a retreat. Having

Figure C.1. Alliance for a Safe and Diverse D.C. presents initial findings from its research on policing of prostitution to community members for insight, spring 2008. Photograph by PJ Starr.

Figure C.2. Members of the Survivor Caucus of CAST (Coalition to Abolish Slavery and Trafficking) with words that hold special meaning to them, 2011. Photograph by John Skalicky.

a network to tap into by phone and Facebook will not solve the inevitable struggles ahead.[6] But it is a start.

Formerly trafficked persons are making their own decisions off-stage as well. It is these stories I have tried to bring to light. When Maria tells employers she should be paid during their vacation in Europe, and Flo holds down two jobs to support her extended family back home, and Suzanne juggles driving her children to afterschool activities while working full time, they move forward, further away from their time in forced labor. They take charge of their lives. Suzanne assures, "I like my life in the United States. So do my kids. This is our home."

Appendix Ideas and Resources for Action

How to Get Involved

With so much interest in the fight against trafficking, I have a few suggestions on how individuals might get involved. The ideas for action are centered on making workplaces safer and more secure for all workers. There is no silver bullet, but a range of activities can build awareness and move us toward more just and sensible policies. They involve attending local, state, and national commissions and hearings on immigration issues and labor protections; and volunteering with workers' rights and migrants' rights organizations in local communities. They also include protesting efforts to criminalize vulnerable workers through ordinances that affect day laborers and sex workers and supporting efforts that regulate unregulated labor sectors, raise wages, and protect workers from retaliation if they call out abuse. These strategies address the wide range of structural factors that make worker exploitation possible. They aim to empower workers and offer greater security and respect to all those living in our communities.

Consider getting involved in the following issues:

1. Fight for immigration reform that includes a possibility for citizenship for all current and future workers, including workers in the informal economy who perform day labor.
2. Monitor worker recruitment programs that tie workers' visas to one employer or involve recruitment agencies that charge high fees.

Figure A.1. Kanthi Salgadu, a member of CAST Survivor Caucus, speaking at a Los Angeles City Hall press conference in July 2011 in support of the California Domestic Workers Bill of Rights, A.B. 889. After vetoing the bill in 2012, Governor Jerry Brown signed it into law in September 2013. Photograph courtesy of Vanessa Lanza and CAST.

3. Work to close the FSLA loophole that excludes some agricultural workers and workers who clean or provide child and elder care in private homes.

4. Support domestic workers' bill of rights introduced in state legislatures.

5. Fight to end immunity for diplomats who abuse workers in their employ.

6. Lobby for immigration relief for whistleblowers.

7. Fight to rescind state- and local-level law enforcement practices that target migrants in your community.

8. Assist and support migrants in their efforts to organize to protect their rights.

9. Assist and support sex workers in their efforts to organize to protect their rights.

10. Assist and support low-wage workers in their efforts to organize to protect their rights.

Consider unearthing information through research on the following:

1. The hiring practices and payment structure of your employer or of services you use (such as landscaping and housecleaning). How does your employer or the businesses you use guarantee employees' payment, safety, and benefits? Do they use recruiting agencies that extract fees from workers seeking visas and work?
2. The credentials of "experts" who are cited in the media.
3. Antitrafficking organizations' history, programs, and staff biographies. Before donating money, find out how they have evaluated the success of their past programs.
4. The supply chains of the companies that make the products you use daily.

Resources

Following is a list of organizations that conduct innovative rights-based organizing or provide legal and social services (including to trafficking clients). This list is by no means exhaustive but rather is intended to serve as a model of the kind of organizations that may be in your community.

Adhikaar
New York, N.Y.

Americans for Immigrant Justice
Miami, Fla., and Washington, D.C.

Asian Pacific Islander Legal Center
San Francisco, Calif.

Ayuda
Washington, D.C.

BAYSWAN (Bay Area Sex Worker Advocacy Network)
San Francisco, Calif.

Boat People, SOS
Falls Church, Va.

Break the Chain Campaign, Institute for Policy Studies
Washington, D.C.

CASA de Maryland
Hyattsville, Md.

CAST (Coalition to Abolish Slavery and Trafficking)
Los Angeles, Calif.

Causa
Salem, Oreg.

Center for Labor Research and Education, UCLA Labor Center
Los Angeles, Calif.

Chinese Staff and Workers' Association
New York, N.Y.

CHIRLA (Coalition for Humane Immigrant Rights of Los Angeles) Los Angeles, Calif.

Coalition of Immokalee Workers Immokalee, Fla.

Colorado Legal Services Denver, Colo.

Damayan New York, N.Y.

Domestic Workers United New York, N.Y.

Florida Immigrant Coalition Miami, Fla.

Heartland Alliance Chicago, Ill.

ICIRR (Illinois Coalition for Immigrant and Refugee Rights) Chicago, Ill.

Immigrant Women and Children Project, Association of the Bar of the City of New York Fund, Inc. City Bar Justice Center New York, N.Y.

Lideres Campesinas Oxnard, Calif.

Michigan Immigrant Rights Center Kalamazoo, Mich.

MIRA (Massachusetts Immigrant and Refugee Advocacy Coalition) Boston, Mass.

Mosaic Family Services Dallas, Tex.

New Orleans Workers' Center for Racial Justice New Orleans, La.

PCUN (Pineros y Campesinos Unidos del Noroeste) Woodburn, Ore.

Sex Workers Project, Urban Justice Center New York, N.Y.

Safe Horizon New York, N.Y.

Southern Migrant Legal Services Nashville, Tenn.

Tahirih Falls Church, Va.

Tenants and Workers United Alexandria, Va.

Tennessee Immigrant and Refugee Rights Coalition Nashville and Memphis, Tenn.

Worker Justice Center of New York Rochester and Albany, N.Y.

Workers Interfaith Network Memphis, Tenn.

National-level Organizations and Online Resources Related to Workers' Rights, Forced Labor and Trafficking, Immigration Reform, and Racial Profiling

ACLU Immigrants' Rights Project
http://www.aclu.org/immigrants-rights/
about-aclus-immigrants-rights-project

BAJI (Black Alliance for Just Immigration)
http://www.blackalliance.org/

BPPP (Best Practices Policy Project)
http://www.bestpracticespolicy.org/

Desiree Alliance
www.desireealliance.org

Detention Watch Network
http://www.detentionwatchnetwork.org/

Equal Justice Initiative
http://www.eji.org/

Families for Freedom
http://familiesforfreedom.org/

The Freedom Network
http://freedomnetworkusa.org

The Human Trafficking Pro Bono Legal Center
www.htprobono.org

The Interdisciplinary Project on Human Trafficking
American University
Washington College of Law
http://traffickingroundtable.org/

Jobs with Justice
http://www.jwj.org/

The Leadership Conference on Civil and Human Rights
http://www.civilrights.org/

MPI (Migration Policy Institute)
http://www.migrationpolicy.org/

National Council of La Raza
http://www.nclr.org/

National Domestic Workers Alliance
http://www.domesticworkers.org/

National Guestworker Alliance
www.guestworkeralliance.org

The National Immigration Forum
http://www.immigrationforum.org/

National Immigration Project of the National Lawyers Guild
www.nationalimmigrationproject.org

NDLON (National Day Laborer Organizing Network)
http://www.ndlon.org/en

NILC (National Immigration Law Center)
http://nilc.org/

NNIRR (National Network for Immigrant and Refugee Rights)
www.nnirr.org/

One America
http://weareoneamerica.org/

Presente.org
http://presente.org/

Rights Work
http://rightswork.org/

Rights Working Group
http://www.rightsworkinggroup.org/

Solidarity Center
www.solidaritycenter.org

Southern Poverty Law Center
http://www.splcenter.org/

Students Working for Equal Rights
http://www.swer.org/

SWOP-USA (Sex Workers Outreach
Project)
http://www.swopusa.org/about-us/

United WE DREAM Network
http://unitedwedream.org/

We Belong Together
http://www.webelongtogether.org/

Notes

Introduction

1. Eva is a rare exception: her brother was living in the United States at the time she was in forced labor. We will learn that having family who live in the United States is unusual for individuals who were trafficked into forced labor.

2. I use the term *undocumented* to describe individuals who do not have U.S. citizenship, a green card, or any kind of work visa. I also have chosen to use the terms *migrant* and *migration* rather than *immigrant* and *immigration* (other than when referring to U.S. government policy) to move away from the negative associations that anti-immigration activists and policymakers have attached to the language of immigration. The anthropologist Patricia Zavella (2011: xiii) eloquently sums up this language choice: "By using the neutral term 'migrant,' I contest the disparaging meanings of the terms 'illegal alien,' 'illegal,' or 'alien.'" She quotes Eithne Luibhéid on how the term *migrant*, which "makes no distinction among legal immigrants, refugees, asylum seekers, or undocumented immigrants," "do[es] not reflect empirically verifiable differences among migrants, who often shift from one category to another. Rather, the distinctions are imposed by the state and general public on migrants in order to delimit the rights that they will have or be denied, and the forms of surveillance, discipline, and normalization to which they will be subjected" (xiii, quoting Luibhéid 2005: xi).

3. Not only are those without documentation vulnerable to coercion. Many trafficking cases in the United States have involved migrants with visas. A report by a working group of workers' organizations documents the abuses these low-wage workers (such as in agriculture and landscaping) and higher-wage workers (such as in technology, nursing, and teaching) endure (International Labor Recruitment Working Group 2013). Entering the United States on a "dizzying array of visas," these international workers, "regardless of visa category, employment sector, race, gender, or national origin" face "disturbingly common patterns of recruitment abuse, including fraud, discrimination, severe economic coercion, retaliation, blacklisting and, in some cases, forced labor, indentured servitude, debt bondage and human trafficking" (2013: 5). One of the most notorious examples of abuse of recruited workers is the Signal Inter-

national trafficking case. Between 2004 and 2006, five hundred Indian guest workers came to the United States with H-2B visas to work as welders and pipefitters in Signal's shipyards in Pascagoula, Mississippi, and Orange, Texas. Hundreds of the guest workers paid Signal's recruiters as much as $25,000 for travel, visa, recruitment, and other trumped-up fees. They were told these jobs would lead to green cards and permanent U.S. residency. Once in the United States the men had to pay approximately $1,050 per month to live in fenced labor camps where as many as twenty-four men shared a single trailer. Visitors were not allowed to visit the camps, company employees regularly searched the men's trailers, and those who complained were threatened with deportation (Southern Poverty Law Center 2013a).

4. The passage of the Trafficking Victims Protection Act (TVPA) in 2000 kicked off antitrafficking efforts in the United States. Since 2000, Congress has reauthorized the TVPA three times: in 2003, 2005, and 2008. Three key aspects of federal government activity are the cornerstone of U.S. efforts to combat trafficking in persons: protection, prosecution, and prevention (commonly known as the "3 P's") (U.S. Department of Justice 2011).

The 2012 *Trafficking in Persons Report*, an annual report issued by the U.S. Department of State as required by the TVPA, includes the following vague update on the total number of T visas issued to date: "To protect against fraud, a cap of 5,000 approvals per year was placed on the special status designated for trafficking victims—the 'T' nonimmigrant status, also commonly referred to as 'T visas' and named after section 1101(a)(15)(T) of title 5 of the U.S Code. The feared rush on T visas, however, has not materialized. Although the number of applications for T nonimmigrant status is increasing every year, less than half of the yearly allotment of T visas for one year has been approved since 2002" (U.S. Department of State 2012a). The total number of T visas issues to date is not printed anywhere, but requires adding up figures from different U.S. government sources. Only by adding up the number of T visas approved from 2002–2011 in a chart in the Attorney General's Annual Report to Congress—2635—can one find the number of T visas issued through 2011 (U.S. Department of Justice 2011:56). With the most recent TIP Report listing 674 T nonimmigrant visas granted in 2012, this puts the total number of T visas issued at 3309 (U.S. Department of State 2013a). Throughout the book I only refer to approximately 3500 T visas issued thus far, not applications in the pipeline. See the following U.S. Department of State, Bureau of Consular Affairs instructions on how to apply for a T visa: http://travel.state.gov/visa/temp/types/types_5186.html#denial.

Another form of immigration relief is a U nonimmigrant visa, which protects victims of crime who are assisting law enforcement in the investigation or prosecution of that crime, including human trafficking and domestic violence (U.S. Department of Justice 2011: 6, 56). Many attorneys explain that they apply for U visas for their clients since they are easier to secure than the T visas. The number of U visas issued thus far reflect this: Fiscal Year 2011 was the second time the statutory cap was reached—10,000 (which does not include eligible family members) (U.S. Department of Justice 2011: 57).

5. The scope of trafficking to the United States has long been in dispute. The U.S.

Department of State's Office to Monitor and Combat Trafficking In Persons (TIP Office) has revised its own estimate downward from 50,000 in 2000 to 18,000 to 20,000 in 2003, and to 14,500 to 17,500 in 2004 (O'Neill Richard 2000; U.S. Department of State 2004b, 2005). The original 50,000 number was extrapolated from media sources by a CIA analyst and was never meant for publication. It has been widely discredited (Farrell et al. 2010; Markon 2007; U.S. Government Accountability Office 2007; Webber and Shirk 2005). Described by the anthropologist Carole Vance (2011b: 936) as a "numerical vampire that cannot be killed off," these figures have set U.S. government antitrafficking policy in motion. We have been left with a "hodgepodge of numbers," observes the sociologist Ronald Weitzer, "that hardly lend themselves to evidence-based policymaking" (Weitzer 2012: 1354). On the lack of reliable data also see Burnovskis and Surtees 2010, Chuang 2010a, Zhang 2009, and a 2005 volume of *International Migration* in which I have an article, Brennan 2005, along with Gozdziak and Collett 2005 and Laczko 2005. The scope of trafficking still remains uncertain; so much so that the U.S. government avoids citing any figure today.

6. The nonpartisan think tank Migration Policy Institute estimates that there are 11 million unauthorized immigrants currently living in the United States (Meissner et al. 2013).

7. This book focuses on international migrants to the United States, not U.S. citizens who according to the TVPA, also can qualify as "trafficked"—but, of course, do not need visas to remain in the United States or to qualify for social services. In its most recent documents, the U.S. Department of State has emphasized that "movement" across borders is not necessary to be trafficked: "Over the past 15 years, 'trafficking in persons' and 'human trafficking' have been used as umbrella terms for activities involved when someone obtains or holds a person in compelled service.

The United States Government considers trafficking in persons to include all of the criminal conduct involved in forced labor and sex trafficking, essentially the conduct involved in reducing or holding someone in compelled service. Under the Trafficking Victims Protection Act as amended (TVPA) and consistent with the United Nations Protocol to Prevent, Suppress, and Punish Trafficking in Persons, Especially Women and Children (Palermo Protocol), individuals may be trafficking victims whether they once consented, participated in a crime as a direct result of being trafficked, were transported into the exploitative situation, or were simply born into a state of servitude. Despite a term that seems to connote movement, at the heart of the phenomenon of trafficking in persons are the many forms of enslavement, not the activities involved in international transportation" (U.S. Department of State, "What is Modern Slavery?" 2013c).

8. The anthropologist and medical doctor Seth Holmes who crossed the U.S.-Mexico border with undocumented Triqui migrants from San Miguel, sees the dangers inherent in crossing as less risky than staying in Mexico without work, money, food, or education. Crossing the border "is not a choice to engage in a risk behavior but rather a process necessary to survive, to make life *less* risky" (Holmes 2013: 21).

9. In *What's Love Got to Do With It? Transnational Desires and Sex Tourism in the Dominican Republic*, I explore the pivotal role the imagination plays in shaping poten-

tial migrants' plans to move to a new country. Sex workers in Sosúa, the Dominican Republic, imagined a life of greater economic security for them and their children through marriage to German clients and migration to Germany (Brennan 2004).

10. A Congressional Research Service report notes the role of a range of actors involved in trafficking: "Human trafficking operations often require the participation of unscrupulous recruiters and employment agency managers and corrupt immigration and consular officials" (Siskin and Wyler 2013: 6). Trafficking also involves criminal entities that "vary in terms of their leadership structure, level of organizational sophistication, transnational reach, membership size, ethnic and social composition, dependence on human trafficking as a primary source of profit, use of violence, and level of cooperation with other organized crime groups" (2013: 5).

11. To be clear, if individuals pay someone to help them travel without authorization across international borders this is not trafficking, but smuggling. As the legal scholar Janie Chuang succinctly explains: "Smuggling stops at the border. Trafficking involves exploitation" (Chuang 2013). Also see the sociologist Sheldon Zhang's book on smuggling (2007).

12. The legal scholar Kathleen Kim (2009: 278) emphasizes labor and migration in her description of human trafficking as a "broader global phenomenon involving the migration of workers for the purpose of exploitation." While exploitation may include "previously recognized forms of unfree labor," "more characteristic of human trafficking are new forms of exploitation that utilize psychological means to coerce labor."

13. On vulnerable migrant workers, see Constable 2007; Cheng 2010; Gardner 2010; Mahdavi 2011; Simmons 2010.

14. The historian Stanley Engerman observes that the term *slavery* now is used "to indicate a wide range of always distasteful and abhorrent behaviors and is frequently applied to major abuses of human and labor rights today, whether permitted by law or not" (Engerman 2007: 2). While some use terms such as *wage slavery, debt slavery, child slavery, spousal slavery,* and *sex slavery* for "rhetorical purposes aimed at advocating the suppression of something evil," others suggest that "legally and otherwise, today's slavery is like slavery in the past" (2007: 12). Kevin Bales, cofounder of the organization Free the Slaves, estimates that 20–30 million people live in modern slavery. But, many of those he considers slaves are "enslaved for only a few months," whereas Engerman notes that "the most crucial and frequently utilized aspect of enslavement, and the most widely accepted, is the right to buy and sell individuals, its permanent or at least lifelong condition, and the inheritability of the status" (Engerman 14 on Bales 1999: 15; and Engerman 18).

In 2010 President Obama declared January "National Slavery and Human Trafficking Prevention Month." In his speech, he commemorated the Emancipation Proclamation and the Thirteenth Amendment, and called on the American people to fight against "modern slavery" (Administration of Barack Obama 2010). Most recently, the U.S. government has recast all trafficking as slavery, clearly signaled by a fact sheet issued by the Office to Monitor and Combat Trafficking in Persons, "What Is Modern Slavery?," and the language in the 2012 Trafficking in Persons (TIP) Report (U.S. Department of State 2013c and 2012a). At the launch of the 2012 TIP Report, U.S. Secretary of State Hillary Clinton explains why the U.S. government adopted the language of slavery: "when we started, we called it trafficking. And we were particularly concerned about what we saw as an explosion of the exploitation of people, most especially women, who were being quote, 'trafficked' into the sex trade and other forms of servitude. But I think labeling this for what it is, slavery, has brought it to another dimension.

I mean trafficking, when I first used to talk about it all those years ago, I think for a while people wondered whether I was talking about road safety—(laughter)—what we needed to do to improve transportation systems. But slavery, there is no mistaking what it is, what it means, what it does" (U.S. Department of State, Remarks by Secretary of State Hilary Rodham Clinton 2012c).

Chuang outlines a genealogy of this "embrace of 'slavery' as a conceptual frame" and questions whether and how a labor-rights perspective might be incorporated into already established criminal justice antitrafficking regimes at the national and international level. The U.S. government's practice of "crying slavery" entrenches the criminal justice paradigm, intensifies a focus on perpetrators—instead of the victims—and absolves states' role in enabling recruiters to subject migrant workers to coercive exploitation (Chuang 2013: 39). The sociologist Julia O'Connell Davidson (2012: 1) also writes about how the metaphor of slavery "mudd[ies] the moral water" and "depoliticizes what is actually a highly political issue."

15. Johnson 1999: 15–16. Historian Johnson recounts the slave William Johnson's remark on his owner: "If we didn't suit him he would put us in his pocket quick—meaning that he would sell us" (19).

16. Johnson 1999: 23.

17. Johnson (1999: 30) writes that slaveholders "had every advantage their considerable resources could support—state power, a monopoly on violence, and a well-developed propaganda network that stretched from church pulpits to planter-class periodicals like *DeBow's Review*—to enforce their ideologically situated account as a transparent truth."

18. While today's traffickers abuse and profit in secret, owning slaves was central to colonial slaveholders' public identity, and status-seeking whites wanted to be seen and thought of as slaveholders (Johnson 1999: 30). In fact slaveholders' letters to one another included "so much about the slave market," that one of Johnson's central arguments is that "slaveholders often represented themselves to one another by reference to their slaves" (13). For whites, the "slave market held dreams of transformative possibilities," "they imagined who they could be by thinking about whom they could buy" (78, 79). Far from being out of sight, Johnson writes, "the outward face of a slaveholding household—the driver of a carriage, the greeting given at the door, the supervision of the child, the service at the table—was often a slave" (89).

19. A worker with a temporary work visa who resigns or is fired is no longer authorized to remain in the United States and the employer is required to inform the Department of Homeland Security of the termination. Those who return to their home countries and complain risk being "blacklisted by recruiters who control access to future employment opportunities" (International Labor Recruitment Working Group

2013: 7). Diplomatic immunity also can be used "to shield flagrant abuse" (Vandenberg and Levy 2012: 78).

20. The International Labor Recruitment Working Group reports that "high debts combined with exploitative working conditions make workers extremely vulnerable to human trafficking" (2013: 7). Since international labor recruiters "often have a virtual monopoly over the job market in which they recruit," they can get away with charging workers high fees (2013: 7). Workers' debts accrue from paying recruitment, visa processing, and travel costs. Borrowing money at high interest rates, or using their homes as collateral, workers who arrive in the United States in debt "are much less likely to leave the job, whatever the conditions, without first earning enough to repay their debt" (2013: 7). In the case of Filipino teachers recruited to teach in Louisiana on H-1B visas, for example, Universal Placement International (UPI) charged them up to $15,000 to pay for visa applications and paperwork, and 10 percent of their monthly salaries for two years (amounting to 37 percent of teachers' salaries) (Dorning and Fanning 2012: 49). Two hundred Filipino teachers with the Louisiana Federation of Teachers sued UPI and the Louisiana Workforce Commission ordered UPI to pay about $1.8 million in illegally charged placement fees (Dorning and Fanning 2012). Workers also may be charged "breakage fees" as penalties if they do not complete the full contract period as has been the case with many nurses whose contracts stipulate fees ranging from $8,000 to $50,000 (International Labor Recruitment Working Group 2013: 7 n. 6).

21. Southern Poverty Law Center 2013b: 11. After being charged monthly interest rates of between 5 and 10 percent on the money they borrowed to pay recruitment fees and other pre-employment costs, "many workers left their jobs in even greater debt as interest on their loans continued to accrue" (2013b: 11). The threat of losing ownership of one's property back home also keeps workers from registering complaints. The Southern Poverty Law Center has represented Guatemalan clients who had left their property deeds as collateral with an agent in Guatemala, a "tactic" that is so "enormously effective at suppressing complaints about pay, working conditions, or housing" that it is "almost inconceivable that a worker would complain in any substantial way while a company agent holds the deed to the home where his wife and children reside" (2013b: 11).

22. Gordon 2005: 15.

23. Such labor abuses violate the International Labour Organization's definition of decent work as "work that is productive and delivers a fair income, security in the workplace and social protection for families, better prospects for personal development and social integration, freedom for people to express their concerns, organize and participate in the decisions that affect their lives and equality of opportunity and treatment for all women and men" (Siddiqui 2005).

24. Forms of wage theft include minimum wage violations sometimes "disguised by complicated piece-rate schemes, underreporting of hours, failure to pay overtime," and unlawful deductions (Southern Poverty Law Center 2013b: 18).

25. Formerly trafficked persons who have participated in empowerment workshops and those who are leaders in antitrafficking activities, including testifying in local, state, and national legislative settings or speaking publically at conferences and other

venues, use the terms *victim* or *survivor*. Similarly in my research with sex workers in the Dominican Republic, leaders in the activist community of sex workers adopted a sex workers' rights organization's use of the term *trabajadora sexuale* (sex worker), while other sex workers called themselves *prostitutas* (prostitutes) (Brennan 2004).

26. To qualify for the nonimmigrant status T-1 visa, "applicants must be in the United States, American Samoa, the Commonwealth of the Northern Mariana Islands, or at a U.S. port of entry due to trafficking" (U.S. Department of State 2011c).

"Certification" from the Department of Health and Human Services qualifies them "access to federally funded benefits and services to the same extent as refugees" (U.S. Department of Health and Human Services, Office of Refugee and Resettlement 2011a: 8). Certification cannot be obtained until a T-visa application is filed, or the trafficked person is granted "Continued Presence" (CP). Law enforcement sponsors CP, which allows individuals to remain in the United States during the course of an investigation or prosecution as well as obtain an employment authorization document (U.S. Department of Health and Human Services, Office of Refugee and Resettlement 2011a: 8). The U.S. Department of Health and Human Services (HHS) is the federal agency authorized to certify foreign adult victims of human trafficking for eligibility for federal and state benefits and services. Certification and eligibility letters are issued by HHS Office of Refugee Resettlement. U.S. citizens and Lawful Permanent Residents (LPR) do not need to be certified or receive a letter of eligibility to receive similar benefits.

Trafficking victims with a certification or eligibility letter can apply for the following: Temporary Assistance for Needy Families (only for families with children under eighteen); Supplemental Security Income (only for people over sixty-five or with severe disability); Refugee Cash Assistance; Supplemental Nutrition Assistance Program, formerly food stamps; Women, Infants and Children nutrition program; Medicaid; Children's Health Insurance Program; Refugee Medical Assistance; medical screening; One-Stop Career Center System; Job Corps (only available to those age sixteen to twenty-four); Matching grants (administered through private agencies as an alternative to public assistance to "enable clients to become self-sufficient within four to six months from the date of certification or eligibility"). T visa recipients can receive employment authorization, can apply to adjust status to Lawful Permanent Resident, and can petition to bring over family members as T visa derivatives (U.S. Department of Health and Human Services, Administration for Children and Families, The Campaign to Rescue and Restore Victims of Human Trafficking 2012).

27. Section 103(8) of the TVPA defines "severe forms of trafficking in persons" to mean:

(A) sex trafficking in which a commercial sex act is induced by force, fraud, or coercion, or in which the person induced to perform such act has not attained 18 years of age; or (B) the recruitment, harboring, transportation, provision or obtaining of a person for labor or services, through the use of force, fraud, or coercion for the purpose of subjection to involuntary servitude, peonage, debt bondage, or slavery (Section 103(8) U.S. Congress 2000; Sisken and Wyler 2013: 2).

28. Chacón 2010: 1635. The U.S. government is not willing to provide protections

to the large numbers of undocumented workers who endure a range of abusive labor practices. The legal scholar Jennifer Chacón (2006: 2980) explains that, by limiting the TVPA's assistance to a "narrowly defined subset of trafficking victims," Congress "deliberately chose to exclude a broad range of labor exploitation from the reach of the TVPA."

29. At a panel at a Freedom Network (a coalition of organizations that provide services to trafficked persons) conference in Washington, D.C., in 2010, an attorney from the U.S. Department of Justice admitted that an individual whose abuse is not deemed severe enough to qualify as a "trafficking victim" risks deportation.

30. A report on workplace abuse of documented and undocumented low-wage workers found widespread minimum wage and overtime violations and threats of employer retaliation for workers attempting to unionize (Bernhardt et al. 2009: 2–4).

31. In a study on exploitation of undocumented workers in San Diego, the sociologist Sheldon Zhang considers why so few trafficked persons have been found to date. He points to the "front and center" attention "sex trafficking" has received, noting in particular that the reauthorization of the TVPA authorized block grants to states and local enforcement "to investigate and prosecute buyers of commercial sex, educate individuals charged with or attempting to purchase commercial sex, and collaborate with local NGOs to provide services to victims" (Zhang 2012: 29).

32. The sociologist Wendy Chapkis explains that distinguishing trafficking victims defined as "vulnerable women and children forced from the safety of their home or homelands into gross sexual exploitation" from "economic migrants who are understood to be men and who have willfully violated national borders" was "useful in rallying public support for victims of migrant abuse in a climate generally hostile to undocumented workers in America's factories and fields" (Chapkis 2005: 52, 54).

33. Srikantiah asserts that an iconic victim is a passive one. She locates years of ignoring forced labor in labor sectors other than the sex sector to the early days of the TVPA's passage and lawmakers' descriptions of trafficking victims as "meek, passive objects of sexual exploitation" (2007: 160). This political rhetoric, subsequently, "has seeped into prosecutors' and investigators' identification of actual trafficking victims with tragic consequences for victims" who "do not describe their stories consistently with it" (2007: 160). This process of victim identification also leaves enormous discretion up to individuals to make determinations based on their "own conception of who is a deserving victim" leading to "non-uniform results" (Srikantiah 2007: 160).

34. The Obama administration ushered in more of a focus on trafficking cases not involving sex, as well as an evaluation of the U.S. government's own antitrafficking activities in the State Department's annual TIP Report, which the Bush administration glaringly had left out of this yearly report card. Nonetheless, Chuang (2013: 17) cautions that while the Obama administration appears to have embraced a labor perspective, "closer examination" reveals "a set of moves, that, intentionally or not, risk limiting the reach and impact of a labor approach to human trafficking." Also see Davis, Kingsbury, and Merry (2012) on "global governance indicators" such as the TIP Report.

35. The sociologist Peter Kwong's research in Chinese communities in the United

States (particularly with individuals from Fruzhou) reveals widespread acceptance of a range of labor abuses that occur within a highly orchestrated, profitable, violent, and underground system of indentured labor. These are workers, he emphasizes, that do not want assistance, but rather agree to work for below-minimum wages to pay off their debts. As one worker, Zhen, explained: "I hate to owe people money. These debts are hurting me like nails stuck into my body" (Kwong 1997: 38).

36. Attorney Kathleen Kim explains that she first met trafficking clients while giving know your rights presentations. At a community-organizing meeting for domestic workers a woman raised her hand and in Spanish said, "I think what you are talking about happened to me" (Kim, Song, and Panchalam 2009: 36).

37. I have been inspired by terrific examples of activist or engaged research, such as Adams 2013; Biehl 2005; Bourgois 2009; Checker 2005; Farmer 1992, 2003; Garcia 2010; Gill 2004; Hale 2001, 2008; Holmes 2013; Lassiter 2005; Lyon-Callo 2008; Pratt 2012; Rappaport 2005; Stuesse 2010b; and Theidon 2013.

38. The cases of teachers and nurses are examples of well-educated, highly skilled workers who were trafficked (Dorning and Fanning 2012).

39. Constable 2007; Pratt 2012; Parreñas 2001.

40. Rothenberg 1998; Chavez 1992; Bowe 2007.

41. The Victims of Trafficking and Violence Protection Act of 2000 states that the T visa "allows victims of human trafficking to remain in the U.S. to assist in investigations or prosecutions of human trafficking violators." The visa allows trafficked persons to remain for up to four years, during which time they can apply for a change of status (from nonimmigrant to immigrant) in order to receive a green card. (U.S. Department of State 2011c).

42. Children, spouses, siblings, and parents of trafficked persons are eligible to apply as derivatives of the primary T visa applicant (T-2: spouses, T-3: children, T-4: parents, T-5: unmarried siblings under the age of eighteen). With this visa they are granted permission to stay in the United States for up to four years and can apply for a green card (U.S. Department of State 2011b).

43. States also have a primary role in the return of refugees and migrants to their home countries. Oxfeld and Long (2004: 14) observe, "State policies are critical to determining whether a return is only imagined or becomes physically possible and under what conditions. States construct the legal, social, and political parameters and interpretations of return."

44. To be eligible for social services and legal assistance while waiting for a T visa, individuals must receive "certification" and "be willing to assist in every reasonable way in the investigation and prosecution of severe forms of trafficking or be unable to cooperate due to physical or psychological trauma" (U.S. Department of Health and Human Services, Administration for Children and Families 2011: 1). In an amendment to the TVPA in 2008, individuals could be exempt from complying with investigators' requests: "Persons unable to cooperate with law enforcement requests due to physical or psychological trauma are exempted from the requirement of compliance with those requests and remain eligible for T nonimmigrant status." Anyone who was under eigh-

teen at the time of trafficking is also exempt from the cooperation requirement (U.S. Department of Homeland Security, Citizenship and Immigration Services 2010). Also see U.S. Congress 2008.

45. The wait for green cards today is considerably shorter.

46. Children twenty-one years old and under are eligible under the TVPA to live in the United States with a trafficked parent. A series of bureaucratic mishaps in the Philippines prevented Maria's son from moving to the United States to live with her while he was still under twenty-one.

47. Das and Kleinman 2001: 4. With an array of memoirs and scholarship on life after atrocities, a place to begin reading is with Primo Levi's (1988) *The Drowned and the Saved*, a masterful autobiography that looks at life after surviving Auschwitz.

48. Das 2000: 208.

49. There is excellent scholarship on exploitative labor practices in a number of industries where migrants labor, for example, on factories (Louie 2001; Rosen 2002; Bonacich and Appelbaum 2000; Ross 1997, 2004); domestic work (Hondagneu-Sotelo 2001; Chang 2000), agriculture (Griffith and Kissam 1995; Rothenberg 1998), poultry processing (Striffler 2005; Fink 2003; Stull and Broadway 2004), commercial cleaning (Zlolniski 2006; Pellow and Park 2002), and day labor (Gordon 2005; The Homeless Persons Representation Project and CASA de Maryland 2004; Valenzuela et al. 2006).

50. For research on the difficulty of climbing out of poverty, see Dohan 2003; Newman 1999; Ehrenreich 2001; Shipler 2004; Wilson 1997; and Katz 1989.

51. Otherwise the U.S. government would pay for their return to their home country. In some instances, consulates have helped underwrite repatriation costs.

52. Oxfeld and Long 2004: 7. Imagining returning home "compensates for the chaos of the refugee experience," an image that grows "seemingly inversely proportional to the disintegration of the refugee's immediate social surroundings" (Janzen 2004: 32).

53. Returning refugees and migrants take leaps as well, hoping their fields will be able to produce crops, their homes will be intact and not occupied by interlopers, and they can survive their former enemies. They weigh the risks and fears of return against the uncertainty and deprivations of remaining displaced (Oxfeld and Long 2004: 7).

54. McSpadden (2004: 36) summarizes the difference between refugee and immigrant: "Being a refugee ('I am forced to be here') — as distinct from being an immigrant ('I choose to be here')."

55. Malkki's (1995) research with Hutu refugees in Tanzania reminds us, however, that not all refugees want to go home again. While those in refugee camps conceptionalized "home" as Burundi, the country they had fled, others who lived in town saw Tanzania as their new "home." Constable (1999: 208) too found "ambivalence" about permanent return among Filipina domestic workers living in Hong Kong: "At times for some, life abroad is overwhelmingly experienced with sorrow and feelings of loss and deprivation. For others, however . . . their native Philippines may be the space where their affections center, yet also Hong Kong is experienced as a source of satisfaction, as a place where they participate in meaningful activities: It can serve as a refuge of sorts."

56. Nostalgia for lost ways of life through forced displacement is a common reaction

of refugees, asylees, and migrants. For example, Palestinian refugees told Ilana Feldman (2006: 19) about their lost "sweet life" and described their village as a "paradise" where "grapes were like gold."

57. Stefansson (2004: 183) found that dual citizenship makes the possibility of refugee repatriation to Bosnia-Herzegovina more attractive. Being able to return to their host countries through newly acquired citizenship is a strategy "to retain as many economic channels, social networks and future opportunities [as possible]."

58. Biehl and Locke 2010: 319.

59. Hammond 2004: 10. I also like Lucia Ann McSpadden's (2004: 47) description of home as "a social space that provides safety, dignity, valued resources, power and belonging."

60. Collins 1991. Collins writes about the "false dichotomy between scholarship and activism, between thinking and doing" (15).

61. Through multisite ethnography, anthropologists can have a "sense of doing more than just ethnography" but actually taking an "ethnographer-activist" position within their field sites (Marcus 1995: 113–14).

62. Hannerz 2003.

63. The psychiatrist Judith Herman (1997: 34, 8) describes how trauma can produce significant and lasting alterations in "physiological arousal, emotional cognition, and memory." London-based researchers on trafficked women's mental health found that they were "likely to be suffering pain and distress, especially memory problems," which may hinder their ability to participate in an investigation or "make considered decisions" until some time has passed (Zimmerman et al. 2008: 58). While traumatic experiences can affect memory, throughout the book I write about trauma from a critical perspective of the overapplication of post-traumatic stress disorder (PTSD) (Summerfield 2001; Gozdziak 2005; Kleinman 1995; Young 1995).

64. In contrast to David Stoll's (1999) book that served to challenge the "factual" basis of human rights activist Rigoberta Menchú's account of living through violence in Guatemala (Burgos-Debray 1984), this project does not seek to catch anyone in an inconsistent or contradictory story. Rather any inconsistencies and contradictions may reflect effects of emotional and physical abuse. See historian Greg Grandin's article and book on Menchú's place in Guatemalan history (2010 and 2011).

65. Jeremy MacClancy (2002: 6) captures the unplanned benefits of participant observation when he describes the "serendipity," "chance events," and "accidental encounters" that can unfold.

66. Talking or writing about one's life and experiences can be restorative. Caterina, one of the patients that the anthropologist João Biehl (2007: 416) met in a facility in Brazil where poor families "abandon" infirm family members, writes and writes in what she calls her "dictionary." In so doing, she makes "herself heard in a place where silence is the rule."

67. Kleinman and Kleinman 1997: 3. Describing "writing with care," the anthropologist Angela Garcia points to the responsibilities inherent in writing about suffering that go beyond simply changing names and identifying details, but also involve captur-

ing the "humanity, vulnerability, and hopefulness of lives" that she "came to know and care about" (Garcia 2010: 34, 35). Kimberly Theidon (2013: 12–13) also proceeds with care as she conducts research "amid terror's talk" in post–civil war Peru. When "we ask people to speak about life and death, about pain and how it etches the heart," the "possibility of distance and impartiality must be surrendered."

68. See Hochshild (2005).

69. See Ross's (2003: 48) discussion on how "words are symbols" "that pull one toward culture's centre." She explains, "Testifying threatens culture's limits. Testimony and its performance are paradoxical, compounded by the strictures of language and memory in the face of suffering."

70. Ross 2003: 1, 5.

71. Theidon 2007: 104. In contexts where people "have lived through violent times" and "fiercely guard stories, secrets, and silences," Theidon asks "Where to begin? Where to tease out the multiple registers of truth" (Theidon 2013: 8).

72. Brennan 2014. Writing about forms of proof that asylum seekers in France must present, Fassin and D' Halluin (2005: 606, 597–98) note the "overindividualized corporeality" in the asylum process as asylum seekers "are expected to unveil themselves, to recount their histories, and to exhibit their wounds." Whether the subject is the "poor who have to exhibit the stigmas of indigence to benefit from public welfare or private charity" or the role of medical certificates to attest to torture as part of applications for asylum in France, "the body has become the place that displays the evidence of truth" (598).

73. Olujic 1995: 196.

74. Power 2003.

Chapter One

1. A 2006 survey of 286 domestic workers in Maryland reported that 75 percent of the respondents did not receive overtime pay and half earned below the minimum wage (Keyes et al. 2007: 1). Wage theft is also rampant in day labor. A survey conducted in 2004 of 476 day laborers in the Metro D.C. area revealed that 58 percent had not been paid at least once, and 55 percent had been underpaid (Keyes et al. 2007: 1). Another study of 140 day laborers found that 62 percent had not been paid at one point (Washington Lawyers' Committee 2008: 7). Human Rights Watch (Meng 2012: 3) found that nearly all of the 52 women farmworkers they interviewed said they had experienced sexual violence or harassment or knew others who had. Those who report abuse to management risk retaliation, including losing their jobs and getting shut out of jobs on other farms. Since many work with family members, all of their jobs hang in the balance. Those living in employer-provided housing can end up homeless.

2. As a board member of the nonprofit organization Different Avenues, I was part of the panel at a press conference for the release of the report "Move Along: Policing Sex Work in Washington, D.C." (Alliance for a Safe and Diverse D.C. 2008). Since then,

Human Rights Watch (2012) issued a report documenting how law enforcement targets sex workers throughout the United States.

3. "End-demand" policies have been widely criticized by sex workers, researchers involved in peer-reviewed research, and migrants' rights advocates for putting sex workers in danger by pushing them to work underground as well as for their ineffectiveness in reducing clients' interest in commercial sex. Criticism of end-demand policies include a reference brief on laws and policies affecting sex work by the Open Society Foundations (2012), assessments of the failures of the "Swedish model," a law passed in 1999 in Sweden that criminalized the purchase of sexual services (Danna 2012; Jordan 2012; Dodillet and Ostergren 2011; Di Tommaso et al. 2009; Harcourt et al. 2005), and assessments of Swedish model–type policies in Canada (Fischer et al. 2002; Kelly and Pacey 2011; van der Meulen 2011). On the implementation of end-demand policies in the United States see Berger (2012) and Thrupkaew (2012). See Weitzer (2010b) on the criminalization of sex work, and Ditmore (2009) on the harmful effects of raids. For a global focus, see Agustín (2007) on the "rescue industry," and the Global Alliance Against Traffic in Women (GAATW) (2007) on the harmful consequences of antitrafficking activities.

4. See Nathan 2005.

5. Administered by the Department of Justice, 287(g) agreements deputize local police officers to enforce federal immigration laws. They have been widely criticized, including by the Police Foundation (2009), which details that the costs of the 287(g) program outweigh the benefits. Other reports include Rights Working Group 2013; Theodore 2013; Kee 2012; American Friends Service Committee et al. 2011; Shahani and Greene 2009; and the National Commission on ICE Misconduct 2009. The Secure Communities program links the FBI's criminal database and the Department of Homeland Security's records to reveal immigration status every time someone is arrested (U.S. Department of Homeland Security, Immigration and Customs Enforcement 2011). The Rights Working Group (2011: 1), a civil liberties organization, finds that "the lack of due process sets the stage for racial profiling without any proper training or real consequences for police agents." Consequently many counties have tried to opt out of the program. National Council of La Raza (2012) also has called this program racial profiling and raised concerns about trust between communities and law enforcement: "SCOMM (Secure Communities) is a federal program imposed on county governments without county approval which allows local jails to check the immigration status of those they believe to be undocumented. The implementation of such programs in other jurisdictions has opened the door to racial profiling and decreased community willingness to contact the police in the event of an emergency." As the National Campaign Coordinator for the National Day Laborer Organizing Network (NDLON) describes it, "s-comm turns every police officer into a gateway for deportation by using pre-conviction arrest data to conduct immigration checks" (Uribe: 2013).

6. Many of these workers have visas to work in the United States, for example on a farm or in someone's house as a domestic worker. These visas are not "portable" but tie workers to one employer. If they leave their employer they become undocumented.

7. Meng 2012; Cho and Smith 2013.

8. Coutin 2007: 5. Coutin also writes writes about the space of "nonexistence" and "subjugation" that "excludes people, limits rights, restricts services, and erases personhood" (Coutin 2003b: 172). Also see the anthropologist Nicholas De Genova on living with "deportability" (2002) and the deportation regime (with Peutz 2010). Migrants have become more vulnerable as targets of crime because of the likelihood they won't report it (Weissman et al. 2009).

9. Chacón (2010: 134, 133) worries about the "growing rights deficit" and the policing practices that the nation relies on to document belonging. See Pamela Constable (2012) on battered immigrant women's fear of calling the police.

10. A report by the Southern Poverty Law Center on Latinos in low-income jobs in the South documents chronic abuse of both documented and undocumented migrants (Bauer 2009).

11. Lennard 2013. The Pew Research Hispanic Center reports an annual average of nearly 400,000 deportations since 2009 (Lopez, Gonzalez-Barrera, and Motel 2011).

12. Hsu 2008. Three hundred and six workers were charged with Social Security fraud, which carries a five-month sentence and aggravated identity theft, which carries a mandatory two-year sentence. Most agreed to Social Security fraud and a stipulated order of removal (Leopold 2008).

13. Camayd-Freixas 2008: 8. This translator wrote, "The sad specter of 9/11 has come back to haunt illegal workers and the local communities across the USA" (20). There was "immediate collateral damage" following the raid, for nearly half the town's population had worked in the meatpacking plant. "Several families had taken refuge at St. Bridget's Catholic Church, terrified, sleeping on pews and refusing to leave for days" (7). The day following the raid, 120 children were absent from the elementary and middle school (out of a total of 363 students). "Some American parents complained that their children were traumatized by the sudden disappearance of so many of their school friends. The principal reported the same reaction in the classrooms, saying that for the children it was as if ten of their classmates had suddenly died. Counselors were brought in. American children were having nightmares that their parents too were being taken away. The superintendant said the school district's future was unclear: 'This literally blew our town away'" (7–8). Camayd-Freixas (2013) further outlines the violence of this deportation regime in his new book.

14. Nossiter 2008. Between July 1, 2010, and September 31, 2012, 205,000 parents with U.S.-born children were deported (Wessler 2012). ICE reported that they deported 46,486 parents of U.S.-born children in just the first half of 2011 (U.S. Department of Homeland Security, Immigration and Customs Enforcement 2012). A report issued by the Department of Homeland Security, Office of Inspector General (2009), recounts that approximately 108,434 "alien parents" of U.S.-citizen children were removed between 1998 and 2007. A number of reports document the effects of parents' deportation on children: Wessler 2011; Kremer et al. 2009; Human Rights Watch 2007; Capps et al. 2007.

15. See the following reports by civil liberties organizations and in the media that

document racial profiling and compromised trust between communities and law enforcement: Rights Working Group 2010 and 2013; Rights Working Group and Penn State Law 2012; Aizenman 2008a; Brulliard 2008; Vargas 2008; Preston 2008; Nossiter 2008; and Cave 2008.

16. See Weissman (2009: 33) on the effects of 287(g) agreements: undocumented individuals are refrained from coming forward with information on crimes, even "heinous" ones.

17. Boarding buses and trains without reasonable suspicion of unlawful activity, Border Patrol agents arrested 2,788 passengers in the Rochester, New York, area alone between October 2005 and September 2009. Such "show me your papers" tactics inhibit individuals' "freedom to travel freely about the country without having to prove their citizenship to goverment agents" and are "more commonly associated with police states than robust democracies" (New York School of Law et al. 2011: 4).

18. Alabama State Representative Mickey Hammon made clear the intent of state-wide anti-immigrant legislation, HB 56: "[The proposed law] attacks every aspect of an illegal alien's life. . . . This bill is designed to make it difficult for them to live here so they will deport themselves" (Human Rights Watch 2011: 1). Following the law's passage in September 2011, migrants began to live "underground" lives. According to one woman, "We live in terror" (2011: 5). During the first month the new law was in effect, the state Department of Education reported over 5,000 Hispanic children absent when normally 1,000 absences were expected. Community members reported not pursuing unpaid wages, going to church, or bringing children to the doctor because of the risk of driving (2011).

19. This phrase was repeated by some speakers at a public hearing I attended on immigration to Virginia, convened by the Virginia Commission on Immigration on May 22, 2008, and held at George Mason University. In contrast Debra Shutika's (2008) research with a community in Pennsylvania is a model of how community members decide to work with migrant newcomers.

20. Lacey 2011.

21. Southern Poverty Law Center 2013b: 15.

22. Southern Poverty Law Center 2013: 14.

23. U.S. Department of State 2004b: 23. A Congressional Research Service report notes that no new U.S. government estimates have been circulated since 2004 (Siskin and Wyler 2013: 16).

24. A number of reports document widespread exploitation of migrants; see the Southern Poverty Law Center's report on rebuilding New Orleans after Katrina (2006b), their report on tree planters (2006a), and their report on migrant women in the food industry (2010). Also see reports on the exploitation of migrant farm-workers' in New York's Hudson Valley (Gray 2007), migrant women in the crab industry (American University, Washington College of Law 2010), and sheepherders with H-2A visas (Lee and Endres 2010). And see the following reports on exploitation of low-wage workers in general: Bernhardt et al. 2009; Milkman et al. 2010; Restaurant Opportunities Centers United 2013; Jayaraman 2013; Pitts 2008.

25. Bonacich and Appelbaum (2000: 25) describe southern California as resembling "the old South," when both race and immigration status were used "to create a workforce without rights."

26. Rights Working Group (RWG) launched the "Racial Profiling: Face the Truth" campaign to fight all types of racial and religious profiling. From May to July 2010, working with community partners in six communities, RWG organized public hearings on racial profiling and produced a report based on those hearings (Rights Working Group 2010).

27. Bauer 2009: 16.

28. Bauer 2009: 10–12.

29. Holmes observes that growers blame workers for their plight, telling Holmes that "pickers *wanted* to work all day without a lunch break" (Holmes 2013: 168).

30. Rothenberg (1998: 154) writes about contractors who search for the chronically homeless and substance abusers: "It is common knowledge among African American farmworkers that there are places throughout the rural South where you can be taken, forced to work in the fields, and paid no wages for your labor. The crew leaders who run these labor camps typically send family members or trusted henchmen to homeless shelters, soup kitchens, and poor neighborhoods to find new workers. Recruiters strike up conversations with men and women who have fallen on hard times, promising good jobs with free housing, cheap food, and high wages. For those seeking a break from the day-to-day struggles of life on the streets, the offer seems almost too good to be true. Some workers are drawn in by the possibility of a decent place to live, the opportunity to save a little money, and the dream of starting life anew. Others are won over by the promise of easy access to wine, beer, and crack cocaine. For alcoholics and drug users, labor camp life provides a chance to slip anonymously into the numbing comfort of addiction, safe from the violence and uncertainty of the street."

This cycle of what Rothenberg calls "debt peonage" among African American workers grows out of "the direct link between the development of the farm labor system in the rural South and the legacy of slavery" (159).

31. Rothenberg 1998: 157, 158.

32. Quoted in Rothenberg 1998: 158.

33. Bonacich and Appelbaum (2000: 197) observe that when garment workers leave factory work, "chances are they will only get equally dead-end jobs"; some, "either serially or simultaneously, hold other, low-wage jobs: hotel and restaurant work, domestic service, janitorial service, gardening, and street vending, none of which provides high wages or job security."

34. Writing about low-wage workers in California, Hondagneu-Sotelo (2001), Dohan (2003), and Zlolniski (2006) found that workers sometimes stay in low-paying jobs because they cannot go without pay while looking for a new job that may not pay much better.

35. The anthropologist Daniel Dohan (2003) describes recently arrived migrants in northern California who, eager to work, put up with low earnings. Steve Striffler, (2005: 103) heard the same pressure among newly arrived poultry workers in North Carolina; one worker, Arturo, explained to him, "I [had] little money. The trip is very

costly. So I need to get a job immediately. I cannot spend two weeks in a hotel waiting for the right job. I take what I can get."

36. Chacón (2006: 2979) asserts that these U.S. border interdiction strategies, combined with "harsh" penalties for undocumented migrant workers and weak labor protections for all workers, actually "interact to facilitate trafficking." Undocumented workers working in San Diego County told Sheldon Zhang that increased security since 9/11 has made it more difficult for them to travel. "Left with few choices but to take whatever jobs are available," they increase their "risk of exposure to trafficking violations or other forms of exploitation" (Zhang 2012: 87).

37. Striffler 2005: 103.

38. Washington Lawyers' Committee 2008: 8.

39. A study of 4,387 workers in low-wage industries reveals widespread workplace law violations, regardless of documentation; 26 percent of the workers in the sample were "paid less than the legally required minimum wage in the previous work week," and foreign-born workers were nearly "twice as likely as their U.S.-born counterparts to have a minimum-wage violation" (Bernhardt et al. 2009: 2). Minimum-wage violations for foreign-born respondents were "concentrated among women — especially women who are unauthorized immigrants" (5).

40. Hahamovitch 2011. The history of the guest worker program in the United States, Hahamovitch writes, "is a tale of exploitation, protest, litigation and mass deportation" (7).

41. Holzer 2011: 17. Thus many legal temporary workers "become unauthorized residents" when their guest term expires (17). Holzer proposes that a provisional visa should be established that would create the option for temporary guest workers to pursue permanent status and change jobs after a period of time in the United States (17).

42. In his research on the poultry industry, Striffler (2005: 5) has observed that the "food system" in the United States not only relies on "cheap labor" but also "requires an easily exploitable workforce to produce and process unhealthy foods." Writing on the garment industry, Bonacich and Appelbaum (2000: 166, 2) have described the return of sweatshops as not "confined to the underground economy" but "a prominent way of doing business."

43. Bonacich and Appelbaum 2000: 198. Rather their "political vulnerability as noncitizens" allows for the "disciplining effects of global, flexible capitalism" (198–99).

44. Bonacich and Appelbaum 2000: 189. Workers also report not being allowed to go to the restroom or to get a drink, having to use old, slow machines, and having their pay cut (189). One worker in a focus-group meeting said that the employer "throws stuff in the faces of the workers when he gets angry. He treats us like we are animals" (190).

45. The Fair Labor Standards Act (FLSA) establishes standards for minimum wage, overtime pay, record keeping, and child labor. The U.S. Department of Labor, Wage and Hour Division (2011b) administers and enforces the FLSA with respect to private employment and most government employees (except for those in some Executive Branch agencies and the Legislative Branch). Domestic service workers living in their employers' residence are exempt from overtime pay, and farmworkers are exempt from

minimum wage and overtime pay (U.S. Department of Labor 2011b; U.S. Department of Labor 2011a).

46. Bonacich and Appelbaum (2000: 4) argue for a broad definition of *sweatshop* to include factories that fail to pay a "'living wage,' meaning a wage that enables a family to support itself at a socially defined, decent standard of living." Earning a living wage means "that people should be able to afford decent housing given the local housing market, and that a family should be covered by health insurance. If wages fail to cover these minima and if families with working members still fall below the official poverty line, they are, we claim, working in sweatshops" (4). Andrew Ross (2004: 22) argues that *sweatshop* should refer to "all exploitative labor conditions," not just "a subpar outfit." He elaborates, "Installing proper fire exits may turn sweatshops into a legal workplace, but it remains a low-wage atrocity" (22).

47. Riis documented the last decades of the nineteenth century, when new immigrants arrived daily and U.S. cities gave rise to unregulated industrial workplaces. His photographs of rag pickers, stale bread vendors, piece workers around tenement kitchen tables, people sleeping in attics and in basements next to coal bins, homeless "tramps" and "waifs" curled up in back alleys, and police station lodgers provide a window into life on the margins for new arrivals and other low-wage workers.

48. Described as the "spiritual leader of documentary photography" (Bezner 1999: 20), Hine sums up his dedication to photography as a vehicle for social change: "If I could tell the story in words, I wouldn't need to lug a camera" (9).

49. Friendly 1960.

50. Many news stories on the plight of farmworkers today have referred to this documentary (e.g., Evelyn Nieves [2005]), "Florida Tomato Pickers Reap 'Harvest of Shame': Boycott Helps Raise Awareness of Plight." The CIW (2010b) produced a discussion guide to accompany the movie, which explains that Florida tomato pickers are paid at a rate that has not significantly risen since 1978 (45 cents/32 lbs.). Workers today have to pick "over twice the number of buckets per hour" as they did in 1980, and over two and a half tons of tomatoes just to earn the equivalent of Florida's minimum wage for a ten-hour workday. For the fiftieth anniversary of the release of the movie, CBS reported that the problems documented in 1960 still exist today, but the hardships are experienced by a different group: "The faces in the fields have changed from poor white and poor blacks to poor Hispanics." Gerardo Reyes of the CIW is quoted as saying, "It doesn't have to be a harvest of shame anymore. It can be a harvest of hope" (Pitts 2010).

51. Walmart and Home Depot, for example, hire firms to run their warehouses, and these firms subcontract employment agencies to hire workers and manage payroll. In this system, "perma-temp" workers are "laid off and rehired every few months by temporary-staffing agencies" (Lydersen 2010). In another case, twenty-two ditch-diggers sought unpaid wages from a subcontractor that hired them at a day-laborer site in Chantilly, Virginia. It turns out that the contractor who hired them, Anthony Maxwell in Hagerstown, Maryland, was hired by KCS Communications Inc., based in Fairfax County, Virginia, which had been hired by S&N Communications Inc. in Kernersville, North Carolina. At the top of this subcontracting chain was the communications

giant Verizon. The plight of these men "casts light on the low-tech backbone of a high-tech project—the casual laborers who are rounded up by subcontractors, sometimes bused across state borders to job sites and set to work digging ditches" (Silverman 2006). As part of the "estimated $20 billion fiber-optic cable system" that Verizon was building, the men were promised $100 a day with no contract or paperwork. Following pressure by advocacy groups, Verizon announced that it would withhold work from contractors not paying workers. CASA de Maryland, the Washington Lawyers' Committee, and seven laborers filed a class-action suit in June 2008 against one of Verizon's prime contractors and several of its subcontractors (Lazo 2008).

52. Riis 1971: 97–98.

53. Subcontracting organizes more than just the workplace. The anthropologist Christian Zlolniski (2006: 3) asserts that this form of production "permeates" migrant workers' lives, "from the survival strategies they develop to make ends meet, to the variety and instability of their domestic arrangements, to the severe problems they confront in barrios." Since the system of subcontracting often relies on social networks of communities and family, newcomers can capitalize on the opportunities subcontracting opens while also use its reliance on these social networks as a basis for collective mobilization (8).

54. Goldstein and Ruckelshaus 1999: 8.

55. Since 2010, the Campaign for Fair Food resulted in the creation of CIW's Fair Food Program (FFP), a partnership among farmworkers, Florida tomato growers, and participating buyers. A third-party monitor ensures compliance with the FFP. Participating buyers pay a "penny per pound" premium, which tomato growers pass onto workers as a line-item bonus on their paychecks. Between January 2011 and May 2013, over $10 million in Fair Food Premiums were paid. And, under the FFP, the CIW conducts worker-education sessions, held on the farm and on the clock (CIW 2013).

56. Angela Stuesse, an anthropologist and a founding collaborator of the Mississippi Poultry Workers' Center, tells of poultry workers squaring off against Tyson Foods when it began firing immigrant workers. Workers expressed "fear, uncertainty, humiliation, anger and worthlessness" and constantly worried that they would be fired. One worker told Stuesse (2010b: 22), "I go to work every day wondering if today will be my day"; another said, "What they are doing is very ugly. . . . They really just consider us machines for working." Summarizing the impasse with Tyson Foods, Stuesse argues, "All involved in the discussions were silenced by IRCA's [Immigration Reform and Control Act] misguided employer sanctions policy, which has obliged undocumented workers to purchase false 'papers' in order to be hired, incentivized companies to be 'unaware' of their employees' undocumented status to avoid legal liability, and compelled immigrant and workers' rights defenders to pressure companies to adopt more humane policies defined by the boundaries of current laws" (23).

57. Writing about new migration destinations in the United States, the demographer Douglas Massey (2008: 8) argues that an expansion of "poorly paid jobs that are difficult, dirty, and sometimes dangerous in small towns and rural areas is a common thread in many 'new destination' areas."

58. While picking strawberries alongside migrant farmworkers, Holmes describes

danger signs (in English only) posted on several large canisters containing insecticides located next to the handwashing stations. Working without gloves, pickers' hands were stained by visible pesticide residue. If they ate anything, they did so while in the fields without washing their hands so they could continue to work and pick the minimum weight (Holmes 2013: 172).

59. In one survey (Washington Lawyers' Committee for Civil Rights and Urban Affairs 2008) of 140 day laborers in Washington, D.C., 39 percent reported sustaining injuries on the work site, and 46 percent reported being required to complete jobs without the necessary safety equipment. Only 13 percent of those injured workers received some form of medical compensation from their employers.

60. Gordon 2005: 77, 15. A hundred sixty workers sought help from the clinic in its first six months. "Once people knew their rights, they realized they were being violated in spades" (76).

61. One way enterprising low-wage workers cultivate job security—and respect—is by managing their image as hard workers. Writing about the strategies of undocumented Mexican restaurant workers in Chicago, the anthropologist Ruth Gomberg-Muñoz (2010: 299) found that they were willing to be "pliant" because doing so could "make the difference between keeping or losing a job." These male networks of workers pushed one another to "echandole ganas" (put your back into it; 299). Such impression management yielded possibilities. One seasoned and respected worker, Alejandro, lobbied his employer to replace an all-white bus staff with his friends (300). But their strategies also had limits. Alejandro explained, "The bosses know you don't have papers, and they use [that knowledge]. That's why they pay you what they pay you, because you cannot ask for more money" (302).

62. See the following sources, in which the CIW's work has been profiled: Estabrook (2011) on the Navarrete case; Bowe (2007) and Rondeaux (2002), on the Ramos trafficking case; Asbed (2003), and Nieves (2005) on the CIW's campaign against Taco Bell's use of subcontractors to pay tomato pickers poverty wages; Hundley (2006) on the CIW's negotiations with the McDonald's Corp; Schlosser (2007), and Greenhouse (2007) on the CIW's campaign to pressure Burger King to have their tomato suppliers pay more to their pickers; Durbin, Sanders, and Brown (2008) on the Senate Health, Education, Labor and Pensions Committee hearing on the working conditions and poverty wages in Florida's tomato fields; and food writer Mark Bittman (2011), and McLaren (2011) on workers' rights as a critical part of the Fair Food movement.

63. Drivers who ferry laborers from farm to farm also have served as sources of information. Described as "the eyes and ears of a modern-day underground railroad," one van driver, José Martinez-Cervantes, was pistol-whipped for helping workers escape (Rondeaux 2002).

64. The CIW's investigations also led to the prosecutions in 2000 of a trafficker who ran down an escaping worker with his car, and prosecutions in 1997 of employers who held hundreds of workers under the constant watch of armed guards. Those who tried to escape were beaten, pistol-whipped, and shot (see Bowe 2003; Benitez 2004).

65. Gurwitt 2004: 24.

66. Describing the TVPA as appearing "at first glance" to be an "inexplicable if wel-

come break from a series of anti-immigration, antipoor, and antiprostitution policies in the United States," the sociologist Wendy Chapkis (2005: 51) lamented that the "new law actually serves as a soft glove covering a still punishing fist." For more on the history of the TVPA, see Jo Doezema's (1998) and Allison Murray's (1998) essays on pre-TVPA discussions on trafficking as sex trafficking; and Anthony DeStefano (2007) on the development of U.S. policy.

67. In President Bush's remarks at the signing of the TVPA of 2005, for example, he placed ending sexual exploitation — of children and youth in particular — at the centerpiece of fighting trafficking: "The Bill I sign today will help us to continue to investigate and prosecute traffickers and provide new grants to state and local law enforcement. Yet, we cannot put the criminals out of business until we also confront the problem of demand. Those who pay for the chance to sexually abuse children and teenage girls must be held to account" (Administration of George W. Bush 2006).

68. Lerum, McCurtis, Saunders, and Wahab 2012: 81. Hickey had been nominated by a broad coalition of activists, Human Rights For All: Concerned Advocates for the Rights of Sex Workers and People in the Sex Trade, to represent the U.S. sex workers' rights movement. That afternoon the U.S. Department of State announced its new position that: "no one should face violence or discrimination in access to public services based on sexual orientation or their status as a person in prostitution" (Lerum 2011). Also see the statement this coalition submitted to the Office of the United Nations High Commissioner for Human Rights (Best Practices Policy Project 2010).

69. The sociologist Elizabeth Bernstein (2007: 129) describes self-identified "modern-day abolitionists" as part of a "broad coalition of evangelical Christian and secular feminist activists" who rally against a "diverse yet intertwined array of human rights abuses" that include human trafficking and commercial sex. Eliminating all forms of sexual labor, regardless of context, is the core of feminist abolitionism. Bernstein (2010: 46) observes that the term *abolitionism*, which was used to describe feminist efforts to eradicate prostitution in the late nineteenth century, has been "reclaimed by those sectors of the contemporary feminist movement that share the conviction that prostitution constitutes a harm tantamount to slavery that nation-states should work to extinguish."

70. Writing "in defense of feminist abolitionism," the legal scholar Michelle Dempsey (2010: 1730) explains, "Abolitionists seek to end both sex trafficking and prostitution . . . while nonabolitionists seek to end sex trafficking while allowing prostitution to continue." Dempsey and other feminist abolitionists embrace what the legal scholar Janet Halley describes as governance feminism — "very state-centered, top-down, sovereigntist feminist rule preferences" (Halley et al. 2006: 341). This approach, which emphasizes criminal enforcement, "speaks the language of total prohibition" (341).

71. Cheng 2010; Shah 2008; Kempadoo 2005; Bernstein 2008; Agustín 2007; Kotiswaran 2008; Brennan 2004.

72. Ditmore 2009; Alliance for a Safe and Diverse D.C. 2008. Critics of the end-demand policies implemented in Sweden point out that they isolate workers from one another, making it difficult for them to evaluate clients. Such isolation may also

present obstacles for health initiatives to reach sex workers, drives wages down, and can lead to an increase in violent encounters (Berger 2012: 549–50).

73. U.S. Department of State 2004a: paragraph 1. The fact sheet continues: "Prostitution and related activities — including pimping and patronizing or maintaining brothels — fuel the growth of modern-day slavery by providing a façade behind which traffickers for sexual exploitation operate. Where prostitution is legalized or tolerated, there is a greater demand for human trafficking victims and nearly always an increase in the number of women and children trafficked into commercial sex slavery" (paragraphs 2, 3).

74. PROS Network and Sex Workers Project at the Urban Justice Center 2012.

75. Bernstein (2010: 53) provides a detailed genealogy of the players — including "pioneers of the early women's movement" and long-time Republican Party faithful — who shaped antitrafficking policy during the Bush administration.

76. Bernstein 2007: 131. Also see Shapiro 2004.

77. Vance 2011c: 139. Commenting on sex panics past and present, Vance writes, "Like dangerous radioactive substances, trafficking has a long half-life. The resurgence of campaigns against trafficking, still popularly understood as women forced into prostitution, makes clear that archaic battles return in new forms" (140). Bernstein (2007: 132) also traces this legacy of saving women: "By the beginning of the twentieth century . . . narratives of women's sexual enslavement abounded, drawing upon both the nation's legacy of race-based, chattel slavery and a resonance with biblical notions of 'slavery to sin.' Such narratives conjured scenarios of seemingly irrefutable moral horror: the widespread abduction of innocent women and girls who, en route to earn respectable livelihoods in metropolitan centers, were seduced, deceived, or forced into prostitution, typically by foreign-born men." Thus, the fight against white slavery operated as a "useful stepping stone and surrogate for a host of additional causes, from social purity and moral reform to temperance and suffrage" (132). The sociologist Kamala Kempadoo (2005) outlines racialized and gendered moral panics from early in the twentieth century to contemporary times, as does fellow sociologist Jo Doezema (2000), what legal scholar Alice Miller aptly terms "pouring new wine into old bottles" (2005: 23).

78. Feingold 2005: 27.

79. Brinkley 2008. Also see Nathan 2005. Weitzer (2006: 33) has described moral crusades as "tak[ing] the form of 'moral panics' if the targeted evil is blown out of proportion, if the number of alleged victims is far higher than what is warranted by the available evidence, and if the claims result in exaggerated anxiety or alarm among at least a segment of the population. In a moral panic, the gravity and scale of a menace or threat far exceeds its objective reality."

80. The text for NPSD-22 can be found at http://www.combat-trafficking.army.mil/documents/policy/NSPD-22.pdf.

81. In June 2013, the U.S. Supreme Court struck down the United States Leadership Against HIV/AIDS, Tuberculosis, and Malaria Act of 2003, which required every group that accepted federal money to combat these diseases to adopt a policy opposing prostitution (the "anti-prostitution pledge"). In a 6–2 opinion, Chief Justice John Roberts

ruled that Congress was not merely attaching strings to the distribution of federal money, but imposing a blanket restriction on the positions of health organizations, a restriction that violated their free speech rights. See Agency for International Development v. Alliance for Open Society International, 133 S. Ct. 2321 (2013).

82. Cohen 2005: 12. Also, see Crago (2008) on the effects antiprostitution policies have had on sex workers throughout the globe.

83. Weitzer (2006: 33) marvels at how antiprostitution views were "institutionalized remarkably quickly, judging from developments in U.S. law and government policy."

84. U.S. Department of Justice 2005: 15. The attorney general's annual report on trafficking in 2005 also reveals an emphasis in fiscal year 2004 on prosecuting cases related to sexual exploitation, with eleven of the twelve cases filed for trafficking prosecutions charted in the category *sex* (U.S. Department of Justice 2005: 22). During Bush's second term, there were almost twice as many prosecutions of "sex" cases than "labor" cases. Of thirty-two cases filed in 2006, twenty-two were sex cases; of thirty-two in 2007, twenty were sex cases; and of thirty-nine cases in 2008, twenty-seven were sex cases (U.S. Department of Justice 2010: 48). Under the Obama administration, the number of non-sexual labor cases filed rose significantly. Of forty-three cases filed in 2009, twenty-two were cases of "sex trafficking" and twenty-one were cases of "labor trafficking" (U.S. Department of Justice 2010: 48). Note that the U.S. government uses language that distinguishes between "sex trafficking" and "labor trafficking" and thus singles out sexual harms as distinct.

85. Benczkowski 2007: 1, 9. In a letter to U.S senators regarding the reauthorization under review, a group of service providers, advocates, scholars, and human rights lawyers noted that the new sex trafficking statute federalizing prostitution-related crimes "will instantaneously and dramatically increase the estimated and actual number of 'trafficking' victims in the U.S." because the "estimated number of prostitution-related arrests is around 100,000 a year (Alexandria House et al. 2008: paragraph 8). The number of "trafficking victims" would increase such that "those engaged in prostitution would outnumber true trafficking victims nearly six to one" (paragraph 8). Consequently they would have to "compete for access to funding, resource programs and every other aspect of assistance to the real trafficked individuals," and "fewer true victims" would be identified (paragraph 8). I was one of the signatories to this letter.

86. Brennan 2008.

87. In his book on U.S. antitrafficking policy, journalist Anthony DeStefano (2007: xxi) describes "anti-prostitution zealots" who "single out sex work as a particular evil" finding "ready allies in the Bush administration which has advanced legislation and policies to conform to the anti-prostitution agenda."

88. Brennan 2008.

89. The attorney general's report in 2006 on activities to combat trafficking from 2001 to 2005 calculates that grants "totaling more than $30 million to institute 32 multidisciplinary anti-human trafficking task forces and 21 victim service providers in communities across the nation" were awarded (U.S. Department of Justice 2006: i).

90. The NYPD's Human Trafficking Squad, for example, is housed within the vice division of the department's Organized Crime Control Bureau (Kemp 2013). During

her research on antitrafficking initiatives in New York, the anthropologist Alicia Peters interviewed a federal prosecutor who told her: "We really haven't done as many forced labor cases. . . . There's already mechanisms locally to find sex trafficking. You have vice squads out there all the time. So that's where we get a lot of our stuff." A local agent told Peters: "Labor's not one of our strong points. . . . Dealing with prostitution— that's easier for us to get into" (Peters 2013: 243). Agents explained to Peters that they "*responded*" to labor cases, but did not "*look*" for them. An agent elaborated: "I target brothels, because it would be offensive if I knocked on doors looking for domestics. . . . I don't want to go into a worksite without a specific lead" (2013: 244).

91. To be clear, the TVPA defines an adult as a victim of trafficking if he or she is induced to perform a commercial sex act or other form of labor through "force, fraud or coercion." For a person under the age of eighteen, no force, fraud, or coercion is necessary to meet the statute's definition of a victim of sex trafficking; for minors, inducement into a commercial sex act, in itself, is sufficient to to meet the statute's definition of trafficking (U.S. Congress 2000).

92. Berger 2012.

93. Grant 2013.

94. Bernstein 2010; Grant 2013.

95. Mathias 2012; Kemp 2013.

96. Mathias 2012; Grant 2013.

97. As discussed in note 5 in the Introduction to this book, estimates of the scope of trafficking to the United States have fluctuated significantly over the past decade, from 50,000 in 2000 to 18,000–20,000 in 2003 to 14,500–17,500 in 2004 (O'Neill Richard 2000; U.S. Department of State 2004b, 2005). A 2007 GAO report noted that "pursuing trafficking in persons crimes continues to present special challenges to federal investigators and prosecutors" since "victims are often hidden from view, employed in legal or illegal enterprises, do not view themselves as victims, or are considered to be criminals or accessories to crimes" (U.S. Government Accountability Office 2007: 2). Consequently "trafficking in persons cases are difficult to pursue because they are multifaceted, complex, and resource intensive" (2). The GAO (2006) also found estimates of global trafficking "questionable" because of "methodological weaknesses, gaps in data, and numerical discrepancies."

98. Landler 2006.

99. Landesman (2004, 30). For a critique of the article, see Young (2004) and a series of articles by Jack Shafer on *Slate* (Shafer 2004a, 2004b, 2004c, 2004d, 2004e). The *New York Times Magazine* cover story provoked so much criticism regarding the author's claims about the girls whom he allegedly had met and on the data he cited that an editors' note in the February 15, 2004, edition of the *New York Times* detailed Landesman's methodology.

100. Brennan 2005.

101. Kotz (2011). Kotz's news organization had phoned police sergeants in cities that had hosted past Super Bowls. The police sergeant in Phoenix, which had hosted the 2008 Super Bowl, said he "didn't notice any sort of glitch in the number of prostitution arrests leading up to the Super Bowl." A police spokeswoman for Tampa, host of the

2009 Super Bowl, also reported that despite their special operations on the sex trade, "the arrests were not a lot a higher. They were almost the same."

102. As an article in the *Chronicle of Higher Education* reports, an antiprostitution activist and researcher, Melissa Farley, dismissed responses of sex workers she interviewed that do not align with her viewpoint that sex work is always harmful. In her book, published by her advocacy group, Prostitution Research and Education, she explained sex workers' answers as the product of disassociation: "I knew that they would minimize how bad it was, not only to make prostitution seem like a reasonable job choice to the interviewers, but especially to justify it to themselves" (Schmidt 2011).

103. There is robust peer-reviewed scholarship that recognizes sexual labor as labor and disputes claims that sexual labor leads to trafficking: Bernstein 2007 and 2010; Vance 2012, 2011b, 2011c; Chuang 2010a; Kotiswaran 2011; Cheng 2008; Halley et al. 2006; Weitzer 2010 and 2012; Soderlund 2005; Parreñas 2011; Feingold 2010; Kempadoo 2005; Doezema 2010; Brennan 2008.

104. Writing about the new trafficking laws' "vulnerability to capture by antiprostitution activists (both evangelical and feminist)," Vance (2011c: 139) observes that the "flood of documentary, exposé, investigation, and made-for-TV dramas about trafficking has been robust and the structure for telling the alleged story—melodrama— excessive."

105. Cizmar, Conklin, and Hinman (2011).

106. Cizmar et al. quoting Estes and Weiner 2001: 143–44. Estes and Weiner quote a report from the group End Child Prostitution, Child Pornography, and the Trafficking of Children for Sexual Exploitation (ECPAT) that claims the estimated "number of prostituted children" to be "between 100,000 and 300,000" (4). Other researchers, such as David Finkelhor of the University of New Hampshire, point out that the Estes and Weiner report was not subject to peer review and "has no scientific credibility" (Cizmar et al. 2011).

107. Feingold 2010: 49. In the process, these antiprostitution actors were able to dominate the rhetoric, policy, and programmatic activities that had demanded and produced "a flight from complexity . . . an almost overwhelming craving for a simple narrative of innocence debauched, a wrong that can be righted by the apprehension of an evildoer" (61).

108. Brunovskis and Surtees (2008: 59) found that presenting a "good girl" image— through "clothing, behavior and demeanor"—can be "key" to being "seen as a victim" by service providers, police, and prosecutors in the antitrafficking care regime in southeastern Europe (also see Miller 2004). They interviewed "rescued" trafficked women living in shelters and found them subjected to "restrictions on freedom of movement and rules on communication and contact outside of shelters" that seemed "excessive" (Brunovskis and Surtees 2008: 54). This moralizing approach to change "victim behavior" implicitly blamed these women for their experiences in forced sexual labor.

109. A coalition of organizations that provide services to trafficked persons holds an annual conference and shares information in conference calls and email listservs, the

Freedom Network has enabled staff at social service organizations to learn from one another's experiences with different clients. The most seasoned social workers and attorneys, in turn, conduct training sessions for service providers through the Freedom Network Training Institute on Human Trafficking. Attending these trainings are potential frontline responders such as paramedics and hospital personnel, as well as attorneys, and nongovernmental and community-based organization staff. (I attended one of these trainings in Washington, D.C.) The Freedom Network also has produced a manual, *Human Trafficking and Slavery: Basic Tools for an Effective Response Participant Tool Kit*, which is continually updated and has been distributed widely.

110. Bernstein (2007) points out that when organizations conduct their own investigations of brothels or massage parlors, the assumed "victims" may feel captured by their rescuers. This type of "undercover and mass-mediated model of activism" has emerged as the "emulated standard" for rescue-oriented organizations (139). On an international level, brothel raids have had violent consequences for the assumed "victims," such as "disrupting HIV-outreach efforts, heightening the potential for police brutality and subjecting adult sex workers and trafficking victims to possible deportation or long involuntary stays in shelters" (Thrupkaew 2009: 1). By partnering with local law enforcement to conduct the raids, "state power [is] used to prey on, rather than protect, its populace" (1). As one "rescued" sex worker by the nonprofit organization International Justice Mission (IJM) asked, "How can this be a rescue when we feel like we've been arrested?" (2). Writing about a televised brothel raid in Cambodia by "rescuers" hired by IJM, Gretchen Soderlund (2005: 65) notes that since six of the thirty-seven women and girls "rescued" ran away from the safe house in Phnom Penh, the line "between rescuers and captors has become increasingly blurry." The safe house manager reports that at least 40 percent of the women and girls taken there eventually escape and return to brothel work (66). After another IJM raid—in Chiang Mai, Thailand—a sex workers' advocacy program, Empower, documented that within a month more than half of the "rescued" Burmese women had escaped from the shelter in which IJM had placed them. Empower's report on the Thai raid reads like a story of capture, not assistance to freedom: "They are only permitted to use their phones for a short time each evening and must hide in the bathroom to take calls outside that time. They report that they have been subjected to continual interrogation and coercion by Trafcord [an antitrafficking NGO formed in 2002 with U.S. financial support]" (Empower 2003 cited in Soderlund 2005: 66).

111. During workplace raids and "rescues" within the sex sector, workers have been placed in immigration detention until their trafficking status could be determined (Ditmore 2009). While workers who are deemed to be possible trafficking "victims" begin receiving legal and social services, those who are not designated as trafficked—and are undocumented—have been deported. Sixty-seven Korean women, for example, were "rounded up and interviewed to determine whether they were involuntarily part of the (trafficking) ring" (Lengel 2006). During this nationwide sting some of the women workers at a Dallas spa were classified as "nonvictims" and sent to immigration court (Meyer 2006). During police raids of eight massage parlors in Dallas in 2007, twenty-seven women were detained. Of those detained nineteen were released,

one was identified as a possible "victim of human trafficking," and "several women, all South Korean, were being held for immigration reasons." Four of the detained women were eventually arrested on warrants related to the investigation (Eiserer 2007).

112. A report by the National Guestworker Alliance describes widespread retaliatory actions against workers' attempts to bargain for better workplace conditions. For example, Cumberland Environmental Resource Co. fired H-2B employees who requested a meeting with their boss to discuss the company's failure to provide them with work for weeks at a time (National Guestworker Alliance 2012: 11). Decatur Hotels in New Orleans fired a recognized worker leader, Daniel Castellanos Contreras, in retaliation for standing up to Decatur's refusal to provide the promised wages, hours, and working conditions (10, 11). Decatur also threatened to blacklist the workers—which blocks workers' ability to apply for future H-2B visas or extensions (10). Ignacio Zaragoza, an H-2B worker from Mexico, explains why workers fear coming forward: "Guestworkers are afraid to report abuse: I've known people in Mississippi that have even been assaulted and didn't report it because they were so afraid of losing everything—their job, their visa, everything. Guestworkers are really afraid of retaliation" (11). Also see Harris (2013) on the firing and arrest of workers who reported abuse.

113. "A Failure of Discretion," editorial, *New York Times*, June 8, 2012. The Southern 32 is a group of immigrant workers involved in labor organizing who are in deportation proceedings (Cho and Smith 2013). They have been pressuring the New Orleans regional ICE office (which has jurisdiction over Alabama, Arkansas, Louisiana, Mississippi, and Tennessee) to cancel the deportation orders ("ICE Official Travels from D.C. to New Orleans for In-person Meeting with Southern 32," Stand Up 2012, www.makejusticereal.org, accessed July 19, 2013). Since June 2011, ICE officials have, under the practice of prosecutorial discretion, the ability to suspend deportation of an immigrant worker who is either cooperating with federal labor officials in an investigation or engaging in a nonfrivolous lawsuit to contest wage violations or secure workplace protections or other civil liberties. Also, see Milkman (2000, 2011) on the relationship between the U.S. labor movement and migrant workers.

Chapter Two

1. Kim 2007: 972. In a dialogue with fellow attorney, Charles Song, Kim explains what distinguishes between a trafficking victim and an individual who is experiencing egregious wage/hour violations: "Generally, one of the first questions I would have to ask and answer, based on the circumstances of the client's case, is if he/she felt forced or coerced. Even if the victim liberated himself/herself and ultimately left by his/her own free will, was there any point in time that the individual felt like he/she had little choice but to comply with the exploitive conditions? If the employer coerced compliance with threats, intimidation, and other abuse, I would consider that person's situation to be trafficking" (Kim, Song, and Panchalam 2009: 38).

2. In the opening of her book on the history of Jamaican guest workers in the United States, the historian Cindy Hahamovitch (2011: 1) wonderfully captures recollections

of a would-be guest worker, Leaford Williams, who was also eager to make a bold move. He describes the excitement when American recruiters came to his small town in 1943: "Everywhere we went during the days and weeks that followed, small groups gathered under the eaves of someone's house or on the front porch of the local shops sharing news about the recruiting program 'for going to foreign.'"

3. In their interviews with service providers working with trafficked persons in southeastern Europe, Brunovskis and Surtees (2008) found widespread assumptions that all victims come from an abusive past. These assumptions "infantilize program beneficiaries and potentially rob them of their agency and ability to dissent and negotiate within the program framework" (72).

4. Ong 1999. Flexible citizenship describes "the strategies and effects of mobile managers, technocrats, and professionals seeking to both circumvent *and* benefit from different nation-state regimes by selecting different sites for investments, work, and family relocation" (112).

5. Ong 1999: 112.

6. While I was conducting research for *What's Love Got to Do with It: Transnational Desires and Sex Tourism in the Dominican Republic*, all of the Dominican sex workers I met had inflexible citizenship (Brennan 2004). They did not have access to legal migrating networks off the island and thus created them by seeking to marry their foreign clients. As single mothers with limited income-earning opportunities available to them in the Dominican Republic, they imagined Germany and German men as offering more economically secure lives for them and their children.

7. There is excellent scholarship on the structural conditions that shape global workers' opportunities and labor conditions: Ehrenreich and Hochschild 2002; Sassen 2000; Constable 2007; Parreñas 2001; Kwong 1997; Mahdavi 2011; Gardner 2010.

8. Constable 2004: 108. The overseas labor that Filipina domestic workers perform, for example, is "inextricably connected with global economic and historical processes (particularly the labor export policy of the Philippines, and the demand for cheap household labor in Hong Kong)" (108).

9. I accompanied an outreach worker from a Dominican nongovernmental organization, Centro de Orientación e Investigación Integral, that conducted trafficking-prevention workshops in communities where many women leave to find work overseas.

10. To give an idea of how much money this is for low-wage earners in the Dominican economy, a report on garment workers there found that they earn a minimum wage of RD$5,400 a month, equivalent to US$148 (Kline 2010: 16).

11. Control over food is not only used in situations of forced labor. Constable (2007) writes poignantly of a wide range of Filipina domestics in Hong Kong who describe often being hungry and losing weight.

12. Ortner 1995: 182.

13. Constable 1997: 14.

14. Constable 1997: 14.

15. Finnegan 2008.

16. Attorney Charles Song is clear that "Trafficking does not involve loyalty to the

trafficker so much as it involves plain old fear of him/her" (Kim, Song, and Panchalam 2009: 42).

17. Kim asks basic questions to build a trafficking case, beginning with "What was the pay?" and "What were the hours?" She also looks for "circumstances that indicate that the employer is exercising more control than is reasonable over the workers," such as living conditions with twelve workers in a one-bedroom apartment with no furniture, no utilities, and no running water. Other indications of forced labor include if the employer is "monitoring the workers closely both during working hours and non-working hours" (Kim, Song, and Panchalam 2009: 40).

18. Bales and Lize 2005: 55–56.

19. Abu-Lughod 1990: 47. In this way, resistance can be a "diagnostic of power," revealing how "power relations take many forms, have many aspects, and interweave" (48).

20. Abu-Lughod 1990: 48.

21. Kim 2007: 967, 943, 966. In the TVPA Congress adopted a broad concept of coercion as "threat of serious harm" (U.S. Congress [2000]; Kim 2007: 966).

22. Kim 2007: 942–43. Kim describes cases "characterized by subtle power dynamics that did not involve physical force, but were nonetheless debilitating" (941).

23. Kim 2007: 970–72.

24. Kim (2007: 955) points to the TVPA's insufficient guidance on "discerning the scope of prohibited coercion" and thus finds that its "persistent ambiguity" "falls short of adequately defining psychological coercion for purposes of legal enforcement."

25. Haynes 2007: 360. Haynes is concerned both about the "enormous" discretion law enforcement officials have to determine who is trafficked, and their inadequate training in how to exercise "the power that comes with that discretion" (370). Kim echoes that "bias against victims depending on the types of industries they are involved in and also their gender" comes into play when law enforcement determines "who counts as a victim and who does not" (Kim, Song, and Panchalam 2009: 44). Kim also comments that without "law enforcement interest in the case, a trafficked person will have a tough time accumulating enough evidence to convince immigration services that they qualify for a T visa" (2009: 49).

26. Haynes 2007: 350. In fact, to prove victimhood, individuals often must present themselves as "easily identifiable victim subject(s), without the clutter and complication of a story in which the victim(s) also had some agency" (354).

27. Lukes 2005: 126, quoting Scott 1990: 72.

28. Abu-Lughod 1990: 47.

29. Scott 1985: 39. When a "given group is exploited," the "coercive force at the disposal of the elites and/or the state makes any open expression of discontent virtually impossible" (39).

30. Scott 1985: 38.

31. Lukes 2005: 129.

32. Lukes 2005: 127.

33. Lukes 2005: 150.

34. Song describes clients "who did escape and found out that they had nowhere to go or were too scared to go anywhere, so they actually went back to their traffickers" (Kim, Song, and Panchalam 2009: 41).

35. There is extensive scholarship on the perpetrators of violence, torture, and genocide. See Hinton (2004) and Gourevitch (1999) on orchestrating the Cambodian and Rwandan genocides; Gill (2004) on training would-be torturers at the School of the Americas; and Scarry (1985) on torturers' intended effects on the body.

36. Herman 1997: 76. Abusive practices can have such "uncanny sameness," writes Herman, that Amnesty International published "a chart of coercion" (76 on Amnesty International 1973).

37. In a report on trafficking from Mexico (Ditmore, Maternick, and Zapert 2012: 39), the researchers found that the majority of those interviewed met their trafficker through a family member, friend, or neighbor.

38. Skinner 2008: 135–36.

39. In *What's Love Got to Do With It?*, I recount a similar story of a husband (in a consensual union) in the Dominican Republic who siphoned off all of his wife's overseas earnings. She had sent these remittances believing that they were going into a savings account. Upon returning to the Dominican Republic, she was stunned to learn that he had spent all her earnings (Brennan 2004: 166–67).

40. Morel 2008.

41. Herman 1997: 79. The context of captivity, in which abusers inflict methods of psychological domination, includes domestic violence, political imprisonment, and concentration camps (77–79). When the "victim is brought into prolonged contact with the perpetrator," it "creates a special type of relationship, one of coercive control" (74). As a result, "the perpetrator becomes the most powerful person in the life of the victim, and the psychology of the victim is shaped by the actions and beliefs of the perpetrator" (75).

42. Over time, the guards used escalating brutal physical beatings to keep workers from trying to leave. When the guards used pipes to beat workers, described by some of the workers as a "bloodbath," one worker lost an eye (U.S. Department of Justice, Criminal Section on Selected Case Summaries).

43. Herman 1997: 77.

44. Free the Slaves and Human Rights Center 2004: 39–40.

45. Su 1997: 145.

46. Preston 2008.

47. Although there are trainings for law enforcement throughout the United States to recognize signs of forced labor, Peters found in her interviews with law enforcement that what "counted" as trafficking was "sex trafficking." "Like many members of the broader public, individual law enforcement agents often assumed trafficking victims should fit the image propagated by the media of a damsel in distress." Jim, a federal agent and the head of a human trafficking unit, told Peters: "Sex trafficking sickens me. Most of the labor trafficking victims they wanted to come here in the first place" (Peters 2013: 245). He told Peters: "In my opinion it's worse than murder-

ing someone, to continuously degrade someone like that. I think about my sisters, my wife, and my daughters, what would I do?" (2013: 222).

48. In a story for the *New Yorker*, William Finnegan (2008) cites a report by the Organization for Security and Cooperation in Europe on monitoring trials in Chisinau, Moldova, that documents courtroom intimidation. In one instance, during the seconds that the trial judge turned his head, the accused trafficker threatened his accuser by slicing his finger across his throat.

49. As with other identifying information throughout the book, I am not disclosing her trafficker's sentence.

Chapter Three

1. Das 2000: 222. Once trafficking clients like Gladys and Tatiana put their trust in assistance-givers and decide to resettle in the United States, they — like others who have suffered through brutal experiences — struggle for what the anthropologist Sverker Finnström (2008: 10) calls "comprehensible life."

2. Between 2006 and 2011, the U.S. government had arranged a single national "Per Capita Victim Services" contract with the U.S. Conference of Catholic Bishops, which used subcontractors to provide social services to internationally trafficked persons in the United States. The subcontractors had to have the capacity to provide all of the needs of the client through comprehensive case management, which involves a social worker assessing the needs of the client and his or her family and coordinating the package of services that the client receives. Subcontracted service providers were expected to have experience working with trafficked persons or "populations with similar needs, such as refugees, undocumented individuals, and survivors of domestic violence," and they must have complied with the financial reporting protocol of the Conference (U.S. Conference of Catholic Bishops 2007). Subcontractors were reimbursed by the Conference on a per client basis — and could receive up to $1,300 per month for precertified clients for up to nine months, and up to $900 per month for certified clients. Once clients received certification from HHS/ORR, they could receive the same federal benefits as refugees for up to three months (U.S. Conference of Catholic Bishops "Anti-Trafficking Services Program" 2011). The USCCB contract with the U.S. government was not renewed in September 2011 since they had been restricting trafficking clients' access to full reproductive care (Mencimer 2012). Subcontractors could not discuss contraception or abortion or use staff time to refer clients for such services, even though as Florrie Burke the chair emeritus of the Freedom Network explained: "We're talking about a group of people [who] have endured rape and no health care, so many of them have untreated infections." "Many of them have been exposed to HIV. They've had forced abortions. The gynecological issues are horrendous" (2012). The ACLU sued the Department of Health and Human Services claiming that it was unconstitutionally forcing recipients of federal money to comply with Catholic beliefs. Judge Richard G. Stearns ruled in favor of the ACLU on March 23, 2012, noting, "this is a case about the limits of the government's ability to delegate

to a religious institution the right to use taxpayer money to impose its belief on others (who may or may not share them)" (2012). In January 2013, a federal appeals court vacated Judge Stearns's ruling arguing that the case had become moot because the contract had expired (Sadowski 2013).

Currently, the dispersal of victim-assistance funds in the United States is administered by three NGOs overseeing three geographic regions. The 2013 Trafficking in Persons Report (U.S. Department of State 2013a: 384) describes this new system: "HHS awarded $4.8 million in FY 2012 to three NGOs for the provision of case-management services to foreign national victims through a nationwide network of NGO subrecipients. Under the HHS victim-assistance program, there is a maximum reimbursement amount allowed per month for each victim for the twelve months during which time that victim can be assisted." Assistance includes: case management and referrals, medical care, dental care, mental health treatment, sustenance and shelter, translation and interpretation services, substance abuse treatment, immigration and legal assistance, employment and training services, transportation assistance, and other essential services (2013a: 384). The government assesses its own track record: "Federal funding streams and grants for victim services remain inadequately structured for providing comprehensive care options for all types of trafficking victims, resulting in disparate treatment of victims, including turning some away" (2013a: 384).

A social worker in New York explains that in their region they have $2,400 to use for each client. "This amount has not changed in ten years. Often, the fund runs out of money before the end of the year." Large organizations with multiple funding sources try to not enroll trafficking clients in the victim-assistance program until they have T visas, so that they can use other funds until that point. "This way they have assistance longer. But this is a real problem for smaller organizations in smaller cities than New York."

3. Ann Jordan (2002: 30), a human rights attorney, criticizes governments and NGOs that "are sincerely concerned about the situation of trafficked women" and "often treat the women as vulnerable, passive objects who are incapable of making reasoned judgments, and, consequently, need to be rescued and 'rehabilitated.'" Writing on the "politics of rescue," Carol Harrington (2005) argues that the diagnosis of posttraumatic stress disorder (PTSD) is applied broadly to women who were in the sex trade to trump any possibility that they may have chosen this form of labor. Humanitarian workers in Bosnia-Herzegovina and Kosovo, for example, "appear to have adopted PTSD discourse because of its capacity to establish 'innocence' in a context hostile to 'prostitutes'" (188). Harrington is careful to "recognize that humanitarian workers who adopt its premises are hampered by bureaucratic and funding considerations that limit their intervention strategies," and thus these "beleaguered workers are doing their best to frame problems in pragmatic ways both to mitigate an immediate problem and to raise funds" (188).

4. While formerly trafficked persons prioritize economic security above all other needs, some organizations instead cite relief from trauma and restoring dignity as a core mission. Here I am not referring to the social service providers that provide direct services to trafficking clients with funding from the U.S. government. There is a dif-

ference between organizations that have received government contracts to oversee the resettlement of trafficking clients and other nonprofit organizations that have no formal relationship with the U.S. government to aid in this resettlement process. Restoration Ministries (2011), for example, puts healing front and center in their mission statement: "Restoration Ministries seeks to bring healing to men, women and children who are trapped in the slavery of sex trafficking and lead them into the freedom of Jesus Christ." Even a U.S. government program that offers social services to trafficked persons and raises awareness of human trafficking has *restore* in its name: The Campaign to Rescue and Restore Victims of Human Trafficking (U.S. Department of Health and Human Services, Administration for Children and Families, The Campaign to Rescue and Restore Victims of Human Trafficking 2012).

5. If there is a "dire need," explains a case manager at a large social service organization in New York City, they can find funds within the organization but "we really have to advocate for it." "Most of the time, however, we cannot pay." Since this large organization has an in-house counseling center, they also can offer counseling free of charge on a first-come, first-serve basis. Smaller organizations would not have the flexibility or resources.

6. Of course, I cannot measure how much one person suffered compared to another. While the "incommunicability of pain" can make it impossible to truly know another's pain, we can seek to understand "how such suffering is produced in societies and how acknowledgement of pain, as a cultural process, is given or withheld" (Kleinman et al. 1997: xiii).

7. Kleinman and Kleinman (1997: 2) emphasize that there "is no single way to suffer, there is no timeless or spaceless universal shape to suffering." In her interviews with the translators of the testimonies given to Peru's Truth and Reconciliation Commission, Theidon (2013: 25) found that they had been trained to "code for trauma." They collapsed Quechua-speaking *campesinos'* varied and poetic language such as "soul loss," "painful memories that fill the body and torment the soul," and "irritation of the heart" into one simple category: "trauma."

8. The overuse of a PTSD diagnosis has produced a lively critique. This one-size-fits-all diagnosis, developed by psychiatrists in the United States after the Vietnam War, has birthed therapies that can be overly zealous and ill-fitting. As the medical anthropologist Allan Young (1995: 5) cautions, "The disorder is not timeless, nor does it possess an intrinsic unity. Rather, it is glued together by the practices, technologies, and narratives with which it is diagnosed, studied, treated, and represented and by the various interests, institutions, and moral arguments that mobilized these efforts and resources." The psychiatrist Patrick Bracken and Cecilia Petty, an advisor with Save the Children, explain, "There is a growing concern that the models developed in Western psychiatry with regard to the effects of trauma should not be exported uncritically. The explosion of interest in this area has happened so quickly and with such an urgency that there has been little critical reflection upon its relevance to non-Western societies" (Bracken and Petty 1998: 4). While soldiers had been the "primary subjects of the psychotherapeutic discourses and practices," in the early 1990s therapeutic interventions were applied to "war traumatized" communities (Moon 2009: 74–75). The

psychiatrist Derek Summerfield (2001: 96) assesses Western societies' conflation of "distress" with "trauma" and the "spectacular" rise in a PTSD diagnosis to those seeking victim status "and its associated moral high ground—in pursuit of recognition and compensation." The anthropologist Nancy Scheper-Hughes (2008: 42) observes that as this "medical—social science—psychiatric pendulum has swung in recent years toward a model of human vulnerability" it has excluded "the awesome ability of people—adults and children—to withstand, survive, and live with horrible events."

9. The abuses that formerly trafficked persons suffered fit Summerfield's (2001: 98) description of human pain as "a slippery thing" that is not easily "registered and measured." Nonetheless the psychiatric sciences "have sought to convert human misery and pain into technical problems that can be understood in standardized ways and are amenable to technical interventions by experts" (98). This immeasurability, however, challenges relief regimes premised on providing assistance only to the most in need. Since the "trauma" of survivors of a range of experiences—accidents, rape, torture—is "universally acknowledged" and "confers a form of social recognition," trauma today is a "moral judgment" rather than a "clinical reality" (Fassin and Rechtman 2009: 284). The physician and anthropologist Didier Fassin and the psychiatrist and anthropologist Richard Rechtman describe trauma as "more a feature of the moral landscape serving to identify legitimate victims than it is a diagnostic category which at most reinforces that legitimacy" (284).

10. Often hearing the expression "my memories suffocate me" among grieving women in Peru, Theidon comments on the relationship between memory, the body, and affliction (Theidon 2013: 41, 40).

11. Das and Kleinman 2001: 18 on Langer 1991.

12. Talking or writing about past abuses is not always therapeutic. This issue of "telling trauma" has been hotly debated. Writing about the role of truth and reconciliation commissions in "post atrocity politics," human rights scholar Claire Moon (2009) critiques the defense of amnesty laws on therapeutic grounds. South Africa's Truth and Reconciliation Commission, for example, centered around a "therapeutic order with amnesty at its core" (72). In this "therapeutic order," unless trauma is "healed" or "laid to rest," lack of resolution leads to resurgent violence (76). Moon critiques legal scholar Martha Minow for "conflat[ing] deliberative, institutionalized criminal justice with its emotional point of origin—vengeance" and contrasts Minow's work with anthropologist John Borneman's writing on Eastern Europe, in which he shows that in new states that had retributive justice, violence was "dampened or diverted" (Moon 2009: 81 on Borneman 1997: 6). With this therapeutic approach in mind, the World Health Organization recommends "methods of trauma-healing" as part of the "social process of reconciliation and peace-building" (Moon 2009: 76). Trauma telling, often framed as "truth telling," thus becomes integral to state building. In sharp contrast, critics like anthropologist Sharon Abramowitz (2009) have found that this "cultural critique of trauma healing and mental health services" has compromised the ability of international organizations that do not embrace this approach to obtain funding. Abramowitz summarizes anthropology's critique: "Anthropologists have successfully pointed out that (a) 'traumatic responses' are often normal responses to extreme con-

ditions of violence and vulnerability; (b) the development of mass-scale trauma healing programs pathologizes entire populations; (c) Western clinical definitions of trauma are often inappropriate in non-Western contexts" (14–15). As a consequence, "NGOS have dedicated their psychosocial interventions to specific 'at-risk' groups which overwhelmingly tend to be children and civilian victims of war rather than ex-combatants or veterans" (14).

13. Commenting on Marcelo Suárez-Orozco's idea of "percepticide" during the Argentine military dictatorship, Theidon observes how even one's senses cannot be trusted in times of constant violence. "The sensation of not recognizing one's own body or trusting one's own perceptions reflects extreme experiences that surpassed the frames of reference that defined life" (Theidon 2013: 211; on Suárez-Orozco 1995: 243).

14. Benjamin 1968: 257.

15. Green 1999: 6, 4. Building on Iris Young's (1990) "five faces of oppression" (exploitation, marginalization, powerlessness, cultural imperialism, and random acts of violence), Green (1999: 13) explains structural violence as a "multidimensional conceptualization of social injustice," not just exploitation. Moreover "humiliation and fear, as well as denial of dignity and integrity," are also "crucial components" of structural violence (13).

16. This woman, Julia, recounted watching helplessly as the Senderistas (members of Sendero Luminoso) shot her husband such that "he didn't have a face—it was just a hole. I cried like crazy. We walked like crazy people seeing so many dead people, scattered everywhere. It was another life. We were like crazy people! I saw the dead scattered, without pants. They'd taken their good shirts" (Theidon 2013: 63). This invocation of "collective madness" helps explain the unexplainable by emphasizing a "disorder larger than one's own" while it also refers to living with profound distrust among neighbors and family members "capable of treachery" (2013: 63, 64).

17. Robben and Nordstrom 1995: 4 drawing on Feldman 1991. Violence is never completely overcome; it can be subject-making as it "seeps into the ongoing relationships and becomes a kind of atmosphere that cannot be expelled to an 'outside'" (Das 2007: 62). Das and Kleinman (2000: 1) also foreground violence in shaping subjectivity by considering how "subjectivity—the felt interior experience of the person that includes his or her positions in a field of relational power—is produced through the experience of violence."

18. Individuals and communities must: "'cope' with—read, endure, work through, break apart under, transcend—both traumatic violence and other, more insidious forms of social suffering" (Das and Kleinman 2001: 3).

19. Theidon 2013; Manz 2002; Malkki 1995. I have turned to enslaved individuals' narratives such as Jacobs (2001) and memoirs from Holocaust survivors (Levi 1996) and from survivors of torture (Partnoy 1998) for insights into being held against one's will. Recent accounts from child soldiers (Coulter 2009; Beah 2007), powerfully describe being surrounded by violence and not knowing if one will be free in the future. Accounts of life under other forms of captivity, such as prisoner-of-war camps and political prisons (Khan 2008; Solzhenitsyn 1974–78), allow insights into how indi-

viduals endure — and resist — the loss of control over even the most basic features of life, such as eating and sleeping.

20. Green 1999. While the violence in trafficking is often hidden, cases of state-sponsored violence and terror have been spectacularly public to create an atmosphere of fear. Green describes "horror, fear, and spectacle, along with murder and brutality" as "weapons of control" used against the Mayan population living in the western highlands of Guatemala. Disappearances, "scorched earth campaigns" that burn and raze villages and displace entire communities, and massacres are all public acts of horror meant to scar the survivors (173). However, although community members may have been caught up in public violence, they may not talk about it with each other. Such silence is what Green found in Guatemala, where the civil war was referred to in "public discourse simply as la violencia or la situacion," and "public discussions about widows or orphans were nonexistent" (3).

21. As an example of efforts to publicly heal and break the silence about violence, members of a community in Guatemala wrote and performed a play about the violence they experienced as a community (Manz 2004).

22. In an article on the "controversial and hotly debated" concept of immigrant and refugee integration, Ager and Strang (2008: 166–67) identify four key domains "central to perceptions of what constitutes 'successful' integration": "achievement and success across the sectors of employment, housing, education, and health; assumptions and practice regarding citizenship and rights; processes of social connections within and between groups within the community; and structural barriers to such connection related to language, culture and the local environment."

23. Rosaldo 1997.

24. There is a robust literature in refugee scholarship on the gap between what refugees need and what policy programmers imagine that they need (Loescher 1993). In repatriation initiatives, for example, aid providers try to incorporate "refugees' own meanings of repatriation and their perceptions and expectation of 'home'" (Black and Koser 1999: 9–10). Yet the anthropologist Laura Hammond (1999: 228) asserts that they are "largely shooting in the dark" as they develop assistance packages: "Social scientists . . . fail to appreciate the lessons that returnees can teach them about culture change, the construction of communities, and the multiple meanings of, and connections between, notions of identity, culture, home and geographical space."

25. Hammond 2004: 12. In fact Hammond emphasizes that since repatriation is "a new beginning" that may require "significant assistance," the best solution to forced migration may not be return (27).

26. Hammond 2004: 12.

27. Community membership is an essential aspect of building a sense of home. As Hammond (2004: 83) writes, communities are formed through the everyday practices of life and shared experiences, which strengthen cohesion.

28. Feldman 2006: 14, 11, 41.

29. Charles Hirschman and Douglas Massey (2008: 5) note that pioneers are a "rare species" since "most migrants follow in the footsteps of friends and family members who have already made the journey and can offer advice, encouragement, and funds

to subsidize the costs of transportation and settlement." Formerly trafficked persons do not benefit from the process of "cumulative causation" through which the costs of migration lower over time as the social networks of family and friends broadens (5).

30. Daniel and Knudsen 1995.

31. In his book on Guatemalan migration to Morganton, North Carolina, the historian Leon Fink (2003: 23–24) writes that the local police, "slowly, and only after some serious blunders," learned how to work with this new migrant population that had fled civil war and violence. One police officer offered the insight that there is an "inherent problem with the Guatemalan people trusting anyone in uniform. Coming from their home culture, they were faced with two types of [cops]: those that were corrupt and looking for money, or someone who was going to put them in the army" (23). This fear of law enforcement can be manipulated. For example, when the police enlisted the help of a translator to find out about a fight between two Guatemalan men, the men initially refused to cooperate. But after the translator took one man into a separate room without the police, he opened up. A police officer asked the translator what he had done to persuade the man to talk; he told Fink that the translator reported, "I told him that you were going to have him executed if he didn't tell the truth" (24).

32. The investigative journalist Noy Thrupakew (2009: 8) wrote about these unholy alliances between corrupt governments, law enforcement, and traffickers. In this context, initiatives to train police in countertrafficking techniques, such as International Justice Mission's program in Cambodia, funded with a $1 million grant from the U.S. Department of Justice, face extraordinary challenges since the "police are notorious for their involvement in trafficking, through extorting protection money from brothel owners, or through assault and rape of sex workers and trafficking victims."

33. Cooperation with law enforcement is not required to apply for a т visa for victims who demonstrate "physical or psychological trauma" and for victims under eighteen (U.S. Department of Justice 2010: 29). However, in a dialogue between two attorneys with years of experience representing trafficking clients, they remark that they do not know anyone who has successfully used this exception. Song comments: "Many trafficked persons may be too scared to attempt to use this exception because it is going to be the government deciding whether you meet the exceptional circumstances" (Kim, Song, and Panchalam 2009: 52). Since Kim and Song's dialogue, attorneys have sought and won this exemption.

34. Buijs 1993; Eastmond 1993.

35. Attorney Song describes his trafficking clients as "fearful of everyone" because "the trafficker consistently reinforces in them that they cannot trust anyone other than the trafficker. The trafficker will tell victims that they cannot trust the neighbors or the police, because they will, for example, report them to immigration, rape them, beat them, lock them up, and more." He and fellow attorney Kathleen Kim "both had clients who did not tell even us, their attorneys who are on their side, the whole story, because they do not know who we are. To them, we are random attorneys who are telling them to trust us and tell us everything. And they are afraid because this is how they got into their terrible situation in the first place—trusting random strangers" (Kim, Song, and Panchalam 2009: 41).

36. Turner 1995: 66. Turner notes that the role doctors and other health professionals had played in torture likely produced "alienation" from health professionals (67).

37. Alba and Nee 2003; Waldinger and Lichter 2003; Fong 1994; Repak 1995.

38. Knudsen 1995: 26–27.

39. Turner 1995: 66.

40. See Muecke 1995.

41. In some cases it is the reverse: social service providers are the first point of contact, and they then notify law enforcement.

42. This shelter assists adult women who are not U.S. citizens, while there also are shelters throughout the United States that offer housing to trafficking victims who are U.S. citizen youth who were in the sex trade.

43. Individuals who enter the United State as refugees receive social services provided by voluntary agencies (VOLAGS) funded by the U.S. Department of State. The Department enters into cooperative agreements with ten entities (nine national VOLAGS and one state). In turn, these organizations contract with their local VOLAG affiliates to provide reception and placement services during the first thirty days refugees are in the country. The services include providing basic food, clothing, shelter, orientation, and referrals to other organizations. The VOLAGS are required to conduct one home visit and ensure that, during the thirty-day period, the refugees apply for a Social Security card; apply for cash assistance, medical assistance, and Food Stamps, as appropriate; and register their children for school (U.S. Department of Health and Human Services, Office of Refugee Resettlement 2008).

44. Domestic violence shelters' locations are confidential. I therefore am vague about the location and other identifying characteristics about the shelters that I mention, referring instead to a shelter "in Orange County" or "in New York City."

45. See note 2 above on the USCCB's past role in the U.S. government's funding structure for trafficking victim assistance.

46. This is a pseudonym for the community-based organization in which Maria is active.

47. In *Buddha Is Hiding*, Aihwa Ong (2003: 47) describes that many people living during the Pol Pot years became "adept at dissimulation and dual consciousness in order to escape unwelcome attention or detection," and thus often relied on lies and silence in order to survive.

48. The anthropologist Susan Hirsch (2006: 39) movingly describes how, in the immediate aftermath of her husband's death in the bombing of the U.S. Embassy in Tanzania, she "craved company and feared being alone" but also "flinched at every encounter, as if my whole being were a raw wound exposed to harsh wind." "I told a friend that whenever I went out, which was rare, I actually wished I could wear a veil so that no one would recognize me."

49. On diplomatic immunity see Chuang 2010b; Vandenberg and Levy 2012; and Narushima 2013.

50. Sofia's daughter recently moved to the United States to live with her mother.

Chapter Four

1. Bourgois 2009: 18. Das and Kleinman (2000: 1) specifically consider subjectivity, "the felt interior experience of the person that includes his or her positions in a field of relational power," when it is "produced through the experience of violence."

2. Trafficking clients are expected to cooperate in a case until it is complete. According to a handbook for lawyers representing trafficking clients, "If an official certifies your client, and at a later date the client stops cooperating, the official has the ability to revoke the certification"—but the requests of law enforcement must be "reasonable," as judged by the court. For example, a request by law enforcement that puts the trafficked client's family in danger "could be unreasonable" (Bruggeman and Keyes 2009: 36).

3. Writing about asylees in France, Fassin and D'Halluin (2005: 600) observe, "Foreigners, thus, discover that although they were nothing 'without papers,' they were hardly more once they had obtained them." They describe the unending suspicion that asylee claimants face: "Today, the government administration's ethos regarding asylum is dominated by suspicion. People's case histories are questioned, facts are challenged, and evidence is disqualified" (606).

4. In *Buddha Is Hiding*, Aiwha Ong (2003) writes about the knowledge that traveled through refugee camps on how to be a desirable and compliant refugee worthy of resettlement to the United States.

5. To be clear, criminal restitution is "money owed to the victim because of the crime committed against the victim. Civil damages, pursued through the civil justice process, may be greater than restitution because it may include punitive damages in addition to compensatory damages" (Kim, Song, and Panchalam 2009: 58). Attorney Martina Vandenberg (2012) who has represented trafficking clients in civil suits writes that with only sixty-one trafficking survivors having filed civil suits, more pro-bono attorneys are needed to pursue civil action. Whether through settlement or judgments, civil recoveries place these individuals "on much firmer footing" (2012). Werner and Kim (2008) provide guidance on civil litigation.

6. Kim, Song, and Panchalam 2009: 58.

7. Kim, Song, and Panchalam 2009: 59–60.

8. Zetter 2007: 182.

9. Burke 2010: 23. I co-organized this conference at the Woodrow Wilson International Center with the anthropologist Pardis Mahdavi. Conference participants' contributions are in an edited volume, *Rethinking Trafficking* (Brennan and Mahdavi forthcoming).

10. A group of seasoned social workers and attorneys in New York City have been reaching out to microfinancing programs and other innovative opportunities to help facilitate greater economic mobility for their trafficking clients. Loosely called the Economic Empowerment Working Group—whose meetings I have attended—they exchange work, school, and loan opportunities for their clients while they also court the interest of established microfinance lenders.

11. Kibria 1993. Since formerly trafficked persons usually resettle on their own, without family or deep networks of kin in the United States, they miss out on the many

forms of reciprocal social relations that Carol Stack elegantly describes in her classic book on kin-based networks, *All Our Kin* (1974).

12. Writing about the working poor in the fast-food industry, anthropologist Katherine Newman observes that they did not have "vertical networks" to produce upward mobility (Newman 1999: 171).

13. Green 1999: 8. See Rylko-Bauer et al. (2009) bullet-point list of the effects of violence and war, such as the disruption of families and communities and the "stress of living with fear and uncertainty" (9).

14. Paul Farmer's (1992, 2001, and 2003) work on structural violence from the dual vantage point of medical doctor and anthropologist documents the interrelated sources and effects of marginalization, exploitation, abuse, and humiliation that the poor endure throughout the world. The anthropologists Nancy Scheper-Hughes and Philippe Bourgois (2003: 1) describe structural violence as "the violence of poverty, hunger, social exclusion and humiliation." They emphasize that violence "can never be understood solely in terms of its physicality—force, assault, or the infliction of pain—alone" but also includes "assaults on the personhood, dignity, sense of worth or value of the victim" (2003: 1). Green's (1999: 8) description of the economic, social, and political forces at work in the lives of the Guatemalan widows she interviewed is a vivid example of structural violence: "I saw that to understand the choices they were making necessitated an exploration of how violence has marked their lives on a daily basis, not only in their memories of the tragic individual deaths of their husbands but in the way violence, both structural and political, operated locally." This "violence of everyday life" grows out of "political violence and repression of the past decade and the long-term systemic violence connected with class and gender inequalities and ethnic oppression" (8).

15. Refugees in Britain, for example, felt "at home" when they felt safe (Ager and Strang 2008: 182–83).

16. In his book on migrant farmworkers, anthropologist and medical doctor Seth Holmes devotes considerable attention to migrant health. He echoes the frustration of the doctors and social workers I interviewed, "The difficult circumstances and limited gaze of the migrant clinic make it impossible for even the most idealistic clinicians to provide effective treatment" (2013: 154). He found that physicians both are unable to recommend "appropriate interventions" as well as often "prescribe ineffective treatments with unintended harmful effects" such as returning a patient with a knee injury to "full duty work" (2013: 154).

17. Women in a variety of contexts may stay silent about sexual abuse in particular. Muecke (1995: 44) found that Khmer women's silence about abuse may be a "cultural strategy for survival in their communities, for face-saving of their families, and for honoring lost parents."

18. With close to two hundred guests attending, this party was not held at the shelter but in a large room at a local college.

19. Since most trafficking clients around the country do not go to events with other trafficked persons or have ongoing contact with organizations, there is no institutional mechanism that brings them together to thank and to celebrate with the individu-

als who have assisted them. Staff at a shelter in Orange County, for example, describe former clients dropping by with food as thank-you's: "They don't write notes—many are illiterate—so they bring the entire staff food! Mole, Philippine specialties, food from around the world."

20. Ager and Strang 2008: 177, 180. Although formerly trafficked persons may develop networks that can "make a difference in the scramble for jobs," the volunteers that they meet through this organization may introduce them to networks that can "facilitate mobility" (Newman 1999: 161).

21. In Dave Eggers's (2007) fictionalized memoir of Valentino Achak Deng, one of the "lost boys" settled in the United States, several families figure prominently in Deng's life. They take him under their care, advise him, help him out financially, and act as surrogate families by regularly having him join in their family activities. Thus, even after refugees time out of their government benefits, informal assistance—and caring support networks—may continue through the communities in which they settle.

22. Ager and Strang (2008: 180) found that the refugees they interviewed cited participation in a wide range of shared activities—"sports, college classes, religious worship, community groups and political activity"—as indicating the depth of their "integration."

23. In her research with a mushroom farming community in Pennsylvania, the folklorist Debra Shutika (2011: 16) describes a sense of belonging as a two-way street between the Mexican newcomers and the English-speaking residents: "The emplacement and belonging experience is not exclusively the project of the newly arrived immigrant; it is a shared process between newcomers and longer-term residents, and it reveals how local populations are simultaneously transformed as migrant settlers establish themselves in the community and become part of it."

24. Geographer Geraldine Pratt's ethnography of Filipina domestic workers in Canada foregrounds "the pain and trauma of family separation," including the effects on children (Pratt 2012: xvi).

Chapter Five

1. These resilient individuals "think of life in terms of both limits and crossroads—where new intersections of technology, interpersonal relations, desire, and imagination can sometimes, against all odds, propel unexpected futures" (Biehl and Locke 2010: 318).

2. Willis (1977: 102) describes a "moment" in working-class culture when work "represents both a freedom, election and transcendence" that "promises the future," while working-class people simultaneously also enter into a "system of exploitation and oppression" and "gates shut on the future." "It is the future in the present which hammers freedom to inequality in the reality of contemporary capitalism" (1977: 120).

3. Dohan 2003: 71, 77. Cognizant of abuse when they encounter it, these recent migrants may have "objections to specific aspects of lousy jobs" without "condemning the desirability or necessity of work" (2003: 67).

4. 2003: 71. Dohan contrasts these newcomers' acceptance of low-wage work with some U.S.-born Mexican Americans' rejection of "futile dead-end jobs" in favor of what Dohan calls "hustling": participation in an active illicit economy and forms of public assistance. Distinguishing themselves from new migrants, these residents of the nearby barrio "Chavez" make clear that the "most demeaning and demanding jobs" are "jobs for immigrants" and thus unacceptable to them (Dohan 2003: 71, 68).

5. Formerly trafficked person live with what economist Guy Standing describes as ". . . chronic insecurity associated not only with teetering on the edge, knowing that one mistake or one piece of bad luck could tip the balance between modest dignity and being a bag lady" (Standing 2011: 20). According to Standing, the "precariat" lack seven forms of labor-related security that social democrats, labor parties, and unions pursued after the Second World War: labor market security, employment security, job security, work security (protections against accidents and illness at work), skill reproduction security, income security, and representation security (2011: 10).

6. Dohan (2003: 35) writes that the jobs available to new migrants pay too poorly to meet their ideal of work as providing the "economic foundation for personal advancement and community stability." As a result, while jobs are an "important source of income and stability," they are also "a source of great challenges and frustration" (35).

7. Fink 2003: 45.

8. In earlier chapters I have written that Maria has lost a number of jobs when her employers moved or their children aged out of child care, and Carmen has endured furloughs during slow occupancy rates.

9. Newman 1999: 162. Even if these contacts work in minimum-wage jobs, "lateral movement in the low-wage labor market certainly beats being unemployed" (1999: 163).

10. Newman asks if skills learned at minimum-wage jobs can ever translate into upward mobility or is the "ghetto worker stuck permanently in employment that will never pull his family above the poverty line?" (Newman 1999: xv). For too many workers "stuck in a job that will never pay a living wage," "the future ends up looking just like the present" (Newman 1999: 151).

11. In a report commissioned by the National Institute of Justice, the authors write about Emilio, who, while waiting for a decision on his T visa application, had turned to "illegal work in unsafe conditions" since his "most important concern" was not "safety, health, housing, or food stamps" but "to earn an income he can live on, and ideally, to send money home to his child" (Bales and Lize 2005: 130).

12. Newman sums up how poverty "tends to be overdetermined:" "Problems that drive people into life at the bottom come from all directions. Trying to cope with children alone, with no help from their fathers, adds to the stress that physically demanding jobs visit on women who are having trouble making ends meet. Worrying about being evicted or making the car payments that enable them to get to work at all does not help. Above all, though, a debilitating health condition, one that instantly compromises a parent's job, creates a powerful downdraft right into homelessness or the need to throw oneself into the arms of anyone who will offer some help" (Newman and O'Brien 2011: xxii–xxiii).

Closing Comments

1. Boff 2012. A detailed report by a conservative London Assembly member, Andrew Boff (2012: 4), commissioned by Mayor Boris Johnson, found "no strong evidence that trafficking for sexual exploitation does in fact increase during sporting events nor that such trafficking or prostitution had increased in London." The report asserts that the police "have been proactively raiding sex establishments without complaints or significant intelligence that exploitation takes place" (5). Quite remarkably the report notes that the raids increase safety and health risks to sex workers who fear reporting crimes and suggests classifying crimes against sex workers as hate crimes.

2. Since 1980 over 1.8 million refugees have been invited to live in the United States (U.S. Conference of Catholic Bishops 2013).

3. The Not for Sale Campaign (2010), a nonprofit organization, recently offered a one-week course at their San Francisco Abolitionist Academy, where "attendees learn how to identify possible cases of human trafficking, how to properly record and document high-probability locations, and how to liaison [sic] and work with partners such as law enforcement, service providers, legal teams, and others."

4. Some of the participants in the two-day conference have articles in a special edition of the *University of Pennsylvania Law Review* 158 (6) 2010.

5. For an example of media stories written in close collaboration with formerly trafficked persons, see Kandasamy 2012a and b.

6. Those just exiting forced labor would find out about the new national network through their social workers and attorneys—who are not part of these private phone calls and Facebook discussions.

References

Abramowitz, Sharon. 2009. "Healing in Peril: A Critical Debate over Ex-Combatant Rehabilitation." *Anthropology News* 50 (5): 14–15.

Abu-Lughod, Lila. 1990. "The Romance of Resistance: Tracing Transformations of Power through Bedouin Women." *American Ethnologist* 17 (1): 41–55.

Adams, Vincanne. 2013. *Markets of Sorrow, Labors of Faith: New Orleans in the Wake of Katrina.* Durham: Duke University Press.

Administration of Barack Obama, Office of the Press Secretary. 2010. "Obama on National Slavery and Human Trafficking Prevention Month." January 4. Accessed May 4, 2012, http://www.america.gov/st/texttrans-english/2010/January/201001051 05309xjsnommiso.6237757.html.

Administration of George W. Bush, Office of the Press Secretary. 2006. "President Signs H.R. 972, Trafficking Victims Protection Reauthorization Act." January 10. Accessed July 27, 2013, http://georgewbush-whitehouse.archives.gov/news/releases /2006/01/20060110-3.html.

Ager, Alistair, and Alison Strang. 2008. "Understanding Integration: A Conceptual Framework." *Journal of Refugee Studies* 21 (2): 166–91.

Agustín, Laura María. 2007. *Sex at the Margins: Migration, Labour Markets and the Rescue Industry.* New York: Palgrave Macmillan.

Ainslie, Ricardo. 1998. "Cultural Mourning, Immigration and Engagement: Vignettes from the Mexican Experience." In *Crossings: Mexican Immigration in Interdisciplinary Perspectives,* ed. Marcelo Suárez-Orozco. Cambridge: Harvard University Press.

Aizenman, N. C. 2008a. "In N. Va., a Latino Community Unravels." *Washington Post.* March 27.

———. 2008b. "42 Workers Detained in ICE Raids at Dulles." *Washington Post.* August 14.

Alba, Richard, and Victor Nee. 2003. *Remaking the American Mainstream: Assimilation and Contemporary Immigration.* Cambridge: Harvard University Press.

Alexandria House et al. 2008. "Letter from Human Rights Activists." Accessed May 3, 2012, http://www.bayswan.org/traffick/HR3887.html#2.

Alliance for a Safe and Diverse D.C. 2008. "Move Along: Policing Sex Work in Washington, D.C." Report. Washington, D.C.: Different Avenues.

American Civil Liberties Union. 2006. "Bush Global AIDS Gag Is Harmful to Public Health, Groups Tell Appeals Court." Press release. November 14. Accessed Oct. 14, 2011, http://www.aclu.org/print/lgbt-rights_hiv-aids/bush-global-aids-gag-harmful-public-health-groups-tell-appeals-court.

American Friends Service Committee et al. 2011. *Restoring Community: A National Community Advisory Report on ICE's Failed "Secure Communities" Program.* August. Report prepared by a commission of national and community-based organizations.

American University, Washington College of Law. 2010. "Picked Apart: The Hidden Struggles of Migrant Worker Women in the Maryland Crab Industry." Report. Washington, D.C.: International Human Rights Law Clinic and Centro de Los Derechos Del Migrant.

Amnesty International. 1973. *Report on Torture.* New York: Farrar, Straus and Giroux.

Andreas, Peter. 2013. *Smuggler Nation: How Illicit Trade Made America.* New York: Oxford University Press.

Asbed, Greg. 2003. "For Pickers, Slavery Tastes Like Tomatoes." *The Palm Beach Post.* March 30.

Baker, Al, and Tim Stelloh. 2012. "As Other Crimes Recede, Street Prostitution Keeps Its Wily Hold." *New York Times.* February 12. Accessed June 8, 2013, http://www.nytimes.com/2012/02/13/nyregion/as-other-crimes-recede-police-crack-down-on-street-prostitution.html?pagewanted=all&_r=0.

Baldwin, S. B., D. P. Eisenman, J. N. Sayles, G. Ryan, and K. S. Chuang. 2011. "Identification of Human Trafficking Victims in Health Care Settings," *Health & Human Rights: An International Journal* 13 (1): 36–49.

Bales, Kevin. 1999. *Disposable People: New Slavery in the Global Economy.* Berkeley: University of California Press.

Bales, Kevin, and Ron Soodalter. 2010. *The Slave Next Door: Human Trafficking and Slavery in America Today.* 2nd ed. Berkeley: University of California Press.

Bales, Kevin, and Steven Lize. 2005. "Trafficking in Persons in the United States." Report to the National Institute of Justice. Croft Institute for International Studies, University of Mississippi.

Bauer, Mary. 2009. *Under Siege: Life for Low-Income Latinos in the South.* Montgomery, Ala.: Southern Poverty Law Center.

Beah, Ishmael. 2007. *A Long Way Gone: Memoirs of a Boy Soldier.* New York: Farrar, Straus and Giroux.

Benczkowski, Brian A. 2007. Letter written as Principal Deputy Assistant Attorney General on behalf of U.S. Department of Justice, Office of Legislative Affairs. Addressed to The Honorable John Conyers Jr., Chairman, Committee on the Judiciary. http://www.justice.gov/olp/pdf/dept-view-letter-hjc-on-hr3887.pdf.

Benitez, Lucas. 2004. "Modern Day Slavery in the U.S. Agriculture Industry: Testimony before the U.S. House of Representatives Government Reform Committee, Subcommittee on Human Rights and Wellness." In *The Ongoing Tragedy* of *International Slavery and Human Trafficking: An Overview 2004*. Washington, D.C.: U.S. Government Printing Office.

Benjamin, Walter. 1968. *Illuminations: Essays and Reflections*. New York: Schocken Books.

Berger, Stephanie. 2012. "No End in Sight: Why the 'End Demand' Movement is the Wrong Focus for Efforts to Eliminate Human Trafficking." *Harvard Journal of Law & Gender* 35 (2012): 524–70.

Bernhardt, Annette, Ruth Milkman, Nik Theodore, Douglas Heckathorn, Mirabai Auer, James DeFilippis, Ana Luz González, Victor Narro, Jason Perelshteyn, Diana Polson, and Michael Spiller. 2009. *Broken Laws, Unprotected Workers*. Chicago: Center for Urban Economic Development.

Bernstein, Elizabeth. 2007. "The Sexual Politics of the 'New Abolitionism.'" *Differences* 18 (3): 128–51.

———. 2008. "Sexual Commerce and the Global Flow of Bodies, Desires, and Social Policies." *Sexuality Research and Social Policy* 5 (4): 1–5.

———. 2010. "Militarized Humanitarianism Meets Carceral Feminism: The Politics of Sex, Rights, and Freedom in Contemporary Antitrafficking Campaigns." *Signs: Journal of Women in Culture and Society* 35 (1): 45–71.

Best Practices Policy Project. 2010. Questionnaire on Human Rights Challenges and Responses in the Context of HIV and AIDS. Submitted September 15, 2010, to Civil Society Section, Office of the United Nations High Commissioner for Human Rights. Accessed July 10, 2013, http://www.bestpracticespolicy.org/wp-content/uploads/2013/01/UNReportonHIV_Sept15_2010.pdf.

Bezner, Lili Corbus. 1999. *Photography and Politics in America: From the New Deal into the Cold War*. Baltimore: Johns Hopkins University Press.

Biehl, João. 2005. *Vita: Life in a Zone of Social Abandonment*. Berkeley: University of California Press.

———. 2007a. "A Life." In *Subjectivity: Ethnographic Investigations*, ed. J. Biehl, B. Good, and A. Kleinman. Berkeley: University of California Press.

———. 2007b. *Will to Live: AIDS Therapies and the Politics of Survival*. Princeton: Princeton University Press.

Biehl, João, Byron Good, and Arthur Kleinman, eds. 2007. *Subjectivity: Ethnographic Investigations*. Berkeley: University of California Press.

Biehl, João, and Peter Locke. 2010. "Deleuze and the Anthropology of Becoming." *Cultural Anthropology* 51 (3): 317–51.

Bittman, Mark. 2011. "The True Cost of Tomatoes." *The New York Times*. June 14.

Black, Richard, and Khalid Koser, eds. 1999. *The End of the Refugee Cycle? Refugee Repatriation and Reconstruction*. Oxford: Berghahn Books.

Boff, Andrew A. M. 2012. "Silence on Violence: Improving the Safety of Women. The Policing of Off-street Sex Work and Sex Trafficking in London." March. Report to London Assembly.

Bonacich, Edna, and Richard P. Appelbaum. 2000. *Behind the Label: Inequality in the Los Angeles Apparel Industry*. Berkeley: University of California Press.

Boris, Eileen, and Rhacel Salazar Parreñas, eds. 2010. *Intimate Labors: Cultures, Technologies, and the Politics of Care*. Stanford: Stanford University Press.

Borneman, John. 1997. *Settling Accounts: Violence, Justice and Accountability in Postsocialist Europe*. Princeton: Princeton University Press.

Bosniak, Linda. 2006. *The Citizen and the Alien: Dilemmas of Contemporary Membership*. Princeton: Princeton University Press.

Bourgois, Philippe. 2009. *Righteous Dopefiend*. Berkeley: University of California Press.

Bowe, John. 2003. "Nobodies: Does Slavery Exist in America?" *New Yorker*, April 21, at 106.

———. 2007. *Nobodies: Modern American Slave Labor and the Dark Side of the New Global Economy*. New York: Random House.

Bracken, Patrick J., and Celia Petty. 1998. Introduction to *Rethinking the Trauma of War*, ed. Patrick J. Bracken and Celia Petty. London: Free Association Books.

Brennan, Denise. 2004. *What's Love Got to Do with It? Transnational Desires and Sex Tourism in the Dominican Republic*. Durham: Duke University Press.

———. 2005. "Methodological Challenges in Research with Trafficked Persons: Tales from the Field." *International Migration* 43 (1/2): 35–54.

———. 2008. "Competing Claims of Victimhood? Foreign and Domestic Victims of Trafficking in the United States." *Sexuality Research and Social Policy* 5 (4): 45–61.

———. 2010a. "Key Issues in the Resettlement of Formerly Trafficked Persons in the United States." "Trafficking in Sex and Labor: Domestic and International Responses." *University of Pennsylvania Law Review* 158 (6): 1581–1608.

———. 2010b. "Securing Migrants' Rights as Anti-Trafficking Work." In *Rethinking Human "Trafficking."* Occasional Paper Series. Washington, D.C.: Middle East Program and United States Studies, Woodrow Wilson International Center for Scholars.

———. 2010c. "Thoughts on Finding and Assisting Individuals in Forced Labor in the USA." "Sexual Labors: Interdisciplinary Perspectives toward Sex as Work." Special edition, *Sexualities* 13 (2): 139–52.

———. Forthcoming. "Trafficking, Scandal, and Abuse of Migrant Workers: Measuring Exploitation in Argentina and the United States." *Annals of the American Academy of Political and Social Science*.

Brennan, Denise, and Pardis Mahdavi, eds. Forthcoming. *Rethinking Trafficking*. Durham: Duke University Press.

Bridge to Freedom Foundation. 2010. "Programs." Accessed Feb. 24, 2012, http://www .bridgetofreedomfoundation.org/programs.html.

———. 2012. "Identifying Recovery Hurdles—Nutritional Habits Survey." Accessed July 27, 2013, http://survey.constantcontact.com/survey/ao7e2yro2dwgbf3pyvd /ao17xhjgjs9jq1/questions.

———. 2013. "Our Team." Accessed July 21, 2013, http://www.bridgetofreedomfoun dation.org/Our%20Team.html.

Brinkley, Joel. 2008. "Enslaved by Definition." *San Francisco Chronicle*. January 13.

Bruggeman, Jean, and Elizabeth Keyes. 2009. "Meeting the Legal Needs of Human Trafficking Victims: An Introduction for Domestic Violence Attorneys and Advocates." Chicago: American Bar Association.

Brulliard, Karin. 2008. "Crackdown on Illegal Immigration Quiets Soccer Fields in Pr. William." *Washington Post*. March 12, 2008.

Brunovskis, Anette, and Rebecca Surtees. 2008. "Agency or Illness—The Conceptualization of Trafficking: Victims' Choices and Behaviors in the Assistance System." *Gender, Technology and Development* 12 (1): 53–76.

———. 2010. "Untold Stories: Biases and Selection Effects in Research with Victims of Trafficking for Sexual Exploitation." *International Migration* 48 (4): 1–37.

Buijs, Gina. 1993. Introduction. In *Migrant Women: Crossing Boundaries and Changing Identities*, ed. G. Buijs. Oxford: Berg.

Burgos-Debray, Elisabeth, ed. 1984. *I, Rigoberta Menchú: An Indian Woman in Guatemala*. Trans. Ann Wright. London: Verso.

Burke, Florrie. 2010. "Notes from the Field." In *Rethinking Human "Trafficking."* Occasional Paper Series. Washington, D.C.: Middle East Program and United States Studies, Woodrow Wilson International Center for Scholars.

Burns, Crosby, Ann Garcia, and Philip E. Wolgin. 2013. "Living in Dual Shadows: LGBT Undocumented Immigrants." Washington, D.C. Center for American Progress. March 8. Accessed June 19, 2013, http://www.americanprogress.org/issues/immigration/report/2013/03/08/55674/living-in-dual-shadows/.

Cadet, Jean-Robert. 1998. *Restavec: From Haitian Slave Child to Middle-Class American*. Austin: University of Texas Press.

Camayd-Freixas, Erik. 2008. "Statement at the U.S. District Court for the Northern District of Iowa Regarding a Hearing on 'The Arrest, Prosecution, and Conviction of 297 Undocumented Workers in Postville, Iowa, from May 12 to 22, 2008.'" Accessed May 4, 2012, http://judiciary.house.gov/hearings/pdf/Camayd-Freixas080724.pdf.

———. 2013. *U.S. Immigration Reform and Its Global Impact: Lessons from the Postville Raid*. New York: Palgrave Macmillan.

Capps, Randy, Rosa Maria Castañeda, Ajay Chaudry, and Robert Santos. 2007. "Paying the Price: The Impact of Immigration Raids on America's Children." Report. Washington, D.C.: Urban Institute for the National Council of La Raza.

Capps, Randy, James Bachmeier, Michael Fix, and Jennifer Van Hook. 2013. "A Demographic, Socioeconomic, and Health Coverage Profile of Unauthorized Immigrants in the United States." Accessed July 19, 2013, http://www.migrationpolicy.org/pubs/CIRbrief-Profile-Unauthorized.pdf. Issue Brief No. 5. May. Washington, D.C.: Migration Policy Institute.

Cave, Damien. 2008. "Local Officials Adopt New, Harder Tactics on Illegal Immigrants." *The New York Times*. June 9.

Chacón, Jennifer. 2006. "Misery and Myopia: Understanding the Failures of U.S. Efforts to Stop Human Trafficking." *Fordham Law Review* 74 (6): 2977–3040.

———. 2010. "Tensions and Trade-Offs: Protecting Trafficking Victims in the Era of Immigration Enforcement." *University of Pennsylvania Law Review* 158 (6): 1609–53.

Chang, Grace. 2000. *Disposable Domestics: Immigrant Women Workers in the Global Factory*. Cambridge, Mass.: South End Press.

Chapkis, Wendy. 2005. "Soft Glove, Punishing Fist: The Trafficking Victims Protection

Act of 2000." In *Regulating Sex: The Politics of Intimacy and Identity*, ed. E. Bernstein and L. Schaffner. New York: Routledge.

Chavez, Leo. 1992. *Shadowed Lives: Undocumented Immigrants in American Society*. Orlando: Holt, Rinehart and Winston.

Checker, Melissa. 2005. *Polluted Promises: Environmental Racism and the Search for Justice in a Southern Town*. New York: New York University Press.

Cheng, Sealing. 2008. "Muckraking and Stories Untold: Ethnography Meets Journalism on Trafficked Women and the U.S. Military." *Sexuality Research and Social Policy* 5 (4): 6–18.

———. 2010. *On the Move for Love: Migrant Entertainers and the U.S. Military in South Korea*. Philadelphia: University of Pennsylvania Press.

Cho, Eunice Hyunhye, and Rebecca Smith. 2013. "Workers' Rights on ICE: How Immigration Reform Can Stop Retaliation and Advance Labor Rights." The National Employment Law Project. February. Accessed July 29, 2013, http://www.nelp.org /page/-/Justice/2013/Workers-Rights-on-ICE-Retaliation-Report-California.pdf ?nocdn=1. Oakland, Calif.: National Employment Law Project California Office.

Chuang, Janie A. 1998. "Redirecting the Debate over Trafficking in Women: Definitions, Paradigms, and Contexts." *Harvard Human Rights Journal* 11: 65–107.

———. 2006. "The United States as Global Sheriff: Using Unilateral Sanctions to Combat Human Trafficking." *Michigan Journal of International Law* 27 (2): 437–94.

———. 2010a. "Rescuing Trafficking from Ideological Capture: Prostitution Reform and Anti-Trafficking Law and Policy." *University of Pennsylvania Law Review* 158 (6): 1655–728.

———. 2010b. "Achieving Accountability for Migrant Domestic Worker Abuse." *North Carolina Law Review* 88 (5): 1627–56.

———. 2013. "Exploitation Creep and the Unmaking of Human Trafficking Law." Presentation at American University Washington College of Law, May 28.

Cizmar, Martin, Ellis Conklin, and Kristen Hinman. 2011. "Real Men Get Their Facts Straight." *The Village Voice*. June 29.

Clawson, Heather, et al. 2003. "Needs Assessment for Service Providers and Trafficking Victims." Report for U.S. Department of Justice, National Institute of Justice. OJP-99-C-010. Fairfax, Va.: Caliber Associates.

Clawson, Heather J., Nicole Dutch, Amy Solomon, and Lisa Goldblatt Grace. 2009. "Human Trafficking Into and Within the United States: A Review of the Literature." Washington, D.C.: U.S. Department of Health and Human Services. Accessed July 29, 2013, http://aspe.hhs.gov/hsp/07/HumanTrafficking/LitRev/.

CNN Freedom Project. 2011a. "Clinton: We Are a Shining Light." June 27. Accessed May 4, 2012, http://thecnnfreedomproject.blogs.cnn.com/2011/06/27/clinton-we -are-shining-a-light/.

———. 2011b. "Life in Slavery." Accessed Sept. 28, 2011, http://thecnnfreedomproject .blogs.cnn.com/category/life-in-slavery/.

Coalition of Immokalee Workers. 2009. "Putting an End to Tomatoes Tinged with the Bitter Taste of Exploitation: Coalition of Immokalee." Joint press release: CIW and Bon Appétit Management Company.

———. 2010a. "ARAMARK and Coalition of Immokalee Workers Sign Agreement to Improve Wages, Working Conditions in Tomato Fields of Florida." *CIW News*, April 1. Accessed Oct. 31, 2011, http://www.ciwonline.org/CIW_Aramark_release.html.

———. 2010b. "Campaign for Fair Food Discussion Guide." CIW Online. Accessed Nov. 3, 2011, http://www.ciwonline.org/Resources/tools/HoS%20Discussion%20Guide.pdf.

———. 2010c. "Sodexo and Coalition of Immokalee Workers Sign Fair Food Agreement." *CIW News*, August 24. Accessed Oct. 31, 2011, http://www.ciwonline.org/ciw_sodexo_joint_release.html.

———. 2010d. "If there are some atrocities going on, it's not our business." CIW Online. Accessed July 27, 2013, http://ciw-online.org/2010/12/14/acceptable_atrocities/.

———. 2011. "About the CIW." Accessed Dec. 14, 2011, http://ciwonline.org/Resources/about/11CIWwho.pdf.

———. 2012. "Campaign for Fair Food." CIW Online. Accessed July 28, 2013, http://ciw-online.org/campaign-for-fair-food/.

———. 2013. "Consciousness + Commitment = Change." CIW Online. Accessed July 29, 2013, http://ciw-online.org/about/.

Cohen, Susan A. 2005. "Ominous Convergence: Sex Trafficking, Prostitution, and International Family Planning." *Guttmacher Report on Public* Policy 8 (1): 12–14.

Coll, Kathleen M. 2010. *Remaking Citizenship: Latina Immigrants and New American Politics*. Stanford: Stanford University Press.

Collins, Patricia Hill. 1991. *Black Feminist Thought: Knowledge, Consciousness, and the Politics of Empowerment*. New York: Routledge.

Constable, Nicole. 1999. "At Home but Not at Home: Filipina Narratives of Ambivalent Returns." *Cultural Anthropology* 14 (2): 203–28.

———. 2003. *Romance on a Global Stage: Pen Pals, Virtual Ethnography, and "Mail Order" Marriages*. Berkeley: University of California Press.

———. 2004. "Changing Filipina Identities and Ambivalent Returns." In *Coming Home? Refugees, Migrants and Those Who Stay Behind*, ed. Ellen Oxfeld and Lynellyn D. Long. Philadelphia: University of Pennsylvania Press.

———. 2007. *Maid to Order in Hong Kong: Stories of Migrant Workers*. Ithaca: Cornell University Press. Second edition.

———. 1997. *Maid to Order in Hong Kong: Stories of Filipina Workers*. Ithaca: Cornell University Press.

Constable, Pamela. 2012. "For Battered Immigrant Women, Fear of Deportation Becomes Abusers' Weapon, But 2 Laws Can Overcome That." *The Washington Post*. February 8.

Coulter, Chris. 2009. *Bush Wives and Girl Soldiers: Women's Lives through War and Peace in Sierra Leone*. Ithaca: Cornell University Press.

Coutin, Susan Bibler. 2003a. *Legalizing Moves: Salvadoran Immigrants' Struggle for U.S. Residency*. Ann Arbor: University of Michigan Press.

———. 2003b. "Illegality, Borderlands, and the Space of Nonexistence." In

Globalization Under Construction: Governmentality, Law, and Identity. Minneapolis: University of Minnesota Press.

————. 2007. *Nations of Emigrants: Shifting Boundaries of Citizenship in El Salvador and the United States.* Ithaca: Cornell University Press.

Crago, Anna-Louise. 2008. *Our Lives Matter: Sex Workers Unite for Health and Rights.* Sexual Health and Rights Project. New York: Open Society Institute.

Daniel, E. Valentine, and John C. H. R. Knudsen. 1995. Introduction to *Mistrusting Refugees,* ed. Daniel Valentine and John Knudsen. Berkeley: University of California Press.

Danna, Daniela. 2012. "Client-Only Criminalization in the City of Stockholm: A Local Research on the Application of the 'Swedish Model' of Prostitution Policy." *Sexuality Research and Social Policy* 9 (1): 80–93.

Das, Veena. 2000. "The Act of Witnessing: Violence, Poisonous Knowledge, and Subjectivity." In *Violence and Subjectivity,* ed. Veena Das, Arthur Kleinman, Mamphela Ramphele, and Pamela Reynolds. Berkeley: University of California Press.

————. 2007. *Life and Words: Violence and the Descent into the Ordinary.* Berkeley: University of California Press.

Das, Veena, and Arthur Kleinman. 2000. Introduction to *Violence and Subjectivity,* ed. Veena Das, Arthur Kleinman, Mamphela Ramphele, and Pamela Reynolds. Berkeley: University of California Press.

Das, Veena, and Arthur Kleinman. 2001. Introduction to *Remaking a World: Violence, Social Suffering, and Recovery,* ed. Veena Das, Arthur Kleinman, Margaret Lock, Mamphela Ramphele, and Pamela Reynolds. Berkeley: University of California Press.

Davis, Kevin E., Benedict Kingsbury, and Sally Engle Merry. 2012. "Introduction: Global Governance by Indicators." In *Governance by Indicators: Global Power through Classification and Rankings,* ed. K. Davis, B. Kingsbury, and S. Merry. Oxford: Oxford University Press.

De Genova, Nicholas P. 2002. "Migrant 'Illegality' and Deportability in Everyday Life." *Annual Review of Anthropology* 31: 419–47.

De Genova, Nicholas P., and Nathalie Peutz, eds. 2010. *The Deportation Regime: Sovereignty, Space, and the Freedom of Movement.* Durham: Duke University Press.

Dempsey, Michelle. 2010. "Sex Trafficking and Criminalization: In Defense of Feminist Abolitionism." *University of Pennsylvania Law Review* 158: 1729–75.

DeStefano, Anthony M. 2007. *The War on Human Trafficking: U.S. Policy Assessed.* New Brunswick, N.J.: Rutgers University Press.

Ditmore, Melissa. 2009. "Kicking Down the Door: The Use of Raids to Fight Trafficking in Persons." Report. New York: Sex Workers Project at the Urban Justice Center.

Ditmore, Melissa, Anna Maternick, and Katherine Zapert. 2012. "The Road North: The Role of Gender, Poverty and Violence in Trafficking from Mexico to the US." Report. New York: Sex Workers Project at the Urban Justice Center.

Di Tommaso, Maria, et al. 2009. "As Bad as It Gets: Well-being Deprivation of Sexually Exploited Trafficked Women." *European Journal of Political Economy* 25: 143–62.

Dodillet, Susanne, and Petra Ostergren. 2011. "The Swedish Sex Purchase Act: Claimed Success and Documented Effects." Paper presented at the International Workshop Decriminalizing Prostitution and Beyond: Practical Experiences and Challenges. The Hague, March 3 and 4.

Doezema, Jo. 1998. "Forced to Choose: Beyond the Voluntary v. Forced Prostitution Dichotomy." In *Global Sex Workers: Rights, Resistance, and Redefinition*, ed. K. Kempadoo and J. Doezema. New York: Routledge.

———. 2000. "Loose Women or Lost Women? The Re-emergence of the Myth of 'White Slavery' in Contemporary Discourses on 'Trafficking in Women.'" *Gender Issues* 18 (1): 23–50.

———. 2010. *Sex Slaves and Discourse Masters: The Construction of Trafficking*. New York: Zed Books.

Dohan, Daniel. 2003. *The Price of Poverty: Money, Work, and Culture in the Mexican American Barrio*. Berkeley: University of California Press.

Dorning, Jennifer, and Charlie Fanning. 2012. "Gaming the System 2012: Guest Worker Visa Programs and Professional and Technical Workers in the U.S." Department for Professional Employees.

Duguay, Christian, director. 2005. *Human Trafficking*. 176 min. Montreal: Lifetime TV.

Durbin, Dick, Bernie Sanders, and Sherrod Brown. 2008. "We Must Treat Farmworkers Fairly." *The Miami Herald*. April 21.

Eastmond, Marita. 1993. "Reconstructing Life: Chilean Refugee Women and the Dilemmas of Exile." In *Migrant Women: Crossing Boundaries and Changing Identities*, ed. G. Buijs. Oxford: Berg.

Eggers, Dave. 2007. *What Is the What*. San Francisco: McSweeney's.

Ehrenreich, Barbara. 2001. *Nickel and Dimed: On (Not) Getting By in America*. New York: Picador.

Ehrenreich, Barbara, and Arlie Hochschild, eds. 2002. *Global Woman: Nannies, Maids, and Sex Workers in the New Economy*. New York: Metropolitan Books.

Eiserer, Tanya. 2007. "8 Spas Raided in Prostitution Sting." *The Dallas Morning News*. April 18.

Empower. 2003. "A Report by Empower Chiang Mai on the Human Rights Violations Women Are Subjected to When 'Rescued' by Anti-Trafficking Groups Who Employ Methods Using Deception, Force and Coercion." Network of Sex Work Projects. June. Accessed Feb. 18, 2012, http://www.nswp.org/resource/report-empower -chiang-mai-the-human-rights-violations-women-are-subjected-when-rescued-anti.

Engerman, Stanley L. 2007. *Slavery, Emancipation and Freedom: Comparative Perspectives*. Baton Rouge: Louisiana State University Press.

Estabrook, Barry. 2011. *Tomatoland: How Modern Industrial Agriculture Destroyed Our Most Alluring Fruit*. Kansas City: Andrews McMeel.

Estes, Richard J., and Neil Alan Weiner. 2001. "The Commercial Sexual Exploitation of Children in the U.S., Canada, and Mexico." Report. Philadelphia: University of Pennsylvania School of Social Work and Center for the Study of Youth Policy.

Farmer, Paul. 1992. *AIDS and Accusation: Haiti and the Geography of Blame*. Berkeley: University of California Press.

————. 2001. *Infections and Inequalities: The Modern Plagues.* Berkeley: University of California Press.

————. 2003. *Pathologies of Power: Health, Human Rights, and the New War on the Poor.* Berkeley: University of California Press.

Farrell, Amy, Jack McDevitt, and Stephanie Fahy. 2008. "Understanding and Improving Law Enforcement Responses to Human Trafficking: Final Report." Report to U.S. Department of Justice, National Institute of Justice. June 1. Accessed July 29, 2013, http://www.ncjrs.gov/pdffiles1/nij/grants/222752.pdf. Boston: Northeastern University.

Farrell, Amy, Jack McDevitt, Noam Perry, Stephanie Fahy, Kate Chamberlain, William Adams, Colleen Owens, Meredith Dank, Michael Shively, Ryan Kling, and Kristin Wheeler. 2010. "Review of Existing Estimates of Victims of Human Trafficking in the United States and Recommendations for Improving Research and Measurement of Human Trafficking." Report. Washington, D.C.: The Alliance to End Slavery and Trafficking.

Farrell, Amy, et al. 2012. "Identifying Challenges to Improve the Investigation and Prosecution of State and Local Human Trafficking Cases." Report for U.S. Department of Justice, National Institute of Justice, Northeastern University, Institute on Race and Justice; Urban Institute, Justice Policy Center. Accessed Aug. 1, 2013, http://www.urban.org/UploadedPDF/412593-State-and-Local-Human-Trafficking -Cases.pdf.

Fassin, Didier. 2010. "Ethics of Survival: A Democratic Approach to the Politics of Life." *Humanity* 1 (1): 81–95.

Fassin, Didier, and Estelle D'Halluin. 2005. "The Truth from the Body: Medical Certificates as Ultimate Evidence for Asylum Seekers." *American Anthropologist* 107 (4): 597–608.

Fassin, Didier, and Richard Rechtman. 2009. *The Empire of Trauma: An Inquiry into the Condition of Victimhood.* Princeton: Princeton University Press.

Feingold, David. 2005. "Human Trafficking." *Foreign Policy* 150: 26–30.

————. 2010. *Sex, Drugs, and Body Counts: The Politics of Numbers in Global Crime and Conflict.* Ed. Peter Andreas and Kelly M. Greenhill. Ithaca: Cornell University Press.

Feldman, Allen. 1991. *Formations of Violence: The Narrative of the Body and Political Terror in Northern Ireland.* Chicago: University of Chicago Press.

Feldman, Ilana. 2006. "Home as a Refrain: Remembering and Living Displacement in Gaza." *History and Memory* 18 (2): 10–47.

Fink, Leon. 2003. *The Maya of Morganton: Work and Community in the Nuevo New South.* Chapel Hill: University of North Carolina Press.

Finnegan, William. 2008. "The Countertraffickers: Rescuing the Victims of the Global Sex Trade." *New Yorker*, May 5.

Finnström, Sverker. 2008. *Living with Bad Surroundings: War, History, and Everyday Moments in Northern Uganda.* Durham: Duke University Press.

Fischer, Benedikt, Scot Wortley, Cheryl Webster, and Maritt Kirst. 2002. "The Socio-legal Dynamics and Implications of 'Diversion': The Case Study of the Toronto 'John

School' Diversion Programme for Prostitution Offenders." *Criminology and Criminal Justice* 2 (4): 385–410.

Fong, Timothy. 1994. *The First Suburban Chinatown: The Remaking of Monterey Park.* Philadelphia: Temple University Press.

Fraser, Nancy. 2008. *Scales of Justice: Reimagining Political Space in a Globalizing World.* New York: Columbia University Press.

Free the Slaves and Human Rights Center. 2004. *Hidden Slaves: Forced Labor in the United States.* Report. Berkeley: University of California.

Freedom Network USA. 2012. "About Us." Accessed Feb. 24, 2012, http://freedom networkusa.org/about-us/.

Friendly, Fred, producer. 1960. "Harvest of Shame." *CBS News,* November 25.

Gallagher, Anne T. 2001. "Human Rights and the New UN Protocols on Trafficking and Migrant Smuggling: A Preliminary Analysis." *Human Rights Quarterly* 23 (4): 975–1004.

————. 2012. *The International Law of Human Trafficking.* Cambridge: Cambridge University Press.

Garcia, Angela. 2010. *The Pastoral Clinic: Addiction and Dispossession along the Rio Grande.* Berkeley: University of California Press.

Gardner, Andrew. 2010. *City of Strangers: Gulf Migration and the Indian Community in Bahrain.* Ithaca: Cornell University Press.

————. Forthcoming. "Construction Workers in the Gulf States: Human Trafficking Revisited." In *Rethinking Trafficking,* ed. Denise Brennan and Pardis Mahdavi.

Gill, Lesley. 2004. *The School of the Americas: Military Training and Political Violence in the Americas.* Durham: Duke University Press.

Global Alliance Against Traffic in Women. 2007. "Collateral Damage: The Impact of Anti-Trafficking Measures on Human Rights around the World." Report. Accessed July 28, 2013, http://www.gaatw.org/Collateral%20Damage_Final/singlefile_Collat eralDamagefinal.pdf. Bangkok: Global Alliance Against Traffic in Women.

Goldstein, Bruce, and Catherine K. Ruckelshaus. 1999. "Lessons for Reforming 21st Century Labor Subcontracting: How 19th Century Reformers Attacked 'The Sweating System.'" Accessed Dec. 21, 2011, http://nelp.3cdn.net/541b69ad88a3a26317_7c m6bx6g4.pdf.

Gomberg-Muñoz, Ruth. 2010. "Willing to Work: Agency and Vulnerability in an Undocumented Immigrant Network." *American Anthropologist* 112 (2): 295–307.

Gordon, Jennifer. 2005. *Suburban Sweatshops: The Fight for Immigrant Rights.* Cambridge: Belknap Press of Harvard University Press.

Gourevitch, Philip. 1999. *We Wish to Inform You that Tomorrow We Will Be Killed with Our Families: Stories from Rwanda.* New York: Picador.

Gozdziak, Elzbieta M. 2005. "Refugee Women's Psychological Response to Forced Migration: Limitations of the Trauma Concept." Report. Washington, D.C.: Institute for the Study of International Migration, Edmund A. Walsh School of Foreign Service, Georgetown University.

Gozdziak, Elzbieta M., and Elizabeth A. Collett. 2005. "Research on Human

Trafficking in North America: A Review of the Literature." *International Migration* 43 (1/2): 99–128.

Grandin, Greg. 2010. "It Was Heaven That They Burned: Who Is Rigoberta Menchú?" *The Nation*. September 27.

———. 2011. *Who Is Rigoberta Menchú?* London: Verso.

Grant, Melissa Gira. 2013. "The War on Sex Workers." *Reason.com*, January 21. Accessed January 24, 2013, http://reason.com/archives/2013/01/21/the-war-on-sex-workers.

Gray, Margaret. 2007. "The Hudson Valley Farmworker Report: Understanding the Needs and Aspirations of a Voiceless Population." Annandale-on-Hudson, N.Y.: Bard Migrant Labor Project.

Green, Linda. 1999. *Fear as a Way of Life: Mayan Widows in Rural Guatemala*. New York: Columbia University Press.

Greenhouse, Steven. 2007. "Tomato Pickers' Wages Fight Faces Obstacles." *The New York Times*. December 24.

Griffith, David, and Ed Kissam. 1995. *Working Poor: Farmworkers in the United States*. Philadelphia: Temple University Press.

Gurwitt, Rob. 2004. "Power to the Pickers: Lucas Benitez Demands a Harvest without Shame." *Mother Jones* 29 (4): 24.

Hahamovitch, Cindy. 2011. *No Man's Land: Jamaican Guestworkers in America and the Global History of Deportable Labor*. Princeton: Princeton University Press.

Hale, Charles. 2001. "What Is Activist Research?" Social Science Research Council, *Items and Issues* 2 (1–2): 13–15.

Hale, Charles, ed. 2008. *Engaging Contradictions: Theory, Politics, and Methods of Activist Scholarship*. Berkeley: University of California Press.

Halley, Janet. 2008. *Split Decisions: How and Why to Take a Break from Feminism*. Princeton: Princeton University Press.

Halley, Janet, Prabha Kotiswaran, Hila Shamir, and Chantal Thomas. 2006. "From the International to the Local in Feminist Legal Responses to Rape, Prostitution/Sex Work, and Sex Trafficking: Four Studies in Contemporary Governance Feminism." *Harvard Journal of Law and Gender* 29 (2): 335–423.

Hammond, Laura. 1999. "Examining the Discourse of Repatriation: Toward a More Proactive Theory of Return Migration." In *The End of the Refugee Cycle?: Refugee Repatriation and Reconstruction*, ed. Richard Black and Khalid Koser. New York: Berghahn Books.

———. 2004. *This Place Will Become Home: Refugee Repatriation to Ethiopia*. Ithaca: Cornell University Press.

Hannerz, Ulf. 2003. "Being There . . . and There . . . and There! Reflections on Multi-Site Ethnography." *Ethnography* 4 (2): 201–16.

Harcourt, Christine, et al. 2005. "Sex Work and the Law." *Sexual Health* 2 (3): 121–28.

Harrington, Carol. 2005. "The Politics of Rescue: Peacekeeping and Anti-trafficking Programmes in Bosnia-Herzegovina and Kosovo." *International Feminist Journal of Politics* 7 (2): 175–206.

Harris, Paul. 2013. "Undocumented Workers' Grim Reality: Speak Out on Abuse and Risk Deportation." *The Guardian*. March 28.

Haynes, Dina Francesca. 2004. "Used, Abused, Arrested and Deported: Extending Immigration Benefits to Protect the Victims of Trafficking and to Secure the Prosecution of Traffickers." *Human Rights Quarterly* 26: 221–72.

———. 2006. "Client-Centered Human Rights Advocacy," *Clinical Law Review* 13: 379–416.

———. 2007. "(Not) Found Chained to a Bed in a Brothel: Conceptual, Legal, and Procedural Failures to Fulfill the Promise of the Trafficking Victims Protection Act." *Georgetown Immigration Law Journal* (21): 337–82.

———. 2008. "Good Intentions Are Not Enough: Four Recommendations for Implementing the Trafficking Victims Protection Act." *University of St. Thomas Law Journal* 6: 77–95.

———. 2009. "Exploitation Nation: The Thin and Grey Legal Lines between Trafficked Persons and Abused Migrant Laborers." *Notre Dame Journal of Law, Ethics and Public Policy* 23 (1): 41–45.

———. 2010. "Lessons from Bosnia's Arizona Market: Harm to Women in a Neoliberalized Postconflict Reconstruction Process." *University of Pennsylvania Law Review* 158: 1779–829.

Herman, Judith. 1997. *Trauma and Recovery: The Aftermath of Violence — from Domestic Abuse to Political Terror*. New York: Basic Books.

Hinton, Alexander Laban, ed. 2004. *Why Did They Kill? Cambodia in the Shadow of Genocide*. Berkeley: University of California Press.

Hirsch, Susan F. 2006. *In the Moment of Greatest Calamity: Terrorism, Grief, and a Victim's Quest for Justice*. Princeton: Princeton University Press.

Hirschman, Charles, and Douglas S. Massey. 2008. "Places and Peoples: The New American Mosaic." In *New Faces in New Places: The Changing Geography of American Immigration*, ed. Douglas S. Massey. New York: Russell Sage Foundation.

Hochschild, Adam. 2005. *Bury the Chains: Prophets and Rebels in the Fight to Free an Empire's Slaves*. New York: Mariner Books, Houghton Mifflin Company.

Holmes, Seth M. 2013. *Fresh Fruit, Broken Bodies: Migrant Farmworkers in the United States*. Berkeley: University of California Press.

Holzer, Harry J. 2011. "Immigration Policy and Less-Skilled Workers in the United States: Reflections on Future Directions for Reform." Migration Policy Institute, January. Accessed Nov. 3, 2011, http://www.migrationpolicy.org/pubs/Holzer -January2011.pdf.

The Homeless Persons Representation Project and CASA de Maryland. 2004. *Baltimore's Day Laborer's Report: Their Stolen Sweat*. Baltimore: Homeless Persons Representation Project and CASA de Maryland.

Hondagneu-Sotelo, Pierrette. 2001. *Doméstica: Immigrant Workers Cleaning and Caring in the Shadows of Affluence*. Berkeley: University of California Press.

Hsu, Spencer S. 2008. "Raid's Outcome May Signal a Retreat in Immigration Strategy, Critics Say." *The Washington Post*. September 2.

Hundley, Kris. 2006. "Fast Food Fight: Tomato Pickers vs. Big Mac." *St. Petersburg Times*. March 5.

Human Rights Watch. 2007. "Forced Apart: Families Separated and Immigrants Harmed by United States Deportation Policy." New York: Human Rights Watch.

—. 2011. *No Way to Live: Alabama's Immigrant Law.* New York: Human Rights Watch.

—. 2012. *Sex Workers at Risk: Condoms as Evidence of Prostitution in Four U.S. Cities.* New York: Human Rights Watch.

International Labor Organisation. 2012. "ILO 2012 Global Estimate of Forced Labour." Geneva, Switzerland. Accessed May 27, 2013, http://www.ilo.org/wcmsp5/groups /public/—ed_norm/—declaration/documents/publication/wcms_181921.pdf.

The International Labor Recruitment Working Group. 2013. "The American Dream Up for Sale: A Blueprint for Ending International Labor Recruitment Abuse." February.

Jacobs, Harriet. 2001. *Incidents in the Life of a Slave Girl.* New York: Norton.

Janzen, John. 2004. "Illusions of Home in the Story of a Rwandan Refugee's Return." In *Coming Home? Refugees, Migrants and Those Who Stay Behind,* ed. Ellen Oxfeld and Lynellyn D. Long. Philadelphia: University of Pennsylvania Press.

Jayaraman, Sarumathi. 2013. *Behind the Kitchen Door.* Ithaca: Cornell University Press.

Johnson, Walter. 1999. *Soul by Soul: Life inside the Antebellum Slave Market.* Cambridge: Harvard University Press.

—. 2003. "On Agency." *Journal of Social History* 37 (1): 113–24.

Jordan, Ann D. 2002. "Human Rights or Wrongs? The Struggle for Rights-Based Response to Trafficking in Human Beings." *Gender and Development* 10 (1): 28–37.

—. 2012. "The Swedish Law to Criminalize Clients: A Failed Experiment in Social Engineering." Issue Paper 4. April. Washington, D.C.: American University Washington College of Law. Accessed July 29, 2013, http://rightswork.org/wp -content/uploads/2012/04/Issue-Paper-4.pdf.

Kandasamy, Ambikaa. 2012a. "U.S. Victims Help Trafficking Victims, If Applicants Can Vault Legal Hurdles." *San Francisco Public Press.* February 21.

—. 2012b. "Without Long-Term Support, Human Trafficking Survivors at Risk of Re-Exploitation." *San Francisco Public Press.* August 30.

Katz, Michael B. 1989. *The Undeserving Poor: From the War on Poverty to the War on Welfare.* New York: Pantheon Books.

Kee, Lindsay. 2012. *Consequences & Costs: Lessons Learned from Davidson County, Tennessee's Jail Model 287(g) Program.* Report. American Civil Liberties Union of Tennessee (ACLU-TN). December. Accessed June 14, 2013, http://www.aclu-tn.org /pdfs/287g%28F%29.pdf.

Kelly, Lisa M., and Katrina Pacey. 2011. "Why Anti-John Laws Don't Work," *Toronto Star,* Oct. 19. Accessed Nov. 1, 2011, http://www.thestar.com/opinion/editorial opinion/article/1072845—why-anti-john-laws-don-t-work.

Kemp, Joe. 2013. "NYPD Sting Charges 156 Johns in Second Massive Prostitution Bust in Metro Area This Week." June 6. *New York Daily News.* Accessed June 8, 2013, http://www.nydailynews.com/new-york/nypd-sting-busts-156-johns-massive-bust -week-article-1.1365548.

Kempadoo, Kamala. 2005. "From Moral Panic to Global Justice: Changing Perspectives on Trafficking." In *Trafficking and Prostitution Reconsidered: New Perspectives on Migration, Sex Work, and Human Rights*, ed. K. Kempadoo. Boulder, Colo.: Paradigm.

Keyes, Elizabeth, Eliza Leighton, Jessica Salsbury, and Kimberley Propeack. 2007. *Wage Theft: How Maryland Fails to Protect the Rights of Low-Wage Workers*. Silver Spring, Md.: CASA de Maryland.

Khan, Mahvish. 2008. *My Guantánamo Diary: The Detainees and the Stories They Told Me*. New York: Public Affairs Books.

Kibria, Nazli. 1993. *Family Tightrope: The Changing Lives of Vietnamese Americans*. Princeton: Princeton University Press.

Kim, Kathleen. 2007. "Psychological Coercion in the Context of Modern-Day Involuntary Labor: Revisiting *United States v. Kozminski* and Understanding Human Trafficking." *Toledo Law Review* 38: 941–72.

———. 2009. "The Trafficked Worker as Private Attorney General: A Model for Enforcing the Civil Rights of Undocumented Workers." *University of Chicago Legal Forum* (2009): 247–316.

Kim, Kathleen C., Charles Song, and Srividya Panchalam. 2009. "Conversation with Two Anti-Trafficking Advocates: Kathleen C. Kim and Charles Song, Reported by Srividya Panchalam." *Los Angeles Public Interest Law Journal* 1: 31–64.

Kleinman, Arthur. 1995. *Writing at the Margin: Discourse between Anthropology and Medicine*. Berkeley: University of California Press.

Kleinman, Arthur, Veena Das, and Margaret Lock, eds. 1997. *Social Suffering*. Berkeley: University of California Press.

Kleinman, Arthur, and Joan Kleinman. 1997. "The Appeal of Experiences, The Dismay of Images: Cultural Appropriation of Suffering in Our Times." In *Social Suffering*, ed. A. Kleinman, V. Das, and M. Lock. Berkeley: University of California Press.

Kline, John M. 2010. "Alta Gracia: Branding Decent Work Conditions. Will College Loyalty Embrace 'Living Wage' Sweatshirts?" Report for the Kalmanovitz Initiative for Labor and the Working Poor and the Karl F. Landegger Program in International Business Diplomacy. Washington, D.C.: Georgetown University.

Knudsen, John. 1995. "When Trust Is on Trial: Negotiating Refugee Narratives." In *Mistrusting Refugees*, ed. E. V. Daniel and J. C. Knudsen. Berkeley: University of California Press.

Kotiswaran, Prabha. 2008. "Born unto Brothels—Towards a Legal Ethnography of Sex Work in an Indian Red-Light Area." *Law and Social Inquiry* 33 (3): 579–629.

———. 2011. *Dangerous Sex, Invisible Labor: Sex Work and the Law in India*. Princeton: Princeton University Press.

Kotz, Pete. 2011. "The Super Bowl Prostitute Myth: 100,000 Hookers Won't Be Showing Up in Dallas." *Dallas Observer*. January 27.

Kremer, James D., Kathleen A. Moccio, and Joseph W. Hammell. 2009. *Severing a Lifeline: The Neglect of Citizen Children in America's Immigration Enforcement Policy*. Minneapolis: Dorsey and Whitney LLP to the Urban Institute.

Kwong, Peter. 1996. *The New Chinatown*. New York: Hill and Wang.

———. 1997. *Forbidden Workers: Illegal Chinese Immigrants and American Labor*. New York: New Press.

Lacey, Marc. 2011. "Smugglers Guide Illegal Immigrants with Cues via Cellphone." *New York Times*, May 9.

Laczko, Frank. 2005. Introduction to "Data and Research on Human Trafficking: A Global Survey," *International Migration* 43 (1/2): 5–16.

Landesman, Peter. 2004. "The Girls Next Door." *The New York Times*. January 25.

Landler, Mark. 2006. "World Cup Brings Little Pleasure to German Brothels." *The New York Times*. July 3.

Langer, Lawrence L. 1991. *Holocaust Testimonies: The Ruins of Memory*. New Haven: Yale University Press.

Lassiter, Luke E. 2005. *The Chicago Guide to Collaborative Ethnography*. Chicago: University of Chicago Press.

Lazo, Alejandro. 2008. "Verizon to Press Contractors on Immigrant Workers' Pay." *The Washington Post*. June 24.

Leach, Mark A., and Frank D. Bean. 2008. "The Structure and Dynamics of Mexican Migration to New Destinations in the United States." In *New Faces in New Places: The Changing Geography of American Immigration*. New York: Russell Sage Foundation.

Lee, Jennifer L., and Kyle Endres. 2010. "Overworked and Underpaid: H-2A Herders in Colorado." Report. Denver, Colo.: Migrant Farmworker Division of Colorado Legal Services.

Lengel, Allan. 2006. "31 Arrested in Reputed Korean Sex-Slave Trafficking along East Coast." *The Washington Post*. August 17.

Lennard, Natasha. 2013. "Obama Deportation Toll on Track to Pass 2 Million." *Salon*, Feb. 1. Accessed May 27, 2013, http://www.salon.com/2013/02/01/obama_deporta tion_toll_on_track_to_pass_2_million/.

Leopold, David Wolfe. 2008. "Statement On Behalf of the American Immigration Lawyers Association Before the Subcommittee on Immigration, Citizenship, Refugees, Border Security, and International Law. Committee on the Judiciary, United States House of Representatives. Hearing on the Arrest, Prosecution, and Conviction of Undocumented Workers in Postville, Iowa from May 12 to 22, 2008." July 24. Accessed June 14, 2013, http://judiciary.house.gov/hearings/pdf/Leopold 080724.pdf.

Lerum, Kari. 2011. "For Sex Workers, Recommendation #86 Will Go Down in History." *Ms. Magazine*, March 15. Accessed July 8, 2013, http://msmagazine.com/blog/2011 /03/15/for-sex-workers-recommendation-86-will-go-down-in-history/.

Lerum, Kari, Kiesha McCurtis, Penelope Saunders, and Stephanie Wahab. 2012. "Using Human Rights to Hold the US Accountable for its Anti-Sex Trafficking Agenda: The Universal Periodic Review and New Directions for US Policy." *Anti-Trafficking Review* 1: 80–103.

Levi, Primo. 1996. *Survival in Auschwitz*. New York: Touchstone.

———. 1998. *The Drowned and the Saved*. New York: Simon and Schuster.

Loescher, Gil. 1993. *Beyond Charity: International Cooperation and the Global Refugee Crisis*. Oxford: Oxford University Press.

Loescher, Gil, and John A. Scanlan. 1986. *Calculated Kindness: Refugees and America's Half-Open Door, 1945 to the Present*. New York: Free Press.

Lopez, Mark Hugo, Ana Gonzalez-Barera, and Seth Motel. 2011. "As Deportations Rise to Record Levels, Most Latinos Oppose Obama's Policy." Pew Hispanic Center, Washington, D.C. December 28. Accessed July 29, 2013, http://www.pewhispanic.org/2011/12/28/as-deportations-rise-to-record-levels-most-latinos-oppose-obamas-policy/.

Louie, Miriam Ching Yoon. 2001. *Sweatshop Warriors: Immigrant Women Workers Take on the Global Factory.* Cambridge, Mass.: South End Press.

Luibhéid, Eithne. 2005. "Introduction: Queering Migration and Citizenship." In *Queer Migrations: Sexuality, U.S. Citizenship, and Border Crossings,* ed. Eithne Luibhéid and Lionel Cantú Jr. Minneapolis: University of Minnesota Press.

Lukes, Steven. 2005. *Power: A Radical View.* 2nd ed. New York: Palgrave Macmillan.

Lydersen, Kari. 2010. "A Thriving Industry Built on Low-Compensated Temp Workers." *The New York Times.* August 26.

Lynn, Stephen. 2007. *Transborder Lives: Indigenous Oaxacans in Mexico, California, and Oregon.* Durham: Duke University Press.

Lyon-Callo, Vincent. 2008. *Inequality, Poverty, and Neoliberal Governance: Activist Ethnography in the Homeless Sheltering Industry.* Toronto: Higher Education University of Toronto Press. Originally published by Broadview Press, 2004.

MacClancy, Jeremy. 2002. "Introduction: Taking People Seriously." In *Exotic No More: Anthropology on the Front Lines,* ed. J. MacClancy. Chicago: University of Chicago Press.

Mahdavi, Pardis. 2011. *Gridlock: Labor, Migration, and Human Trafficking in Dubai.* Stanford: Stanford University Press.

Malkki, Liisa H. 1995. *Purity and Exile: Violence, Memory, and National Cosmology among Hutu Refugees in Tanzania.* Chicago: University of Chicago Press.

Manz, Beatriz. 1995. "Fostering Trust in a Climate of Fear." In *Mistrusting Refugees,* ed. E. V. Daniel and J. C. Knudsen. Berkeley: University of California Press.

———. 2002. "Terror, Grief, and Recovery: Genocidal Trauma in a Mayan Village in Guatemala." In *Annihilating Difference: The Anthropology of Genocide,* ed. A. Hinton. Berkeley: University of California Press.

———. 2004. *Paradise in Ashes: A Guatemalan Journey of Courage, Terror, and Hope.* Berkeley: University of California Press.

Marcus, George E. 1995. "Ethnography in/of the World System: The Emergence of Multi-Sited Ethnography." *Annual Review of Anthropology* 24: 95–117.

Markon, Jerry. 2007. "How Widespread Is Human Trafficking? U.S. Estimates Thousands of Victims, But Efforts to Find Them Fall Short." *Washington Post,* Sept. 23.

Markowitz, Fran, and Anders H. Stefansson. 2004. *Homecomings: Unsettling Paths of Return.* Lanham, Md.: Lexington Books.

Massey, Douglas. 2002. "A Validation of the Ethnosurvey: The Case of Mexico-U.S. Migration." *International Migration Review* 34 (3): 776–94.

———. 2008. *New Faces in New Places: The Changing Geography of American Immigration.* New York: Russell Sage Foundation.

Mathias, Christopher. 2012. "Undercover NYPD Cops Pose As Prostitutes, Arrest Nearly 200 in 'Operation Losing Proposition.'" *Huffington Post.* January 17. Accessed

June 8, 2013, http://www.huffingtonpost.com/2012/01/17/undercover-nypd-cops
-pose-as-prostitutes_n_1210702.html.

McLaren, Brian D. 2011. "Dirty Tomatoes: A Spiritual and Dietary Proposal." *Huffington Post*. August 25.

McSpadden, Lucia Ann. 1999. "Assessing Essential Qualities of Community: Eritrean Refugees' Resistance and Return." In *Negotiating Power and Place at the Margins*, ed. J. G. Lipson and L. A. McSpadden. Arlington, Va.: American Anthropological Association.

————. 2004. "Contemplating Repatriation to Eritrea." In *Coming Home? Refugees, Migrants, and Those Who Stay Behind*, ed. Ellen Oxfeld and Lynellyn D. Long. Philadelphia: University of Pennsylvania Press.

Meissner, Doris, Donald M. Kerwin, Muzzafar Chishti, and Claire Bergeron. 2013. "Immigration Enforcement in the United States: The Rise of a Formidable Machinery." Migration Policy Institute.

Mencimer, Stephanie. 2012. "The War on Women: Sex-Trafficking Edition." *Mother Jones*. April 24. May/June Issue. Accessed Dec. 11, 2012, http://www.motherjones.com/politics/2012/04/catholic-bishops-war-on-contraception-sex-trafficking?page=1.

Meng, Grace. 2012. "Cultivating Fear: The Vulnerability of Immigrant Farmworkers in the U.S. to Sexual Violence and Sexual Harassment." Report. New York: Human Rights Watch.

————. 2013. "Turning Migrants into Criminals: The Harmful Impact of U.S. Border Prosecutions." Report. May. Accessed July 29, 2013, http://www.hrw.org/sites/default/files/reports/us0513_ForUpload_2.pdf. New York: Human Rights Watch.

Meyer, Paul. 2006. "Asian Spa Arrests Fuel Debate on Human Trafficking." *The Dallas Morning News*. May 15.

Milkman, Ruth. 2000. *Organizing Immigrants: The Challenge for Unions in Contemporary California*. Ithaca: Cornell University Press.

————. 2011. "Immigrant Workers, Precarious Work, and the US Labor Movement." *Globalizations* 8 (3): 361–72.

Milkman, Ruth, Ana Luz González, and Victor Narro. 2010. *Wage Theft and Workplace Violations in Los Angeles*. Los Angeles: Institute for Research on Labor and Employment.

Miller, Alice. 1999. "Human Rights and Sexuality: First Steps toward Articulating a Rights Framework for Claims to Sexual Rights and Freedoms." Proceedings of the 93rd Annual Meeting. *American Society of International Law* 288–303.

————. 2004. "Sexuality, Violence against Women, and Human Rights: Women Make Demands, and Ladies Get Protection," *Health and Human Rights* 7 (2): 16–47.

————. 2005. "Pouring New Wine into Old Bottles: Understanding the Dilemmas of Contemporary Trafficking Work." *Minerva* 29: 23–25.

Moon, Claire. 2009. "Healing Past Violence: Traumatic Assumptions and Therapeutic Interventions in War and Reconciliation." *Journal of Human Rights* 8 (1): 71–91.

Morel, Pierre, director. 2008. *Taken*. 93 min. Los Angeles: 20th Century Fox.

Muecke, Marjorie A. 1995. "Trust, Abuse of Trust, and Mistrust among Cambodian

Refugee Women: A Cultural Interpretation," In *Mistrusting Refugees*, ed. E. V. Daniel and J. C. Knudsen. Berkeley: University of California Press.

Murray, Alison. 1998. "Debt-Bondage and Trafficking: Don't Believe the Hype." In *Global Sex Workers: Rights, Resistance, and Redefinition*, ed. K. Kempadoo and J. Doezema. New York: Routledge.

Narushima, Yuko. 2013. "Diplomatic Impunity: Trafficking Women to the United States." *Washington Spectator*. March 1.

Nathan, Debbie. 2005. "Oversexed: Anti-Trafficking Efforts Place Undue Emphasis on Commercial Sex Work and Downplay Other Forms of Forced Labor." April 29. *The Nation*.

National Commission on ICE Misconduct and Violations of 4th Amendment Rights. 2009. "Raids on Workers: Destroying Our Rights." N.p.: Report of the National Commission on ICE Misconduct and Violations of Fourth Amendment Rights. http://www.icemisconduct.org/docUploads/UFCW%20ICE%20rpt%20FINAL%20 150B_061809_130632.pdf.

National Council of La Raza, Action Network. 2012. "Thank Your Arlington County Board Members for Rejecting SCOMM!" Accessed May 4, 2012, http://action.nclr .org/p/dia/action/public/?action_KEY=2561.

National Guestworker Alliance and Pennsylvania State University, The Dickinson School of Law. 2012. "Leveling the Playing Field: Reforming the H-2B Program to Protect Guestworkers and U.S. Workers." Report. Accessed June 20, 2013, http:// www.guestworkeralliance.org/wp-content/uploads/2012/06/Leveling-the-Playing -Field-final.pdf.

Newman, Katherine. 1999. *No Shame in My Game: The Working Poor in the Inner City*. New York: Vintage Books and Russell Sage Foundation.

Newman, Katherine, and Rourke L. O'Brien. 2011. *Taxing the Poor: Doing Damage to the Truly Disadvantaged*. Berkeley: University of California Press.

New York School of Law Immigrant Rights Clinic, New York Civil Liberties Union, and Families for Freedom. 2011. *Justice Derailed: What Raids on Trains and Buses Reveal about Border Patrol's Interior Enforcement Practices*. Report by the New York University School of Law Immigrant Rights Clinic, the New York Civil Liberties Union, and Families for Freedom. November. Accessed July 29, 2013, http://www .nyclu.org/files/publications/NYCLU_justicederailedweb_0.pdf. New York: New York Civil Liberties Union.

Nieves, Evelyn. 2005. "Florida Tomato Pickers Reap 'Harvest of Shame': Boycott Helps Raise Awareness of Plight." *Washington Post*. Feb. 28.

Nossiter, Adam. 2008a. "Hundreds of Factory Workers Are Held in Immigration Raid: Mississippi Plant Is Latest Target of Federal Agents." *New York Times*. August 26.

———. 2008b. "Nearly 600 Were Arrested in Factory Raid, Officials Say." *New York Times*. August 27.

Not for Sale Campaign. 2010. "The Academy: Academy Curriculum." Accessed July 24, 2013, http://www.notforsalecampaign.org/news/2010/03/18/not-for-sale-abolitionist -academy-apply-now-for-summer-2010/.

O'Connell Davidson, Julia. 2012. "Absolving the State: The Trafficking-Slavery Metaphor." *Global Dialogue* 14(2).

Olujic, Maria B. 1995. "The Croatian War Experience." In *Fieldwork Under Fire: Contemporary Studies of Violence and Survival*, ed. C. Nordstrom and A. C. G. M. Robben. Berkeley: University of California Press.

O'Neill Richard, Amy. 2000. "International Trafficking in Women to the United States: A Contemporary Manifestation of Slavery and Organized Crime." Monograph. Washington, D.C.: Center for the Study of Intelligence.

Ong, Aiwha. 1999. *Flexible Citizenship: The Cultural Logics of Transnationality*. Durham: Duke University Press.

———. 2003. *Buddha Is Hiding: Refugees, Citizenship, the New America*. Berkeley: University of California Press.

Open Society Foundations. 2012. "Laws and Policies Affecting Sex Work: A Reference Brief." Open Society Public Health Program. New York: Open Society Foundations.

Organization for Refuge, Asylum and Migration (ORAM). 2013. "Blind Alleys: The Unseen Struggles of Lesbian, Gay, Bisexual, Transgender and Intersex Urban Refugees in Mexico, Uganda and South Africa." Report. February. Accessed June 19, 2013, http://www.oraminternational.org/en/publications/264-blind-alleys. San Francisco: Organization for Refuge, Asylum and Migration.

Ortiz, Paul. 2002. "From Slavery to Cesar Chavez and Beyond: Farmworker Organizing in the United States," in *The Human Cost of Food: Farmworkers' Lives, Labor, and Advocacy*, ed. Charles Thompson and Melinda Wiggins. Austin: University of Texas Press.

Ortner, Sherry. 1995. "Resistance and the Problem of Ethnographic Refusal." *Comparative Studies in Society and History* 37 (1): 173–93.

Oxfeld, Ellen, and Lynellyn D. Long. 2004. "Introduction: An Ethnography of Return." In *Coming Home? Refugees, Migrants, and Those Who Stay Behind*, ed. Lynellyn D. Long and Ellen Oxfeld. Philadelphia: University of Pennsylvania Press.

Parreñas, Rhacel Salazar. 2001. *Servants of Globalization: Women, Migration, and Domestic Work*. Stanford: Stanford University Press.

———. 2011. *Illicit Flirtations: Labor, Migration, and Sex Trafficking in Tokyo*. Stanford: Stanford University Press.

Partnoy, Alicia. 1998. *The Little School: Tales of Disappearance and Survival*. Berkeley: Cleis Press.

Pellow, David, and Lisa Sun-Hee Park. 2002. *The Silicon Valley of Dreams: Environmental Injustice, Immigrant Workers, and the High-Tech Global Economy*. New York: New York University Press.

Peteet, Julie. 2005. *Landscape of Hope and Despair: Palestinian Refugee Camps*. Philadelphia: University of Pennsylvania Press.

Peters, Alicia. 2013. "'Things that Involve Sex Are Just Different: US Anti-Trafficking Law and Policy on the Books, in Their Minds, and in Action." *Anthropological Quarterly* 86 (1): 221–56.

Pitts, Byron. 2010. "'Harvest of Shame' 50 Years Later." *CBS News*, Nov. 25.

Pitts, Steven C. 2008. "Job Quality and Black Workers: An Examination of the San

Francisco Bay Area, Los Angeles, Chicago, and New York." Center for Labor
Research and Education, Institute for Research on Labor and Employment.
Berkeley: University of California.

Police Foundation. 2009. "The Role of Police: Striking a Balance between Immigration
Enforcement and Civil Liberties." Washington, D.C.: Police Foundation.

Power, Samantha. 2003. *A Problem from Hell: America and the Age of Genocide*. New
York: Basic Books.

Pratt, Geraldine. 2012. *Families Apart: Migrant Mothers and the Conflicts of Labor and
Love*. Minneapolis: University of Minnesota.

Pratt, Mary Louise. 2002. Oral presentation at Symposium on Gender, Cultural
Citizenship, and Transnationalism. New York University, October 11.

Preston, Julia. 2008. "After Iowa Raid, Immigrants Fuel Labor Inquiries," *New York
Times*. July 27.

PROS Network and Leigh Tomppert of the Sex Workers Project at the Urban
Justice Center. 2012. "Public Health Crisis: The Impact of Using Condoms as
Evidence of Prostitution in New York City." April. Accessed June 19, 2013, http://
sexworkersproject.org/downloads/2012/20120417-public-health-crisis.pdf. New
York: Sex Workers Project, Urban Justice Center.

Rappaport, Joanne. 2005. *Intercultural Utopias: Public Intellectuals, Cultural
Experimentation, and Ethnic Pluralism in Colombia*. Durham: Duke University Press.

Repak, Terry. 1995. *Waiting on Washington: Central American Workers in the Nation's
Capital*. Philadelphia: Temple University Press.

Restaurant Opportunities Centers United. 2013. "Realizing the Dream: How the
Minimum Wage Impacts Racial Equality in the Restaurant Industry in America."
New York.

Restoration Ministries. 2011. "Who We Are." Accessed July 22, 2013, www.restoration
ministriesdc.org/who-we-are/letter-from-director.html.

Rights Working Group. 2008. *Equal Treatment Denied: United States Immigration
Enforcement Policies*. Shadow Report to the UN Committee on the Elimination of
Racial Discrimination. Washington, D.C.

———. 2010. "Faces of Racial Profiling: A Report from Communities Across
America." September. Accessed July 29, 2013, http://www.rightsworkinggroup.org
/sites/default/files/ReportText.pdf. Washington, D.C.: Rights Working Group.

———. 2011. "BREAKING: DHS Announces Investigation of the Misnamed 'Secure
Communities' Program." May 20. Accessed Sept. 28, 2011, http://www.rights
workinggroup.org/content/breaking-dhs-announces-investigation-misnamed
-%E2%80%9Csecure-communities%E2%80%9D-program.

———. 2013. "The Minority Reports: How the Intersection of Criminal Justice,
Immigration and Surveillance Undermines Freedoms in California." Report. March.
Accessed July 29, 2013, http://rightsworkinggroup.org/sites/default/files/RWG
_MinorityReports_2013.pdf. Washington, D.C.: Rights Working Group.

Rights Working Group, American-Arab Anti-Discrimination Committee, Asian
American Justice Center, Center for Constitutional Rights, National Immigration
Law Center, UNC School of Law, Immigration and Human Rights Policy Clinic.

2010. "The Persistence, in the United States, of Discriminatory Profiling Based on Race, Ethnicity, Religion and National Origin." Submitted as Shadow Report for the United Nations Universal Periodic Review. November. Accessed July 29, 2013, http://www.rightsworkinggroup.org/sites/default/files/Racial%20Profiling%20 Joint%20Report%20USA.pdf.

Rights Working Group and Center for Immigrants' Rights, Pennsylvania State University, Dickinson School of Law. 2012. "The NSEERS Effect: A Decade of Racial Profiling, Fear, and Secrecy." Report. May. Washington, D.C. Accessed July 29, 2013, http://www.rightsworkinggroup.org/sites/default/files/RWGPenn_NSEERSReport _060412.pdf. Washington, D.C.: Rights Working Group and Penn State Law.

Riis, Jacob A. 1971. *How the Other Half Lives*. New York: Dover. Originally published in 1890.

Robben, Antonius C. G. M., and Carolyn Nordstrom. 1995. "The Anthropology and Ethnography of Violence and Sociopolitical Conflict." In *Fieldwork Under Fire: Contemporary Studies of Violence and Survival*, ed. C. Nordstrom and Antonius C. G. M. Robben. Berkeley: University of California Press.

Rondeaux, Candace. 2002. "Fear and Knowing in Immokalee." *St. Petersburg Times*. December 1.

Rosaldo, Renato. 1997. "Cultural Citizenship, Inequality, and Multiculturalism." In *Latino Cultural Citizenship: Claiming Identity, Space, and Rights*, ed. William V. Flores and Rina Benmayor. Boston: Beacon Press.

Rosen, Ellen Israel. 2002. *Making Sweatshops: The Globalization of the U.S. Apparel Industry*. Berkeley: University of California Press.

Ross, Andrew. 1997. *No Sweat: Fashion, Free Trade, and the Rights of Garment Workers*. New York: Verso.

———. 2004. *Low Pay, High Profile: The Global Fight for Fair Labor*. New York: New Press.

Ross, Fiona C. 2003. *Bearing Witness: Women and the Truth and Reconciliation Commission in South Africa*. London: Pluto Press.

Ross, Robert J. S. 2004. *Slaves to Fashion: Poverty and Abuse in the New Sweatshops*. Ann Arbor: University of Michigan Press.

Rothenberg, Daniel. 1998. *With These Hands: The Hidden World of Migrant Farmworkers Today*. New York: Harcourt Brace.

Rylko-Bauer, Barbara, Linda Whiteford, and Paul Farmer. 2009. "Prologue: Coming to Terms with Global Violence and Health." In *Global Health in Times of Violence*, ed. Barbara Rylko-Bauer, Linda Whiteford, and Paul Farmer. Santa Fe, N.M.: School for Advanced Research Press.

Sadowski, Dennis. 2013. "Federal Court Panel Dismisses ACLU Challenge of USCCB Trafficking Grant." *National Catholic Reporter*. January 17. Accessed Jan. 22, 2013, http://ncronline.org/news/politics/federal-court-panel-dismisses-aclu-challenge -usccb-trafficking-grant.

The Salvation Army. 2011. "Salvation Army Services to Trafficking Survivors." Accessed Sept. 28, 2011, http://www.salvationarmyusa.org/usn/www_usn_2.nsf/vw-dynamic index/309857EA653289748525744000681 3E6?Opendocument.

Sassen, Saskia. 2000. *Guests and Aliens.* New York: New Press.

Saunders, Penelope. 2005. "Identity to Acronym: How 'Child Prostitution' Became 'CSEC.'" In *Regulating Sex: The Politics of Intimacy and Identity,* ed. Elizabeth Bernstein and Laurie Schaffner. New York: Routledge.

Scarry, Elaine. 1985. *The Body in Pain: The Making and Unmaking of the World.* New York: Oxford University Press.

Scheper-Hughes, Nancy. 2008. "A Talent for Life: Reflections on Human Vulnerability and Resilience." *Ethnos* 73 (1): 25–56.

Scheper-Hughes, Nancy, and Philippe Bourgois. 2003. "Making Sense of Violence." In *Violence in War and Peace: An Anthology,* ed. Nancy Scheper-Hughes and Philippe Bourgois. Malden, Mass.: Blackwell.

Schleifer, Rebecca, and Darby Hickey. 2013. "Partners, not pledges, needed to fight HIV." Special to CNN. May 23. Accessed June 19, 2013, http://globalpublicsquare .blogs.cnn.com/2013/05/23/partners-not-pledges-needed-to-fight-hiv/.

Schlosser, Eric. 2007. "Penny Foolish." *The New York Times.* November 29.

Schmidt, Peter. 2011. "Scholars of Legal Brothels Offer a New Take on the 'Oldest Profession.'" *Chronicle of Higher Education,* Sept. 18. Accessed Oct. 26, 2011, http:// chronicle.com.proxy.cecybrary.com/article/Scholars-of-Legal-Brothels/129047/.

Schwenken, Helen. 2005. "'Domestic Slavery' versus 'Workers' Rights': Political Mobilization of Migrant Domestic Workers in the European Union." Working Paper 116. San Diego: Center for Comparative Immigration Studies, University of California at San Diego.

Scott, James. 1985. *Weapons of the Weak: Everyday Forms of Peasant Resistance.* New Haven: Yale University Press.

———. 1990. *Domination and the Arts of Resistance: Hidden Transcripts.* New Haven: Yale University Press.

Shafer, Jack. 2004a. "Doubting Landesman: I'm Not the Only One Questioning the *Times Magazine's* Sex-Slave Story, 'The Girls' Next Door.'" January 27. *Slate.* Accessed June 24, 2008, http://www.slate.com/articles/news_and_politics/press_box/2004/01 /doubting_landesman.html.

———. 2004b. "Enslaved by His Sources." *Slate,* Feb. 3. Accessed July 28, 2013, http:// www.slate.com/articles/news_and_politics/press_box/2004/02/enslaved_by_his _sources.html.

———. 2004c. "How *Not* to Handle Press Critics." *Slate,* Jan. 29. Accessed July 28, 2013, http://www.slate.com/articles/news_and_politics/press_box/2004/01/how _not_to_handle_press_critics.html.

———. 2004d. "Sex Slaves of West 43rd Street." *Slate,* Jan. 26. Accessed July 28, 2013, http://www.slate.com/articles/news_and_politics/press_box/2004/01/sex_slaves _of_west_43rd_street.html.

———. 2004e. "The *Times Magazine* Strikes Back." *Slate,* Jan. 28. Accessed July 28, 2013, http://www.slate.com/articles/news_and_politics/press_box/2004/01/the _times_magazine_strikes_back.html.

Shah, Svati P. 2008. "South Asian Border Crossings and Sex Work: Revisiting the

Question of Migration in Anti-Trafficking Interventions." *Sexuality Research and Social Policy* 5 (4): 19–30.

Shahani, Aarti, and Judith Greene. 2009. *Local Democracy on ICE: Why State and Local Governments Have No Business in Federal Immigration Law Enforcement.* New York: Justice Strategies.

Shapiro, Nina. 2004. "The New Abolitionists." *Seattle Weekly.* August 25–31.

Shared Hope. 2011. "Rescue and Restore." Accessed July 5, 2011, http://www.shared hope.org/WhatWeDo/RescueRestore.aspx.

Shipler, David. 2004. *The Working Poor: Invisible in America.* New York: Vintage Books.

Shutika, Debra Lattanzi. 2008. "The Ambivalent Welcome: Cinco de Mayo and the Symbolic Expression of Local Identity and Ethnic Relations." In *New Faces in New Places: The Changing Geography of American Immigration,* ed. D. Massey. New York: Russell Sage Foundation.

———. 2011. *Beyond the Borderlands: Migration and Belonging in the United States and Mexico.* Berkeley: University of California Press.

Siddiqui, Tasneem. 2005. "International Labour Migration from Bangladesh: A Decent Work Perspective." Working Paper 66. Geneva: Policy Integration Department, National Policy Group, International Labour Office.

Silverman, Elissa. 2006. "Pay Fight in Tech's Trenches." *The Washington Post.* February 16.

Simmons, David. 2010. "Structural Violence as Social Practice: Haitian Agricultural Workers, Anti-Haitianism, and Health in the Dominican Republic." *Human Organization* 69 (1): 10–18.

Siskin, Alison, and Liana Sun Wyler. 2013. "Trafficking in Persons: U.S. Policy and Issues for Congress." Washington, D.C.: Congressional Research Service. February 19.

Skinner, Benjamin. 2008. *A Crime So Monstrous: Face-to-Face with Modern Day Slavery.* New York: Free Press.

Soderlund, Gretchen. 2005. "Running from the Rescuers: New U.S. Crusades against Sex Trafficking and the Rhetoric of Abolition." *NWSA Journal* 17 (3): 64–87.

Solzhenitsyn, Aleksandr I. 1974–78. *The Gulag Archipelago, 1918–1956: An Experiment in Literary Investigation.* Trans. Thomas P. Whitney. New York: Harper and Row.

Southern Poverty Law Center. 2013a. "SPLC Spearheads Unprecedented Legal Collaboration to Seek Justice for Indian Guest Workers." Press Release. May 21. Accessed May 27, 2013, http://www.splcenter.org/get-informed/news/splc-spearheads -unprecedented-legal-collaboration%2523.UZqjyIJW5vM#.UaN5xmTwLEU.

———. 2013b. "Close to Slavery: Guestworker Programs in the United States" (2013 ed.). Montgomery, Ala.: Southern Poverty Law Center.

———. 2006a. "Beneath the Pines: Stories of Migrant Tree Planters." Montgomery, Ala: Immigrant Justice Project.

———. 2006b. "Broken Levees, Broken Promises: New Orleans' Migrant Workers in Their Own Words." Montgomery, Ala.: Immigrant Justice Project.

———. 2010. "Injustice on our Plates: Immigrant Women in the U.S. Food Industry." Montgomery, Ala.: Immigrant Justice Project.

Srikantiah, Jayashri. 2007. "Perfect Victims and Real Survivors the Iconic Victim in Domestic Human Trafficking Law." *Boston University Law Review* 87 (2007): 157–211.

Stack, Carol. 1974. *All Our Kin*. New York: Basic Books.

Standing, Guy. 2011. *The Precariat: The New Dangerous Class*. London: Bloomsbury Academic.

Stefansson, Anders H. 2004. "Returns to Sarajevo and Contemporary Narratives of Mobility," In *Coming Home? Refugees, Migrants, and Those Who Stay Behind*, ed. Ellen Oxfeld and Lynellyn D. Long. Philadelphia: University of Pennsylvania Press.

Stoll, David. 1999. *Rigoberta Menchú and the Story of All Poor Guatemalans*. Boulder, Colo.: Westview Press.

Striffler, Steve. 2002. "Inside a Poultry Processing Plant: An Ethnographic Portrait." *Labor History* 43 (2): 305–13.

———. 2005. *Chicken: The Dangerous Transformation of America's Favorite Food*. New Haven: Yale University Press.

Stuesse, Angela C. 2010a. "Challenging the Border Patrol, Human Rights and Persistent Inequalities: An Ethnography of Struggle in South Texas." *Latino Studies* 8 (1): 23–47.

———. 2010b. "What's 'Justice and Dignity' Got to Do With It? Migrant Vulnerability, Corporate Complicity, and the State." *Human Organization* 69 (1): 19–30.

Stull, Donald D., and Michael J. Broadway. 2004. *Slaughterhouse Blues: The Meat and Poultry Industry in North America*. Belmont, Calif.: Wadsworth.

Su, Julie A. 1997. "El Monte Thai Garment Workers: Slave Sweatshops." In *No Sweat: Fashion, Free Trade, and the Rights of Garment Workers*, ed. Andrew Ross. New York: Verso.

Su, Julie A., and Chanchanit Martorell. 2001. "Exploitation and Abuse in the Garment Industry: The Case of the Thai Slave-Labor Compound in El Monte." In *Asian and Latino Immigrants in a Restructuring Economy: The Metamorphosis of Southern California*, ed. Marta López-Garza and David R. Diaz. Palo Alto, Calif.: Stanford University Press.

Suárez-Orozco, Marcelo. 1995. "A Grammar of Terror: Psychocultural Responses to State Terrorism in Dirty War and Post–Dirty War Argentina." In *The Paths to Domination, Resistance, and Terror*, ed. Carolyn Nordstrom and JoAnn Martin. Berkeley: University of California Press.

Summerfield, Derek. 2001. "The Invention of Post-Traumatic Stress Disorder and the Usefulness of a Psychiatric Category." *British Medical Journal* 322 (7278): 95–98.

Theidon, Kimberly. 2006. "Intimate Enemies: Toward a Social Psychology of Reconciliation." In *The Psychology of Resolving Global Conflicts: From War to Peace*, ed. M. Fitzduff and C. E. Stout. Westport, Conn.: Praeger Security International.

———. 2007. "Gender in Transition: Common Sense, Women, and War." *Journal of Human Rights* 6: 453–78.

———. 2013. *Intimate Enemies: Violence and Reconciliation in Peru*. Philadelphia: University of Pennsylvania Press.

Theodore, Nik. 2013. *Insecure Communities: Latino Perceptions of Police Involvement in Immigration Enforcement*. May. Department of Urban Planning and Policy, University

of Illinois at Chicago. Accessed June 14, 2013, http://www.uic.edu/cuppa/gci/docu
ments/1213/Insecure_Communities_Report_FINAL.pdf.

Thrupkaew, Noy. 2012. "A Misguided Moral Crusade." *The New York Times*. September 22.

———. 2009. "The Crusade against Sex Trafficking." *Nation*, Oct. 5. Accessed July 26,
2011, http://www.thenation.com/article/crusade-against-sex-trafficking.

Ticktin, Miriam. 2011. *Casualties of Care: Immigration and the Politics of Humanitarianism
in France*. Berkeley: University of California Press.

Turner, Stuart. 1995. "Torture, Refuge, and Trust." In *Mistrusting Refugees*, ed. E. V.
Daniel and J. C. Knudsen. Berkeley: University of California Press.

Urban Justice Center, Sex Workers Project. 2009. "Raids and Trafficking in Persons:
The Facts." Accessed May 3, 2012, http://www.urbanjustice.org/pdf/publications
/KDTD_Fact_Sheet.pdf.

Uribe, Sarahí. 2013. "Opinion Nation: Immigration Activists and Experts on Their
'Dealbreakers' on Immigration Reform: The Federal Government Must Ditch Its
Discredited Deportation Programs." *The Nation*. April 15. Accessed June 1, 2013,
http://www.thenation.com/blog/173832/opinionnation-immigration-activists-and
-experts-their-dealbreakers-immigration-reform#axzz2X3BzBsZU.

U.S. Conference of Catholic Bishops. 2007. "Services for Survivors of Human
Trafficking." Accessed Feb. 24, 2012, http://www.usccb.org/mrs/trafficking/docs
/traffickingbrochuremarch07.pdf.

———. 2011. "Anti-Trafficking Services Program." Accessed July 28, 2013, http://
www.usccb.org/about/anti-trafficking-program/index.cfm.

———. 2013. "Refugee 101." Accessed Apr. 1, 2013, http://www.brycs.org/about
Refugees/refugee101.cfm.

U.S. Congress. 2008. *William Wilberforce Trafficking Victims Protection Reauthorization
Act of 2008 U.S. Code*. Title 22 §§ 7105. 110th Congress. Washington, D.C.:
Government Printing Office.

U.S. Congress, House of Representatives. 2000. *Victims of Trafficking and Violence
Protection Act of 2000*. Report 106–939, Section 103. 106th Congress, 2nd Session.
Washington, D.C.: Government Printing Office.

U.S. Department of Health and Human Services, Administration for Children and
Families. 2011. *Fact Sheet: Certification for Victims of Trafficking*, Accessed: April 17,
2011, http://www.acf.hhs.gov/trafficking/about/Certification_for_Victims_of
_Trafficking_Fact_Sheet.pdf.

U.S. Department of Health and Human Services, Administration for Children and
Families, The Campaign to Rescue and Restore Victims of Human Trafficking. 2012.
Fact Sheet: Victim Assistance. Aug. 7. Accessed May 24, 2012, http://www.acf.hhs.gov
/trafficking/about/victim_assist.html.

U.S. Department of Health and Human Services, Office of Refugee Resettlement.
2008. "Synthesis of Findings from Three Sites." Accessed July 23, 2013, http://
archive.acf.hhs.gov/programs/orr/resources/synthesis_of_finding.htm#_TOC
178156650.

———. 2011a. *Services Available to Victims of Human Trafficking: A Resource Guide for Social Service Providers.* June. Accessed Sept. 21, 2011, http://www.acf.hhs.gov /trafficking/HHS_Trafficking_Svcs_Booklet_6_6_11_508_compliant.pdf.

———. 2011b. "Voluntary Agencies Matching Grant Program FY 2012." 2012. Accessed Feb. 27, 2012, http://www.acf.hhs.gov/programs/orr/programs/match _grant_prg.htm.

U.S. Department of Homeland Security, Citizenship and Immigration Services. 2010. Policy Memorandum, 602–0004. Accessed Sept. 21, 2011, http://www.uscis.gov /USCIS/Laws/Memoranda/2010/William%20Wilberforce%20TVPRAct%200f%20 2008%20July%20212010.pdf.

———. 2012. "USCIS Service and Office Locator." Accessed Feb. 24, 2012, https:// egov.uscis.gov/crisgwi/go?action=offices.detail&office=VSC&OfficeLocator.office _type=SC&OfficeLocator.statecode=VT.

U.S. Department of Homeland Security, Immigration and Customs Enforcement. 2011. "Secure Communities." Accessed Sept. 28, 2011, http://www.ice.gov/secure _communities/.

———. 2012. "Deportation of Parents of Parents of U.S.-Born Citizens: Fiscal Year 2011 Report to Congress Second Semi-annual Report." March 26.

U.S. Department of Homeland Security, Office of the Press Secretary. 2008. "Fact Sheet: DHS End-of-Year Accomplishments." December 18. Accessed Feb. 2, 2012, http://www.dhs.gov/xnews/releases/pr_1229609413187.shtm.

U.S. Department of Homeland Security, Office of Inspector General. 2009. *Removals Involving Illegal Alien Parents of United States Citizen Children.* Washington, D.C.: U.S. Government Printing Office.

U.S. Department of Justice. 2005. *Assessment of U.S. Government Activities to Combat Trafficking in Persons in Fiscal Year 2004.* Accessed Aug. 5, 2013, http://www.justice .gov/archive/ag/annualreports/tr2005/assessmentofustipactivities.pdf.

U.S. Department of Justice. 2006. *Report on Activities to Combat Human Trafficking: Fiscal Years 2001–2005.* Washington, D.C.: U.S. Government Printing Office.

———. 2009. *Attorney General's Annual Report to Congress and Assessment of U.S. Government Activities to Combat Trafficking in Persons.* Washington, D.C.: U.S. Government Printing Office.

———. 2010. *Attorney General's Annual Report to Congress and Assessment of U.S. Government Activities to Combat Trafficking in Persons.* Washington, D.C.: U.S. Government Printing Office.

———. 2011. *Attorney General's Annual Report to Congress and Assessment of U.S. Government Activities to Combat Trafficking in Persons.* Washington, D.C.: U.S. Government Printing Office.

———. N.d. "Criminal Section on Selected Case Summaries." Civil Rights Division. Accessed June 20, 2013, http://www.justice.gov/crt/about/crm/selcases.php#human trafficking.

U.S. Department of Labor, Wage and Hour Division. 2011a. "Fact Sheet #12: Agricultural Employers under the Fair Labor Standards Act (FLSA)." Accessed Dec. 14, 2011, http://www.dol.gov/whd/regs/compliance/whdfs12.pdf.

————. 2011b. "Handy Reference Guide to the Fair Labor Standards Act." Sept. Accessed Dec. 14, 2011, http://www.dol.gov/whd/regs/compliance/hrg.htm.

————. 2013. "Exemptions." Accessed July 27, 2013, www.dol.gov/whd/regs /compliance/hrg.htm#8.

U.S. Department of State. 2003. *Trafficking in Persons Report*. Washington, D.C.: U.S. Government Printing Office.

————. 2004a. "Fact Sheet: The Link between Prostitution and Sex Trafficking." Washington, D.C.: U.S. Government Printing Office.

————. 2004b. *Trafficking in Persons Report*. Washington, D.C.: U.S. Government Printing Office.

————. 2005. *Trafficking in Persons Report*. Washington, D.C.: U.S. Government Printing Office.

————. 2006. *Trafficking in Persons Report*. Washington, D.C.: U.S. Government Printing Office.

————. 2007. *Trafficking in Persons Report*. Washington, D.C.: U.S. Government Printing Office.

————. 2008. *Trafficking in Persons Report*. Washington, D.C.: U.S. Government Printing Office.

————. 2009a. "Remarks at Release of the Ninth Annual Trafficking in Persons Report alongside Leaders in Congress." Presented by Hillary Rodham Clinton. June 16. Accessed May 4, 2012, http://www.state.gov/secretary/rm/2009a/06/124872.htm.

————. 2009b. *Trafficking in Persons Report*. Washington, D.C.: U.S. Government Printing Office.

————. 2010. *Trafficking in Persons Report*. Washington, D.C.: U.S. Government Printing Office.

————. 2011a. *Trafficking in Persons Report*. Washington, D.C.: U.S. Government Printing Office.

————. 2011b. "Visas for Victims of Human Trafficking: Filing Applications for Immediate Family Members (T-2, T-3, T-4, OR T-5 Visa Categories)." Accessed Sept. 21, 2011, http://travel.state.gov/visa/temp/types/types_5186.html#filing.

————. 2011c. "Visas for Victims of Human Trafficking: T-1 Non-Immigrant Status." Accessed Sept. 21, 2011, http://travel.state.gov/visa/temp/types/types_5186.html #status.

————. 2012a. *Trafficking in Persons Report*. Washington, D.C.: U.S. Government Printing Office.

————. 2012b. "Release of the 2012 Trafficking in Persons Report." News release. Accessed July 21, 2013, www.state.gov/secretary/rm/2012/06/193368.htm.

————. 2012c. "Release of the 2012 Trafficking in Persons Report." Remarks by Secretary of State Hillary Rodham Clinton. June 19. Video and transcript. Accessed July 21, 2013, http://www.state.gov/secretary/rm/2012/06/193368.htm.

————. 2013a. *Trafficking in Persons Report*. Accessed July 29, 2013, http://www.state .gov/j/tip/rls/tiprpt/2013/.

————. 2013b. "Visas for Victims of Human Trafficking." Travel.State.Gov, a service of the Bureau of Consular Affairs. Accessed June 20, 2013, http://travel.state.gov/visa/temp/types/types_5186.html#denial.

———. 2013c. "What is Modern Slavery?" Fact sheet, Office to Monitor and Combat Trafficking in Persons. Accessed July 21, 2013, www.state.gov/j/tip/what/.

U.S. Government Accountability Office. 2006. "Human Trafficking: Better Data, Strategy and Reporting Needed to Enhance U.S. Antitrafficking Efforts Abroad." Report GAO-06-825. Washington, D.C.: Government Accountability Office.

———. 2007. "Human Trafficking: A Strategic Framework Could Help Enhance the Interagency Collaboration Needed to Effectively Combat Trafficking Crimes." Report GAO-07-915. Washington, D.C.: Government Accountability Office.

Valenzuela, Abel, et al. 2006. On the Corner: Day Labor in the United States. Los Angeles: UCLA Center for the Study of Urban Poverty.

Vance, Carole. 2011a. Remarks at Radcliffe. "Beyond Ideology: Research on Trafficking, Forced Labor and Migration." Radcliffe Exploratory Seminar. Cambridge, Mass. February 4–5.

———. 2011b. "States of Contradiction: Twelve Ways to Do Nothing about Trafficking while Pretending To." Social Research 78 (3): 933–48.

———. 2011c. "Thinking Trafficking, Thinking Sex." GLQ: A Journal of Lesbian and Gay Studies 17 (1): 135–43.

———. 2012. "Innocence and Experience: Melodramatic Narratives of Sex Trafficking and Their Consequences for Law and Policy." History of the Present 2 (2): 200–218.

Vandenberg, Martina E. 2012. "Giving Back: Combating Human Trafficking." GPSolo 29 (5). http://www.americanbar.org/publications/gp_solo/2012/september_october/giving_back_combating_human_trafficking.html.

Vandenberg, Martina E., and Alexandra F. Levy. 2012. "Human Trafficking and Diplomatic Immunity: Impunity No More?" Intercultural Human Rights Law Review 7: 77–101.

van der Meulen, Emily. 2011. "Sex Work and Canadian Policy: Recommendations for Labor Legitimacy and Social Change." Sexuality Research and Social Policy 8 (4): 348–58.

Vargas, Theresa. 2008. "Team Will Track Pr. William's Illegal Immigration Crackdown." Washington Post. March 17.

Vine, David, Melissa Checker, and Alaka Wali. 2010. "A Sea Change in Anthropology? Public Anthropology Reviews." American Anthropologist 112 (1): 5–6.

Waldinger, Roger, and Michael I. Lichter. 2003. How the Other Half Works: Immigration and the Social Organization of Labor. Berkeley: University of California Press.

Washington Lawyers' Committee for Civil Rights and Urban Affairs. 2008. Wages Denied: Day Laborers in the District of Columbia. October 22. Washington, D.C.: Washington Lawyers' Committee for Civil Rights and Urban Affairs.

Waslin, Michelle. 2004. "Immigration Reform: Comprehensive Solutions for Complex Problems." Issue Brief. National Council of La Raza. Accessed Nov. 5, 2011, http://www.nclr.org/images/uploads/publications/28596_file_IB_13_Immigra_ionReform_FNL.pdf.

Webber, Alexandra, and David Shirk. 2005. "Hidden Victims: Evaluating Protections for Undocumented Victims of Human Trafficking." *Immigration Policy in Focus* 4: 1–10.

Weissman, Deborah M., Rebecca C. Headen, and Katherine Lewis Parker. 2009. "The Policies and Politics of Local Immigration Enforcement Laws: 287(g) Program in North Carolina." February. American Civil Liberties Union of North Carolina Legal Foundation and Immigration and Human Rights Policy Clinic of University of North Carolina at Chapel Hill. Accessed June 15, 2013, http://www.law.unc.edu/documents /clinicalprograms/287gpolicyreview.pdf.

Weitzer, Ronald. 2006. "Moral Crusade against Prostitution." *Society* 43 (3): 33–38.

———. 2007. "The Social Construction of Sex Trafficking: Ideology and Institutionalization of a Moral Crusade." *Politics and Society* 35 (3): 447–75.

———. 2010a. "The Mythology of Prostitution: Advocacy Research and Public Policy." *Sexuality Research and Social Policy* 7: 15–29.

———. 2010b. "The Movement to Criminalize Sex Work in the United States." *Journal of Law and Society* 37 (1): 61–84.

———. 2012. "Sex Trafficking and the Sex Industry: The Need for Evidence-Based Theory and Legislation." *The Journal of Criminal Law & Criminology* 101 (4): 1337–70.

Werner, Daniel, and Kathleen Kim. 2008. "Civil Litigation on Behalf of Victims of Human Trafficking." Montgomery, Ala.: Immigrant Justice Project, Southern Poverty Law Center.

Wessler, Seth Freed. 2011. *Shattered Families: The Perilous Intersection of Immigration Enforcement and the Child Welfare System*. November. New York: Applied Research Center.

———. 2012. "Nearly 205k Deportations of Parents of U.S. Citizens in Just over Two Years." December 17. Accessed June 14, 2013, http://colorlines.com/archives /2012/12/us_deports_more_than_200k_parents.html#obtained.

Willis, Paul. 1977. *Learning to Labor: How Working Class Kids Get Working Class Jobs*. New York: Columbia University Press.

Wilson, Richard A. 1997. "Human Rights, Culture and Context: An Introduction." In *Human Rights, Culture and Context: Anthropological Perspectives*, ed. R. A. Wilson. London: Pluto Press.

Wilson, William Julius. 1996. *When Work Disappears: The World of the New Urban Poor*. New York: Knopf.

Women's Commission for Refugee Women and Children, International Rescue Committee. 2007. *The U.S. Response to Human Trafficking: An Unbalanced Approach*. New York: Women's Commission for Refugee Women and Children.

Young, Allan. 1995. *The Harmony of Illusions: Inventing Post-Traumatic Stress Disorder*. Princeton: Princeton University Press.

Young, Cathy. 2004. "Was Story about Sexual Trafficking Exagerrated?" *Boston Globe*. Accessed June 24, 2008, http://www.boston.com/news/globe/editorial_opinion /oped/articles/2004/02/09/was_story_about_sexual_trafficking_exagerrated/.

Young, Iris. 1990. *Justice and the Politics of Difference*. Princeton: Princeton University Press.

Zarembka, Joy M. 2002. "America's Dirty Work: Migrant Maids and Modern-Day Slavery." In *Global Woman: Nannies, Maids, and Sex Workers in the New Economy*, ed. Barbara Ehrenreich and Arlie Russell Hochschild. New York: Henry Holt.

Zavella, Patricia. 2011. *I'm Neither Here nor There: Mexicans' Quotidian Struggles with Migration and Poverty*. Durham: Duke University Press.

Zetter, Roger. 2007. "More Labels, Fewer Refugees: Remaking the Refugee Label in an Era of Globalization." *Journal of Refugee Studies* 20 (2): 172–92.

Zhang, Sheldon X. 2007. *Smuggling and Trafficking in Human Beings: All Roads Lead to America*. Westport, Conn.: Praeger.

———. 2009. "Beyond the 'Natasha' Story—A Review and Critique of Current Research on Sex Trafficking." *Global Crime* 10 (3): 178–95.

———. 2012. "Looking for a Hidden Population: Trafficking of Migrant Laborers in San Diego County." Report to the U.S. Department of Justice, Office of Justice Programs, National Institute of Justice. November. San Diego: San Diego State University.

Zimmerman, Cathy, et al. 2008. "The Health of Trafficked Women: A Survey of Women Entering Posttrafficking Services in Europe." *American Journal of Public Health* 98 (1): 55–59.

Zlolniski, Christian. 2006. *Janitors, Street Vendors, and Activists: The Lives of Mexican Immigrants in Silicon Valley*. Berkeley: University of California Press.

Index

anthropology, anthropologists, 217n56, 232–33n12; as activists, 209n61; on experience of suffering, 29, 209–10n67; fieldwork of, 5; language of, 20–21; participant observation and, 24–25. *See also names of specific anthropologists*

anti-immigration, 33, 41, 42, 138; activists of, 199n2; antimigrant measures and, 24, 213n18; legislation on, 37; policies of, 5, 39, 43, 60, 219n66

antiprostitution, 38, 219n66, 220n77, 221n83; activists and advocates of, 61, 62, 78, 190, 223n102, 223n107; of Bush administration, 63, 64, 221n87; frame of, 66; lobby, 67; organizations of, 68–69; researchers on, 187; of United States Leadership Against HIV/AIDS, Tuberculosis, and Malaria Act, 220–21n81

antitrafficking community, 25; activists and advocates in, 33, 62, 125, 126, 134; assistance givers in, 185; events of, 23; fundraising campaigns, 71; leaders of, 204n25; legal regime and, 11, 23, 71, 203n14; NGOS in, 224n110; organizations in, 68, 190, 195–98; policy concerning, 65; resources for, 195–98; statistics on, 221n89; work of, 13, 19, 122, 146

anxiety, anxiousness, 217n56: of trafficking victims, 112, 117–18, 123; of T visa holders, 146, 150

Appelbaum, Richard P., 213n25, 215n43; on sweatshops, 48, 214n33, 215n42, 215n44, 216n46

Argentina, 29–30, 58, 232n13

assaults, 2, 238n14; sexual, 38, 54, 235n32; unreported, 225n112; verbal, 103

assistance for formerly trafficked persons, 4, 130, 152; limits of, 117, 127; providers of, 26, 70; U.S. government and, 116, 152. *See also specific types of service providers*

attorneys and lawyers, 116, 235n33, 235n35, 237n10, 241n6; assistance of, 21, 23, 25, 27; civil litigation and, 148–49; forced domestic laborers and, 8; Freedom Network and, 224n109; as friends, 22; for human rights, 230n3; inexperienced in trafficking, 130; in Justice Department, 206n29; nonidentification of, 28; of trafficking clients, 14, 19–20;

32, 146–47, 186, 188, 207n36, 237n2, 237n5; T visa recipients and, 10; in Washington, 217n51

automobile ownership, 55, 100, 141–42, 154, 160, 183, 188, 190. *See also* driver's license

Ayuda, 71

Bales, Kevin, 202n14, 240n11

Beatrice, as forced domestic laborer, 8–9, 32–33

Benitez, Lucas, of CIW, 60

Bernstein, Elizabeth, 66, 219n69, 219n75, 220n77, 223n110, 224n110

Biehl, João, 165, 207n37, 209n66, 238n1

body: lack of control over, 103; language of suffering inscribed on, 29–30, 210n72

Bonacich, Edna, 213n25, 215n43; on sweatshops, 48, 214n33, 215n42, 215n44, 216n46

border, borders: children at risk of forced prostitution near, 67–68; corrupt guards at, 6; crossing of, 6, 47, 78–79, 167, 201n8; interdiction strategies at, 215n36; smuggling at, 202n11

Border Patrol agents, 42, 213n17; local law enforcement functioning as, 42

Borneman, John, 232n12

Bosnia-Herzegovina, 209n57, 230n3

Bourgois, Philippe, 147, 238n14

Boycott the Bell, 53

Brazil, 209n66, 104

Break the Chain Campaign, 71

brothels, 9, 39, 66, 142, 220n73, 224n110; burden of proof for trafficking and, 85; in New York City, 95, 150, 153; NYPD and, 222n90; police corruption and, 235n32; in public imagination, 12, 31; raids on, 224n10; trafficking and, 31, 220n73. *See also* prostitution, prostitutes; sexual labor; sex work, workers

brutality, 15, 97, 234n20; of police, 224n110; against trafficked persons, 17, 86, 102, 228n42

bureaucracy, bureaucracies, 33, 117, 120, 131, 147, 166, 207n46, 230n3

Burger King, campaign against, 218n62

Burke, Florrie, 152, 229n2

Bush, George W., administration, 60–66, 221n87; antitrafficking efforts, 68, 71, 72,

Flo (Africa), 3, 81, 105, 166, 168, 192; abuser and, 127, 140–41, 150; accomplishments of, 32, 105–10, 149, 165, 180, 184; assertiveness of, 173; driver's license obtained by, 141; fears of, 140; living arrangements of, 138; memory of, 26; social network of, 124, 160–61

Florida, 21; attorneys in, 14; farmworkers in, 50, 52, 53, 216n50, 217n55, 218n62

food: control over, 226n11; exploitation in industry of, 215n42; of old country, 1, 239n19

forced labor, 14; divergent experiences of, 117; escape from, 8, 31; indications of, 227n17; lasting effects of, 112; training to recognize, 228n47; treatment of victims of, 103–4

France, asylum seekers in, 210n72, 237n3

Francisco, 8, 138, 151

Freedom Network, 70, 223–24n109; annual conferences of, 23, 68, 187, 206n29

Freedom Network Training Institute on Human Trafficking, 83, 224n109

Free the Slaves, 202n14

friendship, friends: between formerly trafficked persons, 1, 160; importance of, 18, 26, 161; making of, 4, 133, 135. See also social networks

future for formerly trafficked persons, 17, 20, 118, 151, 176, 177, 183

Garcia, Angela, 207n37, 209–10n67

GED (General Educational Development) test, 2, 32, 116, 167, 168, 179, 180

gender, 15, 23; balance of, 22; ideologies of, 83; power differentiated by, 30; of victims, 227n25

generational identity of formerly trafficked persons, 15, 158, 169, 181

Germany, Germans, 51; Dominican sex workers and, 202n9, 226n6; prostitution and sex trafficking in, 66, 67

Gladys (Mexico), 95, 117, 139, 229n1; English skills of, 103, 112; excited for future, 115, 167, 177; living on own terms, 116

global worker, workers, 7, 79, 82; Elsa as, 87–93; trafficking and, 222n97

Good Samaritans, 161

Gordon, Jennifer, 9, 49, 55

Grant, Melissa Gira, 65

gratitude of formerly trafficked persons, 16, 132

Great Britain, 165; refugees in, 238n15; sex trafficking in, 187, 241n1

Great Depression, rural poverty during, 50

Green, Linda, 119, 155, 238n14

green cards, 200n3, 207n41; costs of, 32; parties for, 145, 158–59, 162; received by T visa recipients, 10, 16, 17, 33, 105, 132, 135, 139, 146, 147, 149, 162, 207n41; restrictions of, 6; for T visa derivatives, 207n42

Guatemala, 119; exploitation of workers from, 204n21; guest workers from, 225n112; migrants and migration from, 43, 235n31; violence in, 209n64, 234n20, 234n21, 238n14

guest workers, 215n41; abuse and exploitation of, 48, 215n40; from Guatemala, 225n112; from India, 200n3; from Jamaica, 225–26n2

H-1B visas, 203n20, 204n20

H-2B visa holders, 43, 200n3, 225n112

Hahamovitch, Cindy, 48, 215n40, 225–26n2

Hammon, Mickey, Alabama anti-immigrant legislation and, 213n18

Hammond, Laura, 20–21, 121, 234n24, 234n25, 234n27

hardships faced by formerly trafficked persons, 19, 146, 166, 216n50. See also challenges of formerly trafficked persons

Harrington, Carol, 230n3

Haynes, Dina, 85, 227n25, 227n26

health care, 2, 18, 156; lack of insurance for, 19, 145. See also medical benefits

Herman, Judith, 93, 98, 209n63, 228n36, 228n41

heroes, heroism, 30, 189

Hickey, Darby, 61, 219n68

Hine, Lewis, 49–50, 50, 208n50, 216n48

Hirsch, Susan, 236n48

Hispanics and Latinos, 44, 212n10, 213n18, 216n50

Holmes, Seth, 201n8, 214n29, 217–18n58, 238n16

home country: imagining return to, 20, 208n52; not returning to, 149. See also repatriation

Home Depot, labor subcontractors and, 216n51

homeless, homelessness, 155; formerly traf-

La Strada, 95

Latinos and Hispanics, 44, 212n10, 213n18, 216n50

law, laws: child-labor, 50; immigration, 78, 120; labor, 5, 11, 39; of the land, 7; trafficking and, 9–10, 30, 62, 63. *See also* attorneys and lawyers; court system; justice system

law enforcement, 212n19; agents of, 23, 65, 85, 123, 127, 148, 228n47; as border patrol agents, 42; building legal cases with, 123; cooperation with, 235n33, 237n2; corruption in, 6; deportation and, 8; discretion of, 227n25; employers and, 9; encounters with, 16; fear and mistrust of, 43, 44; of federal immigration, 211n5; racial profiling by, 33, 44; rescues of trafficked persons by, 8, 127, 148; sex workers and, 62, 64, 222n90, 224n110; training of, 15, 23, 122, 228–29n47. *See also* police officers

Lawful Permanent Resident (LPR) status, 16, 205n26

lawyers. *See* attorneys and lawyers

leadership training institute, 56

legal clinics, 24

legal protection, protections, for workers, 5, 24, 49

legal status of formerly trafficked persons: as individualize pursuit, 120; in limbo, 116, 146–47; sense of home and belonging tied to, 121. *See also* T visas

Lideres Campesinas, 14, 56, 57

living conditions, 18, 49–50, 54, 227n17

living wage, 216n46, 240n10

Liza (Indonesia), 77–78, 85, 105, 127, 180

Locke, Peter, 165

Long Island, 2, 3, 21, 55

Los Angeles, 21, 22, 40, 42, 95, 138, 163; anti-trafficking work in, 23, 120, 157–60; City Hall, 194; Filipinos in, 49; formerly trafficked persons in, 132, 141, 183; migrant rights organizers in, 37, 38, 56; shelters in, 124, 125, 133, 135, 136, 151, 169, 177, 182

Louisiana, 8, 204n20, 213n24, 225n112, 225n113

love and relationships, 3, 4, 21; with abusers, 14, 94, 95, 98, 111–12, 149, 185; boyfriends and, 15, 28, 100, 137, 138, 139, 142, 164; danger of, 97; loverboy phenomenon and, 95

low-wage work, workers, 18, 24, 31, 32, 82, 154, 214n33, 214–15n35; challenges of, 187, 214n34, 240n6; competition for, 179; demand for, 5; in Dominican Republic, 226n10; exploitation and, 9, 12–13, 24, 48, 53, 206n30; lack of respect for, 33, 190; lateral movement and, 240n9; Latinos and, 212n10; migrants and, 240n4; rights for, 25; statistics on, 215n39; unreported abuse of, 49; vulnerabilities of, 178

Mann Act, 64

Maria (Philippines), 168, 192, 208n46; abuse of, 81; apartment of, 2; attitude of, 82, 132, 163–64, 166, 172; conversation with, 1–2; as early T visa recipient, 10, 16–17; education and, 181; employment of, 146, 151, 240n8; financial insecurity of, 146, 164; food and, 103; green card received by, 16, 146; Philippines and, 81, 85, 145, 164–65, 184; social network of, 124, 172; son of, 16, 164, 208n46

Martinez-Cervantes, José, heroics of, 218n63

Maryland: 108, 109, 142, 216n51; domestic workers in, 210n1; migrants' rights organizations in, 13, 24. *See also* CASA de Maryland; Washington, D.C.: suburbs of

massage parlors, 39, 224n110, 224–25n111

Massey, Douglas S., 217n57, 234–35n29

media, 33, 34, 187; antiprostitution frame in, 66–67; attention of, 25, 150; as inflammatory, 33; on "modern-day slavery," 5; mythic notions of trafficking victims and, 31; on trafficking, 4, 63, 66, 72, 130, 149, 188, 190, 223n104, 228n47

medical benefits, 186; full-time employment and, 147; lack of, 19, 145, 178

memory: burden of, 146; formerly trafficked persons and, 25–26; trauma and, 209n63

mental health, 30, 117, 130, 230n2, 232n12; chronic worry, 119; deferring counseling for, 116; integrated treatment for, 156; trauma and, 209n63

mentoring, mentors, 116, 157, 159–61, 177

methodology of book, 21–31

Mexican Americans, 179, 240n4

Mexico, Mexicans, 44, 165, 184, 228n37; border of, with United States, 42, 68, 201n8; formerly trafficked persons from, 95,

outreach, 58, 60; author and, 80, 226n9; creative and innovative, 23, 28; for HIV, 224n110; peer-led, rights-based, 13, 14, 55, 56, 57, 72

Palermo Protocol, 201n7
Palestinian refugees, 121, 209n56
paranoia, in victims of trafficking, 112, 139
participant observation, 25, 209n65
Pennsylvania, 213n19, 239n23
permanent residence (LPR) status, 16
perm-temp workers, 216–17n51
persecution, state-sponsored, 119
Peru, 119, 210n67, 231n7, 232n10, 233n16n
Peters, Alicia, 222n90, 228n47
Philippines, 15, 81, 85, 88, 122, 125, 132, 181, 239n19; celebration of independence of, 145; families of formerly trafficked persons in, 1, 16–17, 146, 164, 184, 208n46; Hong Kong and, 226n8; teachers from, 204n20. *See also* Filipinas
Philippine Connections, 132, 145, 146
photography: of Hine, 216n47; of Riis, 216n46
physicians and doctors, 124, 201n8, 232n9, 238n14, 238n16; farmworkers and, 238n16; trafficking patients and, 6, 10, 17, 155–59, 235–36n36
pioneers: first T visa recipients as, 10; migrants as, 121, 234n29
place-making, 20, 115
Planned Parenthood, 156
poems, poetry, by formerly trafficked persons, 3, 118
police officers: corruption and, 6, 87, 105; immigration law and, 42, 84, 139, 211n5; migrant workers and, 43, 73, 235n31; profiling by, 37, 43; prostitution and, 62, 67, 222–23n101, 241n1; rescue of traffickers by, 8, 86; surveillance by, 187. *See also* law enforcement
posttraumatic stress disorder (PTSD), 118, 230n3, 231–32n8
poultry industry, 47, 48, 214–15n35, 215n42, 217n56
poverty: about access and social networks, 154; on edge of, 183; of formerly trafficked persons, 5, 22, 126, 146, 151, 189; health issues

resulting from, 155; overdetermination of, 240n12; radiating effects of, 154
power, 30, 227n19
prevention of trafficking into forced labor, 28, 31, 42, 53, 200n4, 202n14; immigration policy and, 4, 72; workshops on, 78, 80, 226n9
privacy: of formerly trafficked persons, 139; lack of, in homeless shelters, 128; as power, 133
prosecution of traffickers, 11, 64, 66, 200n4, 218n64, 221n84; trafficking victims and, 12, 123, 200n4, 204n26, 207n41, 207–8n44
prostitution, prostitutes, 64, 220n73; children as, 223n106; ending demand for, 67; feminism and, 219n69, 219n70; legalization of, 62; NYPD and, 221–22n90; "rescue" of, 31, 220n77, 224n110; rights of, 219n68; Super Bowls and, 222–23n101; as term, 205n25; TVPA implementation as crusade against, 12. *See also* sexual labor; sex work, workers
protections: against extreme exploitation, 11; for migrant workers, 7, 10, 31, 73, 215n36
pseudonyms, 27–28, 236n46

Queens, 1, 2, 151

race: discrimination by, 43–44; of formerly trafficked persons, 15; in old South, 214n25; power differential by, 30; profiling by, 33, 187, 211n5, 214n26; slavery and, 7, 220n77
recession, economic, 19, 32, 38, 104, 151
recruiters, recruitment agencies: abuse by, 199n3; blacklisting of complainers, 203n19; at homeless shelters, 214n30; indebtedness to, 9, 18; in Jamaica, 226n2; migrants and, 6, 7, 172, 190; monopoly of international, 204n20; unscrupulous, 202n10
refugees, 160, 208n54, 208n55, 237n4; assistance for, 69, 152, 234n24, 236n43; asylees and, 237n3; in Britain, 238n15; building social networks, 121, 128; community of, 21; controlled poverty of, 152; integration of, 234n22; as mentors and guides, 160; Palestinian, 209n56; research on resettlement of, 121; resettlement of, 128, 152; social services for, 10; statistics on, 241n2. *See also* repatriation
religion, religious identity: Catholic church,

theory, theories, 6; action and, 24

Thirteenth Amendment, 202n14

Thrupakew, Noy, 235n32

TIP Office, 201n5; annual report of, 23, 202n14, 206n34

traffickers, 228n37; court trials of, 148; police corruption and, 235n32; prison terms for, 18; prosecution of, 30, 64, 218n64, 221n84. *See also* abuse, abusers

trafficking: care regime, 68–71; debt and, 204n20; designation of, 9, 11, 16, 29, 33, 201n7; of highly skilled workers, 207n38; human rights and, 33; involves criminal entities, 202n10; language of, 10, 29; laws against, 111, 200n4; for sex, 31, 64, 206n31, 219n70, 220n73, 222n91, 223n104, 228–29n47; statistics on, 222n97; as term, 7; TVPA definition of, 205n27, 222n91

trafficking assistance regime, 16–17, 23, 68–71, 130

Trafficking in Persons Report, 200n4

trafficking into forced labor, defined and described, 6–10

trafficking plus, defined and described, 150–51

Trafficking Victims Protection Act (2000). *See* TVPA

transcripts of taped conversations, 26

transgendered people, 37, 61

trauma, 117, 209n63, 231n7, 231–32n8, 235n33; as moral judgment, 232n9; telling, 232–33n12

travel brokers, 7, 18, 77, 101

travel restrictions of T visas, 6, 16

trust, 120, 122–26; difficulty with, 27, 120, 122; of formerly trafficked persons, 21, 26, 97, 100, 102, 126, 143, 160, 176, 235n35; law enforcement and, 42, 43, 211n5, 213n15, 235n31; migrant workers and, 53, 56, 78; of one's perceptions, 233n13; service providers and, 69, 130–31, 134–35, 229n1

"Truth behind Sex Trafficking, The," 67

truth commissions, 29, 231n7, 232n12

T visas, 8, 9, 11, 17, 69, 123, 182, 186, 189, 200n4, 205n26, 229n2; applicants for, 240n11; derivatives of, 207n42; first recipients of, 10, 16, 146, 157; LPR status and, 168; paucity of, 5, 12, 31; qualifying for, 13, 24,

83, 227n25, 237n2; time limits on, 32, 33, 207n41, 207n42; travel restrictions of, 6

TVPA (Trafficking Victims Protection Act; 2000), 65, 201n7, 207n41; binary conceptualization of, 13, 30; Bush administration and, 11–12, 219n67; coercion in, 227n21, 227n24; criticisms of, 218–19n66; definition of trafficking in, 205n27, 222n91; passage of, 9, 70, 200n4; reauthorization of, 64, 206n31, 221n85; T visas and, 43

Tyson Foods, 217n56

uncertainty, 208n53; of chattel slaves, 8; economic, 116; fear and, 86; of forced laborers, 94, 109–10, 111, 127; of formerly trafficked persons, 17, 87, 121, 147, 162, 217n56

underclass, 155

undocumented migrants, 7, 11, 39, 46, 187; in Chicago, 218n61; definition of, 199n2; effects of IRCA on, 217n56; hesitation of, to report crimes, 213n16; hostility to, 206n32; in San Diego County, 215n36; as sex workers, 12, 224n111

UN Human Rights Council, 61, 219n68

United Nations Protocol to Prevent, Suppress, and Punish Trafficking in Persons, Especially Women and Children, 201n7

United States Citizenship and Immigration Services. *See* USCIS

United States Leadership Against, HIV/AIDS, Tuberculosis, and Malaria Act(2003), 64, 220–21n81

Universal Placement International (UPI), 204n20

U nonimmigrant visa, 200n4

USCIS (United States Citizenship and Immigration Services), Vermont Service Center of, 147

U.S. Conference of Catholic Bishops (USCCB), as contractor for U.S. government, 229–30n2

U.S. Congress: TVPA and, 23, 64, 206n28, 221n85, 227n21; United States Leadership Against HIV/AIDS, Tuberculosis, and Malaria Act of, 220–21n81

U.S. Department of Health and Human Services (HHS), 205n26, 229–30n2; Administration for Children and Families, 230–31n4

U.S. Department of Homeland Security, 12, 203n19, 211n5

U.S. Department of Justice, 12, 25, 60, 64, 235n32; antitrafficking and, 65, 221n84, 221n89; attorneys of, 206n29; TVPA reauthorization and, 64; 287(g) agreements and, 211n5

U.S. Department of Labor, 215–16n45

U. S. Department of State, 219n68; Bureau of Public Affairs of, 62; on prostitution, 220n73; VOLAGS and, 236n43

U.S. Government Accountability Office reports on trafficking, 222n97

U.S. State Department, Office to Monitor and Combat Trafficking in Persons. *See* TIP Office

U.S. Supreme Court, 220–21n81

Vance, Carol, 63, 201n5, 220n77, 223n104

Verizon: labor subcontractors and, 216–17n51

Vermont Service Center of USCIS, as processing center for T visas, 69, 147

veterans, 156

victimhood, victims, 232n8; agency of, 226n3, 227n26; assistance for, 65, 69, 71, 230n2; currency of, 28–31; frame of, 186–87, 188, 223n108; legal proof of, 11; mantle of, rejected, 118; passiveness of, 206n33; psychology of, 228n41; as term, 205n25; trafficked persons as, 10, 31, 126, 222n91, 224n110, 224–25n111; as witnesses, 12, 112

Victims of Trafficking and Violence Protection Act (2000). *See* TVPA

Vietnam, Vietnamese, 27, 101, 125, 166

violence, 119, 155, 233n17; coercion without, 11; community, 155; consequences of experiencing or witnessing, 210n71; of deportation regime, 212n13; domestic, 22; families and, 238n13; fear and, 234n20; in Guatemala, 234n20, 234n21; structural, 233n15, 238n14; subjectivity and, 237n1; against women workers, 2, 115, 210n1

Virginia, 21, 24, 142, 213n19, 216n51; day laborers in, 38, 55, 58; 287(g) agreements in, 138–39. *See also* Washington, D.C.: suburbs of

visa, visas: no protection from coercion,

199n3; work, 40, 211n6. *See also specific types of visas*

voluntary agencies (VOLAGS), 236n43

volunteers, 157, 239n20; antitrafficking, 21, 158–61; author as, 24; at shelters, 129, 158

vulnerability, vulnerabilities, 5, 14, 15, 18, 178, 206n32

wages, 47, 58; highest for those in sex sector, 179; living, 216n46; poverty-level, 9, 12; nonstandard, 49; slavery, 202n14. *See also* low-wage work, workers; minimum wage; wage theft

wage theft, 11, 14; complaints about, 47; as crime against migrants, 24, 40, 45; day labor and, 210n1; decades of lost income and, 19–20, 58; fake fees as, 47–48; forms of, 204n24; in Washington, D.C., area, 49

waiting by formerly trafficked persons, 146–47

Walmart, labor subcontractors and, 216n51

Washington, D.C., 21, 149, 168, 177; attorneys in, 19, 56, 126, 149; author in, 23, 24; day laborers in, 47–48, 218n59; domestic workers organizations in, 3, 12, 13, 38, 56, 58, 124, 162, 176, 180; Freedom Network conferences in, 224n109; police in, 37, 38; sex workers' rights in, 61; Smithsonian Institution in, 140; social workers in, 70, 130, 138, 152; suburbs of, 78, 90, 98, 105; wage theft in, 49

Washington Lawyers Committee, 217n51, 218n59

Weitzer, Ronald, 201n5, 220n79, 221n83

white slavery, 220n77

Willis, Paul, 165, 239n2

witnesses, trafficking victims as, 12, 15, 16, 29, 73, 134, 148, 186

women, 15, 94–96; abuse and exploitation of, 65, 97; as farmworkers, 54, 56, 210n1; as forced domestic laborers, 8, 82; as formerly trafficked persons, 19–23, 29–30, 127, 209n63; as migrant workers, 213n24; as needing "rescue," 12, 63, 189, 220n77, 224n110; rights of, 185; in sex trade, 62, 66; as single mothers, 240n12; vulnerability of, 206n32 workers' rights, 24, 28, 71, 111, 218n60, trafficking and, 33; workers' comp as, 49

working conditions, 165; abusive, 47; bargaining for improvements in, 225n112; complaints about, 54; expectations of formerly trafficked persons, 163, 169; of low-wage migrants, 9, 48; of Mayan workers in North Carolina, 171; unsafe, 12, 48, 49, 51, 55–56, 72, 218n59

Zetter, Roger, 152

Zhang, Sheldon, 202n11, 206n31, 215n36

DATE DUE

DEC 2 0 2016			
			PRINTED IN U.S.A.